D0870053

Arduino™ Sketches

Arduino™ Sketches

Tools and Techniques for Programming Wizardry

James A. Langbridge

FOUNTAINDALE PUBLIC LIBRARY

300 West Briarcliff Road
Bolingbrook, IL 60440-2894
(630) 759-2102

WILEY

Arduino™ Sketches: Tools and Techniques for Programming Wizardry

Published by
John Wiley & Sons, Inc.
10475 Crosspoint Boulevard
Indianapolis, IN 46256
www.wiley.com

Copyright © 2015 by John Wiley & Sons, Inc., Indianapolis, Indiana

Published simultaneously in Canada

ISBN: 978-1-118-91960-6
ISBN: 978-1-118-91962-0 (ebk)
ISBN: 978-1-118-91969-9 (ebk)

Manufactured in the United States of America

10 9 8 7 6 5 4 3 2 1

No part of this publication may be reproduced, stored in a retrieval system or transmitted in any form or by any means, electronic, mechanical, photocopying, recording, scanning or otherwise, except as permitted under Sections 107 or 108 of the 1976 United States Copyright Act, without either the prior written permission of the Publisher, or authorization through payment of the appropriate per-copy fee to the Copyright Clearance Center, 222 Rosewood Drive, Danvers, MA 01923, (978) 750-8400, fax (978) 646-8600. Requests to the Publisher for permission should be addressed to the Permissions Department, John Wiley & Sons, Inc., 111 River Street, Hoboken, NJ 07030, (201) 748-6011, fax (201) 748-6008, or online at http://www.wiley.com/go/permissions.

Limit of Liability/Disclaimer of Warranty: The publisher and the author make no representations or warranties with respect to the accuracy or completeness of the contents of this work and specifically disclaim all warranties, including without limitation warranties of fitness for a particular purpose. No warranty may be created or extended by sales or promotional materials. The advice and strategies contained herein may not be suitable for every situation. This work is sold with the understanding that the publisher is not engaged in rendering legal, accounting, or other professional services. If professional assistance is required, the services of a competent professional person should be sought. Neither the publisher nor the author shall be liable for damages arising herefrom. The fact that an organization or Web site is referred to in this work as a citation and/or a potential source of further information does not mean that the author or the publisher endorses the information the organization or website may provide or recommendations it may make. Further, readers should be aware that Internet websites listed in this work may have changed or disappeared between when this work was written and when it is read.

For general information on our other products and services please contact our Customer Care Department within the United States at (877) 762-2974, outside the United States at (317) 572-3993 or fax (317) 572-4002.

Wiley publishes in a variety of print and electronic formats and by print-on-demand. Some material included with standard print versions of this book may not be included in e-books or in print-on-demand. If this book refers to media such as a CD or DVD that is not included in the version you purchased, you may download this material at http://booksupport.wiley.com. For more information about Wiley products, visit www.wiley.com.

Library of Congress Control Number: 2014948616

Trademarks: Wiley and the Wiley logo are trademarks or registered trademarks of John Wiley & Sons, Inc. and/or its affiliates, in the United States and other countries, and may not be used without written permission. Arduino is a trademark of Arduino, LLC. All other trademarks are the property of their respective owners. John Wiley & Sons, Inc. is not associated with any product or vendor mentioned in this book.

To my loving girlfriend, Anne-Laure, who once again put up with entire evenings and weekends spent on my PC. This is the second time I've done that to her, but she put up with me anyway and kept on smiling (most of the time). I still don't know how.

To my wonderful daughter, Eléna: I have to admit, I'm addicted to your laugh and smile, something you did every time I showed you the projects I was working on. Again you found a way of telling me when I needed to stop and spend more time playing with you (by unplugging and randomly rewiring my breadboard projects), but coming back home at the end of a long and difficult day to see you smiling and jumping into my arms gave me more energy than you can imagine.

About the Author

James A. Langbridge does not like talking about himself in the third person, but he will try anyway. James was born in Singapore and followed his parents to several countries before settling down in Nantes, France, where he lives with his partner and their daughter.

James is an embedded systems consultant and has worked for more than 15 years on industrial, military, mobile telephony, and aviation security systems. He works primarily on low-level development, creating bootloaders or optimizing routines in assembly, making the most of small processors. When not on contract, James trains engineers on embedded systems, or he makes new gizmos, much to the dismay of his partner.

James wrote his first computer program at age 6 and has never stopped tinkering since. He began using Apple IIs, ZX80s and ZX81s, and then moved to BBC Micros and the Amiga before finally having no other option but to use PCs.

About the Technical Editor

Scott Fitzgerald is an artist and educator working with technology and its relationship to people, approaching digital tools from a human-centric perspective. His work has been featured in numerous books and publications such as *The New York Times* and *IDN Magazine*. He has edited several books on Arduino and communication technologies, is the author of the book that accompanies the Arduino Starter Kit, and is responsible for documentation of the Arduino platform at `http://arduino.cc`. Scott is currently an assistant arts professor and head of the interactive media program at New York University Abu Dhabi. He enjoys tormenting his cat and partner with early morning work sessions.

Credits

Project Editor
Christina Haviland

Technical Proofreader
Ying Chin

Production Editor
Rebecca Anderson

Copy Editor
San Dee Phillips

**Manager of Content Development
and Assembly**
Mary Beth Wakefield

Marketing Director
David Mayhew

Marketing Manager
Carrie Sherrill

**Professional Technology and
Strategy Director**
Barry Pruett

Business Manager
Amy Knies

Associate Publisher
Jim Minatel

Project Coordinator, Cover
Patrick Redmond

Proofreader
Sarah Kaikini, Word One New York

Indexer
Johnna VanHoose Dinse

Cover Designer
Michael E. Trent/Wiley

Cover Image
© iStock.com/johnbloor

Acknowledgments

Writing a book is a huge project. When I was at school, I used to shudder at the thought of writing 1,000 words for an essay, and I was alone to do it. This book is, of course, much longer, and I enjoyed every minute of it, thanks to the team of professionals who helped me every step of the way. Take a quick look at the people involved in this project, and you will soon see what I'm talking about.

I can't thank everyone involved personally; there are just too many people, but there are a few names that I will never forget. My thanks go out to Christina Haviland, my project editor. When I knew that I would be working with her again, I was thrilled. She actually managed to put up with me for the entire duration and didn't even shout at me when I was late, despite the fact that some of the chapters were very, very late. I was also thrilled to know that I'd be working with San Dee Phillips, my copy editor. The job they did transforming raw data coming out of my brain into something readable is outstanding. Then there is Scott Fitzgerald, my technical editor, who made sure that I didn't make any mistakes. Believe me, nothing slipped by, and despite all the grumbling I did when I received the corrections, thank you! This wouldn't have been possible without you.

I would also like to thank Atmel for their time and effort, for the engineers I was in contact with to get more information, and to Tom Vu who kept on encouraging me along the way and sending me new evaluation boards to play with. My thanks also go out to Silicon Labs for its excellent UV sensor that is presented in this book and for the time it spent helping me. Thanks to Materiel .net who managed to get me a new computer, camera, and components in record time when mine broke, allowing me to get the job done. Your coffee mug is still on my desk!

Of course, this book would not have been possible without the amazing people at Arduino. I don't know if they know just how much they have changed the world of makers. Your boards have brought back the joy I had in creating gizmos and contraptions.

This has been a huge adventure, and I've met a lot of amazing people along the way. Thank you to every one of you—for your time, your suggestions, and your encouraging messages.

Contents at Glance

Contents

Introduction

Arduinos have opened up a new world to us. Both makers and professionals use Arduino-based systems to create wonderful and complex devices to help to create fascinating gizmos. From the simplest device that turns on a light when you press a button to advanced 3-D printers, you can use Arduinos in just about every application.

To power all this, Arduinos use *sketches*—software programs that you design to complete your device. They communicate with the outside world and are logic behind your projects. To assist you, the Arduino environment has *libraries*—software that you can add as required, depending on your application or the hardware that you add. Each library is explained in this book with examples for each library.

This book introduces you to Arduino sketches, the software routines that you can use and the different libraries available for the different Arduinos that you will encounter.

The Arduino can be your canvas, and your sketch can be your digital masterpiece.

Overview of the Book and Technology

This book covers everything you need to start using Arduinos. It presents the most common Arduinos on the market today, explains how to get your software up and running, and how to program the Arduino, but most important, it explains the Arduino programming languages and the different libraries that you can add to your designs to provide extra functionality. It also gives a primer in electronics to help you in the numerous examples throughout the book.

How This Book Is Organized

This book is designed to give as much information as possible to someone who is starting Arduino programming. It is separated into four parts.

Part I, "Introduction to Arduino," (Chapters 1–3) gives an overview of Arduinos—where they came from and why they are here to stay. It gives a primer on electronics and C programming, and also goes into the Arduino Language, the common elements that you will use for every project.

Part II, "Standard Libraries," (Chapters 4–17) is dedicated to the libraries available for every Arduino, that is, the different software components you can include to add functionality and hardware support. Each library is presented in its own chapter, and an example is provided for each library to help you understand its use.

Part III, "Device-Specific Libraries," (Chapters 18–23) is dedicated to libraries that are specific to different Arduinos; software you can add to a particular Arduino to access hardware or perform specific tasks. Again, each library is presented in its own chapter, and examples are provided.

Part IV, "User Libraries and Shields," (Chapters 24–26) is all about going even further with your Arduino; it explains how to import user libraries and how to design and distribute your own libraries. It also shows how to create your own shield, an electronic board that you can add to your Arduino to provide even more functionality.

Who Should Read This Book

This book is primarily for makers—people with ideas on how to create amazing applications or automate everyday tasks—and also for developers who want to get into the amazing world of Arduino programming.

Tools You Need

Each chapter has an example, and the exact components needed for that chapter are listed at the beginning of the chapter. To follow every example in this book, you need the following hardware:

- Computer
- USB cable and micro-USB cable
- 5-V power supply

- Breadboard with connector cables
- Several Arduinos:
    - 2 x Arduino Uno
    - Arduino Due
    - Arduino Mega 2560
    - Arduino Esplora
    - Arduino Robot
    - Arduino
- SainSmart LCD Shield
- SainSmart Ethernet Shield
- LM35 Temperature Sensor
- SD card
- Arduino GSM Shield
- Adafruit ST7735 TFT breakout board
- Adafruit MAX31855 breakout board
- Type-K thermocouple wire
- Adafruit SI1145 UV Sensor board
- SainSmart Wi-Fi shield
- DHT11 Humidity sensor
- HC-SR04 ultrasonic distance sensor
- HYX-S0009 or equivalent servo motor
- L293D
- 5-V bipolar stepper motor
- Red, green, and blue LEDs
- 10-kilohm resistors
- 4.7-kilohm resistors

What's on the Website

The source code for the samples is available for download from the Wiley website at `www.wiley.com/go/arduinosketches`.

Summary

Arduino development is a fascinating subject, one that opens up a whole new world of possibilities. Arduinos are perfectly suited for learning about embedded development, but also for automating everyday tasks or even making amazing gizmos and contraptions. Throughout this book, you'll find numerous examples about how to create simple devices, providing a hardware schematic to get you started, as well as the sketch to get you up and running.

To get the most out of your sketches, each library is introduced and the different functions are explained. Examples are provided for every library, going through the code line by line so you understand what the sketch does. My hope is that this book will serve as a reference for your new projects. Have fun!

Introduction to Arduino

In This Part

Introduction to Arduino

Electronics enthusiasts have always been present. For decades, they have been creating interesting devices and products. Amateur radio enthusiasts typically made their own radio sets using schematics found in magazines or simply from their own design. How many of us built a radio system to discover electronics, only to be hooked? With a few dollars' worth of components, you could create your own radio and listen to glorious long-wave transmissions on a small low-quality speaker, and yet it was better than what could be bought in the shops because it was homemade. If you wanted better sound, you could buy a better speaker. More volume? There were kits for that, too. Audiophiles built their own amplifiers and accessories depending on their needs. Electronics shops proposed books for all levels, from beginner to expert. Kits were also available using the simplest of components all the way to entire computer systems. It was a time in which you could build just about anything, and everything. You could, quite literally, walk into an electronics shop, buy a DIY computer, and spend a few hours soldering memory chips onto a printed circuit board. That's how I started.

In the 1990s, things changed slightly. Most hobbyists had a PC on their desk and could use them to create schematics, simulate parts of a system, and even print circuit board with transparent layouts, making the entire process much easier. However, something was missing. Almost all the devices that could be made were not programmable. Microprocessors were available but were either too expensive or too complicated. At the time, the 68000 microprocessor was one of the most reliable components available and was relatively cheap but complex. The microprocessor by itself was useless; it had to be hooked up to external memory. To run a program on every boot, it had to also have read-only memory. If you wanted interrupts, again, you had to add a chip into the design. The end result was complicated and out of the reach of some enthusiasts. To do without this complexity, enthusiasts that wanted programmable devices tended to use what was already on their desk: a personal computer.

Most PCs at the time used the ISA bus, as shown in Figure 1-1. ISA was a simple bus that allowed components to be added to the processor and general computer system. It was a simple system that allowed users to insert add-on cards into their computer, and it was extremely easy to use. It wasn't hard to create a circuit board that could be plugged into an ISA slot, and complete prototyping boards existed, enabling enthusiasts and engineers to test a solution before making their own board. Some of these boards even included breadboards, a simple system allowing users to place their components and wires without the need to solder. This sparked a small revolution, and many enthusiasts turned to this type of board to do what previously could not be done: create programmable systems. An ISA board could have digital inputs and outputs, analog inputs and outputs, radios, communication devices—just about anything was possible. All this would be controlled by the computer's CPU, using simple programming languages such as C or Pascal. My ISA card kept my student apartment nice and warm by reading data from a thermometer and turning on electric heaters, acting like a thermostat. It also served as an alarm clock, programmed depending on my classes the next day. Although I did manage to miss a few morning classes, in all fairness it was usually my fault; the ISA card worked perfectly on a tight budget.

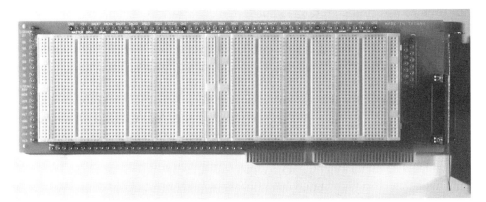

Figure 1-1: ISA prototyping board

Computers became faster, and systems evolved. The industry changed, and so did the expansion ports. Just as enthusiasts became experts on the ISA bus, the industry invented a new system: the VESA Local Bus (VLB). The VLB bus was an extension to ISA, only adding a second connector for memory-mapped I/O and Direct Memory Access (DMA), but it announced a change. Computers were indeed getting faster, and some computer bus systems couldn't keep up. Even VLB couldn't keep up, and after only a year, PCI became the reference. The PCI bus is an advanced bus but requires components and logic to identify itself. It suddenly became increasingly difficult to create homemade boards. Some users decided to use other industry-standard ports, such as the parallel port or RS-232, but most stopped creating such systems. Those that did continue mainly used analog systems or nonprogrammable digital systems. Instead of having a programmable microcontroller, the system was designed using logic gates. For example, a bulb could turn on if both inputs A and B were true, or if input C was false. These tasks became more and more complicated as the number of inputs increased.

Analog systems, such as radios and amplifiers, did not have a form of programming. They were designed with a specific task in mind. Configuration was analog; with a small screwdriver, the designer could "tweak" values with potentiometers, variable resistances. It wasn't possible to program the device to multiply an input signal by a specific value; instead, potentiometers were added to counter the effect of tolerances in the components. Designs therefore added an additional phase, calibration. Specific input signals were fed into devices, and a specific output was expected.

Processors did exist that could be used, and some projects did use them, but integrating a processor into a design generally meant that several components needed to be used. Memory chips, I/O controllers, or bus controllers had to be used, even after a decade of technological advancements, and circuits became more and more complicated. Even when designs worked, programming them proved to be a challenge. Most programming was done via EEPROM devices, short for Electronically Erasable Programmable Read-Only Memory. These devices could contain a computer program and could be programmed using an external programmer attached to a computer. They were called erasable read-only because the contents could indeed be wiped and replaced, but doing so required removal of the circuit and subjecting it to ultra-violet light for 20 minutes. One small error in a program could often take 30 minutes or more to correct.

Atmel AVR

Atmel is an American semi-conductor company, founded in 1984, and the name Atmel is an acronym for Advanced Technology for Memory and Logic. Right from the start, Atmel designed memory chips that used less power than competing designs, but it soon decided to create programmable devices. In 1994, Atmel entered the microprocessor market, creating an extremely fast 8051-based microcontroller. In 1995, Atmel was one of the first companies to license the ARM architecture, giving it access to advanced processor technology.

Atmel didn't use only ARM technology, it also created its own processor, the AVR, in 1996 (see Figure 1-2). What does AVR stand for? Well, that is one of the many mysteries of Atmel. Designed by Alf-Egil Bogen and Vegard Wollan, some say it stands for Alf and Vegard's RISC processor. We will never know, and at the time, people were not interested in understanding the name, but rather getting their hands on this advanced piece of technology. Today, more and more people are curious as to the origin of this curious processor, Atmel continues to tease the public with videos of the inventors explaining the name, only to have the big reveal scrambled by mobile telephone interference.

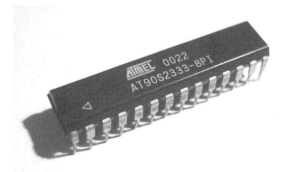

Figure 1-2: Atmel AVR Microprocessor

Previously, programming the read-only memory of a device required some tedious tasks, like subjecting the chip to UV light, or complicated erase techniques. This all changed with Atmel's 8-bit AVR. The AVR was the first microcontroller family to use on-chip flash memory for program storage. It also included Random Access Memory (RAM) directly on the chip, essentially containing everything needed to run a microcontroller on a single chip. Suddenly, all the complicated design could be replaced with a single component. Even better, programming the chip could be done in minutes, using minimal hardware. Some Atmel designs allowed users to plug the microcontroller directly into a USB port and to program it using Atmel's software. From compilation to program execution took less than a minute.

Several learning platforms existed: Parallax's BASIC Stamp and PIC devices were in use, but Atmel's AVR made its appearance and added another alternative for electronics enthusiasts. Previously, on digital systems, the logic was defined before creating the board. Inputs and outputs were connected to logic gates, and the functionality was designed into the product. Now, with the AVR series, enthusiasts and engineers had a new possibility. Instead of designing functionality electronically, systems could be designed to interact with the outside world using computer programming. This simplified electronics; instead of using multiple logic gates, everything was connected directly to the microcontroller, which could then be programmed to react to events from the outside world. Programs could be flashed and re-flashed, and devices could be programmed and re-programmed, opening the gates to a whole new world of electronics. In theory, a device could be made that would adapt to almost every situation possible. The technology existed; all that was left was for someone to create the device.

The Arduino Project

The Arduino project started in 2005, and was a project for the students at the Interaction Design Institute Ivrea in Ivrea, Italy. Students were taught to use a BASIC Stamp, a small microcontroller device programmable in PBASIC (a variation of the BASIC programming language), but the price for this device (almost $75) was considered to be too expensive for students, not only on acquisition, but also to replace damaged units.

Arduino started as a project for design students, targeted as a replacement for the BASIC Stamp. The Atmel 8-bit AVR was chosen for its simplicity and low price, and had the extra advantage of requiring few external components. It also has an impressive amount of inputs and outputs, making it a perfect choice for future designs.

Students and teachers worked together on a new design, one that used the Atmel AVR and that could easily accept external cards. When the original design was completed, researchers worked to make the design lighter, less expensive and easily usable by students, enthusiasts, and engineers. The first Arduino board was born. Improvements on the Arduino's original design, such as replacing the DB-9 serial connector with USB, has helped expand the platform's appeal.

There are two sides to every Arduino. There is, of course, the hardware, but this is only part of an Arduino project. Every Atmel microcontroller used for Arduino comes with a specific firmware, a small program embedded on every device that looks for a program to run or helps install a program using a serial device.

The final design was released as open source and was designed and sold by Arduino. Releasing Arduino as an Open Source Hardware project was an interesting move. Because it was open source, it attracted more and more users to look into their projects. Because the Arduino already had an excellent input/output design, users began to create boards that could be added to the original Arduino. When Arduino designed a new board, it kept the original input/output layout, enabling existing add-ons to be used with new designs.

Originally designed for education, the Arduino project became famous with electronics enthusiasts, and its boards were sold by more and more distributors.

Arduino not only created the hardware—an embedded device that does not have corresponding software and support programs might still be difficult to use—but also spent a lot of time developing its own language and Integrated Development Environment (IDE). The end result is a nice IDE that can work on Windows, MacOS, and Linux and converts the Arduino language (a high level variant of C/C++) to AVR code. The Arduino development environment hides away all the complications linked to embedded systems and mixing software—such as setting up an environment, linkers, pesky command lines—and lets the developer program using simple C language functions through the Arduino Programming Language.

The ATmega Series

Atmel has placed its AVR design into different groups, depending on various factors. There are numerous AVR microcontrollers, and knowing which one to use is essential for projects. Some ATmega devices have more memory, or more digital and analog inputs and outputs, or have a specific package size.

The ATmega Series

The Atmel megaAVR is the muscle of the AVR series. They are designed for applications requiring large amounts of code, with flash memory ranging from 4 k all the way to 512 k, enough for the most demanding of programs. Atmel megaAVR devices come in various sizes, ranging from 28 pins all the way to 100 pins. These devices have an impressive amount of embedded systems: analog to digital converters, multiple serial modes, and watchdog timers, to name but a few. They also have a large amount of digital input and output lines, making them ideal for devices that communicate with numerous components.

There are close to 100 ATmega devices, ranging in flash memory size and package size, and some models have advanced features such as internal LCD Controllers, CAN controllers, USB controllers, and Lightning controllers. ATmega chips are found in almost every Arduino board produced.

You can find more information on the ATmega series on Atmel's website at: `http://www.atmel.com/products/microcontrollers/avr/megaavr.aspx`.

The ATtiny Series

The Atmel tinyAVR series has small-package devices designed for applications that require performance and power efficiency. These devices live up to their name "tiny"; the smallest tinyAVR is 1.5 mm by 1.4 mm. The word "tiny" is only a reference to their size. Their power is comparable to the larger AVRs; they have multiple I/O pins that can be easily configured and a Universal Serial Interface that can be configured as SPI, UART, or TWI. They can also be powered with as little as 0.7 V, making them highly energy-efficient. They can be used in single-chip solutions or in glue logic and distributed intelligence in larger systems.

There are more than 30 ATtiny devices, and they come with between 0.5 k and 16 k of flash memory, and range from 6-pin packages to 32-pin packages. You can find more information on the ATtiny series on Atmel's website at: `http://www.atmel.com/products/microcontrollers/avr/tinyavr.aspx`.

While the ATtiny series are powerful devices given their size, no Arduino uses this device as its microcontroller.

Other Series

Atmel also has different AVR series: The XMEGA series deliver real-time performance, with added encryption using AES and DES modules, and includes an interesting technology, the XMEGA Custom Logic, reducing the need for external electronics.

Atmel also produces a 32-bit version of its AVR microcontroller: the UC3. Supporting fixed-point DSP, a DMA controller, Atmel's famous Peripheral Event System and advanced power management, the UC3 is a formidable microcontroller. You can find more information on Atmel's AVR website at: `http://www.atmel.com/products/microcontrollers/avr/default.aspx`.

The Different Arduinos

The original Arduino was designed for one specific task, and it fit that task perfectly. With the success of the original Arduino board, the company decided to create more designs, some of them for very specific tasks. Also, because the original Arduino design was open source, several companies and individuals have developed their own Arduino-compatible boards, or have followed in the open source tradition, and have proposed their modifications to Arduino. Arduino has begun a certification program to ensure compatibility with boards that use different processors, with the Intel Galileo being the first to receive such a certification. Anyone is free to make their own Arduino-based derivative, but the name and logo of Arduino are trademarked. As such, you'll find a number of boards with names ending in "uino", implying compatibility.

WARNING   Beware of counterfeits! Some companies propose Arduino boards that are cheaper than the original Arduino series, but these boards tend to have less reliable hardware. Arduino boards are cheap but still use good quality electronic components, whereas counterfeit boards may well use components that will not last as long. Paying a few extra dollars for a board helps Arduino finance more research to create new Arduino boards and software, and ensures a better user experience. You can read more about how to spot counterfeit boards at: `http://arduino.cc/en/Products/Counterfeit`.

Arduino made the board design open source, but it still produces its own boards. These boards are known as official boards. Other companies also make Arduino-compatible boards.

Arduino Uno

The Arduino Uno is the "standard" Arduino board and the most readily available. It is powered by an Atmel ATmega328, with a total of 32 KB of flash memory, 2 KB of SRAM, and 1 KB of EEPROM memory. With a total of 14 digital I/O pins and 6 analog I/O pins, this is a very capable device, able to run most programs. An on-board ATmega16u2 chip manages serial communication. It is one of the least expensive boards and the most used. When starting a new project, if you do not know what Arduino to use, start with the Uno, as shown in Figure 1-3.

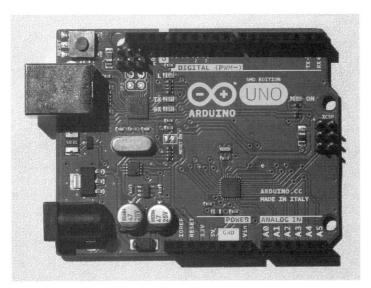

Figure 1-3: The Arduino Uno

Arduino Leonardo

The Arduino Leonardo is slightly different to the Uno. Based on the ATmega32u4, this microcontroller has enhanced USB capabilities and therefore does not require a dedicated microchip for USB serial communication like the Uno. One advantage to this is cost; one less microchip means a cheaper solution. It also means that a developer can use the microcontroller as a native USB device, increasing flexibility in the communication with a computer. The Leonardo can effectively emulate a keyboard and mouse via USB HID, as shown in Figure 1-4.

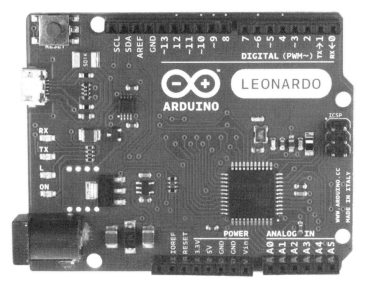

Figure 1-4: The Arduino Leonardo

Arduino Ethernet

The Arduino Ethernet, based on the ATmega328 found in the Uno, can connect to an Ethernet network, a functionality needed in a number of projects. Physically, the Arduino Ethernet has the same 14-digital inputs/outputs as the Arduino Uno, with the exception that 4 are used to control the Ethernet module and on-board micro-SD card reader, limiting the amount of pins available.

It is interesting to note that the Arduino Ethernet has an optional POE module, short for Power Over Ethernet. This option enables the Arduino Ethernet to be powered directly from an Ethernet connection, without the need for an external power source provided that there is a POE supply on the other end of the Ethernet cable. Without POE, the Arduino must be powered by an external source

Another difference from other Arduino boards is the lack of a USB connector. Because most of the space is taken up with an Ethernet connector, this device instead supports a 6-pin serial programming header and is compatible with numerous programming devices (including a device from Arduino, the USB-Serial adapter). The Arduino Ethernet is shown in Figure 1-5.

Arduino Mega 2560

The Arduino Mega 2560 is only slightly larger than the Arduino Uno, but it has more input and output pins. It has a total of 54 digital I/O pins and 16 analog inputs. It also has a large amount of flash memory: 256 KB, capable of storing larger programs than the Uno. It also has generous SRAM and EEPROM: 8 KB and 4 KB, respectively. It also has 4 hardware UART ports, making it an ideal platform for communicating with multiple devices serially.

Figure 1-5: The Arduino Ethernet

Arduino Mega boards are used when large amount of inputs and outputs are required. It is shown in Figure 1-6.

Figure 1-6: The Arduino Mega 2560

Arduino Mini

The Arduino Mini is a tiny device, useful for applications where space is reduced to the absolute minimum (see Figure 1-7). It has 14 digital I/O pins and 4 analog input pins. (Four more are available but are not broken out.) The device has the strict minimum: it does not have a USB connector; it has no power regulator; and it has no headers. Programming is done via an external USB or RS232 to TTL serial adapter. It is shown in Figure 1-7.

Figure 1-7: The Arduino Mini

Arduino Micro

The Arduino Micro lives up to its name; it is one of the smallest Arduino boards available. Despite its small size, it still has a large amount of input and output pins; it has 20 digital input/output pins, of which 7 can be used as PWM outputs. It also has 12 analog inputs.

The Micro is not designed to have shields but it does have an interesting layout, as shown in Figure 1-8. It can be placed directly onto a breadboard.

Arduino Due

The Arduino Due differs from all other Arduino designs in that it is not based on an AVR, but rather uses a microcontroller based on an ARM Cortex-M3, the Atmel SAM3X8E. This advanced microcontroller is clocked at 84 MHz and is a full 32-bit device. It has a large amount of digital and analog I/O: 54 digital pins (12 of which can be used as PWM) and 12 analog inputs. The board has 4 UARTs, an SPI header, a Twin-Wire Interface, and even includes a JTAG header.

Figure 1-8: The Arduino Micro

The Arduino Due has more strict power supply requirements, and the micro-controller itself is powered under 3.3 V. Be careful not to apply 5 V to any of the pins: otherwise, you will damage the board. When choosing a shield for the Due, make sure the shield supports 3.3 V. You can identify if a shield is Due compatible by making sure it conforms to the Arduino R3 layout.

The Arduino Due is an incredibly powerful Arduino. The Due has 512 KB of flash memory and a total of 96 KB of SRAM. It can handle the largest programs at a fast speed. If you have a lot of calculations to perform, this is the Arduino that you need (Figure 1-9).

LilyPad Arduino

The LilyPad Arduino is an interesting device. It strays from the typical Arduino build because it is not rectangular, but round. Secondly, it does not support shields. What it is designed for, however, is to be a small device that is perfect for wearable computing, or e-fabric. The round shape means that connectors are evenly distributed, and its small scale (2 inches in diameter) makes it perfect for wearable devices. This device is easily hidden, and multiple manufacturers have designed devices especially for the LilyPad: Wearable LEDs, light sensors, even battery supply boxes that can be sewn into fabric.

To make the LilyPad as small and as light as possible, some sacrifices were made. The LilyPad does not have a voltage regulator, so it is vitally important to deliver at least 2.7 volts, but more important, no more than 5.5 volts; otherwise, the LilyPad will be destroyed (see Figure 1-10).

Figure 1-9: The Arduino Due

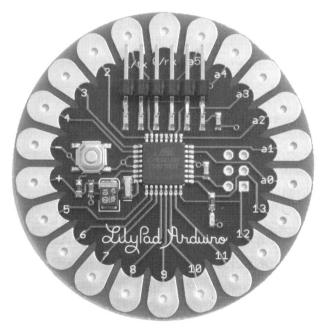

Figure 1-10: The LilyPad Arduino

Arduino Pro

The Arduino Pro exists in two versions, based either on the ATmega168 or the ATmega328. The 168 version operates at 3.3 V with an 8 MHz clock, and the 328 version runs on 5 V at 16 MHz. Both versions have 14 digital inputs/outputs and 6 analog inputs. It has a JST battery power connector, a power switch to select between power modes, and space reserved for a power jack, if needed. It does not have a USB connector but instead uses a FTDI cable for programming.

The Arduino Pro is different from most other Arduinos in that while it is a prototyping board it is designed to be embedded in projects. It does not come with headers—indeed, it does not have any headers at all, as shown in Figure 1-11. All the digital and analog inputs and outputs are placed at the exterior of the board, retaining shield layout, ready to be soldered to wire or connectors if necessary. Instead of being used for prototyping, the Arduino Pro is aimed at semipermanent installation in finished products. The Arduino Pro was not designed by Arduino but was designed and is manufactured by SparkFun Electronics.

Arduino Robot

The Arduino Robot is, simply put, an Arduino on wheels. There are two Arduino boards on the Robot—one controls the on-board motors, and the other contains sensors. The Control board controls the Motor board and gives it instructions on how to operate.

The Control board is powered by an ATmega32u4, with 32 KB of flash, 2.5 KB of SRAM, and 1 KB of EEPROM. It also has an external I2C EEPROM device, providing more storage. It has a compass, a speaker, three LEDs, a five-button key pad, and an LCD screen. It also has three solder points for external I2C devices. It also has I/O capability, with five digital I/Os, six PWMs, and four analog inputs. There is space for eight analog inputs (for distance sensors, ultrasound sensors, or other sensors) and six digital I/O pins for other devices (four of which can be used for analog input).

The Motor board is a fully independent board, powered by an ATmega32u4, the same microcontroller as on the Control board. The Motor board contains two wheels powered independently, five IR sensors, and I2C and SPI ports. It also contains the power supply; it is powered by four rechargeable AA batteries, and contains a jack port to recharge the on-board batteries. The board can also be powered by an on-board USB connector, but in this configuration, for safety reasons, the motors are disabled (Figure 1-12).

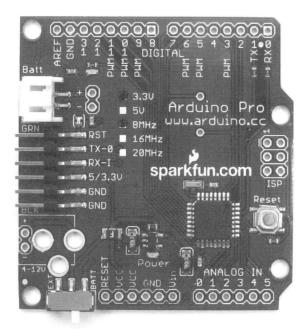

Figure 1-11: The Arduino Pro

Figure 1-12: The Arduino Robot

Arduino Esplora

The Arduino Esplora is a strange device. Where most Arduinos are designed to sit on a table or be placed under fabric, the Esplora is designed to be held in your hand. Based on an ATmega32u4, it is not shield compatible and does not have any solder points for inputs and outputs. Instead, it looks and feels like a game pad; it has thumb inputs in the form of four digital switches, one analog joystick, and a linear potentiometer. For more feedback, the Esplora has a buzzer and an RGB LED. It also features more advanced devices; it has an on-board microphone, a temperature sensor, a connector for an LCD screen, and a three-axis accelerometer.

The Esplora has 32 KB of flash; 4 KB are used by the bootloader. It has 2.5 KB of SRAM, and 1 KB of EEPROM. It is a capable device, and it makes up for its lack of connectors with four TinkerKit connectors: two inputs and two outputs, as shown in Figure 1-13.

Figure 1-13: The Arduino Esplora

Arduino Yún

The Arduino Yún is based on an ATmega32u4, but it also has an Atheros AR9331 on the same board. The Atheros processor has a complete Linux distribution, based on OpenWRT, famous for Linux-based wireless routers.

The Arduino Yún has built-in Ethernet and WiFi, and also has a micro-SD slot. The Yún is different from other Arduinos and shields in that it has advanced network functionality; the Arduino can send commands to OpenWRT and then continue processing its sketch (Figure 1-14). The two processors work independently, the Bridge library facilitates communication between the two processors.

Figure 1-14: The Arduino Yún

Arduino Tre

The not-yet-released Arduino Tre promises to be a phenomenal beast. Up until now, the fastest Arduino was the Arduino Due, based on an ARM-compatible microcontroller. The Tre, created by Arduino and BeagleBoard, combines the power of a full computer with the flexible input and output of an Arduino.

The Tre has a Cortex-A8 class processor, the Sitara AM335X processor, running at 1 GHz. This processor has access to 512 MB of RAM and has an HDMI port capable of displaying Full HD (1920 x 1080). All this power is interfaced by an Atmel ATmega32u4 using the Arduino programming environment that enthusiasts have come to love.

Arduino Zero

The Arduino Zero is a brand new Arduino using Atmel's SAM D21 microcontroller. It has 256 KB of flash memory, 32 KB of RAM, and runs at 48 MHz. The Arduino Zero is designed to handle future requirements from the Maker community, by creating a design that is powerful, robust, and flexible enough to be used in robotics and wearable projects, as well as the IoT. It is also the first design to have an advanced debugger interface.

Your Own Arduino?

Arduino has always created open-source designs, and all the boards listed previously have schematic files available directly from the Arduino website, under a Creative Commons Attribution Share-Alike license. Put simply, this means that you are free to study the Arduino schematics to make your own or to make modifications either for personal use or professional use on the condition that you give credit to Arduino for the original design and release your own design under the same license.

With the exception of the Arduino Due, all Arduino boards are based on the Atmel AVR. These chips can be bought from electronic distributors with the Arduino firmware pre-installed, or if you have the proper tools, you can buy blank chips and load the firmware yourself.

Shields

An Arduino by itself is a capable device and already includes numerous input and outputs, but its power only starts there. Because Arduino designs are open source, numerous companies have developed shields, printed circuit boards that are placed on top of the Arduino board that connect to the Arduino's pins. There shields add functionality by using different inputs and outputs, either digital I/O or through serial communication.

What Is a Shield?

A *shield* is a printed circuit board that can be placed on the top of most Arduino boards. It connects to the Arduino's processor through male header pins. Adding a shield to an Arduino does not necessarily expand the possibilities of an Arduino, but most do.

For most prototyping projects, you connect wires to the Arduino's headers and connect them to a breadboard. This is easy enough for a lot of applications, like outputting data to two or three LEDs. For more complex applications, a breadboard isn't practical due to the complexity of the wiring, or the size of the components. Micro-SD card readers are extremely small and cannot be placed onto a breadboard. Soldering wires to a micro-SD reader isn't particularly easy, so your choices are limited. Writing data to a micro-SD card is something that can happen a lot, so it's fortunate several companies have developed shields with a micro-SD reader. If your application requires data logging, all you have to do is to connect the shield to the top of the Arduino, add a few lines of code, and you are ready to go. It is that simple.

As said previously, not all shields add functionality. Some shields exist to help prototyping— allowing you to solder components onto the shield—without having to make your own PCB. Prototyping on a breadboard is an excellent way to test that your design works, but after the design is proven, it is time to make a better board. For example, if you were creating a doorbell application, it would be complicated to hide a breadboard behind the ringer. Instead, you could solder those components onto a prototyping board, saving space and making your design much more resistant to shock or tampering. The added advantage of this type of board is that you do not need to create your own printed circuit board or do any complicated routing.

The Different Shields

Shields exist for a wide variety of applications: storage on SD cards, network connectivity by Ethernet or WiFi robotics control, enabling displays like LCD and TFT screens, to name but a few.

Most shields can be stacked, so you are not limited to using only one at a time. However, some shields may require input and outputs that will subsequently be unavailable to other designs. Be careful when you choose your shields!

Arduino Motor Shield

When using motors, special care has to be taken. When turned off, motors can induce voltage spikes, and components need to be added to a design account for this possibility. Also, typically, USB power is insufficient for motors. The Arduino Motor Shield takes care of this and enables the programmer independent control of two DC motors, or one stepper motor. This shield can either be powered from the Arduino or rely on an external power supply.

Arduino Wireless SD Shield

The Wireless SD shield is designed for an Xbee module but works with any radio modem with the same footprint. The on-board micro-SD slot allows the shield to act as a data logger. It also has a small prototyping area for adding components.

Arduino Ethernet Shield

The Arduino Ethernet shield does exactly as the name implies; it adds Ethernet connectivity through a W5100 controller, supporting up to four simultaneous socket connections. This module also includes a micro-SD slot for data-logging.

The Arduino Ethernet Shield has an optional POE module. On a POE network, the module (and the parent Arduino) can be powered directly over Ethernet.

Arduino WiFi Shield

The Arduino WiFi Shield includes an HDG104 Wireless LAN controller, enabling an Arduino to access 802.11b/g networks. It can connect to open and encrypted networks. This module also includes a micro-SD slot for data-logging.

Arduino GSM Shield

The Arduino GSM shield connects to the Internet through a GPRS network, at a maximum of 85.6 KBps. It also has voice capabilities; by adding an external microphone and speaker circuit, it can make and receive voice calls. It can also send and receive SMS messages. The modem, an M10 by Quectel, is configured using AT commands, handled in software by the GSM library.

The Arduino GSM Shield comes with a Bluevia SIM card; which allows for machine-to-machine roaming data connections in blocks of 10 or 20 megabytes. However, the GSM shield will work with a SIM card from a different provider.

Your Own Shield

In some cases, you will want to make your own electronics. For prototyping, a breadboard is sufficient, but when you need something more robust and more professional, it is time to make your own shield. There are several software options to assist you, but one of the best is the Fritzing application. In Fritzing, you can create breadboard designs, translate them into electronic schematics, and generate a shield layout directly. Fritzing also has its own shield creation system; just upload your schematic to its website and receive a professionally built shield.

What Can You Do with an Arduino?

This is one of the most commonly asked questions, but the answer is both simple and complicated. Put simply, you can do almost anything you can imagine. The most difficult part of any Arduino project is identifying a need. Maybe you have an aquarium at home and would like to control the lighting in a specific way? Maybe you would like to add a parking assist device onto your car. Some people just want to add some automation to their house, opening and closing motorized shades at the push of a button. Some people come up with even more amazing and fun projects: a remote-controlled lawn mower, even a chess playing robot. The possibilities are almost unlimited. There are a few things that an Arduino cannot do, but that list is becoming shorter every time a new Arduino-compatible board is released.

Arduino is an excellent way to learn about software development and electronics because it is a low-cost, robust device that is easy to program.

Some people use Arduino for hobbyist electronics, with projects ranging from the simple to the incredibly absurd. I know of one person who has entirely automated his house using 10 Arduino Megas, each room communicating with the others to better estimate electrical consumption, heating, and personal comfort.

Arduino is also used professionally because the components are low-cost and highly reliable and have the added flexibility of being open source. When an initial design is completed, developers can make a board much smaller to be included in toys, small embedded systems, and even industrial machines. Several 3-D printers are based on Arduino for their ease of use and reliability.

What You Will Need for This Book

Each chapter has a list of elements required to complete. However, when creating an Arduino project, a few items are required every time. Following is a list:

- **A power supply**—The Arduino Uno accepts an input voltage of 6 to 20 V, with 7 to 12 V being recommended. Any standard AC-to-DC center-positive adapter should work fine, preferably one that can supply up to or over 1 amp of current.

- **Multimeter**—Almost any model. You do not need to buy the most expensive, far from it, but it should test DC voltage, DC amperage and continuity, with optional resistance calculation, and AC voltage and amperage if you plan to interface your Arduino to main's power.

- **Breadboard**—The size depends on your project. Consider a medium-sized board; if it is too small you might not fit all your components (or it might be too cramped, possibly creating short circuits), and large breadboards can cost more and require more space. (I use 680-point breadboards for most of my examples and projects.)

- **Resistors**—A common element of every project. There are numerous values, but there are some values that will be used more often. There are kits on the market that propose 10 of every value, or you can go with the most common, the choice is yours. To start out, ten 220-ohm, ten 1-kilohm, and ten 10-kilohm resistors should suffice.

- **LEDs**—A great way of knowing the output of a pin. Coupled with a resistor, it can instantly show the state of your project.

- **Other electronic components**—Sometimes it is handy to have a small collection of capacitors, switches, and diodes on hand. Each example in this book has a complete list of the required components.

Summary

This chapter briefly talked about some of what an Arduino can do, but there is no way of knowing exactly what everyone will do with it. As I said, your only limitation will be your imagination, and I would love to hear about what you have done with an Arduino! You can contact me on my website at `http://packetfury.net`. I look forward to hearing about your projects!

In the next chapter, you will learn more about programming an Arduino, including how to install the Arduino IDE, how to connect an Arduino to your computer, and uploading your first sketch.

CHAPTER 2

Programming for the Arduino

The Arduino is an embedded system, that is to say it has the minimum amount of hardware to get the job done. That does not mean that it is by any means a weak system; there is no point in having a PCI bus if it will never be used—it will only take up space, energy, and increase the overall cost of the device. Arduinos are lightweight—and inexpensive—and make excellent embedded systems. Just like all embedded systems, programming is done on a host computer, not the Arduino itself.

Programming an embedded system, and indeed programming any sort of system, is the art of writing text that can be understood by a human, and translating it into a binary file that can be understood by a processor. For this, some tools are required. The data written by humans is called *source code*, and because most source code is in text format, sometimes a simple text editor is enough. Most people go with an *Integrated Development Environment* (*IDE*), an augmented text editor with add-ons designed for developers. These add-ons can range from text auto-completion to debugging and often include tools to handle different types of *source files*, which contain source code. Some projects might use only one file, but large projects can sometimes have hundreds of files, if not thousands. After the source code is written, a compiler must be used, which reads in the source code and creates one or more binary files. These binary files are later uploaded onto the Arduino and run by the microcontroller.

Arduino developed all the tools required to get straight to work. With a different embedded system, you may have to make a choice of an IDE, install a compiler, and sometimes even a flasher, and spend precious hours setting up the system. With Arduino, this isn't the case; everything is delivered in a simple package and contains everything needed, from writing your programs to flashing the final binary file.

An Arduino program is known as a *sketch*. There are several definitions of the word sketch such as a brief literary composition or a brief musical composition. Whatever your preference, an Arduino sketch is like a work of art; you, the artist, gather and assemble elements to create your masterpiece. Google X engineer Jeremy Blum, author of the book *Exploring Arduino* (Wiley, 2013), said,

---

I believe that creative engineering is indistinguishable from fine artwork.

The Arduino will be your canvas; you are on your way to making something amazing using sketches and electronics. Your only limitation will be your imagination.

Installing Your Environment

The first thing that you need to do is to install the Arduino IDE. The Arduino IDE is a fully integrated piece of software written in Java. Java can run on multiple platforms, and the IDE is available for Windows, Mac OS X, and Linux. You can get the Arduino IDE free of charge at the Arduino website:

```
http://arduino.cc/en/main/software
```

On this page, you will most likely have several options. The latest stable version will always be listed first. Next, any beta versions available will be listed. Beta versions are test versions that might not be up to the quality of a finished version but that add functionality; it will be up to you to decide if you want to use it. Beta versions sometimes support more hardware, and if you use the latest Arduino boards, you might not have a choice.

Also listed on the site are nightly builds and builds for specific hardware. Nightly builds are installers that are generated every night that contain the latest updates but may in some rare cases also have bugs. Specific builds are builds created for a single board in mind. At the time of writing, there is an IDE available for the Intel Galileo, an Arduino compatible board designed and manufactured by Intel that does not use the same compiler.

Downloading the Software

Time to get to work! You have to download the software, so find the latest version and download it. Figure 2-1 shows what the Arduino site looks like on my development computer.

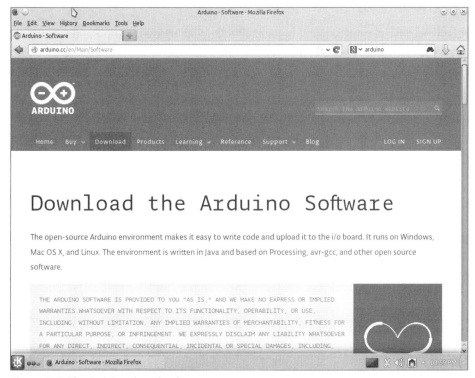

Figure 2-1: The Arduino download page

Windows users have a choice between an installer and an archive. For the installer, simply download the installer, double-click it, and follow the instructions. For more information on installing, please see the Arduino website on installing: `http://arduino.cc/en/Guide/HomePage`.

Mac OS X and Linux users have to download an archive. Simply unpack the archive using your normal tool, and double-click the Arduino icon inside the newly created folder. Everything required is inside this folder.

If you have an operating system that is not listed, or if you are curious about the source code, a source code bundle is also available. You could compile the source code yourself.

Some Linux distributions might bundle the Arduino IDE directly; others might require external repositories. Refer to your distribution's forums or look at Arduino's Playground website, a community edited wiki, at: `http://playground.arduino.cc`.

Running the Software

Once you have downloaded and installed the software, open the application. If everything went well, you should have a window that looks like the one in Figure 2-2.

Figure 2-2: Empty sketch

This is the Arduino IDE, where you will design your sketches. The main window is the sketch editor, which is where you write your code. At the bottom is the status window; you receive information on compilation, uploads, or code errors. In the bottom right of the screen is the device information panel, which shows the device that you are using, as well as the serial port it is connected to.

The sketch editor isn't just a simple text editor; the editor colors and formats text depending on what you write. Comments are greyed out, data types are written in color, and so on. This provides a nice, easy way to read and write source code.

Using Your Own IDE

The Arduino IDE is a capable environment, but some people may want to use their own IDE, either for preference or simply because they are used to another environment. The Arduino community has worked hard on porting the tools to other programs, and you can find a complete list on the Arduino Playground. Eclipse, CodeBlocks, Kdevelop, and the command line are just a few of the environments proposed. Although this book concentrates on the Arduino IDE, check out other IDEs. For more information see `http://playground.arduino .cc/Main/DevelopmentTools`.

Your First Program

It's time to dive in! By default, Arduinos come with a default sketch called Blink. This sketch will blink the on-board LED connected to pin 13, available on most Arduinos. Just plug a USB cable into your computer and your Arduino, and after a few seconds you will see the LED blink, telling you that everything went well. Arduinos are all about getting things done, and what better way to show you just how easy they are than to run your first program. Your first sketch will look like Listing 2-1:

Listing 2-1: Your first sketch

```
/*
  Blink
  Turns on an LED on for one second, then off for one second, repeat

  This example code is in the public domain.
 */

// Pin 13 has an LED connected on most Arduino boards.
// give it a name:
int led = 13;

// the setup routine runs once when you press reset:
void setup() {
  // initialize the digital pin as an output.
  pinMode(led, OUTPUT);
}

// the loop routine runs over and over again forever:
void loop() {
  digitalWrite(led, HIGH);   // turn the LED on (HIGH is the level)
  delay(200);                // wait for 0.2 seconds
  digitalWrite(led, LOW);    // turn the LED off by making the LOW
  delay(200);                // wait for 0.2 seconds
}
```

If this source code doesn't make much sense to you, don't worry; everything will be explained a little later. Seasoned C developers might have a few questions, which will also be answered later.

The previous sketch is an entire program. You can either type it in or use the Arduino IDE directly; this code listing is actually an example from the Arduino IDE. To open it, go to File ➪ Examples ➪ 01.Basics ➪ Blink, and a new window will open with the code. This sketch has *comments*, text zones where the user can write about what he is intending to do, indicated by // at the beginning of the line. Have a quick read through, and try to see what the program is doing.

When you are ready, it is time to upload your first program! *Uploading* means installing the binary code onto the Arduino board. Make sure your Arduino board is connected to your development computer via USB. For this example, use an Arduino Uno or Arduino Mega. This code can run on all the Arduinos, so feel free to use whichever you have. To upload the program, a few simple steps must first be completed. The IDE needs to know what type of board is connected. First, go into the menu; Tools ➪ Board, and select your board. As you can see, there are a lot of different boards to choose from. Select the entry that corresponds to your board; in this example, I have an Arduino Mega 2560, as illustrated in Figure 2-3.

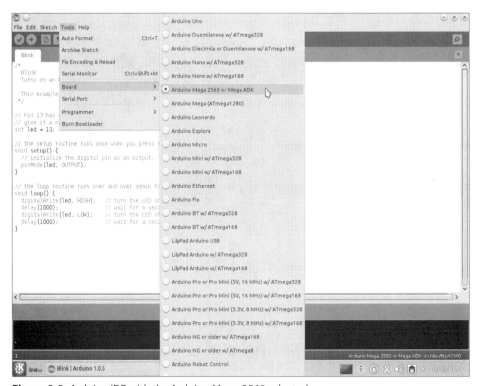

Figure 2-3: Arduino IDE with the Arduino Mega 2560 selected

Next, the IDE needs to know how the board is connected to your computer. Using the Tools ⇨ Serial Port menu, you can select the proper connection. On a Windows machine, the board will appear as a COM port. On a Mac, the Arduino connection will start with "/dev/tty.usbmodem." My development machine is a Linux system, and in this case the Arduino is connected to /dev/ttyACM0. On some systems, there might be several serial ports listed. Figure 2-4 illustrates me selecting my port.

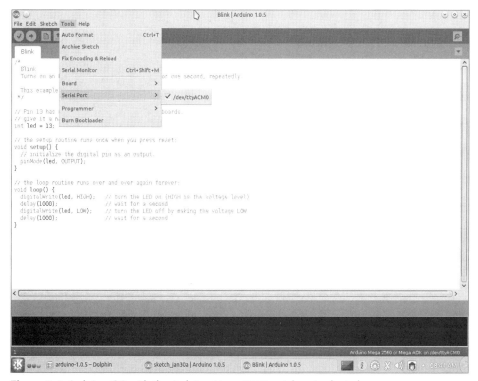

Figure 2-4: Arduino IDE with the Arduino Mega 2560 serial port selected

That's it—as far as configuration goes. You have to do this only once; the Arduino IDE remembers your preferences and keeps them for the next time. You will need to change your settings if you change boards or plug the board into a different USB port.

Next, you may optionally verify the source code. The verification stage actually compiles the source code; the compiler will warn you if anything goes wrong. If there is a problem, the IDE shows a message at the bottom of the screen, indicating a line number and the cause of the problem. For this example, the compiler shouldn't complain, and it will compile your application. To compile, you must click the Verify button (the check mark) in the top left of the IDE or go into the menu Sketch ⇨ Verify/Compile. There is also a keyboard shortcut: Ctrl+R.

There is now one final step: you must *upload* the program onto your Arduino. Simply click the Upload button next to the Verify button, or go to the menu item File ⇨ Upload. Again, a keyboard shortcut is available: Ctrl+U, as shown in Figure 2-5. The upload process also re-verifies the source code before uploading.

Figure 2-5: Successful upload

The Arduino IDE now attempts to contact the Arduino board and transfer the program into the microcontroller's flash memory. A message at the bottom should soon display the text "Done Uploading". Now look at your Arduino board. Next to the USB connector, a small LED should be blinking; the same one used to verify that your Arduino was working in the beginning of the chapter. This time, it should be blinking two to three times per second. Congratulations! You have now successfully uploaded your first Arduino program!

The program has now been written into flash memory, but what does that mean? Like a program on a computer, it has been "installed" into the nonvolatile memory and will be executed every time you turn on the Arduino, so try that right now. Unplug your Arduino from the USB port, wait a few seconds, and then plug it back in. The Arduino will be powered again from the USB port, and after a few seconds, the LED will start to flash. Your program is running.

Although it may appear that the Arduino has simply run your program, it hasn't done only that. Arduinos contain something called a *bootloader*, a small program that is run every time the device starts. This is only one of the strong points of the Arduino system; the bootloader is always available to allow the programmer to reflash a program. Even if you accidentally flash a program that continuously crashes, you will always be able to reflash your Arduino, provided the bootloader is present.

WARNING If you need more program space, you can delete the bootloader and place your own application at the start of the processor's instruction sequence. Doing this has the advantage of freeing the space used by the bootloader and using it for your own application. The bootloader is a small program, about 2 kilobytes in size. If you delete the bootloader, you can still reflash your Arduino, but more specialized equipment will be required.

Understanding Your First Sketch

Now that your sketch works and you have seen the results, it is time to have a closer look at the source code. This is presented step by step. The first part gives some interesting information:

```
/*
  Blink
  Turns on an LED on for one second, then off for one second repeatedly

  This example code is in the public domain.
*/
```

Everything placed between the text /* and */ is considered to be a *comment*, a portion of source code that is ignored by the compiler. Everything within these markers will be ignored, so it is the best place to write natural language text about what the program does, or is doing. It is common to start a source code file with a comment, explaining what the application does. Just by looking at these few lines, you already have an idea about what the program will do.

```
// Pin 13 has an LED connected on most Arduino boards.
// give it a name:
int led = 13;
```

This, again, explains what will happen using comments. Just like the /* and */ markers, when the compiler encounters the marker //, it will ignore everything else after that marker but only for that line. On the first line, the compiler encounters a comment marker and ignores the text. It then attempts to read in the second line but again encounters a comment and ignores that, too. On the third line, there is no comment; this is a real line of code.

It starts with the keyword *int*, short for integer. This is a *variable declaration*; it tells the compiler to reserve space for a *variable*, a named container that can change its contents. Because the variable was declared as an integer, it can hold only whole numbers between -32,768 and 32,767. This variable is named *led*. The compiler will assign the value 13 to the variable. Finally, the line is finished with a semicolon. In C, a semicolon marks the end of an instruction.

Now for the next part:

```
// the setup routine runs once when you press reset:
void setup() {
  // initialize the digital pin as an output.
  pinMode(led, OUTPUT);
}
```

The first line is a comment. It explains what the next portion of the code will do.

The next line is interesting. The keyword `void` means an empty data type. The second word, `setup`, declares the name of a function. Because of the parentheses and curly brackets, you know that this is not a variable but a function. *Functions* are portions of code that can be called inside a program; instead of writing the same code dozens of times, it is possible to write it only once and have the program call this function as required. It is also a way of separating code for special needs.

Inside the parentheses, you would list any *parameters* for the function: these are variables that can be passed to the function. Because there is nothing inside the parentheses of `setup()`, there are no parameters. The function therefore does not need any data to run. Because the function was declared as void, it will not return any data either. When this function is called, it will do its job and then return without any data. But what exactly does it do?

Everything included in the curly brackets is part of the function—in this case, a single line of code. When the setup function is called, it executes one instruction, `pinMode()`. This instruction is not preceded with a data type, meaning that it is not a variable declaration, and it is not a function declaration. Because it has parentheses, it is a function, and unlike `setup` it requires two parameters: `led` and `OUTPUT`. All the standard functions will be listed in Chapter 4, but just to give you an idea, `pinMode()` is a function that tells the microcontroller how a particular pin will be used. Before using a pin, the microcontroller needs to know how it will be used; in this case, it will be sent as an output. The microcontroller can therefore set the output of a pin as `HIGH` or `LOW` and will not attempt to read the status of the pin. The pin in question, identified as *led*, was defined earlier in the code; it is pin number 13.

Now for the final section of code.

```
// the loop routine runs over and over again forever:
void loop() {
  digitalWrite(led, HIGH);   // turn the LED on (HIGH voltage level)
  delay(200);                // wait for a second
  digitalWrite(led, LOW);    // turn the LED off, LOWvoltage
  delay(200);                // wait for a second
}
```

Again, the code starts with a comment, giving you an idea of what this portion of code will do. This is a function declaration for a function called `loop()`. It does not require any parameters to run.

Inside of loop, you'll see the function `digitalWrite()`. As you might have guessed from the name of the function, it performs a write action on a pin in digital format. It sets the pin status to a logical 1 (HIGH) or a logical 0 (LOW). The first time the function is called in this sketch, it sets the pin to a logical 1.

The code then calls the `delay()` function with an argument of 1000. The `delay` function tells the microcontroller to wait for a specified number of milliseconds before proceeding to the next instruction. In this case, it tells the microcontroller to wait for 1 second before proceeding. So, the program turns on a pin and then waits for 1 second. The rest of the code is similar; a digitalWrite is performed, this time setting the pin to a logical 0 (LOW), and then waits for another second.

For those of you used to developing applications in C, you might have noticed that the Arduino code does not have a `main()` function. In C, the `main()` function is used as an entry point; that is to say, it is the function that is called when the program starts. This is true for systems programming, where an operating system takes care of initializing everything required by the program, but this is not the case on embedded systems.

The Arduino requires that two functions be present; `setup()` and `loop()`. These two functions must be present, even if they are empty, but they rarely will be.

The `setup()` function is called when a sketch starts and is used to initialize variables, pin modes, and other components for your sketch. It is good practice to keep initialization code away from the work code, making things clearer. It also has the advantage of making your program more robust. Although it is perfectly possible to set up a pin as required just before performing an action, it is best to have everything completely set up before starting your program. Looking into the `setup()` function can tell you immediately if you have correctly set up a pin, instead of looking through long lines of code in the work section. In this example, `setup()` contained a command to change the status of a pin, setting it to output.

The `loop()` function does exactly what its name implies; it loops continuously, as long as power is applied to the Arduino. In the example, `loop()` set the output of a pin HIGH, waited for 1 second, set the output of the same pin to LOW, and then waited for another second. After this was done, the function ran again. This is also the reason why configuration should not be done inside the `loop()` function; the same code will be run over and over again. If you had put any configuration here, variables could have been overwritten, and setting pin configurations might have slowed down the application.

These two functions are required for any sketch, though you are free to add your own functions as required.

Programming Basics

As said previously, programming is the art of writing something that is readable by humans and that can be converted to be understood by computers. The problem is that computers, despite what people try to tell you, aren't intelligent at all. They need to be told exactly what to do, and require exact instructions. Source code has to be laid out in a precise way.

Variables and Data Types

In your sketches, most of the time you will want to store data and perform some type of calculation. Counting the number of times a button is pushed, storing the voltage on an analog pin, or performing a complex mathematical calculation with vectors: require data to be calculated and stored. This data is saved in a *variable*, a memory location that can be changed as required. By declaring a variable, you are asking the compiler to allocate a specific amount of memory, depending on the data type.

There are different types of data, and you must first tell the compiler exactly what sort of data you want to store. If you define a variable as capable of holding integers, you cannot use the same variable to store floating-point data, or even a string of text. The different data types are listed in Table 2-1.

Table 2-1: Different Data Types

DATA TYPE	CONTENTS
void	No data type
boolean	True or false
char	One character, stored as an ASCII number ('A', 'B', 'C'...)
unsigned char	Decimal numbers, from 0 to 255

DATA TYPE	CONTENTS
byte	Decimal numbers, from 0 to 255
int	Decimal numbers, from –32,768 to 32,767
	(Arduino Due, from –2,147,483,648 to 2,147,483,647)
unsigned int	Decimal numbers, from 0 to 65,535
	(Arduino Due, from 0 to 4,294,967,295)
word	Decimal numbers, from 0 to 65,535
long	Decimal numbers, from –2,147,483,648 to 2,147,483,647
unsigned long	Decimal numbers, from 0 to 4,294,967,295
short	Decimal numbers, –32,768 to 32,767
float	Floating point numbers, from –3.4028235 x 10^{38} 3.4028235 x 10^{38}
double	Floating point numbers
string	An array of char
String	Advanced arrays of char
array	A collection of variables

Also noteworthy, the Arduino Due is a relatively new device that uses a 32-bit microcontroller instead of the 8-bit AVR found in other Arduino boards. Therefore, some of the data types are different to other Arduinos. Integers are coded to 32-bits, meaning they can handle much larger numbers. Also, the data type double is coded to 8 bytes on the Arduino Due and 4 bytes on other Arduinos. Therefore, a double has more precision on an Arduino Due.

When declaring a variable, it is important to first specify the data type and then the variable name. Optionally, you may assign a value by using the equal sign. Finally, finish with a semicolon. The following are legal declarations:

```
long data;
char usertext;
int pin_number = 42;
```

You are free to use just about any variable name, but don't use names that are too vague. In the previous example, usertext hints that the variable contains some text that comes from an external source. The variable pin_number suggests that this is the pin ID for input or output operations, but data? The definition is too vast; does it contain text? Numbers? Later in your sketch, you might start wondering what this variable contains, and you might even confuse it with another variable with unpredictable results.

Data types work on variables but also on functions. This is described later in the "Functions" section.

Control Structures

The power of microprocessors and microcontrollers is their ability to process data. They follow instructions, and can also execute conditional instruction depending on data. Does the variable contain a number greater or equal than 42? If so, execute this portion of code. Otherwise, execute another portion. These instructions come in the form of conditional statements like `if`, `for`, and `while`.

if Statement

The `if` statement is the simplest of branching statements and is used to detect if an expression is equal to a result. It is used as follows:

```
if (expression)
{
    statement;
}
```

Multiple instructions can be used inside an `if` statement, by placing multiple instructions inside curly brackets:

```
if (expression)
{
    statement;
    another_statement;
}
```

It is also possible to execute two sets of instructions using an `if .. else` statement. You can think of it as doing one thing `if` the result is equal to something, `else` performs another action.

```
if (expression)
{
    do_this;
}
else
{
    do_that;
}
```

It is also possible to mix several `if`s using `else`:

```
if (expression)
{
    do_this;
}
else if (expression)
{
    do_that;
}
```

The expression is used to check the veracity of a statement. For example, you can check to see if a variable is equal to a certain value, less than a value, greater than a value, and so on. It is also possible to detect other value types; for example, if a boolean value is true or false.

```
int myval = 42;
if (myval == 42){
    run_this; // myval equals 42; this function will be executed
}else{
    run_that; //This one will not
}
if (myval < 50){
    run_another_function; //This will be run, since 42 is less than 50
}
```

Note that in this example, the myval variable is set to the value 42 with a single equals sign (=), but the value is evaluated with a double equals (==). In C, a single equal sign always sets the value of a variable (or at least tries to). Two equal signs makes an evaluation. Watch out when writing if structures; a single equal sign will force a value into a variable, and the results might not be quite what you expect!

switch Case

The if statement is easy to use and works well in situations in which you need to check a variable against one value, possibly two. What would happen if you need to check against multiple variables? What about a robot that needs to detect how close an obstacle is? In this case, you might use an if statement; if the obstacle is less than 3 inches away, then stop the motors. Some situations are not as simple. Imagine a keypad connected to an Arduino with some stickers on the keypad detailing instructions for the user. If the user presses button one, then the Arduino will turn on the lights. If the user presses button two, then the blinds open. If the user presses button three, some music turns on, and so on. With if statements, this would rapidly get out of hand and would be difficult to read:

```
if (button == 1){
    turn_on_lights();
}
if (button == 2){
    if (blinds_up == false){
        raise_blinds();
        blinds_up = true;
    }
}
if (button == 3)
...
```

A more elegant way of writing this is through the switch/case statement. Just like the if statement, switch/case controls the flow of the program by allowing different sections to be executed depending on a condition. A switch statement checks the value of a variable, and executes different case statements depending on the value.

```
switch(button)
{
    case 1:
        turn_on_lights();
        break;
    case 2:
        if (blinds_up == false)
        {
            raise_blinds();
            blinds_up = true;
        }
        break;
    case 3:
        ...
```

Notice the break instruction; it is typically used at the end of each case and tells the compiler to stop running instructions. Without the break statement, the Arduino would continue to execute the case instructions, even when another case should be used. This can actually be used to your advantage. Imagine that in this application, pushing buttons 4, 6, and 8 actually do the same thing. You can write the following:

```
switch(button)
{
    case 4:
    case 6:
    case 8:
        //code to be run
        break;
}
```

while Loop

The while loop is the most basic loop in C; it will loop over the same code while a condition is satisfied. As long as the condition is true, while continues to execute the same code, checking the condition at the end of the loop.

```
while (button == false)
{
    button = check_status(pin4);
}
```

In this example, the function `check_status` runs until it returns `true`. When that happens, the variable `button` becomes `true`, and the `while` loop will be broken. It might be within a few milliseconds, or the system might wait indefinitely.

for Loop

In cases in which you need a portion of code to loop an exact number of times, the `for` loop is used. It is similar to `while`, only it is written differently. The `for` loop keeps track of the number of times it has run.

```
for (expression1; expression2; expression3)
{
    instructions;
    instructions;
}
```

This might look complicated, but don't worry; it is simple. It requires three expressions:

- `expression1` is the initializer; it will initialize a variable.
- `expression2` is the conditional expression; as long as this condition is `true`, the loop keeps on executing.
- `expression3` is the modifier; when a loop is completed, this action is performed.

For example:

```
for (int i = 0; i < 10; i++)
{
    myfunc(i);
}
```

In this example, a variable is defined with the name `i`. The variable is set to zero, and each time the function `myfunc` is run, `i` is increased by one. Finally, when `i` reaches 10, the loop stops before running `myfunc`. This saves you from writing out all the commands one by one like this:

```
myfunc(0);
myfunc(1);
...
myfunc(8);
myfunc(9);
```

NOTE The name `i` is often used for a temporary variable in `for()` loops. It is shorthand for "index."

Functions

A function is a portion of code that can be called, with parameters if required, and returns data if required. If you write a long list of repeating statements in code, or if you have created code that needs to be called several times, it may be useful to create a function.

The main program is running and then calls a function, called `addTwo()`, with two parameters: `12` and `30`. The function is run and data is returned. The program then returns to where it was.

A function requires a data type, even if it does not return any data. If no data is to be returned, then the data type `void` must be used. The contents of the function are contained within curly brackets. In the `addTwo()` function shown above, it returned an `int` datatype, indicated when it was first declared.

Libraries

The Arduino programming environment comes with a standard library, a library of functions that are included in every sketch. However, the Arduino is also an embedded system, so the standard library contains the strict minimum. By default, it can handle basic mathematical operations, and set pins to digital or analog input and output, but it cannot write data to an SD card, connect to WiFi, or use a TFT screen. These devices that are not standard on Arduino boards. Of course, an Arduino can use these devices when they are available, but to use these devices, a library for the specific device must be imported into a sketch. Otherwise, there is no point in having the extra functionality that could potentially take up space on a device where space is critical.

Adding a library to your sketch adds more functionality and allows you, the programmer, to use new functions. For example, by importing the EEPROM library, you can access the internal EEPROM by using two new functions: `read()` and `write()`. The standard library will be presented in Chapter 4, and different libraries are presented throughout the book.

CROSS-REFERENCE   Chapter 6 explains EEPROM technology and the EEPROM library.

Summary

This chapter showed you how to create your first Arduino sketch and walked you through it step by step. Arduino has developed all the tools required for you to get started programming, and they are delivered in a simple package that contains everything you need, from writing your programs to flashing the final binary file.

An Arduino program is known as a sketch, which is like a work of art. You, the artist, gather and assemble elements to create your masterpiece, and the Arduino is your canvas.

In Chapter 3, you will see some of the most common electronic components, and how to choose their values. Each will be presented, and I will explain how to use them in your sketches.

Electronics Basics

You can have a lot of fun with an Arduino, but without some electronics, you won't get far. Without adding a single electronic component, you could program an Arduino Robot to run around racetracks, or program a games controller with an Arduino Esplora, but how about an Arduino Uno? Of course, you can add shields to add some functionality, but the real fun comes when you add your own electronics. This chapter shows you how to add your own electronics components onto an Arduino. No, don't run away! It is easy, I promise.

Electronics is often shrouded in mystery, conjuring images of highly complex and advanced components requiring weeks of calculating, just to choose the right one. Although some components are indeed incredibly advanced, and although some electronic circuits do indeed require weeks of work, this tends to be true in advanced fields, not basic electronics. At the end of this chapter, you will understand some basic electronic components, and you will be able to create your own electronic circuit.

Electronics is fun, but should be taken seriously. In this chapter, you will see a few warnings for particular components. Some components can't handle high voltage; others may be damaged or destroyed if handled incorrectly. Throughout this book, there are numerous electronic examples, but none of them use high voltage, AC voltage, or any other dangerous factors. Still, be careful! You will not hurt yourself with the 5 volts used in the examples, but a short circuit will damage any components in the circuit.

Electronics 101

Everyone is exposed to electronics in one way or another. You can find electronics inside your television, your computer, your washing machine, and just about any device in your house. The electronic boards inside a television are miniaturized, and look extremely complicated, but every electronic design follows simple laws of physics.

Electricity is the flow of electrons through a conductor. A conductor enables the flow of electricity, and an insulator does not. A resistor restricts the flow of electrical energy.

So, how do electronics relate to electricity? Electronics involve the use of components to manipulate electricity. This manipulation can be used to process information and build logical systems, among other things. For example, your home computer is filled with electronic components. It processes things like input from the keyboard, and by manipulating electricity it renders the characters you type on screen. When discussing circuits, it's good to keep in mind that there are two different types of supplying power. Alternating current (AC) is the type of electricity that comes from a wall socket. It's good for traveling over long distances (like from the power station to your home). In an AC circuit, the direction of electricity switches back and forth rapidly (60 times a second in North America, 50 times a second in most of the rest of the world) Direct current (DC) is the type of electricity for circuits you'll be building in the examples in this book. It's best suited for small electrical components like the ones you'll be using. In a DC circuit, electricity flows in one direction. In most devices in your home, like your personal computer or television, AC from the wall is converted to DC for use by the device.

Voltage, Amperage, and Resistance

Electrons are charged particles that naturally move from a location of higher potential energy to a location of lower potential energy. As the electrons move through a circuit, they can be harnessed to activate electronic devices to do work. Light bulbs, your television set, your coffee machine—all these devices function by harnessing the movement of electrons.

> **NOTE** A circuit is a closed loop that has a power supply and something to use the power (called a *load*). A power supply connected to itself without a load is called a short circuit, which can cause wires to melt or power supplies to catch fire.

When describing electricity, three measurements are used: voltage, amperage, and resistance.

- *Voltage* is the difference in electronic charge between two points.
- *Amperage* is the rate at which electrons flow past a point in a circuit.
- *Resistance* is the amount a component resists the flow of electrical energy.

Voltage

Voltage is defined as the amount of potential energy between two points in a circuit. In all circuits, the direction of the flow of electrons is determined by a location with higher potential electronic energy, and a point with lower potential energy. All available voltage will be used in a circuit.

It is possible to increase the amount of voltage in a circuit by placing power sources in series. For example, one AA battery typically has 1.5 volts of potential energy between the two ends. To have a potential energy of three volts, you can place two AA batteries end to end (so the "+" end of one touches the "-" end of the other). In this way, you would add the voltage of both batteries to create a power supply of three volts.

All electrical devices, have a voltage rating. The voltage rating describes the ideal voltage for that device. It also describes the type of circuit it is designed to be used with. In most cases, all the AC power sockets in your house provide the same voltage. Appliances and devices that are designed to plug into the wall are all rated for this sort of voltage. The power supply for the device will typically step-down the AC voltage to a DC voltage that is appropriate for the device. For example, my DVD player plugs into the wall, but the components inside run on 12 V DC. However, if you bought a device in the United States, flew across the Atlantic and tried to plug it into a socket in the United Kingdom, you may have an unpleasant surprise. Household electricity in the United States is 110V AC, and in Europe it is approximately 230V AC, depending on the country. Because all available voltage is used in a circuit, a device that is rated for 110 V will be overloaded trying to use the excess voltage in a 230 V socket and be damaged as a result. Some devices (like many laptop chargers) can automatically adapt between voltages, but many electronic devices cannot.

The Atmel ATmega328 microcontroller, found on the Arduino Uno, is an electronic device that can function between 1.8 V DC and 5.5 V DC. This describes the component's *tolerance*; it can function with a voltage between the two values. Typically, most devices connected to an Arduino won't work with voltages at the lower end of the range. To simplify design, the Arduino Uno has a voltage regulator: a device that accepts a wide range of input voltage from a power supply and provides a steady output voltage. In the case of the Arduino Uno, the input voltage can range between 6 V DC and 20 V DV and supplies a steady 5 V DC to the ATmega328 and any external components. Five volts is a common voltage for hobbyist electronics and some professional electronics. Some sensors and components use 3.3 V DC for power. The Uno has a separate regulator to power devices that require this voltage.

Providing too much or too little voltage to a component may damage it or destroy it.

Amperage

Amperage describes the amount of current in a circuit, which is the rate at which electric charge flows past a point in a circuit. It is measured in Amperes, or Amps. You'll be using components that use fractions of an amp in the projects in this book. It's common to use the analogy of water flowing through a pipe to illustrate the concept of electricity in a circuit. In this analogy, if voltage is the pressure forcing water through the pipe, amperage would be the amount of water flowing past a specific point in the pipe. The faster the water, the more current. Contrary to voltage, with amperage it is better to provide more than is required by the system because the system uses only the amount it needs.

To illustrate how current is used, imagine a simple circuit with a battery and a lamp. The lamp is the load in the circuit, and the battery is the power supply. The lamp runs off of 5 V DC and 20 milliamps (0.02 amps). The battery can supply up to one amp of current at 5 V DC. All the voltage will be used up, but the lamp will only use the amount of current it needs to turn on. Unlike extra voltage in a circuit, surplus amperage doesn't get used. If too little amperage is available, components will not work as expected: lights will dim, microcontrollers will reset, and all sorts of problems can result. Typically it's a good idea to use a power supply that provides at least two times the amperage your circuit needs.

Resistance

Resistance describes the ability for something to resist the flow of electrical energy. Materials with very high resistance are often used as insulators, like rubber and plastics. It's often necessary to regulate the flow of electrical energy through a circuit by increasing or decreasing resistance. For example, most LEDs used as indicators in hobbyist projects use less than the 5 V DC that the Arduino supplies. Placing a resistive element in series with the Arduino and the LED will decrease the voltage so the LED will function properly.

The practical unit of resistance is called the Ohm and is represented by the Greek letter omega (Ω). A resistance of 1 ohm is considered to be extremely weak, while a resistance of 1 million ohms is considered to be an effective insulator. Even if it's not stated in the documentation, all components have some resistance, even wires for carrying electricity.

Ohm's Law

One of the most frequently used formulas in electronics is Ohm's law, which states that the current that flows through a conductor between two points is directly proportional to the potential difference between the two points. Figure 3-1 depicts Ohm's Law.

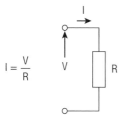

Figure 3-1: Ohm's Law

In this Ohm's Law formula, I is the flow of current, V is the potential difference, and R is the resistance of the conductor in ohms. For example, imagine a 50 Ω resistor placed on the ends of a 1.5 V AA battery. In this case, the formula would appear as shown in Figure 3-2.

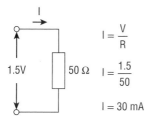

Figure 3-2: Ohm's Law example

I is unknown. However, both V and R are known, so I can be calculated. V is the voltage of the battery (1.5 volts) and R is the resistive value of the resistor (50). Knowing these two values, you can now calculate the current flowing inside the resistor—0.3 amps, or 30 milliamps.

The Basic Components

Looking at a circuit board, you might be afraid of all the different components on the board, all the different types.... How can you possibly understand all that? In truth, there are relatively few electronic components, and most are extremely simple to understand. There are a few complicated components, but they are rarely used and are mostly used in specific situations. The examples used in this book use only common components, ones that are readily available at most electronics shops, and their use is explained here.

Resistors

Resistors are electronic components designed to restrict the flow of electrical energy. There are different resistor values associated with varying resistors.

Different Resistor Values

Manufacturers cannot make every value of resistor possible, instead there is a standard range of values. The Electronic Industries Association (EIA) standard resistor values dictate the values of most resistors. Resistors use the following numbers: 10, 12, 15, 18, 22, 27, 33, 39, 47, 56, 68, and 82, in any power of 10. For example, you can easily find a 10 Ω resistor, or a 220 Ω resistor, or even a 4.7 kΩ resistor, but you will have great difficulty finding a 920 Ω resistor; the closest you will easily find is 820 Ω or 1000 Ω. How would it be possible to obtain a resistor with a value of 920 Ω? Putting resistors in series, that is to say one after the other, adds their values, so an 820 Ω resistor with a 100 Ω resistor combined is the same as a 920 Ω resistor, as illustrated in Figure 3-3. Examples in this book do not use resistors in series, instead standard values will be used. Resistors have various tolerances, typically deviating from 5% to 10% from their stated value.

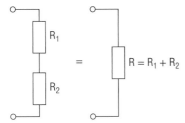

Figure 3-3: Resistors in series

   Putting resistors in parallel, that is to say one next to the other, has a different effect on the value of the total resistance, as shown in Figure 3-4. Again, this configuration will not be used in the examples in this book and is here for reference only.

Identifying Resistor Values

Resistors come in several shapes and sizes, but the ones that you will want to use for your examples are quite common, and can be identified as ¼ watt. This type of resistor has long legs to fit easily into a breadboard for rapid prototyping of circuits. Other kinds of resistors include surface-mounted resistors, available if you need to save space and are working on a printed circuit board, but they can be difficult to solder. The most common resistors look like the component shown in Figure 3-5.

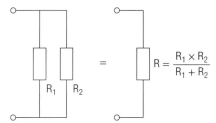

$$R = \frac{R_1 \times R_2}{R_1 + R_2}$$

Figure 3-4: Resistors in parallel

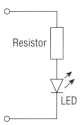

Figure 3-5: A common axial 10% tolerance resistor

Note the bands of color on the resistor; resistors are too small to put any readable text on and are color-coded to indicate their value. Typically, you'll find resistors with 4 stripes on them, though versions with 5 or 6 bands exist as well. Table 3-1 lists the color code.

Table 3-1: Resistor Color Code

COLOR	DIGIT 1	DIGIT 2	MULTIPLIER	TOLERANCE
Black	0	0	x 10^0	
Brown	1	1	x 10^1	
Red	2	2	x 10^2	
Orange	3	3	x 10^3	
Yellow	4	4	x 10^4	
Green	5	5	x 10^5	
Blue	6	6	x 10^6	

Continues

Table 3-1 (*continued*)

COLOR	DIGIT 1	DIGIT 2	MULTIPLIER	TOLERANCE
Violet	7	7	x 10^7	
Gray	8	8	x 10^8	
White	9	9	x 10^9	
Gold				± 5%
Silver				± 10%

The first two bands indicate the value in ohms, the third band is a multiplier for scaling, and the fourth indicates how far the actual value may deviate from the stated value. A resistor with red, violet, orange, and gold stripes has a value of 2.7 KΩ; 2, 7, 10^3, and 10-percent tolerance. A 100 Ω resistor is brown, black, brown, and silver; 1, 0, 10^1, 10 percent.

NOTE Color-blind people might be starting to worry here; don't. Whatever your color vision problems, I can assure you, you will be able to identify resistor values. I have acute achromatopsia, meaning that I see more or less in black and white. All colors are difficult for me to see. This was a problem during my studies, where teachers didn't know how to react, but today, this is never a problem for me. A simple ohmmeter or multimeter can quickly tell you the value of a resistor.

Using Resistors

The current and voltage can be regulated in an electronic circuit by resistors. Imagine an electronic circuit powered by a 5 V DC power supply. You want to add a Light Emitting Diode (LED) to show that the circuit is powered, in this case a red LED. This LED has a *voltage drop* of 1.7 V. A voltage drop means that the voltage of the circuit will be reduced by that amount. Therefore, if you were to place an LED directly between the +5 V and 0 V it would be damaged (remember, all voltage gets used up in a circuit). There must be a component to reduce the voltage across the LED, a resistor is the ideal candidate. The schematic of this circuit is shown in Figure 3-6.

Because you want 1.7 V across the LED, and because the circuit is powered by 5 volts, that means there should be a voltage drop of 3.3 volts across the resistor. Also, the LED is rated for 20 milliamps of current, but for this project 15 milliamps should be enough. Therefore, to have 15 milliamps flow through the LED, you will have to use a 220 Ω resistor. Another example is shown at the end of this chapter.

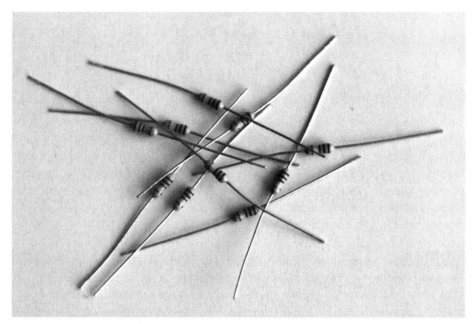

Figure 3-6: A resistor used to power an LED

Capacitors

Where resistors are designed to resist electric current, capacitors are designed to store small amounts of electric energy.

Capacitors are composed of two parallel sheets of conductor separated by a thin nonconductor, which could be made from a number of materials, such as paper, mica, ceramic, plastic, and sometimes even air. When connected to electric potential, electrons are attracted into the capacitor and released when the outside voltage drops. A capacitor is, essentially, a small (and weak) rechargeable battery.

Capacitors come in many shapes and sizes and can be some of the smallest components available to the biggest, capable of dwarfing entire battery packs. Have you ever taken apart an electronic device and seen large, cylindrical components, normally in blue or black plastic? Chances are those are electrolytic capacitors, and you probably have not seen the biggest available.

WARNING   Some capacitors can be connected any way in a circuit; others must be placed in a certain way. Electrolytic capacitors especially have a polarity, and this must be respected. Failure to correctly polarize electrolytic capacitors can result in catastrophic failure; the component will leak or explode, potentially damaging the rest of your circuit. Don't try this at home!

The unit of capacitance is the *farad* (F). Most capacitors are in the microfarad range, but they can be as small as 1 picofarad (10^{-12} F) and as large as 10^4 F in supercapacitors.

Using Capacitors

If capacitors can store energy, how can this be used? First, capacitors can be used to regulate power lines, helping to filter out slight drops in power. Power lines are thought to be stable, but this is not always the case. Especially in motor systems, the power levels in power lines can vary. When motors start, they draw a lot of current, making the voltage temporarily drop. Adding capacitors onto the power supply helps filter out those drops and stabilizes the power for other components. These are described as *decoupling* capacitors.

WARNING   Some capacitors can hold a large charge, and that charge is still there when you remove the power. Be careful when using these devices. Examples in this book are limited to 12V, which do not pose a threat, but larger devices like computer monitors and televisions can contain capacitors that store massive amounts of energy. Be careful!

One other use for capacitors, and one that is the most used on homemade electronics, is to help with one of the most basic components: buttons. A button is a simple mechanical device that will either make an electrical contact or break it. The problem is that these devices are not perfect, and pushing a button to make a contact often results in "bounces," or unwanted spikes, when the metal inside the switch bounces on the contacts. By using a capacitor, the bounces can be filtered out.

Diodes

A diode is a small component that allows electricity to flow in only one direction. A perfect diode would not have any voltage drop and would not allow any electricity to flow in the opposite direction, but we don't live in a perfect world. Diodes do in fact have a voltage drop depending on the type of diode you use. A silicon diode like the 1N4148 have a voltage drop of approximately 0.65 V. Germanium diodes have a voltage drop of about 0.3 V.

Also, diodes have something called a *breakdown voltage*, the reverse voltage at which a diode conducts in reverse and most often breaks the component. The 1N4148 has a breakdown voltage of at least 100 volts, something that you will not encounter in the examples in this book, but it is useful to know.

Different Types of Diodes

There are many types of diodes. This book presents only the most common diode. Other types of diodes exist; Zener diodes have a specific breakdown voltage, and the breakdown state does not destroy the component. Schottky diodes have a low forward voltage drop. Tunnel diodes are extremely interesting because they use quantum tunneling and are used for advanced circuits.

There are also many other common diodes, ones that could deserve their own section. Laser diodes are special types of diodes that create laser lights; you can find these components in consumer electronics like CD players and Blu-ray recorders. Light-emitting diodes (LEDs) work in the same way, producing visible and nonvisible light and are presented in the next section.

Using Diodes

Diodes are used primarily to protect circuits either by avoiding a reverse-voltage or avoiding voltage spikes.

Electric motors can use large amounts of energy to make the motor spin. When there is an interruption of current flow inside the component motor, this can lead to a sharp rise in voltage across the device circuit. If the voltage drawn is beyond what the circuit is designed to handle, it may damage or destroy it.

Light-Emitting Diodes

Light-emitting diodes are exactly what their name implies; diodes, electronic components that let current flow in one direction only and that emit light. LEDs are used as indicators in home electronics, and have started to replace traditional incandescent light bulbs in home and industrial lighting. They are far more robust than light bulbs; they use less energy and exist in many different colors, shapes, and sizes.

Most LEDs emit a single-color with typical colors being red, orange, green, blue, and white. Dual-color LEDs also exist that can be either one of two colors or a mix between two colors, and finally, RGB LEDs exist that can take on almost any color by varying the red, green, and blue components.

LEDs also exist that emit nonvisible light: ultra-violet and infrared. Laser diodes are special types of light-emitting diodes, capable of creating laser light in various wavelengths and powers.

Using LEDs

Using LEDs is remarkably similar to their parent family: diodes. However, the difference is in their power consumption. Care must be taken not to supply too much current to an LED; otherwise it is possible to damage or even destroy the component.

LEDs have a larger voltage drop than their diode counterparts. Most common red LEDs have a voltage drop between 1.8 V–2 V, yellow LEDs 2.0 V, green LEDs 2.2 V, and blue LEDs can have up to a 3.4 V voltage drop. Typical maximum current for LEDs is around 20 mA for all LEDs, though blue versions can draw 30 mA. Your electronics distributor will have more information about the specific model you are using, so consult their documentation.

Transistors

Transistors are largely responsible for the proliferation of digital technologies, as well as many of the advances in computing power and size. A transistor is like a tiny switch but is *solid state*, meaning that there are no moving parts to wear out and can turn on and off much faster than any mechanical device. There are several sorts of transistors, but this tutorial talks only about the most common type in hobbyist electronics: the bipolar transistor.

Using Transistors

Although there are dozens of uses for transistors, examples in this book cover only one possible use: a switch.

Imagine an Arduino system powered by 5 volts. This system is designed to turn on and off an electric motor, one that needs to be powered by a 12-volt power supply. The motor also requires more current than the Arduino can supply. How can the Arduino possibly power a 12-volt motor using only a 5-volt output? The answer is, of course, by using a transistor as a switch.

A bipolar transistor has three leads. The Collector is connected to the positive side of the circuit, and the Emitter is connected to the negative side of the circuit, or the ground. Electrons will flow from the Collector to the Emitter, depending on the voltage at the Base. By supplying a relatively low voltage to the transistor's base, current can flow through the transistor into the collector and out of the emitter. In short, the transistor conducts current through the collector-emitter path only when a voltage is applied to the base. When no base voltage is present, the switch is off. When base voltage is present, the switch is on.

Breadboards

Electronics is fun; there is a joy in assembling components to do a required task; and it is hugely satisfying. When finished, some electronics are akin to digital art, in their function and in their implementation. Some circuit boards are a work of art in their own right, because of placing LEDs at strategic places, and cutting out the board to be the right shape. Have a closer look at your Arduino; notice the pictures printed onto the board, the picture of Italy, and imagine the time that was taken to make this board its current shape. It did take a lot of time, but that is also what frightens some people; do you really have to make one of these boards every time you make a design? Printed circuit boards like the Arduino and shields can either be made at home using some specialized equipment and chemicals, or fabricated professionally. Luckily, when prototyping, you don't need to do all that; there is a much simpler alternative: the breadboard.

Use of the term *breadboard* in this discussion may surprise you; normally it is a flat, wooden board designed to cut bread (or other foods). In the early days of amateur radio, amateurs would nail bare copper wire onto a wooden board (more often than not a breadboard which was readily available), and solder components onto the wires. Because components were much bigger in those days, some components (tubes especially) could actually be screwed onto the breadboard. Amateurs had created an easy prototyping device from an item readily available at any supermarket.

Modern breadboards are sometimes called *solderless breadboards*, implying that they can be reused. They exist in all sizes, from the smallest boards, designed to hold a single component, all the way to huge prototyping boards, designed to include an entire single board computer. Breadboards are normally classed by their number of *connection points*, the number of holes on the board that can accept wires and components.

Typical breadboards have two areas called *strips*. The terminal strip is the main part of any breadboard and is designed to hold components and wires. There is normally a notch in the middle, marking a separation between connectors, but it is also designed to allow air to flow beneath components helping them cool down.

The terminal strip is normally numbered: numbers horizontally and letters vertically. What is important to know is that a single number is connected to all the letters; A0, B0, C0, D0, and E0 are all connected electronically. A component pin placed in E0 connects to a wire connected to A0 but does not connect to a wire placed in A1.

The bus strip is located along the side of the terminal, and serves as a power rail. Normally, two rows are available: one for the supply voltage and one for the ground.

The holes are not placed at random; their spacing is exactly 0.1″, or 2.54 mm, accommodating many electronic components, and all Dual In-Line Package (DIP) chips. Most of the AVR chips exist in DIP format, making it possible to build an Arduino directly on a breadboard.

Inputs and Outputs

The Arduino's digital pins can be configured to be inputs or outputs to either write information or to read it.

There are two types of inputs on Arduino boards, digital and analog. On the digital pins, the Arduino "reads" either a logical zero (0 volts), or a logical 1 (equivalent to the power supply of the Arduino itself). Most Arduinos are powered by 5 volts, but a few are powered by 3.3 volts. If using a 3.3 voltboard like the Due, don't put 5 V on an input pin; you could damage the microcontroller.

Note that in digital mode, there is a reasonable amount of tolerance; an input of up to 2 volts is still considered to be a logical zero.

On the analog pins, things are different. An analog signal has an infinite number of steps between zero volts and the power supply of the Arduino. In practice, it is not possible to sample an infinite amount of values, and the Arduino uses something called an Analog Digital Converter (ADC) to change the analog signal to a discrete number of steps. The Arduino's ADC has a *resolution* of 10-bits, which means there are 1,024 values that can be recognized on an analog input.

Connecting a Light-Emitting Diode

In this chapter, you have learned about basic electronic components, so now put that to the test. In this example, you control an LED placed on a breadboard, connected to an Arduino. The Arduino will be programmed to fade the LED. In this example, I will use an Arduino Uno and also a blue LED. Check the information about the LED you're using to determine the voltage and current requirements. The LED I'm using has a forward voltage of 3.4 V and pulls 30 mA of current.

Calculation

LEDs must be used with resistors, so the first thing that has to be done is to calculate the resistor that will be used. The Arduino Uno outputs 5 V DV, and the LED has a forward voltage of 3.4 volts; therefore, the resistor will have a potential difference of 1.6 volts. It will also let 30 mA of current pass. Because we know the amperage and voltage of the circuit, we can figure out the necessary resistance. My calculation is shown in Figure 3-7.

$$R = \frac{V}{I}$$

$$R = \frac{1.6}{0.020}$$

$$R = 80 \ \Omega$$

Figure 3-7: Calculating the resistor

Even though the LED is rated at an absolute maximum of 30 mA, you should try and aim for less than 30 mA of current. A safe bet would be to let 20 mA of current through the LED; that still makes it nice and bright and will not damage the component. For the time being, let's assume you want to let 30 mA of current pass through the LED, in which case the circuit would require a 53 Ω resistor. This is not a standard resistor value. The closest standard resistor value below 53 ohms is 47 ohms. If you do the math, you'll see that a 47-ohm resistor would allow 34 mA of current through the LED, above its rated tolerance. If you re-do the calculations aiming for 20 mA, the new result is 80 Ω. The closest standard value is 82 Ω, which is close to the target. Therefore, for this example, the schematic will use an 82 Ω resistor.

Software

It's time to code the application. This sketch illustrates a common beginner's task with the Arduino, fading an LED. Listing 3-1 presents the source code.

Listing 3-1: Fade

```
int led = 9;           // the pin that the LED is attached to
int brightness = 0;    // how bright the LED is
int fadeAmount = 5;    // how many steps to fade the LED each loop

// the setup routine runs once when you press reset or power the board:
void setup()  {
  // declare pin 9 to be an output:
  pinMode(led, OUTPUT);
}

// the loop routine runs over and over again forever:
void loop()  {
  // set the brightness of pin 9:
  analogWrite(led, brightness);

  // change the brightness for next time through the loop:
  brightness = brightness + fadeAmount;

  // reverse the direction of the fading when the LED is fully bright
  // or fully off :
  if (brightness == 0 || brightness == 255) {
    fadeAmount = -fadeAmount ;
  }
  // wait for 30 milliseconds to see the dimming effect
  delay(30);
}
```

The led variable is the pin the LED is connected to. You're using pin 9 because it is one of the PWM pins. That is, it is one of the pins you can call analogWrite() on. In the setup() function, the pin is set to become an output. Then, the loop() function adds the value stored in fadeAmount to the variable brightness, looks to see if the value should be inverted, and then waits for 30 milliseconds. Because this function is looped, it constantly updates the output pin value, ranging from

0 to 255, before returning back to zero. This will have the effect of starting with the LED completely off and then slowly increasing brightness to full before fading back to off.

Hardware

The code is done; the next thing to do is to actually create the circuit. This is only a prototype, so you will be using a breadboard. It is one of the simplest circuits you can build: two wires, one resistor, and one LED. The LED will be powered by the Arduino board.

First things first—the breadboard view. My view is shown in Figure 3-8.

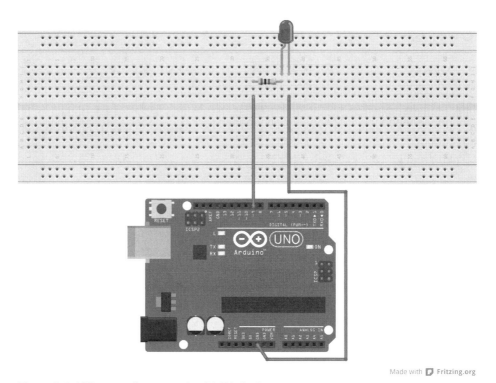

Made with 🄳 Fritzing.org

Figure 3-8: LED output (Image made with Fritzing)

After you re-create this circuit, you are now ready to upload your sketch to the Arduino, wait a few seconds, and look at an LED fading beautifully. Congratulations; you have just created your first hardware design! You now know how to create a sketch, and you know how to create an electronic circuit. The following chapters explain the different libraries in detail with example sketches and circuits to help you along your way.

What Now?

Now, it is all up to you. You might want to make this a permanent application in your house. Breadboards are good for prototyping, but a more permanent solution would require either creating a printed circuit board or maybe even an Arduino shield. A printed circuit board could be placed anywhere, and with enough wires, could even be placed far from the Arduino. You could put this outside in the garden as a night light, for example. Shields require being connected to the Arduino and therefore are not as easy to place outside. With a shield and an enclosure, you could make a night-light for a young child or even add a decoration in the living room. It is easy to add a few additional LEDs to this design to light up a cupboard or to illuminate a decoration. You can even make a small holiday display or welcome sign.

Summary

Welcome to the amazing world of Arduino! This chapter has given you a brief overview of electronics, enough to get you started with the projects contained in this book.

The following chapters explain some of the libraries that can be added to projects to give you an insight to what can be done. In Chapter 4 you will be using the standard library, which has the basic building blocks that you will see and use in every sketch. I will go through the different functions and explain how each one works.

Part

II

Standard Libraries

In This Part

The Arduino Language

Functionality can be added to Arduino programs using libraries, but every Arduino project invariably starts with one library; the Arduino Language. The Arduino Language contains everything required for basic programs, allowing access to input and output pins, mathematical functions, and control structures. This chapter lists those functions and gives an explanation of each one. You can also consult the Arduino reference page at `http://arduino.cc/en/Reference/`.

I/O Functions

An Arduino is a powerful system, but its power comes from interacting with the real world. To do this, the Arduino must use Input and Output, shortened to I/O. Pins can be defined as either being an input or output; it is up to you to decide.

Digital I/O

Digital I/O is defined as using a digital signal to communicate; a logical 1 or logical 0. In Arduino, 1 is defined as having a "high" voltage; normally at or close to the system voltage. 0 is defined as having a "low" voltage, typically 0. A system powered by 5 volts will usually have 5 volts for a logical 1 and 0 volt for a logical 0. A system powered by 3.3 V will usually have 3.3 V and 0.

Examples of digital inputs are switches, like push buttons or contact switches. They are either on or off; there are no values in between.

pinMode()

Before using a pin as a digital input or output, you must first configure the pin, which is done with `pinMode()`. `pinMode()` uses two parameters: `pin` and `mode`.

```
pinMode(pin, mode)
```

The pin parameter is simply the digital pin number you want to set. The mode parameter is one of three constants: `INPUT`, `OUTPUT`, or `INPUT_PULLUP`. The `INPUT` and `OUTPUT` constants set the pin to be a digital input or output, respectively. The `INPUT_PULLUP` constant sets the selected pin to become a digital input but also connects an internal resistor to keep the input level at a logical one if there is no input value.

By default, all digital pins are configured as `INPUT`, but it's considered best practice to explicitly declare the `pinMode()`.

INPUT

Pins configured as `INPUT` can read voltage applied to them. It takes only a small amount of current to change an `INPUT` pin's state. The drawback to this is that pins configured as `INPUT` with nothing connected to them are more likely to change state due to electronic interference like static discharges. It is useful to use a pull-down resistor (going to ground) when connecting a switch to a pin configured as `INPUT`. Ten kilohm is a good resistor value for this.

`INPUT` pins are good at reading logical inputs but cannot be used to input, or *sink*, any current. For example, you cannot use an `INPUT` pin to sink current from an LED.

OUPUT

Pins configured as `OUTPUT` are capable of delivering power to circuits, up to 40 mA. This is more than enough to power an LED but is not enough to power motors. Output pins cannot read sensors. Connecting output pins directly to 5 volts or 0 volts can damage the pin.

INPUT_PULLUP

Pins configured as `INPUT_PULLUP` are configured as output, but with an internal pull-up resistor connected. On most Arduino boards this internal resistor is at least 20 kilohms. This has the effect of setting the input value to HIGH if it is pulled to ground, and LOW if voltage is applied.

digitalRead()

In order to read the state of a digital pin, you must use `digitalRead()`:

```
result = digitalRead(pin);
```

The `pin` parameter is the pin number you want to read from. This function returns either `HIGH` or `LOW`, depending on the input.

digitalWrite()

To write the state of a pin that was declared as an `OUTPUT`, use the `digitalWrite()` function:

```
digitalWrite(pin, value);
```

The `pin` parameter is the pin number you want to write to, and the `value` is the logical level you want to write; `HIGH` or `LOW`.

Analog I/O

Analog is different than digital. Digital signals are one of two states; either true (a logical one), or false (a logical zero). Digital states are not designed to have any other value.

Analog is different in that it has a potentially infinite amount of values between two points. Analog is all around us. A light bulb is normally either on or off, but consider the sun. At nighttime, there is no light, and in daytime, midday, on a sunny day with no clouds, you would think that you have the maximum amount of sunlight. And during sunrise? You can see the amount of sunlight change visibly within a few minutes. During a cloudy day? There is light but not as much as during a clear day. This is no longer digital; it isn't on or off. The sun is analog; there are an infinite amount of possibilities.

Imagine a cruise ship. At the front of most large ships, there is a scale, a *water line*. It is used for several reasons, but to simplify, this marker serves to determine if a ship has been overloaded. Overloaded, a ship is at risk of sinking. The water line, technically called the *Plimsoll Line*, is where the water meets the hull. You can imagine that this line varies between two values: the minimum and the maximum. For this example, imagine between 20 feet and 40 feet. Right now, the ship you are watching is loading passengers, excited to sail to the Mediterranean. Slowly, the Plimsoll line rises: 30 feet, 31 feet, 32 feet.... And it stops at 33 feet. With a maximum Plimsoll line of 40 feet, this ship is safe to sail, but what is the exact value? 33 feet? Exactly? Probably not. It might be 33 feet and 1 inch, or maybe 33 feet and 3/8 of an inch? The point is, it doesn't matter. Humans aren't good with an infinite amount of values, and a docker looking at the ship will fill in the registry with 33 feet; he won't need absolute precision. It doesn't matter if a little bit is lost in the process.

Microcontrollers work in the same way. Microcontrollers are digital, but many can read analog values, including Arduinos. The device used to read analog is called an *ADC*, short for *Analog to Digital Converter*. The ADC cannot handle infinite values. It has a *resolution*. The Arduino divides the range into different equally sized portions. A 10-bit device can distinguish 210 different values—or a total of 1,024 different values. If used on a range between 0 and 5 volts; an input of 0 volts would result in a decimal 0; an input of 5 volts would give the maximum of 1,023. Something in between, such as 2.5 V would yield a value of 512. A 10-bit ADC can sense differences of 5 volts divided by the resolution, or 1,024. This device can therefore have an accuracy of 5 / 1,024, or roughly 0.005 volts.

analogRead()

To read a value from an analog pin, you call `analogRead()`.

```
int analogRead(pin)
```

`analogRead()` reads the voltage value on a pin and returns the value as an `int`. The pin argument denotes the analog pin you want to read from. When referring to an analog pin, call them as A0, A1, A2,…A6.

This function takes approximately 100 microseconds to perform. In theory, you could sample a pin up to 10,000 times a second. However, it's best to let the ADC "settle" for a few milliseconds between reads for more accurate data acquisition.

analogWrite()

`analogWrite()` is used to write an analog output on a digital pin. Wait, analog? On a digital pin? Well, yes, sort of. It's not a true analog value that's being written.

Arduinos use something called *Pulse-width modulation*, *PWM* for short. PWM is digital but can be used for some analog devices. It uses a simple technique to "emulate" an analog output. It relies on two things: a pulse width and a duty cycle. It is a way of simulating any value within a range by rapidly switching between 0 volts and 5 volts.

The pulse width (also called a *period*) is a short duration of time in which the duty cycle will operate. The duty cycle describes the amount of time that the output will be at a logical one in the given period. Depending on the Arduino you're using, the period can range from 490 Hz to 980 Hz. A duty cycle of 50 percent means that during 50 percent of the pulse width, the output will be at a logical one, and the remaining 50 percent of the pulse width, the duty cycle will be at a logical 0. A duty cycle of 0 percent means that the output will always be p, and a duty cycle of 100 percent means that the output will always be 1.

PWM is an excellent method for controlling motors and dimming LEDs; it worked well in the previous chapter. However, some components do not like receiving pulses and want a stable output. For example, another Arduino reading an analog input would read in alternating values of 5 V and 0 V instead of a true analog signal. In this case, adding a capacitor to the circuit will "filter" the output.

Generating Audio Tones

Although most Arduinos are incapable of playing back advanced audio without additional electronics, they can play musical notes and tones natively.

Audio, or sound in general, is simply a vibration that propagates as waves of pressure. To generate sound, speakers and buzzers vibrate at certain frequencies to create sound.

Audio tones generated by Arduinos are variable frequencies, which can range from just a few Hertz up to 20 kHz, around the limits of human audition.

tone()

tone() is used mainly to generate audio tones on devices like buzzers. Although designed to generate audible tones, it is not limited to audio. This function generates a square wave, a signal that alternates instantly between two values, typically the maximum voltage and zero. It generates signals with a fixed 50 percent duty cycle, from frequencies as low as 31 Hz to 80 kHz (humans can typically hear up to 20 kHz). tone() accepts unsigned integers as a parameter.

This function requires either two or three parameters, depending on your use.

```
tone(pin, frequency)
tone(pin, frequency, duration)
```

The pin parameter is the pin number on which to produce a tone. The frequency parameter is the frequency to generate in hertz, passed as an unsigned int. Finally, the optional duration parameter is the duration of the tone in milliseconds, passed as an unsigned long. If this parameter is not specified, the tone will be generated indefinitely, or until the program tells the tone generation to stop.

noTone()

noTone() stops the square wave generation of tone() on the specified pin. If no tone is generated, this function has no effect. This function must be called before generating another tone on the same pin.

Reading Pulses

Arduinos can be told to react to pulses received on digital pins, reading serial data when data becomes available, or to call specific functions when a signal is received. However, in some cases, it is not the change in the signal that is important, but the time the signal stays at a logical state.

Imagine a sensor attached to your door. You want to know if the door was opened, and you want to know exactly how long the door was opened for. By adding a reed switch to your door, you can have a logical 1 (HIGH) if the door is closed, and a logical 0 (LOW) if the door is opened. How long was the door opened for? The Arduino can tell you.

pulseIn()

`pulseIn()` will tell you the length of a pulse. It requires a pin as a parameter and the type of pulse to read. When programmed, the Arduino waits for a signal on the selected pin. For example, you can tell the Arduino to wait for a pin to go HIGH. When it does, it starts a counter. When the signal returns to LOW, it stops the counter, and returns the number of microseconds. If no signal change is received within a set time, the function gives up and returns 0.

```
unsigned long length pulseIn(pin, value)
unsigned long length pulseIn(pin, value, time-out)
```

The `pin` parameter is the pin number to listen on, as an `int` value. The `value` parameter is the type of signal to wait for: either `HIGH` or `LOW`. The optional `timeout` parameter tells the Arduino how long to wait for a signal. It is an `unsigned long` and represents the amount of microseconds to wait. If omitted, it waits for 1 second before timing out.

`pulseIn()` is accurate within 10 microseconds when the time-out is up to 3 minutes long. Pulses longer than 3 minutes may be calculated inaccurately. Also, responding to interrupts can give inaccurate results because the internal timers are not updated during interrupt handling.

Time Functions

Timing is important in electronics projects. Electronics are not instantaneous, and most sensor components require some time before they can be accessed. A typical one-wire humidity sensor requires 100 ms of time between the command to acquire a reading and returning the result. Querying the component before it has had adequate time to complete its task could result in malformed data or cause the component to send a previous result. In either case, your sketch might not work as intended. Fortunately, Arduinos can patiently wait for a specified amount of time, by calling `delay()`.

Another time function on Arduinos is the ability to get the time that the current sketch has been running. When an Arduino is powered on (or reset), two counters begins counting: the number of microseconds that the system has been running and the number of milliseconds.

delay()

`delay()` tells the microcontroller to wait for a specified number of milliseconds before resuming the sketch. This can be used to tell the microcontroller to wait for a specified period of time before reading a sensor, or slowing down a loop that is running too fast.

delayMicroseconds()

delayMicrosecond() is similar to delay(), but instead of waiting for a specified number of milliseconds, it waits for a specific number of microseconds.

This function is accurate to a certain point; values above 16,383 produce inaccurate results. If you need an accurate delay above 16,000 microseconds (or 16 milliseconds), use a mix of delay() and delayMicroseconds(), like in the following snippet of code, where the Arduino is asked to wait for 22.5 milliseconds, or a total of 25,500 microseconds.

```
delay(25); // waits for 25 milliseconds
delayMicroseconds(500) waits for 500 microseconds
```

millis()

millis() returns the number of milliseconds that the sketch has been running, returning the number as an unsigned long. This can be used to check how long the current sketch has been running, but it can also be used to calculate how long a function takes to run, by comparing the number of milliseconds before and afterward.

```
unsigned long timeBefore;
unsigned long timeAfter;

timeBefore = millis(); //Get the time before running a function
aLongFunction(); //Run a function that could take some time
timeAfter = millis(); //And now get the time after running the function
```

This data is stored in a counter that will overflow (go beyond the data capacity and return to zero) after approximately 50 days.

micros()

micros() is almost identical to the millis() function, except it returns the number of microseconds in an unsigned long. The counter overflows far more quickly than millis(); roughly every 70 minutes.

```
unsigned long time;

void setup(){
  Serial.begin(9600);
}
void loop(){
  Serial.print("Time: ");
```

```
time = micros();
//prints time since program started
Serial.println(time);
// wait a second so as not to send massive amounts of data
delay(1000);
}
```

This function has a minimum number of microseconds that can be correctly evaluated. On Arduinos with a clock speed of 16 MHz, the resolution is 4 microseconds. On 8 MHz models, the resolution is 8 microseconds.

Mathematical Functions

The Arduino is a capable calculator, and the Arduino language has a large amount of mathematical functions to help you calculate. They can be used for simple calculations, to quickly analyze the voltage of one pin compared to another, or more advanced functions, to help robots move around and calculate the best path available.

min()

`min()` returns the smaller of two numbers.

```
result = min(x, y)
```

The two values can be of any numerical data type, returning the same data type as the parameter. This is used both as a way of knowing the smaller of two values and also to constrain data range; by using `min()`, you can make sure that an input value never goes over a certain value.

```
int sensorData = 100;
min(sensorData, 255); // Returns 100 (sensorData is smaller)
min(sensorData, 100); // Returns 100
min(sensorData, 64); //Returns 64
```

max()

`max()` is similar to `min()`, except it returns the higher of two values.

```
result = max(x, y)
```

`max()` can take any numerical data type and can be used to obtain a minimum value for sensor data.

```
int sensorData = 100;
max(sensorData, 255); // Returns 255
max(sensorData, 100); // Returns 100 (both values are the same)
```

```
max(sensorData, 64); //Returns 100 (sensorData is larger)
```

constrain()

`constrain()` is like combining parts of `max()` and `min()` at the same time; it constrains data values to a set range.

```
value = constrain(data, min, max)
```

Imagine a light sensor, reading the ambient light inside your living room, letting you turn the lights on or off. Values may vary between dark (you can still vaguely see your way around), and bright (comfortable to see, but not blinding). For a light sensor that gives values between 0 and 1,023, you could set the constrain levels to values between 40 and 127. Values below 40 are considered too dark to have a reliable reading, and values over 127 are too bright. What if a ray of sunlight hits the sensor? It would still be bright enough to see comfortably, but the sensor may return the maximum value: 255. Or what would happen if somebody covered the light sensor, for example, a cat and their incredible sense of disturbing scientific experiments by sleeping on your equipment? With no light at all, the sensor might return 0, and if you ever divide a value by your sensor reading, you could cause an error (because computers can't divide by 0). The following code will make sure you receive the sensor data, but constrained between values of 40 and 127 if the original sensor data was out of those bounds.

```
sensorValue = constrain(sensorData, 40, 127);
```

abs()

`abs()` returns the absolute value of a number, for example, the non-negative value of the number, without regard to its sign. The absolute value of 2 and –2 is 2.

```
value = abs(x);
```

This function is implemented in such a way that only values should be calculated, not the results from mathematical operations or functions.

```
abs(i++); // Do not do this, the result might not be what you expected

i++; // First calculate
abs(i); // Then use the result
```

map()

`map()` remaps a number in one range set to another. It takes a number, a theoretical boundary, and remaps that number as if it were in another boundary.

```
map(value, fromLow, fromHigh, toLow, toHigh);
```

This function takes a value called `value` in a range between `fromLow` and `fromHigh`, and remaps that value to a new range set by `toLow` and `toHigh`.

The clearest way to explain `map()` is with an example. Imagine a sensor, connected to an analog pin. It outputs numbers from 0 to 1,023. How would you convert this to a percentage? The `map()` function could do this in a single line.

```
result = map(sensorData, 0, 1023, 0, 100);
```

Mapping can also be used to invert value ranges:

```
result = map(sensorData, 1, 50, 50, 1);
```

pow()

`pow()` raises a number to the power of *x*.

```
double result = pow(float base, float exponent);
```

The base number and exponent are calculated as `float`, allowing for fractional exponents. The result of this calculation is returned as a `double`.

sqrt()

`sqrt()` calculates the square root of a number.

```
double result = sqrt(x);
```

The number `x` can be of any numerical data type, and the result is expressed as a double.

random()

Arduinos are capable of generating pseudo-random numbers using the `random()` function:

```
result = random(max);
result = random(min, max);
```

This function takes one or two parameters specifying the range for the random number to be chosen. If the `min` parameter is omitted, the result will be a number between zero and `max`, otherwise the number will be between `min` and `max`. The `result` is returned as a `long`.

Computers cannot generate purely random numbers, and instead use complex algorithms. While the output may indeed seem random, it is actually a sequence that is extremely long but always the same. To prevent your Arduino from always starting at the beginning, you can use the `randomSeed()` function to select where in that sequence to start:

```
randomSeed(seed);
```

The `seed` parameter is a `long` and can be any value you choose (either a fixed number or the amount of milliseconds that your sketch has been running).

Trigonometry

Trigonometry is a branch of mathematics that studies relationships between lengths and angles of triangles. Although some students might hate trigonometry at school, complaining that they will never need to calculate the side of a triangle in everyday life, the truth is that trigonometry is used in a great number of things we interact with every day. It is used in electronics, architecture, civil engineering, and a large number of fields.

Consider the triangle shown in Figure 4-1.

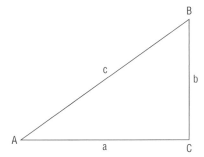

Figure 4-1: Right triangle

This triangle has three angles, called *A*, *B*, and *C*, and three sides, called *a*, *b*, and *c*. If the angle C is a right angle, that is, 90 degrees, you can calculate all the values with a little additional information. When dealing with right triangles, you can compute A, B, C, a, b, and c if you have the values for one side and one angle, or two of the sides.

Why would this be used? There are several reasons why you would want to use trigonometry with an Arduino. For example, the Arduino Robot could calculate a path around an obstacle if the angle and the distance are known. You could create a clock application on an LCD screen. Because you know the angle of the line (the hour), and the length of a line (a fixed value), you can apply the previous formula to draw the hour hand on-screen. In robotics, trigonometry is used extensively to know where the end of an arm will be based on calculations for every segment of the arm.

Trigonometry calculations on the Arduino are accomplished with `sin()`, `cos()`, and `tan()`.

sin()

`sin()` calculates the sine of an angle in radians. The result is returned as a `double` between –1 and 1.

```
result = sin(angle);
```

Here, the `angle` parameter is a `float`, the angle in radians, and the function returns a `double`; the sine of the angle.

cos()

`cos()` calculates the cosine of an angle in radians. The result is returned as a `double` between –1 and 1.

```
result = cos(angle);
```

Once again, this function takes a single parameter, a `float`, the angle in radians, and returns a `double`.

tan()

`tan()` calculates the tangent of an angle in radians. The result is returned as a `double`.

```
result = cos(angle);
```

Constants

The functions used to calculate the sine, cosine, and tangent all require the angle to be expressed in radians, which isn't always what you have. Converting degrees to radians and back again is a simple mathematical formula, but the Arduino goes one step further, proposing two constants; `DEG_TO_RAD`, and `RAD_TO_DEG`:

```
deg = rad * RAD_TO_DEG;
rad = deg * DEG_TO_RAD;
```

Arduino also has another constant; `PI`, which of course is the familiar constant for π.

Interrupts

Interrupts are a way to respond immediately to external signals without having to spend a lot of time looking for changes.

Imagine you are at home, and you are waiting for an important parcel. This parcel will be delivered to your letter box without requiring a signature. The chances are that the postman will not knock on your door. You want to get your hands on it as soon as possible, so you go outside to look at the letter box frequently. It isn't there, so you wait for 10 minutes or so before having another look. You have to decide when to stop working (if you can actually work at all) before looking again, choosing a time that suits you. In computer terms, this continual checking for an event is known as *polling*.

Interrupts are different. A few days later, you wait for another parcel; only this time the parcel requires a signature, so the delivery man knocks on your door. This gives you a little more freedom. Because you don't have to waste time by looking inside the letter box every few minutes, you can get some work done. The delivery man will knock on your door to let you know that he has arrived, and at that time you can stop working for a few minutes to get your parcel. The downside to this is that you have to react quickly; if the delivery man does not get an answer quickly, he will go away. This situation is analogous to an *interrupt*.

Interrupts are a technique to let the processor continue working while waiting for an external event. It might not occur at all, in which case the main program continues, but if an external signal is received, the computer interrupts the main program and executes another routine, known as an *Interrupt Service Routine*, or *ISR*. ISRs are designed to be fast, and you should spend as little time as possible inside an ISR. When servicing an interrupt, some functions will not continue to work; `delay()` and `millis()` will not increment in interrupt context.

All Arduinos have interrupts; most use interrupts internally for serial communication or for timing counters. Some Arduinos have more user-programmable interrupts. Table 4-1 shows which interrupts are available on which pins for different models.

Table 4-1: Interrupt Pins on Arduinos

BOARD	INT.0	INT.1	INT.2	INT.3	INT.4	INT.5
Uno	2	3				
Ethernet	2	3				
Leonardo	3	2	0	1	7	
Mega2560	2	3	21	20	19	18

The Arduino Due is different. It has highly advanced interrupt handling and can effectively be programmed to interrupt on every digital pin.

attachInterrupt()

This function specifies which routine to call when a specified interrupt is received.

```
attachInterrupt(interrupt, ISR, mode)
```

This function attaches a function to the interrupt number `interrupt`, depending on the status of the pin. The `mode` specifies the pin state to trigger the interrupt. Valid states are `LOW`, `CHANGE`, `RISING`, `FALLING`, or `HIGH`. `ISR` names the function you want to run. The ISR can be any function you write, but it cannot have parameters and cannot return information.

The Arduino Due has a slightly different prototype, as shown here:

```
attachInterrupt(pin, ISR, mode) // Arduino Due only!
```

detachInterrupt()

This function detaches a previously attached interrupt handler from `attachInterrupt()`. Interrupts on this ID will now be ignored. All other interrupts remain in place. It requires the interrupt ID to function.

```
detachInterrupt(interrupt);
```

This function is again slightly different for the Arduino Due; the Due requires the pin number to be specified, not the interrupt ID.

```
detachInterrupt(pin); // Arduino Due only!
```

noInterrupts()

`noInterrupts()` temporarily disables interrupt handling. This is useful when you are in an interrupt handler and do not want to be disturbed by other interrupts. It does have a down side; some system functions require interrupts, mainly communication. Do not disable all interrupts just because your code does not require user-made interrupt handlers. Disable interrupts only when there is timing-critical code being performed.

```
// Normal code
noInterrupts();
// Time critical code
interrupts();
// Normal code
```

interrupts()

`interrupts()` re-enables all interrupts. You do not need to reconfigure interrupt handlers; all interrupts will be reconfigured as they were before calling `noInterrupts()`.

Summary

In this chapter you have seen the Arduino Language, a set of instructions and functions that are used on every Arduino and are available for every sketch. In the next chapter, you will see the functions used to communicate with the outside world through serial communications.

Serial Communication

After reading this chapter, you will be familiar with the following functions:

- `if (Serial)`
- `available()`
- `begin()`
- `end()`
- `find()`
- `findUntil()`
- `parseFloat()`
- `parseInt()`
- `peek()`
- `print()`
- `println()`
- `read()`
- `readBytes()`
- `readBytesUntil()`
- `setTime-out()`
- `write()`

The following hardware is required to complete the activities and examples presented in this chapter:

- Arduino Uno
- USB Cable

The code download for this chapter is found at `http://www.wiley.com/go/arduinosketches` on the Download Code tab. The code is in the Chapter 5 folder and the filename is `chapter5.ino`.

Introducing Serial Communication

The original IBM PC, introduced in 1981, came with two serial ports, physical connectors allowing the computer to connect to devices or another computer via the RS-232 protocol. For most people, this was the beginning of the serial port, but in reality, it started much earlier. Early computers had serial ports, and they have even been used on mainframes. They have been in use almost since the beginning of microprocessor-based computers.

The word serial comes from the way data is transmitted; serial devices send bits one at a time on a single wire. This is something that you have seen before; it is like a telephone call. Both users pick up the telephone and a single wire connects them together. Both users can talk at the same time (even if it is considered polite to listen while the other person talks), and words are sent one at a time. Both sides are free to start talking when they want, and also free to stop talking.

While serial devices send bits on a single wire, parallel devices send multiple bits on multiple wires. Although parallel communications can be faster than serial, they were often more expensive, requiring more wires. There are also speed limitations due to physical limitations of conductive wiring. Figure 5-1 shows the difference between serial and parallel communications.

A new standard was born: RS-232. RS-232 serial ports were a standard feature on computers allowing users to connect mice, modems, and other peripherals using a common connector. These connectors allowed computers to talk with peripherals, and even talk with other computers. Software was designed to send data between computers on serial links, but while RS-232 was fast enough for devices like mice and modems, it became too slow to handle large amounts of data.

The original serial ports have been removed from most modern computers in favor of a new standard: USB. USB is short for Universal Serial Bus, and even that, however advanced it may be, still uses the same principle: sending data through a serial line. USB does not use RS-232, instead it uses new techniques to send data serially. It can, however, connect to RS-232 hardware using a special converter, which is required when a computer does not have RS-232 but needs to connect to an RS-232 compatible device. Luckily, Arduinos use USB communications, so an adapter is not required.

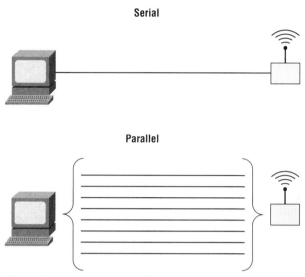

Figure 5-1: Serial versus parallel

Serial ports are extremely simple. This simplicity is one reason why they are used so often. Data is sent on one wire, the transmit wire (TX), and received on another, the receive wire (RX). On the other side of the cable, it is connected to another computer with a TX pin and an RX pin. Inside the cable itself, the TX and RX wires are inverted. The TX pin on one side is connected to the RX pin on the other side. This is illustrated in Figure 5-2.

Figure 5-2: Transmit and receive wires

With all the technological advances made over the years, you could ask the question: Why do systems still use RS-232? There are several reasons. First, it is a proven technology in that it has been used reliably for decades. Second, there are a large amount of cheap electronic components that communicate via RS-232. They are easy to use, requiring only a few lines of code to implement. Third there is the cable distance. Although not necessarily a big advantage for some systems, RS-232 low-capacitance cables can be 1,000 feet long, although most cables limit the distance to 50 feet.

Arduinos use serial ports for communicating with computers and other devices. The USB port of an Arduino is used for serial communication with a computer, with the added advantage that USB can also be used to power the device. USB also has the advantage of auto-configuring most of the parameters. Some Arduinos have other hardware serial ports, enabling communication with up to four other devices. The USB communication is sent to Arduino pins 0 and 1, meaning that those pins are reserved if your device must communicate with a computer.

UART Communications

A Universal Asynchronous Receiver/Transmitter (UART) is a piece of hardware that translates from serial and parallel forms. This is what is used to communicate on a serial interface. Data is sent to the UART device in parallel format, for example, a byte. The UART takes the byte and sends the data 1 bit at a time, adding any required information and line handling. On the receiving end, another UART device decodes the data and returns it to parallel form.

The native UART controller on all Arduinos has a buffer of 64 bytes, meaning the Arduino can receive up to 64 characters while busy with other tasks.

For UARTs to communicate, they must be configured in the same way. This information consists of the following:

- Baud rate
- Data bits
- Parity
- Stop bits

Baud Rate

Originally, the *baud rate* was the amount of times that a signal could be changed per second. Now, it commonly refers to the speed at which information can be transmitted. If you want to send a logical one several times in a row, you do not need to change the signal. The receiving device looks at the input line once every few microseconds or nanoseconds and samples the level. If your sender transmits a series of 1s every millisecond, the receiving device looks at the input line every millisecond. The receiver reads the value and then waits for a millisecond before the next reading. During this time, the sending device has the time to change the logical level (if needed) before the receiver re-samples the data.

It is important that both devices share the same baud rate. If one device is sending faster or slower than another device, the communications will be misinterpreted. If your serial terminal is showing lots of strange characters, then there is a chance that the baud rate is not the same between the two devices.

A baud rate of 1,000 baud is synonymous to a bit rate of 1,000 bits per second. However, that does not mean that 1,000 bits of data are sent. The data is *encapsulated*, placed inside other bits that help the computer identify the data being sent. RS-232 allows asynchronous communications, meaning that the communications line does not require a clock signal, and communications can begin and stop at any time instead of requiring a constant flow. RS-232 needs some way of telling the receiver that they are about to send data and that they have finished sending a packet. For this reason, RS-232 connections almost always have a start bit, 8 data bits, and a stop bit for a total of 10 bits. Some parameters allow for an extra parity bit, or two stop bits, for a total of 12 bits, while only transmitting 8 bits of data. An example data packet is illustrated in Figure 5-3.

Start	Data	Parity	Stop
1 bit	5–9 bits	0–1 bits	1–2 bits

Figure 5-3: A serial packet containing data

Various baud rates exist; most are either multiples of the original baud rate, 75 baud, or multiples of crystal oscillators. Most UART devices are capable of multiple speeds: 300, 1,200, 2,400, 4,800, 9,600, 19,200, 38,400, 57,600, and 115,200 are the most common. Some chips can go even faster. Other devices have non-standard speeds; you need to find a speed supported by both the sender and the receiver. In embedded systems, 9,600, 19,200, and 115,200 are common values.

Data Bits

The number of data bits in each packet can be between 5 and 9 bits. Often this data is used to represent a character or symbol. Five data bits are typically used for Baudot code, a character table predating ASCII that gave baud its name. Seven data bits are used for pure ASCII characters. Most modern systems use 8 bits because that corresponds to 1 byte. Do not try to speed up data throughput by lowering the amount of data bits, even if you are sending only ASCII. It is best to remain compatible with as many devices as possible and to use 8 data bits, unless the other equipment does not let you use the default 8 bits.

Parity

Parity is used as error detection, attempting to detect transmission errors. A parity bit can be added to make the number of 1s in a packet even or odd. Receiving equipment can detect transmission errors and request the sending equipment to re-send data if the data has unexpected information. This was mainly used on older equipment because modern signaling technology no longer needs parity checking, but it is still available if needed.

Stop Bits

Stop bits are automatically sent at the end of every packet. They allow the receiving hardware to detect the end of a character and to resynchronize with the incoming stream. Modern electronic devices usually use 1 stop bit, but older systems can use 1 1/2 or 2 bits.

Debugging and Output

Systems developers have a wide variety of debugging techniques to help them. Programs can be run and "frozen," allowing the developer to look inside the program and see what is happening. You can run a program line by line, watching variables change during a program. In some cases, you can even rewrite lines of code before they are executed, without having to restart your program.

Embedded systems offer an alternative, a physical port that connects directly to the processor that allows a hardware debugger to take control. Again, programs can be run step by step; variables can be examined and modified; and advanced debugging techniques can be used. All this comes at a cost; some debuggers can cost tens of thousands of dollars.

Arduinos forgo these complex and costly implementations for less expensive alternatives. The most common tool used for this purpose is the serial port.

Debugging with a serial port can be effective. It is possible to add a single line to a program, printing out information and simple statements:

```
Debug: We are about to enter the function connectServer()
Debug: Connected!
Debug: Leaving connectServer()
Debug: Connecting to a client...
Debug: Connected with status 2! (should be 1)
```

This is an example of a debug output. First, you can tell that the function `connectServer()` was called and that the program also cleanly exited the function. Don't laugh; this is still in use on lots of development projects!

The last line is where things get interesting. You can use the serial output to display values as shown here. If you can't use a debugger to look at a variable's content, then print it out. In a single line, the developer knows that a return value was not what he expected it to be, and now he has a good idea of where to look for the problem.

NOTE Serial connections depend on correct parameters. If the speed parameter is wrong, the receiving UART device will receive garbled data. You will not get small portions of cleartext with a few wrong characters; the entire text will be unreadable. If your terminal is showing corrupted data, check your settings.

Starting a Serial Connection

All Arduinos have at least one serial port to communicate with a PC called `Serial`. Some boards have several UART devices. The Arduino Mega, for example, has three additional UART controllers called `Serial1`, `Serial2`, and `Serial3`.

The Arduino Leonardo's microcontroller has a built-in USB communication device, separating USB and Serial communication. On the Leonardo, the `Serial` class refers to the virtual serial driver, not the serial device on pins 0 and 1. These pins are connected to `Serial1`.

To do anything with a serial port, you must use the functions available to the `Serial` class.

To begin using a UART device, you must first do some basic configuration. You need to set at least one parameter; the baud rate, or speed. Optionally, you can set the data bits, parity, and stop bits if required. Arduinos, by default, require you to set the speed and set 8N1 as a default configuration. To do this, you use the `begin` function of the `Serial` object.

```
Serial.begin(speed);
Serial.begin(speed, config);
```

For Arduino Megas, you can also use the other serial objects (note that these are not connected to the USB port through the 16U2):

```
Serial1.begin(speed);
Serial1.begin(speed, config);
Serial2.begin(speed);
Serial2.begin(speed, config);
Serial3.begin(speed);
Serial3.begin(speed, config);
```

The `speed` parameter is a long and indicates the baud rate. To communicate with a PC, use one of the following: 300, 600, 1,200, 2,400, 4,800, 9,600, 14,400, 19,200, 28,800, 38,400, 57,600, or 115,200. Typically, 9,600 is an appropriate speed for communicating debug information. You are free to use just about any speed you want as long as both devices are operating at the same speed. For example, some Bluetooth devices can send serial data at speeds much faster than 115,200, in the order of one megabaud (one million baud). Be aware of what the device or computer is expecting.

Serial configuration is normally done in `setup()` because devices tend to not change the speed at which they communicate over time.

```
void setup()
{
  Serial.begin(9600); // Opens the serial port, sets data
// rate to 9600 baud}
void loop() {}
```

For the Arduino Leonardo, you can detect if the USB serial communications channel is open. The `Serial` class can return `true` or `false`, depending on the communication state.

```
if(Serial) // Check to see if the channel is open
```

If you have a number of statements in your `setup()` that you want to send serially, it is useful to wait until the Leonardo's serial port has initialized before proceeding.

```
while(!Serial){ // while there is no serial connection
;; // do nothing
}
```

This works on the Leonardo, Micro, Esplora, and other 32U4-based boards. On all other boards, this function always returns true, even if the device is not connected to USB.

Writing Data

Now that you have established a connection, your Arduino can send data to a receiving device. For debugging, you will probably send ASCII a standard used to transmit text using the English alphabet and some punctuation, and use a terminal emulator for receiving messages. The Arduino IDE integrates a terminal emulator to easily access messages and debugging data. Terminal editors are used to ASCII but will get confused if receiving a non-ASCII character. If a terminal emulator receives a non-ASCII character, for example, something formatted as a raw byte, it will probably produce an unintelligible mess.

Sending Text

To send ASCII data, use `print()`. This function sends data to the serial device as human-readable ASCII format. The data to be printed can be in any format. It can print a single ASCII character or a complete string.

```
Serial.print("Hello, world"); // Output an entire string
Serial.print('!'); // Output a single character
```

It can also print number formats by converting those to ASCII.

```
Serial.print(42); // Outputs the ASCII string "42" to the serial port
Serial.print(1.2345); // Outputs "1.23"
```

By default, numbers are displayed in decimal and rounded to two decimal places. You can change both of these. To print a specific amount of decimal places, just specify the number of digits after the floating-point number to be displayed:

```
Serial.print(1.2345, 0); // Prints "1"
Serial.print(1.2345, 1); // Prints "1.2"
Serial.print(1.2345, 4); // Prints "1.2345"
```

To display numbers in different formats, you need to specify the numerical type constant after the number. There are four possibilities: BIN for binary, DEC for decimal, HEX for hexadecimal, and OCT for octal.

```
Serial.print(42, BIN); // Prints 0010 1010
Serial.print(42, DEC); // Prints 42
Serial.print(42, HEX); // Prints 2A
Serial.print(42, OCT); // Prints 52
```

print() prints data but does not append any special characters to the end of the text. In ASCII, there are a number of these reserved characters. These are escaped with a backslash (\ ). For example, how would you print a quote that has to reside in another quote?

```
Serial.print(""He said "Captain", I said "what""); // Compiler error
```

As far as the compiler understands this line, the text starts at the first quotation mark, and ends at the second, so what is all this noise afterward? The compiler won't understand and will ask you to correct the problem. To show that this is a special character, you must first escape it.

```
Serial.print(""He said \"Captain\", I said \"what\"");
    //reference intact!
```

You need to escape characters like quotation marks, backslashes, and single quotes.

There are also other special ASCII characters to be aware of. Consider the following code:

```
Serial.print("Imagination is more important than knowledge.");
Serial.print("Albert Einstein");
```

At first glance, everything looks good. However, computers are extremely good at doing exactly what you ask for, and nothing more. The result might not quite be what you expect when viewed in a terminal:

```
Imagination is more important than knowledge.Albert Einstein
```

Those lines of text were put on different lines; why didn't the second text start on the next line? Well, the compiler wasn't told to do this. To manually insert a new line, you must use the \n character, for a new line.

```
Serial.print("Imagination is more important than knowledge.\n");
Serial.print("Albert Einstein");
```

Now things look better. The text now appears like this:

```
Imagination is more important than knowledge.
Albert Einstein
```

That's more like it. Now this quotation is readable. Of course, inserting the new line escape sequence is going to get boring, especially if some are forgotten. Luckily, there is a function that can do this for you. The println function automatically adds a new line and a return at the end of the text.

```
Serial.println("Imagination is more important than knowledge.");
Serial.println("Albert Einstein");
```

With citations, the author is frequently added on the bottom of the text, but with an indentation. This too can be added by the tabulation sequence: \t.

```
Serial.println("Imagination is more important than knowledge.");
Serial.print("\tAlbert Einstein");
```

Tabulation can be important for data output, as shown in more detail in the chapter example.

Sending Data

Not all data can be sent as easily as ASCII. If you are trying to output the result of a sensor, it sometimes isn't practical to convert that data to an int and send it as text. It takes up more time and is just as easy to send that data as a byte onto the serial line. Because the default serial connection can send 8 bits of data per packet, you can send a byte in a single data packet. This is exactly what is done when flashing an Arduino; the Arduino IDE doesn't convert your sketch to ASCII before sending the data; it sends the data 1 complete byte at a time.

Luckily, sending data is just as easy as sending text and can be accomplished with the write() function. This function accepts either a single byte or a string to send. It can also accept a buffer as a parameter and a second parameter to indicate the length of the buffer.

```
Serial.write(byte);
Serial.write(string);
Serial.write(buffer, len);
```

Reading Data

It isn't all about sending data through a serial connection; Arduinos can also receive data. Receiving data can be used for many projects; computers can send data, for example, to control the brightness of an LED. Some wireless devices like Bluetooth also use serial ports to transmit data; maybe your telephone can send data to unlock a door or to open a window. Arduinos can also talk to each other over a serial connection, for example, a master Arduino telling a slave Arduino to turn on the lights in the room it controls.

When the UART device receives data, it stores it in an internal buffer. This buffer normally holds 64 characters; any more, and data will be lost. Don't worry; in practice, 64 is more than enough because interrupts can be put in place to tell the microcontroller to retrieve information from this buffer before too much data arrives.

Starting Communications

The first part of any communications is to initiate the connection. Each side must open up a serial port before being able to send and receive data. For the Arduino to initialize a serial communication, you must use the `begin()` function:

```
Serial.begin(speed);
Serial.begin(speed, config);
```

This function requires one or two parameters; the speed parameter is the baud rate for the serial communication. It must be the same on both devices, otherwise they will not be able to communicate. It is expressed as an `int`, and is the exact speed to use. By default, the Arduino IDE will use 9,600, but you are free to choose a different value, so long as both the Arduino serial monitor and the Arduino itself use the same speed.

Is Data Waiting?

You can check the number of bytes in the serial buffer by calling `available()`. This can also let you know if there is any valid data waiting to be read.

```
int bytes = Serial.available();
```

There are two ways people typically use `available()`. One way is to return the result to know the amount of bytes waiting to be read.

```
int inBytes = Serial.available();
```

You can also evaluate if there are a certain number of bytes with an `if()` statement:

```
if (Serial.available() > 0)
{
  // Read in serial data
}
```

Trying to read the serial buffer if no data is available can waste time in your sketch. To avoid a sketch freezing while waiting for data, you can change the duration of the serial time-out, as explained here.

Reading a Byte

You can read a byte from the data buffer using the `read()` function. This function takes 1 byte from the UART buffer and returns it to the program. This function does not return a `byte`, instead, it returns an `int`. There is a good reason for this. What would happen if the buffer were empty? Would the function return 0? That might be the byte waiting for the user in the buffer; there is no way of telling. Instead, the `read()` function returns an `int`. The return values are in the range of 0 to 255, or –1 if no data is available. This function returns immediately and does not wait for data to arrive.

Reading Multiple Bytes

Reading in a single byte at a time can be tedious; fortunately there are other ways of getting data from a serial connection.

`readBytes()` reads multiple bytes from a serial port and places them into a buffer.

```
Serial.readBytes(buffer, length);
```

You must specify the amount of bytes to read, in which case the function stops when all the data has been received. There is also another reason why this function might stop; asking this function for more characters than is available could cause the Arduino to momentarily stall while waiting for data that may never arrive. To avoid this, there is a time-out for waiting to read serial data. The time-out is set by `setTime-out()`. It takes one parameter: a long that contains the number of milliseconds to wait for all the data to arrive. By default, serial ports time out after 1 second.

```
Serial.setTime-out(time);
```

You can now retrieve multiple bytes and time out if no data is available. However, the Arduino still has one trick left. Imagine working with a protocol that allows your computer to send messages to an Arduino: turn on the lights in the bedroom, turn off the TV, and other such instructions. These instructions are sent in small packets, and each packet ends with an exclamation mark. There is a function available that reads in serial data and stops either when all the data is read in, when there is a time-out, or when a special character is received. This function is called `readBytesUntil()` and accepts one argument: the character to wait for.

```
Serial.readBytesUntil(character, buffer, length);
```

Both `readbytes()` and `readBytesUntil()` return a byte of data: the amount of characters read from the serial port. This will be zero if no data was received because a time-out occurred, less than the expected length if some data was received and a time-out occurred while waiting for the full packet, or the same expected length if all the requested data were available. In the case of `read-BytesUntil()`, non-zero values may also indicate that the terminator character was detected.

Taking a Peek

There is a way to get hold of the first byte of data from the UART buffer without modifying the buffer. There are several reasons why this might be useful to you. When you know that data has arrived, what does it contain? Is this ASCII data that needs to be put in a string? Or is this binary data that needs to be put in another buffer? Would it help to know what the first character is? Well, you can. Just like those who cheat when it is their birthday, there is a way to peek at data without changing anything. This will return the first byte from the buffer, but it will not remove the byte from the buffer. Again, it returns an `int`; it returns the first byte of data if it is available; otherwise it returns –1.

```
data = Serial.peek();
```

From here, you can read one or several bytes using the functions listed previously, and the first byte of data read with `peek()` will still be in the buffer.

Parsing Data

You have the data, but what do you do with it? Everything received is either ASCII text or binary data. If it is binary data, then your program must analyze the data and extract the data. ASCII, however, is received as text. This is great if you want to know the user's name, but what if you ask him for his age? What if the serial port receives an instruction to turn on an LED at a specific light setting? It might be text that represents an `int` or `float`, but how do you extract that data? The answer is simple: You parse it.

`parseInt()` and `parseFloat()` scan through text and extract the first `int` or `float` encountered. Any preceding text that is not a number is ignored. Parsing stops when the first non-numerical character is found after a numerical character, as shown in Figure 5-4.

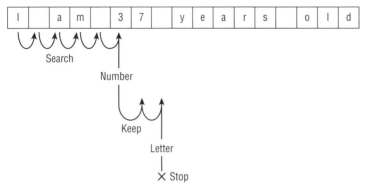

Figure 5-4: Finding numbers in a string

`parseInt()` would ignore the first letters and extract the number 37. The data before the number and the number itself will be removed from the buffer. The rest of the data remains intact.

You can run the `parseInt()` function repeatedly, which can be helpful if data is sent to the Arduino as comma-separated values (CSV). If sending a series of three numbers (`127,255,64`), `parseInt()` can be called three times to extract three numbers. For example, if you want to set the values of an RGB LED.

```
int red = Serial.parseInt(); // Will read 127
int green = Serial.parseInt(); // Will read 255
int blue = Serial.parseInt(); // Will read 64
```

Cleaning Up

The final part of any phone call is to hang up, and it is the same with serial connections. If your application requires you to terminate a serial connection, it can be done by calling `end()`.

```
Serial.end()
```

Input from the USB serial connection is sent to pins 0 and 1, meaning that those pins cannot be used for anything else when a serial connection is established. After calling `Serial.end()`, any pins associated with that serial connection can be used for general input and output. If you need to restart a serial connection, call `begin()` again with the desired baud.

Example Program

For this example, you use an Arduino Uno. It connects via USB to your development PC and is powered via USB. No power supply is needed, and there will not be any components connected this time.

This program demonstrates the principles of a serial connection. The Arduino welcomes the user, asks for her name, and then presents itself. It asks for the user's age and then gives the age. Finally, it prints out a few ASCII characters using tabs.

Listing 5-1: Serial Connection (Filename: `Chapter5.ino`**)**

```
1   char myName[] = {"Arduino"};
2   char userName[64];
3   char userAge[32];
4   int age;
5   int i;
6
7   void setup()
8   {
9     // Configure the serial port:
10    Serial.begin(9600);
11
12    // Welcome the user
13    Serial.println("Hello! What is your name?");
14
15    //Wait for a few seconds, then read the serial buffer
16    delay(10000);
17    Serial.readBytes(userName, 64);
18
19    //Say hello to the user
20    Serial.print("Hello, ");
21    Serial.print(userName);
22    Serial.print(". My name is ");
23    Serial.print(myName);
24    Serial.print("\n");
25
26    //Ask for user's age
27    Serial.print("How old are you, ");
28    Serial.print(userName);
29    Serial.println("?");
30
31    //Wait for a few seconds, then read the serial buffer
32    delay(10000);
33    age = Serial.parseInt();
34
```

Continues

Listing 5-1 (*continued*)

```
35    //Print out the user's age
36    Serial.print("Oh, you are ");
37    Serial.print(age);
38    Serial.println("?");
39    Serial.print("I am ");
40    Serial.print(millis());
41    Serial.println(" microseconds old. Well, my sketch is.");
42
43    //Now print out the alphabet
44    Serial.println("I know my alphabet! Let me show you!");
45    Serial.println("Letter\tDec\tHex\t");
46    for (i = 'A'; i <= 'Z'; i++)
47    {
48      Serial.write(i);
49      Serial.print('\t');
50      Serial.print(i);
51      Serial.print('\t');
52      Serial.print(i, HEX);
53      Serial.print('\t');
54      Serial.print('\n');
55    }
56 }
57
58 void loop()
59 {
60    // put your main code here, to run repeatedly:
61 }
```

Lines 1 to 5 declare the global variables in the program. The myName variable is declared and initialized with the name "Arduino"; the others are only declared.

On line 7, setup() is declared. Because the code runs only once, all the code in this example is placed in setup(). Even though there's nothing happening in loop(), it still needs to be there.

On line 10, the serial device is initialized. The default serial port, Serial, connects to pins 0 and on1e. On an Arduino Uno, these are connected to the USB port. The speed is set to 9,600 baud, and no other parameters are set; therefore the device defaults to 8 data bits, no parity, and 1 stop bit. On line 13, the Arduino greets the user through println(). The program waits for 10 seconds and reads the serial buffer with readBytes(). The data will be put into the userName variable and read up to the size of the buffer, 64 bytes. I hope your name isn't longer than 64 characters! Because it probably isn't, the function will read the bytes in your name and then wait for 1 second to see if there are up to 64 characters. After this, it returns what data it has.

On line 19, the sketch greets the user again, this time with her name. This is done by printing some default text and then printing a variable, the user's name.

Again, it prints out some default text and then prints another variable, its own name. Finally, it prints out the new line character. These four lines of code are printed on a single line of text.

On line 27, the sketch again asks the user a question, and on line 32, it waits for another 10 seconds for the user to enter some text. On line 33, the sketch calls parseInt(), emptying the buffer looking for numbers. The result is stored in the age variable.

On line 36, the sketch again talks to the user, first confirming her age, and then on line 40 calls millis(). This function returns the number of milliseconds that the sketch has been running.

At line 43, the sketch prints out a formatted table, using tabs. The sketch tells the user that it knows its ABCs, and demonstrates its mastery of the alphabet. The first column will be the letter, the second will be the decimal value, and the third will be the hexadecimal value.

Line 46 is a loop that iterates through letters A to Z. These are chars and can be printed as such. In ASCII, capital letters are associated with values from 65 to 90. write() sends these as bytes. The Arduino's serial monitor interprets these as the ASCII equivalent. If print() had been used, the decimal number would have been printed, as on line 50. On line 52, the sketch again prints the value but this time using hexadecimal notation.

The result of the sketch looks like this:

```
Hello! What is your name?
> Elena
Hello, Elena. My name is Arduino

How old are you, Elena?
> I am 8 years old.
Oh, you are 8?
I am 21001 microseconds old. Well, my sketch is.
I know my alphabet! Let me show you!
Letter  Dec     Hex
A       65      41
B       66      42
C       67      43
D       68      44
E       69      45
F       70      46
G       71      47
H       72      48
I       73      49
J       74      4A
K       75      4B
L       76      4C
M       77      4D
```

```
N        78        4E
O        79        4F
P        80        50
Q        81        51
R        82        52
S        83        53
T        84        54
U        85        55
V        86        56
W        87        57
X        88        58
Y        89        59
Z        90        5A
```

To run this sketch, simply upload it from the Arduino IDE. By pressing Ctrl+Shift+M, or by going to Tools ⇨ Serial monitor menu item, you can access the serial monitor that enables you to read the serial data and to input values. Try this out and have fun with it.

This sketch is not perfect, there are a few flaws that were left in. For example, when reading from the serial port, the sketch first waits 10 seconds. This is not a particularly desirable interaction; the user doesn't know how long they have, and they may not react in time. How would you change the sketch so that it waits until data is available? The `available()` function might be useful. You could also try to accomplish the same with `peek()`.

Secondly, the sketch does not check for any problems; it might not receive a name, or it might not receive a correct age. This is also left as an exercise; try to correct this, and re-ask the question if the sketch does not receive a good answer.

How could you add additional columns to display octal values? What about binary?

SoftwareSerial

When no more serial ports are physically available, the SoftwareSerial library can use software to emulate serial communications on other digital pins without the need for a UART. This allows you to have multiple serial ports on a device that would not normally allow it. Because transmission is handled by software and not hardware, only one SoftwareSerial port can receive data at any time. Also, speed is limited to 115,200 baud.

This introduces the concept of libraries. A library is software that can be added as required. It provides functionality and is often not something that you would need every time. If your sketch does not require a library, there is nothing else to do. If your sketch does require a library, you must first *import* it, that is to say tell the Arduino IDE that your sketch requires the functionality provided by a library. To see the list of libraries available, look at the Arduino IDE in the

Sketch ⇨ Import Library menu. There, you will see a list of available libraries. Clicking on one of these will automatically import the library.

Before you can use a software serial implementation, you must first import the library and create an instance of the `SoftwareSerial` class called an object. When instantiating the object, it requires two parameters: the pin used for receiving data and the pin used to send data. Just like the Serial class, you typically call `begin()` in `setup()`. The methods used by SoftwareSerial are just like those used with Serial, so `print()`, `println()`, `available()`, and the rest work the same.

```
#include <SoftwareSerial.h>
#define rxPin 10
#define txPin 11
// set up a new software serial port instance
SoftwareSerial mySerial = SoftwareSerial(rxPin, txPin);

void setup()
{
mySerial.begin(4800);
mySerial.println("Hello, world!");
}
```

The SoftwareSerial object has its own internal buffer of 64 characters. If it receives any more characters, it will overflow. To check the overflow status of the buffer, the call `overflow()` function can be used:

```
bool result = mySerial.overflow();
```

This function checks the internal overflow flag and automatically resets it. Subsequent calls to this function will report no overflow, unless more data has been received, causing another overflow.

SoftwareSerial requires a pin that supports change interrupts, which, depending on your model, is not available on all pins. The Mega2560 can use pins 10 through 15, 50 to 53, and A8 to A15 for RX. On the Leonardo, pins 8 through 11 and 14 to 16 can be used. The transmit pin does not require interrupt support, so any digital pin can be used. For more information about interrupt pins on your Arduino, check Arduino's website for your specific board.

Summary

In this chapter you have seen how to open and close serial communications, allowing you to connect to your Arduino and how to exchange information. In the next chapter you will see how to store long-term data on your Arduino using the EEPROM library.

EEPROM

This chapter discusses the `read()` and `write()` functions of the EEPROM library. The hardware needed to run the examples in this chapter are an Arduino Uno and a USB cable.

You can find the code downloads for this chapter at `http://www.wiley.com/go/arduinosketches` on the Download Code tab. The code is in the Chapter 6 download and the filename is `chapter6.ino`.

Introducing EEPROM

Life would be boring if you had to reinstall software every time you turned off your computer. In the beginning, that is almost exactly what happened. A computer was turned on, and if a floppy disk was not inserted, the computer did not know what to do and just waited. It had no idea of who used it or what programs were available. Ironically, little has changed; instead of a floppy disk, we have hard drives, storing many times more data, but it still relies on the same principle.

Computers typically have two types of memory: volatile and nonvolatile. Volatile memory contains data as long as it is powered. When the power is removed, all the data is lost. This is how RAM works on your home computer. It uses a memory module called DDR. Actually; DDR memory is even more volatile than you might at first think; it needs to be refreshed frequently to keep the data in place. This might sound like poor engineering, but the truth is that Dynamic RAM (DRAM) is extremely fast, dense, and relatively cheap, allowing for inexpensive memory chips that work very well.

Volatile memory is used to store variables and data. The actual program is placed in nonvolatile memory and uses volatile memory to operate. Your alarm clock might have this function. You can set an alarm, but if the power is cut, you have to reprogram the alarm clock; otherwise, you won't wake up on time.

Nonvolatile memory is memory that retains data when power is removed. The first implementation of nonvolatile memory was an implementation of volatile memory with a small cell battery. When that battery ran out, the data would be lost. One solution to this was EPROM memory, as shown in Figure 6-1.

Figure 6-1: EPROM memory chip

Electrically Programmable Read Only Memory (EPROM) is a special memory that retains its data even when power has been removed. Early versions of EPROM required specialized equipment to be programmed. True ROM chips existed well before the arrival of EPROM, but EPROM added something that ROM chips did not have; they could be erased and reprogrammed.

Reprogramming the first EPROM chips was not something particularly easy to accomplish; these devices had a quartz "window" on the top of the chip. By placing the chip under ultraviolet light, the device could be erased within 20 minutes. When fully erased, the device could be reprogrammed.

Although such devices did work well, they were not always practical. They could store programs or nonvolatile variables, but devices became more intelligent and required an increasing number of parameters. How would you feel if your multimedia player couldn't change its name, IP address, or basic configuration? Something had to be done.

Electrically Erasable Programmable Read Only Memory (EEPROM) is a new generation of EPROM devices. EPROMs had to be removed from their circuit to be programmed or erased; however, EEPROM can be erased and reprogrammed in-circuit. Not only can they be reprogrammed, but also the erase and reprogram sequence can be applied to specific memory portions. In short, EEPROM devices can be modified byte by byte, providing an excellent method of storing long-term variables. Data retention for EEPROM devices is normally guaranteed for 10 to 20 years, but that is only a minimum. The real figure is normally much higher. Most EPROM devices were also guaranteed for 10 to 20 years, and a lot of systems built in the 70s are still working fine.

EEPROM does suffer from one flaw; writing data damages the device, ever so slightly. Don't panic! That doesn't mean that the device will stop working minutes after turning it on. Most EEPROM devices support at least 100,000 writes to the same byte, often much more. Writing data once a day to the same memory location will give a lifetime of at least 273 years. Remember; EEPROM is used for configuration data—data that does not often change, for example, serial numbers or IP addresses. Are you actually going to change your IP address 100,000 times?

EEPROMs are slower than other types of memory due to their technology. EEPROM cannot be written to directly; the memory must first be erased before bits can be written, and it is this erase phase that damages the device ever so slightly.

The Different Memories on Arduino

Arduinos have three different memory technologies: RAM, Flash, and EEPROM.

The RAM on Arduinos is exactly like the volatile memory on your computer; it is used to store variables, and the contents are lost when the power is removed.

The Flash memory is used for the sketch itself, as well as a small bootloader. This is the memory that is used when you upload a sketch. Previous contents are erased and replaced. Flash memory supports at least 10,000 write cycles.

The EEPROM memory is a slightly different memory technology, supporting more write cycles. EEPROM memory on ATmega microcontrollers support at least 100,000 writes and can be read and written to byte by byte. This is the memory that will contain long-term settings and is not overwritten by each flash. Updating your sketch won't overwrite your variables.

The EEPROM size varies for each microcontroller. The ATmega8 and ATmega168 found in early versions of the Arduino both have 512 bytes of EEPROM, and the ATmega328 in the Uno has 1,024 bytes. The ATmega1280 and ATmega2560 used in the different versions of the Arduino Mega both have 4 KB of EEPROM.

The EEPROM Library

The EEPROM library is a collection of routines that can access the internal EEPROM memory, reading and writing bytes. The EEPROM library can be imported by manually writing the include statement:

```
#include <EEPROM.h>
```

Optionally, you can add the EEPROM library using the Arduino IDE. Go to the Sketch menu item; select the Import Library submenu, and select EEPROM. This automatically includes the library, as shown in Figure 6-2.

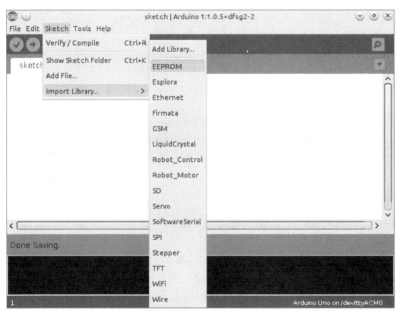

Figure 6-2: Importing the EEPROM library

Reading and Writing Bytes

The entire EEPROM library consists of two functions: `read()` and `write()`. These two functions can read and write bytes from specific memory locations.

The `read()` function reads data from a specified address `adr`, expressed as an `int`, and returns data as a `byte`.

```
EEPROM.read(adr);
```

The `write()` function writes a byte contained in `data` to a specific address `adr`. This function does not return any values.

```
EEPROM.write(adr, data);
```

The Arduino compiler automatically sets the correct start memory location. It doesn't matter if you use an Uno, Mega2560, or Mini; the compiler "translates" the correct address. Reading at memory location 0 read from the first byte of EEPROM.

Consider the following program:

```
byte value;
void setup()
{
  // initialize serial and wait for port to open:
  Serial.begin(9600);
  while (!Serial) {
    // wait for serial port to connect. Needed for Leonardo only
  }
  value = EEPROM.read(0);
  Serial.print("Value at position 0:");
  Serial.print(value, DEC);
  Serial.println();
}
void loop(){}
```

In this program, the Arduino reads the first byte of EEPROM memory and displays it over the serial interface. Yes, it is that simple. Writing a byte into memory is just as straightforward:

```
void setup()
{
  EEPROM.write(0, value);
}

void loop() {}
```

Writing a byte erases the byte in memory before rewriting, and this takes some time. Each write takes approximately 3.3 ms for each byte. Writing the entire contents of a 512-byte EEPROM device takes a little more than 1 1/2 seconds.

Reading and Writing Bits

Bits are used when using true/false values. In some applications there will be relatively few (or sometimes none at all), and in others, you will use boolean variables extensively. An Arduino cannot write individual bits to EEPROM; to store bits, they must first be stored in a byte. There are two possibilities.

If you have a single bit to store, the easiest way is just to code it as a byte, even if you use 1 out of 8 bits.

If you have several bits to store, you might want to try storing them all in 1 byte to save space, for example, a notification LED that the user can program as he wants. If this is an RGB LED, the user can choose a mix of any primary colors for notification. This can be coded into 3 bits; 1 for red, 1 for green, and 1 for blue. A logical 1 means the color is present, and a logical 0 means the color is not present.

You can define this as follows:

```
// primary colors
#define BLUE  4  // 100
#define GREEN 2  // 010
#define RED   1  // 001
```

Did you note that RED was defined as 1, and has the number 001 next to it? Arduinos, like all computer systems, store data as binary—a collection of ones and zeros. It is critical to understand binary when performing bitwise calculations.

Binary is a base-two system; that is to say that each digit can take one of two possible values—0 or 1. The rightmost figure corresponds to 2^0, the number to its left corresponds to 2^1, the next one to 2^2, and so on. In this example, I have used three specific values: 1, 2, and 4. I did not use 3 since in binary, 3 is written as 011, and I wanted each color to be assigned to a bit.

There are five more bits that could be coded into this byte. Each bit could indicate another behavior; maybe the LED should blink? Or maybe a warning beep? You can make this decision.

Also, another important part of bitwise calculations is AND and OR. In binary logic, a result is TRUE if one value AND the second value are both TRUE. TRUE and TRUE would result in TRUE, but TRUE and FALSE would result in FALSE. A result is TRUE if one value OR another value is TRUE. 1 OR 1 is TRUE, as is 1 OR 0, but 0 OR 0 is FALSE.

Let's imagine you want a cyan light to be lit up if something occurs. Cyan is a mix of green and blue. In English, you would say that you want green and blue, but in computer logic, you would say that you want GREEN or BLUE. A logical OR is true if one of the two values being compared is true. In this case, GREEN (010) is compared to BLUE (100), and the answer becomes 110.

So, the result, called CYAN, is 110, but now that you have encoded that, how can you get the data out of it? This time, you will be using a logical AND. A logical AND is true if the both the values being compared are true. So, CYAN AND BLUE? CYAN has a value of 110, and the value of BLUE is 100. The leftmost bit is 1 in both, so that will return as a 1. The second bit is 1 in CYAN and 0 in BLUE. It returns 0. The third bit is 0 in both values; it also returns 0. The result is 100. You can now say that BLUE is present in CYAN because the result was not zero.

Now, time to try that again with RED. The value of CYAN is 110, and RED is 001. The first two bits are 1 in CYAN and 0 in RED. They return 0. The third bit is 0 in CYAN and 1 in RED. The logical AND process returns 000. There is no RED in CYAN because CYAN AND RED returns 0.

To read boolean data, read the byte containing the data from EEPROM and then perform a logical AND with the reference value. To create boolean data, you must take an empty variable (initialized as 0) and then perform logical OR operations with reference values. What happens if you want to update an existing value? You already know how to set a bit, using a logical OR, but to clear a bit, you must use a logical NOT AND. NOT inverts a status; if it was previously TRUE, it will become FALSE. By inverting the reference, you keep every bit that is set except the one you want to clear. To toggle a bit, simply use the logical XOR to invert its status. XOR, short for Exclusive OR, will be true if and only if one of the inputs is TRUE; if they are both TRUE, then the result will be FALSE.

Figure 6-3 shows a table of logical operators, showing the effect of each.

A	B	A | B	A & B	A ^ B	~A
0	0	0	0	0	1
1	0	1	0	1	0
0	1	1	0	1	1
1	1	1	1	0	0
		OR	AND	XOR	NOT

Figure 6-3: Logical operators

Following is a short example of how to perform bitwise operations. A bitwise OR is performed using the | symbol:

```
value |= RED; // Bitwise OR. Sets the BLUE bit
```

To perform a bitwise AND, use the & symbol:

```
vavalue &= ~GREEN; // Bitwise AND. Clears the RED bit (AND NOT RED)
```

And finally, to perform an exclusive OR, use the ^ symbol:

```
value ^= BLUE; // Bitwise XOR. Toggles the GREEN bit
```

Reading and Writing Strings

Strings are generally an array of char values and as such can be easily stored and recalled. In Arduino, it's possible to use a char array as a string, or you can use the String data type for more robust data manipulation, at the cost of program size. With character arrays, you can recall the entire allocated memory and print it out as required.

Suppose you need to store a string, defined as such:

```
char myString[20];
```

You can also set a string to a specific value when you declare it. Note that while this array can contain up to 20 elements, not all of them have data.

```
char myString[20] = "Hello, world!";
```

You can store information in EEPROM like this:

```
int i;
for (i = 0; i < sizeof(myString); i++)
{
  EEPROM.write(i, myString[i]);
}
```

This routine will write the contents of the string to EEPROM memory, one byte at a time. Even if the string is only 5 bytes long, it will store the contents of the entire array. That is, if you declare a `char` array of 20 elements and only have valid data in the first 5 bytes, you'll still be writing 20 bytes to EEPROM. You could make a more optimized routine that automatically stops when it receives a null character: the end of a C string, but because this routine writes to EEPROM memory that is not often (if ever) changed, there is no point to over-complexifying the program. Reading a string is just as easy:

```
int i;
for (i = 0; i < sizeof(myString); i++)
  {
    myString[i] = EEPROM.read(i);
  }
```

Again, the operation is the same; it will take 1 byte from EEPROM and place it into the string, and repeat for each byte in the string.

Reading and Writing Other Values

If the EEPROM can only read and write bytes, how can you save the contents of an integer or a floating point number? At first it might seem impossible, but remember that in computers, everything is just 1s and 0s. Even a floating-point number is written in memory as binary, it just occupies a larger number of bytes. Just like with strings, it is possible to write just about anything in EEPROM memory, by reading and writing 1 byte at a time.

Before beginning, you must know exactly what sort of data you need to read and write. For example, on all Arduinos except the Due, an `int` is written as 2 bytes. By using techniques known as shifts and masks, it is possible to "extract" bytes of data. Shifting takes a binary number and "shifts" data to the left or to the right by a certain number of bits. Masking makes it possible to perform bit-wise operations on a portion of a binary number. Take the following example:

```
void EEPROMWriteInt(int address, int value)
{
  byte lowByte = ((value >> 0) & 0xFF);
  // Now shift the binary number 8 bits to the right
  byte highByte = ((value >> 8) & 0xFF);
  EEPROM.write(address, lowByte);
  EEPROM.write(address + 1, highByte);
}
```

In this example, an int is to be saved into EEPROM. It contains two bytes: the low byte and the high byte. The terminology "low" and "high" bytes is used when a number is stored on several bytes; the low byte contains the least significant part of the number, and the high byte contains the most significant part of the number. First, the lowest byte is extracted. It simply takes the number and performs a bitwise AND with 0xFF. The 0x in front of the letters tells the Arduino IDE that this is a hexadecimal number. Just like binary, hexadecimal is another way of printing a number. Instead of using only two values per figure, hexadecimal uses 16. 0xFF is the hexadecimal representation of 255, the largest number that a byte can hold. Then, the same value is shifted right 8 bits, and again, an AND is performed. This is an elegant solution that can work for integers but will not work for more complex numbers, like a floating-point. You cannot perform shifts with a floating-point, more advanced techniques are required.

Several users have requested EEPROM functions to write any sort of data, one possible solution is available in the Arduino Playground and is called EEPROM Write Anything. If you want to write anything to EEPROM, look at this example from the playground—but be forewarned, it uses advanced programming techniques that are not covered in this book:

http://playground.arduino.cc/Code/EEPROMWriteAnything

Here is an extract of this code:

```
template <class T> int EEPROM_writeAnything(int ee, const T& value)
{
  const byte* p = (const byte*)(const void*)&value;
  unsigned int i;
    for (i = 0; i < sizeof(value); i++)
      EEPROM.write(ee++, *p++);
  return i;
}
```

Again, this code requires specific information: the exact size of the value to save. Be careful when using int values; again, on the Arduino Due, they are a different size than other Arduino boards.

Where possible, try to use byte-size values, but as you can see, it is possible to store just about anything in EEPROM.

Example Program

In the previous chapter, you created a program that would greet the user, ask for his name and age, and write some data to a serial port. However, when the Arduino was unplugged, it forgot everything; the next time it was powered on, it would ask for the same information. We'll build on that same program but now store the responses in EEPROM. The Arduino should first check its EEPROM memory. If no information is found, it will ask the user some questions and then store that information into nonvolatile memory. If the information is found, it will tell the user what information it has and then delete the contents of its memory. It is now clear that an Arduino knows its ABCs, so I removed that portion of code from the example. The program is shown in Listing 6-1.

Listing 6-1: Example program (code filename: `Chapter6.ino`)

```
1    #include <EEPROM.h>
2
3    #define EEPROM_DATAPOS 0
4    #define EEPROM_AGEPOS 1
5    #define EEPROM_NAMEPOS 2
6    #define EEPROM_CONTROL 42
7
8    char myName[] = {"Arduino"};
9    char userName[64];
10   char userAge[32];
11   unsigned char age;
12   int i;
13   byte myValue = 0;
14
15   void setup()
16   {
17     // Configure the serial port:
18     Serial.begin(9600);
19
20     // Does the EEPROM have any information?
21     myValue = EEPROM.read(EEPROM_DATAPOS);
22
23     if (myValue == 42)
24     {
25       // Get the user's name
26       for (i = 0; i < sizeof(userName); i++)
27       {
28         userName[i] = EEPROM.read(EEPROM_NAMEPOS + i);
29       }
30
```

```
31        // Get the user's age
32        age = EEPROM.read(EEPROM_AGEPOS);
33
34        // Print out what we know of the user
35        Serial.println("I know you!");
36        Serial.print("Your name is ");
37        Serial.print(userName);
38        Serial.print(" and you are ");
39        Serial.print(age);
40        Serial.println(" years old.");
41
42        // Write zero back to the control number
43        EEPROM.write(EEPROM_DATAPOS, 0);
44    }
45    else
46    {
47        // Welcome the user
48        Serial.println("Hello! What is your name?");
49
50        // Wait until serial data is available
51        while(!Serial.available())
52        // Wait for all the data to arrive
53        delay(200);
54
55        // Read in serial data, one byte at a time
56        Serial.readBytes(userName, Serial.available());
57
58        // Say hello to the user
59        Serial.print("Hello, ");
60        Serial.print(userName);
61        Serial.print(". My name is ");
62        Serial.print(myName);
63        Serial.println("\n");
64
65        // Save the user's name to EEPROM
66        for (i = 0; i < sizeof(userName); i++)
67        {
68          EEPROM.write(EEPROM_NAMEPOS + i, userName[i]);
69        }
70
71        // Ask for user's age
72        Serial.print("How old are you, ");
73        Serial.print(userName);
74        Serial.println("?");
75
76        // Wait until serial data is available
77        while(!Serial.available())
78        // Wait for all the data to arrive
79        delay(200);
80        age = Serial.parseInt();
```

Continues

Listing 6-1 (*continued*)

```
81
82     // Print out the user's age
83     Serial.print("Oh, you are ");
84     Serial.print(age);
85     Serial.println("?");
86     Serial.print("I am ");
87     Serial.print(millis());
88     Serial.println(" microseconds old. Well, my sketch is.");
89
90     // Now save this to EEPROM memory
91     EEPROM.write(EEPROM_AGEPOS, age);
92
93     // Since we have all the information we need, and it has been
94     //saved, write a control number to EEPROM
95     EEPROM.write(EEPROM_DATAPOS, EEPROM_CONTROL);
96   }
97
98 }
99
100 void loop()
101 {
102   // put your main code here, to run repeatedly:
103 }
```

So, what has changed? Well, the most visible change is that the code concerning Arduino's ABC recital has been removed. This example concentrates on something else.

On line 11, the user's age is now stored in an `unsigned char`. Originally this was stored in an `int`, but this presents a problem for EEPROM memory. Remember that in Chapter 4 you saw that `int` values stored from –32768 to 32767. You won't need all those numbers; humans don't (yet) live that long, and in any case, negative numbers aren't necessary. The problem isn't the range; it is the size of the container. On most Arduinos, an `int` is coded on 2 bytes (in the Due it occupies 4 bytes). If you release your program as open source, you will have no way of knowing which Arduino will be used. In addition, an `int` for an age is a bad idea; it isn't optimal. An unsigned char is always 1 byte and can handle numbers from 0 all the way to 255. This will be easier to write to an EEPROM.

On line 21, the sketch reads data from the EEPROM. The exact location is defined by `EEPROM_DATAPOS`. Of course, the function could have been called directly with the number 0 (and this is exactly what the compiler is going to do), but adding a `#define` makes the code more readable and also allows the developer to change memory location without worrying about forgetting a call. This makes everything neater. This sketch shows the persistence of nonvolatile memory, and as such, it has to have a way of ignoring any data stored. To do this, a "control" byte is allocated. The Arduino reads a value in the EEPROM. If it receives the number 42, it presumes that the EEPROM contains valid information and attempts to read that data. If the Arduino reads any other number, it asks the user for information, writes that data to EEPROM, and then writes the control byte.

Assuming that no valid EEPROM data has been found, the sketch is close to what was already present in the previous chapter. On lines 50 and 76, the serial call has been changed. At the end of the previous example, I asked you to try and find a better way of listening for serial communication. This is one way of waiting for serial data. What did you find?

On line 91, the sketch saves the contents of the variable `age` to EEPROM using a single function call: `EEPROM.write()`. However, on line 65, the string `userName` is saved 1 byte at a time. The entire string memory is written to EEPROM, but you could tweak the code to write only what is needed. What would you write?

This brings the question: How do you organize memory? It is up to you, the engineer and creator, to decide how the memory will be partitioned. This example used position 0 as the control byte, position 1 as the age, and 20 bytes from position 2 onward as a string containing your name. Don't hesitate to use a spreadsheet or some paper notes to map out your memory, to know what will go where. An example is shown in Figure 6-4.

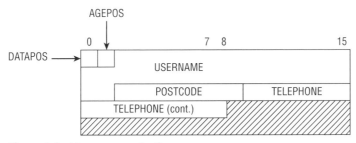

Figure 6-4: Memory organization

Keep in mind that `#define` statements are easier to change rather than looking through your code if you need to change something.

Preparing EEPROM Storage

One of the problems encountered with EEPROM memory happens the first time a sketch is run. This sketch assumes that if a certain number is present in the first block, then the rest of the information is valid. When running this sketch on another system, you do not know what EEPROM contains. If you are unlucky, the first byte will already contain the control number you're looking for, but the rest of the data may not contain a valid age, or a valid name. This could simply result in garbled text, but in another application, it might lead to significant problems. Imagine a small sensor that connects to the Internet to upload temperature readings to a server. If the IP address is stored in EEPROM, and that memory location does not contain valid data, then your application will attempt to upload data to a server that does not belong to you.

To prevent this, some designers add a reset button to their project. By adding a few lines to your sketch, you can erase EEPROM data in the case of a first-time power on, or if the Arduino board were changed. Some applications use the control number for error checking, adding several numbers throughout EEPROM memory for more reliability. Or, you could use a second sketch, one that you upload that sets EEPROM data exactly as you want, before reflashing the final sketch. There are several solutions available; it all depends on what solution is the best for you and your application. Don't trust EEPROM contents on a new system; take the time necessary to prepare the nonvolatile memory.

Adding Nonvolatile Memory

Arduinos have limited EEPROM memory that is sufficient for most programs, but in some cases you might need to add EEPROM memory. Numerous EEPROM components exist, for example the Atmel AT24C01A that adds 1 KB of memory, or the AT24C16A that adds 16 KB of memory. However, these components are connected to the I2C bus (explained in Chapter 8) and cannot be addressed by the EEPROM library. The EEPROM library can handle only the internal EEPROM, not external. If you want more external memory, it must be addressed by the bus that it uses.

If you require large amounts of nonvolatile memory, other solutions exist. Arduino shields exist that can accept SD or micro-SD cards. At the time of writing, micro-SD cards have capacities up to 128 gigabytes, more than enough for most logging applications.

SD cards are based on flash memory, and as such, also inherit flash memory's weakness: write cycles. However, most SD cards have an internal controller that implements something called *wear leveling*, a technique used to limit the amount of write cycles to a specific place in memory. This greatly increases the life expectancy of the flash memory, allowing for normal filesystem use, even when files are frequently updated. If you need nonvolatile memory that is often changed, consider using an SD-card shield. SD-card operation is explained in Chapter 12.

Summary

In this chapter, you have seen how to read and write data to and from an Arduino's internal EEPROM memory. In the next chapter, I will explain SPI communications, another form of serial communication used to talk to sensors and exchange information.

This chapter discusses the following functions of the SPI library:

- `begin()`
- `end()`
- `setBitOrder()`
- `setDataMode()`
- `setClockDivider()`
- `transfer()`

The hardware needed to use these functions includes:

- Arduino Due
- Adafruit MAX31855 breakout board
- Type-K thermocouple wire, from Adafruit Industries

You can find the code download for this chapter at `http://www.wiley.com/go/arduinosketches` on the Download Code tab. The code is in the Chapter 7 folder and the filename is `Chapter7.ino`.

Introducing SPI

Serial data connections have been the backbone for computer communication systems for decades. Reliable and sufficiently fast for most devices, they have been used to communicate with modems, IC programmers, and computer-to-computer communications for most of computing's history. They use few wires compared to other communications systems and are generally robust—qualities that are useful for embedded systems and peripherals.

Serial communications are also used deep inside embedded systems where space is critical. Instead of connecting a device to a 32-bit data bus, a simple temperature sensor can, instead, be connected to the microcontroller via just a few wires. It makes design simpler, cheaper, and more efficient.

Although serial connections have a lot of advantages, they also have disadvantages. Having a modem and a programmer requires a computer with two serial ports; a serial port cannot (easily) handle multiple devices. One serial port, one device. This is the same for microcontrollers and microprocessors; most devices have at least one serial port, but it is difficult to find a device with more than three RS-232 serial ports. Also, more ports mean more software—and more tasks used to check the serial buffers. Also, a modem might be used for long periods of time, but a chip programmer will be used for just a minute or two, tying up a serial port for a single task that is rarely run.

SPI Bus

To allow multiple devices to be used on a single serial port, the SPI bus was created. SPI is short for Serial Peripheral Interface and is indeed an interface to devices, using a synchronous serial line capable of full-duplex communication (meaning that both devices can send and receive at the same time).

SPI is a master/slave protocol; one master communicates with one or more slaves. Communication is made with only one slave at a time; to communicate with another slave, the master must first stop communicating with the first slave. Slaves cannot "talk" on the network without being instructed to by the master.

To connect and talk to a slave, a master requires at least four wires. The "Master Out-Slave In" (MOSI) and "Master In-Slave Out" (MISO) wires are used for data communication; SCLK is a serial clock that regulates the speed of the communication; and SS (short for Slave Select) is used to select the peripheral. It's not uncommon to see SS referred to as CS (for Chip Select) in some documentation.

SS is a wire that "selects" a slave on a logical zero. The MOSI, MISO, and SCLK wires are connected to every device on the SPI bus, and devices listen only to the master and communicate if their SS wire is set to active low. This allows for several slaves to be connected to a master on the same network. A typical SPI bus is shown in Figure 7-1.

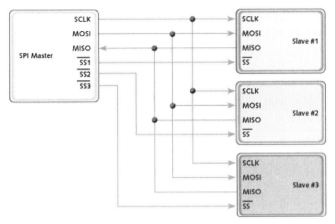

Figure 7-1: An SPI network using several slaves

Comparison to RS-232

SPI is also simpler in design compared to RS-232 communications; RS-232 uses two wires (Tx and Rx), but it requires a set clock speed on both sides of communication. The clock on both devices connected via RS-232 need to be in agreement, preventing configuration problems or desynchronization. SPI masters generate their own clock signal and send that signal to every device. SPI devices are therefore normally simpler to design, cheaper to fabricate, and easier to use.

Another difference between SPI and RS-232 is the way data is sent. RS-232 was designed for long distance communications; SPI is not. It does not need to handle signal noise like RS-232 and therefore does not require checksum bits. This has one major advantage; where RS-232 communications have to send 7-bit or 8-bit data, SPI can select any length it wants. Some devices send 8-bit data, some send 16-bits, even devices using nonstandard lengths like 12-bits can be found on the market.

Configuration

Although SPI does not require explicit configuration like RS-232 devices, it does require a form of configuration. The clock signal is a digital signal, oscillating between a logical one and a logical zero. Some devices will be active on a rising edge (as the clock goes from low to high), and some will be active on a falling edge (as the clock goes from high to low). Also, the clock can be configured to be active low or active high.

Also, because SPI are serial devices, bits are sent one at a time. Because of this, you have to know if the device is expecting the most-significant bit first or the least-significant bit first. Data is normally shifted out with the most significant bit first.

One last configuration is the clock speed. The clock is generated by the master, and as such, it is the master that defines the speed of the bus. Most components have a maximum speed configuration; creating a clock signal above this frequency results in corrupted data.

Communications

SPI is a master/slave protocol, and as such, the master initiates communication with a slave. To do this, it pulls the slave's SS pin low (while maintaining any other SS wires high). This tells the slave that it is being addressed.

To communicate, the slave requires a clock signal, which will be generated by the master. Each clock pulse results in a bit of data being transmitted; however, some sensors (like the DHT-11 used later in this book) require a small timeframe in which the conversion will be made. If this is required, the master must not initiate the clock until the slave has had time to complete the conversion.

When the clock signal is generated, both the master and slave are free to communicate at the same time. In reality both devices do communicate at the same time; the master transmits on the MOSI line, and the slave listens to that line. At the same time, the slave transmits on the MISO line, and the master listens to that line. Both happen at the same time, but some devices do not require meaningful data to be received; a slave device that transmits only data receive data from the master but it ignores all information sent to it.

When the master finishes, either sending the data it requires or retrieving data, it normally stops the clock signal and deselects the slave.

Arduino SPI

The SPI bus on the Arduino is an exception compared to most other ports. On select Arduinos, the SPI bus is present as a dedicated header—the ICSP header, as shown in Figure 7-2.

The ISCP header has several uses, including bypassing the Arduino bootloader to program the microcontroller directly, (ISCP is short for In-Circuit Serial Programming), but this is out of the scope of this book.

The ISCP port also normally exposes the SPI bus, depending on models. The Arduino Uno, the reference model of the Arduino family, uses pin 11 and ICSP-4 for the SPI MOSI signal. These pins are duplicates; they are electrically connected. On the Arduino Leonardo, the MOSI pin is available only on the ICSP header and cannot be output to any digital pins.

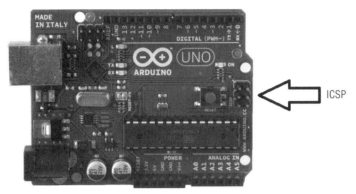

Figure 7-2: The ICSP header on an Arduino Uno

If you move on to designing your own shields, use the ICSP headers. Arduino shields that use SPI cannot function on the Arduino Leonardo if they do not use the ICSP header, and SPI is used for numerous connections (including SD-card readers).

The ICSP header does not include any SS lines; only the MISO, MOSI, and SCLK lines are exposed, together with power and ground connectors. Because the Slave Select pin is not used to transfer data, but used only to tell a slave that it will be addressed, any digital output pin can be used as a Slave Select. This way, you can have an extremely large amount of slaves on your system; however, remember that only one slave can be selected at any time; it is up to you to drive all the outputs high when not talking to a slave.

Arduinos also have the possibility of becoming an SPI slave, and as such, AVR-based Arduinos have an input SS pin. The Arduino SPI library can be only a master, and as such, this pin must be configured as an output. Failure to do so might make the Arduino believe that it is a slave and render the library inoperative. On most Arduinos, this is pin 10, and on the Arduino Mega2560, it is pin 53.

SPI Library

The Arduino SPI library is a powerful library designed to handle SPI communications simply and effectively. Most Arduino boards utilize the SPI library in the exact same way, but there are notable differences if you're using an Arduino

Due. Before discussing these extended methods, let's review the standard functions of the library.

To use the library, you must first import it. In the Arduino IDE, either go to the menu, Sketch ⇨ Import Library ⇨ SPI, or add the library manually:

```
#include <SPI.h>
```

To initialize the SPI subsystem, you must first use `begin()`.

```
SPI.begin();
```

This function automatically sets the SCLK, MOSI, and SS pins to output, pulling SCLK, MOSI LOW, and SS HIGH. It also sets the MISO pin as an input.

To stop the SPI subsystem, call `end()`:

```
SPI.end();
```

Ending the SPI subsystem frees up the I/O lines, letting you use them for other uses.

To configure the SPI bus, three functions are available: `setBitOrder()`, `setDataMode()`, and `setClockDivider()`.

`setBitOrder()` controls the way in which bits are sent on a serial line: the least-significant bit (LSB) first or the most significant bit (MSB) first. This function takes one parameter: a constant, either `LSBFIRST` or `MSBFIRST`.

```
SPI.setBitOrder(order);
```

`setDataMode()` sets the clock polarity and phase. It takes a single parameter, the "mode," for the SPI clock to use.

```
SPI.setDataMode(mode);
```

The `mode` parameter is one of four constants: `SPI_MODE0`, `SPI_MODE1`, `SPI_MODE2`, and `SPI_MODE3`. The difference between these four modes is listed in Table 7-1.

Table 7-1: The Different SPI Clock Modes

MODE	CPOL	CPHA	EFFECT
SPI_MODE0	0	0	Clock base zero, capture on rising, propagation on falling
SPI_MODE1	0	1	Clock base zero, capture on falling, propagation on rising
SPI_MODE2	1	0	Clock base one, capture on falling, propagation on rising
SPI_MODE3	1	1	Clock base one, capture on rising, propagation on falling

CPOL is short for Clock Polarity and tells the device if the clock is active on a logical 1 or a logical 0. CPHA is short for Clock Phase and tells the device if data should be captured on a rising edge (going from 0 to 1) or a falling edge (going from 1 to 0).

Finally, the clock divider function, `setClockDivider()`, is used to set the clock frequency in relation to the system clock.

```
SPI.setClockDivider(divider);
```

For AVR-based systems like the Arduino Uno, the `divider` parameter is a numerical value: 2, 4, 8, 16, 32, 64, or 128. These values are available as constants:

- `SPI_CLOCK_DIV2`

- `SPI_CLOCK_DIV4`

- `SPI_CLOCK_DIV8`

- `SPI_CLOCK_DIV16`

- `SPI_CLOCK_DIV32`

- `SPI_CLOCK_DIV64`

- `SPI_CLOCK_DIV128`

By default, AVR systems using a system clock of 16 MHz use a divider of 4, `SPI_CLOCK_DIV4`, resulting in an SPI bus frequency of 4 MHz.

NOTE The Arduino Due has more advanced SPI features that are explained in the section "SPI on the Arduino Due."

To send and receive data on the SPI bus, use `transfer()`.

```
result = SPI.transfer(val);
```

This function takes a byte as a parameter, the byte to send on the SPI bus. It returns a byte, the byte of data received on the SPI bus. `transfer()` sends and receives only a single byte per call; to receive more data, call this function as many times as needed.

SPI on the Arduino Due

The Arduino Due is not an AVR device but uses Atmel's SAM3X8E: a micro-controller based on ARM's Cortex-ME design. It is a more powerful device and has advanced SPI functionality.

The SPI library is almost the same on AVR devices and ARM-powered devices, but changes slightly. When calling an SPI function, you must also add the SS pin that will be used.

NOTE The Extended SPI library for the Due is only available on Arduino 1.5 and greater.

Most SPI devices are compatible, but as you have seen previously, there are different modes, and sometimes you will have two SPI devices on your system that use different modes. This can complicate designs greatly, forcing you to reconfigure the SPI controller each time you change peripherals. The Arduino Due has a way around this.

The Arduino Due can use pins 4, 10, and 52 as slave select. These pins must be specified on each call, including the setup with SPI.begin():

```
void setup(){
  // Initialize the bus for a device on pin 4
  SPI.begin(4);
  // Initialize the bus for a device on pin 10
  SPI.begin(10);
  // Initialize the bus for a device on pin 52
  SPI.begin(52);

}
```

begin() is written in a different way:

```
SPI.begin(slaveSelectPin);
```

It takes one parameter, the slave select pin, to use. So why is this required? This becomes obvious when configuring the SPI bus:

```
// Set clock divider on pin 4 to 21
SPI.setClockDivider(4, 21);
// Set clock divider on pin 10 to 42
SPI.setClockDivider(10, 42);
// Set clock divider on pin 52 to 84
SPI.setClockDivider(52, 84);
```

Each SS pin can have its own clock frequency, and the Arduino automatically changes the clock frequency when talking to a particular slave. This also applies to any configuration made:

```
// Set mode on pin 4 to MODE0
SPI.setDataMode(4, SPI_MODE0);
// Set mode on pin 10 to MODE2
SPI.setDataMode(10, SPI_MODE2);
```

The SPI system now automatically changes modes when talking to a particular slave. To initiate communications, use transfer(), specifying the pin:

```
result = SPI.transfer(slaveSelectPin, val);
result = SPI.transfer(slaveSelectPin, val, transferMode);
```

Again, it takes a byte, `val`, and sends it on the SPI bus. It returns `result` as a byte. However, you must also indicate the `slaveSelectPin`. This function has an optional parameter, `transferMode`. Because the extended SPI library requires you to specify the slave select pin, the library will change the outputs of the slave select pin. By specifying the SS pin, this output is pulled low to access the selected slave. By default, when a byte has been sent, the extended SPI library will then output a logical one to the SS pin, deselecting the slave. To avoid this, use the `transferMode` parameter. This parameter is one of two possible values, as shown in Table 7-2.

Table 7-2: The Transfer Modes Available on the Arduino Due

TRANSFER MODE	RESULT
SPI_CONTINUE	The SS pin is not driven high; it remains low. The slave is still selected.
SPI_LAST	Specifies that this is the last byte to send/receive. The SS pin is driven high; the slave is deselected.

By default, `SPI_LAST` is used. Please be aware that some SPI devices automatically send data when they are selected; deselecting and reselecting the slave after every byte can result in unexpected data.

To stop the SPI interface for a particular pin, use `end()`:

```
SPI.end(slaveSelectPin);
```

This terminates the SPI interface for this particular slave select pin, freeing the pin for other uses, but keeps the SPI interface active if other slave select pins were configured.

Example Program

For this application, you create a digital thermometer using a thermocouple. A *thermocouple* is a temperature measuring device created by the contact of two different conductors: differences in temperature from different points creates voltage. The voltage generated is extremely small (often a few microvolts per degree Celsius) so they are often coupled with amplifiers.

The major advantage to thermocouples is their price—just a few dollars per cable. Their downside is their accuracy; they can sometimes be off by a few degrees (type K typically has a +/–2° C to +/–6° C accuracy), but their temperature range more than makes up for this. A typical thermocouple can work with temperatures between –200° C and +1000° C (–238° F to +1800° F). Although it is not likely that such a device would be used in medical applications, they are frequently used in the industry to monitor temperatures in ovens. To illustrate the temperatures that thermocouples can support, copper becomes liquid at 1084° C (1983° F) and gold becomes liquid at 1063° C (1946° F). They can therefore be placed in almost every oven, fire or barbecue. If ever you want to create a smokehouse to make smoked salmon, a thermocouple is an excellent way to keep track of the temperature directly inside the fire and on the racks.

Thermocouples do not report a temperature; rather, they report a temperature difference between their hot junction (the tip) and the cold junction (the other end of the thermocouple that is connected to the printed circuit board). To use a thermocouple effectively, it is important to know the temperature on the cold junction, and integrated drivers do this automatically.

The MAX31855 is a thermocouple driver, capable of working with a variety of thermocouples. It has good accuracy, fast conversion, and excellent range. (This device, coupled with a type K thermocouple, can register up to +1350° C (+2462° F). Different thermocouples exist, using different metals and handling different temperature ranges. A thermocouple driver must be connected to the correct thermocouple to function. To communicate this data with another device, the MAX31855 uses the SPI bus and is a read-only device. It outputs the thermocouple temperature, reference junction temperature, and fault indicators. The MAX31855 can warn when a thermocouple short occurs, or when the connection is broken, making it excellent for industrial applications.

The MAX31855 is only available in a surface-mounted format (SO-8), but Adafruit has created a small, reliable breakout board for this component. The MAX31855 itself can support only 3.3 V power, but Adafruit have added voltage shifting onto its breakout board, allowing this component to be used by both AVR (which typically operate at 5 V) and the Cortex-M (running at 3.3 V) based Arduinos.

Hardware

For this example, you use an Arduino Due. The Due is a powerful device, powered by 3.3 V and with advanced SPI functionality. You also use an Adafruit MAX31855 breakout board and thermocouple. This board has two connectors: One is placed on the breadboard and the thermocouple connects to one. It requires some soldering; the connectors are packaged with the card but not connected, but it is easy to do and requires only a few minutes.

The Arduino Due has three slave select pins available; for this example, you use the digital pin 10. The layout is shown in the Figure 7-3.

The layout is extremely simple; the breakout board is connected to the Arduino Due's 3.3 V power and also to the ground. The driver's SS pin is connected to digital pin 10; this is the slave select pin and will be pulled low when the Arduino Due requests information from the MAX31855. The SPI clock on pin 21 is connected to the breakout board's clock connector. To read information from the breakout board, the MISO, pin 74, is connected to the breakout board's data pin (labeled DO). What about the Arduino Due's MOSI, Master Out-Slave In? The MAX31855 is a read-only device, and as such, does not require any data from the master. To simplify the design, this pin was voluntarily omitted. So how does the MAX31855 know when to send information? This device automatically prepares to send data when its slave select pin is driven low. Temperature conversions and fault detection are done continuously when the MAX31855 is not selected, and as soon as the MAX31855 is selected via slave select (as soon as SS is driven low), the conversion process stops, and it begins to transmit data.

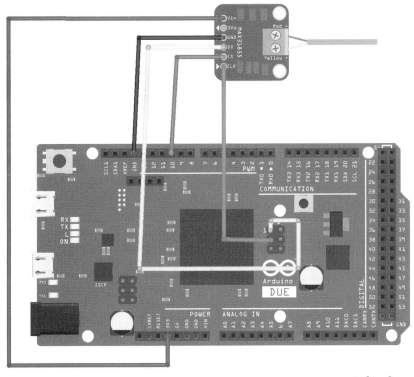

Figure 7-3: Hardware layout image created with Fritzing

The K-type thermocouple is connected to the breakout board, but be careful of the polarity. The Adafruit thermocouple cable and breakout board come with complete documentation on how to connect. Only the tip should be used to sense the temperature. If the cable is too long, do not put more than necessary inside the device you want to get a temperature reading from. Leave the rest of the cable outside.

There are several versions of the MAX31855 chip: one per cable type. The chip on Adafruit's breakout board can use only K-type thermocouples. Connect the wire to the breakout board, being careful to use the correct polarity (red and yellow wires).

Sketch

Now that the hardware is connected, it is time to deal with the software. This sketch communicates with the MAX31855 through the SPI bus. The datasheets explain how the data transmits. The MAX31855 sends 32-bits of data (unless stopped by the slave select pin), corresponding to several pieces of information. The transmission is shown in Table 7-3.

Table 7-3: MAX31855 Data Output

BIT	NAME	FUNCTION
D[31:18]	14-bit thermocouple tempera-ture data	Contains signed 14-bit thermocouple temperature
D17	Reserved	Always reads as 0
D16	Fault	Reads as 1 if a fault is detected, otherwise 0
D[15:4]	12-bit internal temperature data	Contains signed 12-bit cold junction temperature
D3	Reserved	Always reads as 0
D2	SCV Fault	Reads 1 if the thermocouple is shorted to VCC
D1	SCG Fault	Reads 1 if the thermocouple is shorted to ground
D0	OC Fault	Reads 1 if the thermocouple is not connected

The data is delivered in a 32-bit package, but there is something interesting about the layout. It can be seen as two 16-bit values: bits D31 to D16 and D15 to D0. The first 16-bits contains everything that is essential: the temperature detected on the thermocouple and a fault bit. If there is a fault, or if the user wants to know the cold-junction temperature, then the second 16-bit value can be read, but otherwise, it is not required.

Time to write the sketch as follows in Listing 7-1:

Listing 7-1: Digital Thermometer Sketch (filename: Chapter7.ino)

```
1    #include <SPI.h>
2
3    const int slaveSelectPin = 10;
```

```
4
5   void setup()
6   {
7     Serial.begin(9600);
8
9     // Initialize the bus for a device on pin 10
10    SPI.begin(slaveSelectPin);
11  }
12
13  void loop()
14  {
15    // Read in 4 bytes of data
16    byte data1 = SPI.transfer(slaveSelectPin, 0, SPI_CONTINUE);
17    byte data2 = SPI.transfer(slaveSelectPin, 0, SPI_CONTINUE);
18    byte data3 = SPI.transfer(slaveSelectPin, 0, SPI_CONTINUE);
19    byte data4 = SPI.transfer(slaveSelectPin, 0, SPI_LAST); // Stop
20
21    // Create two 16-bit variables
22    word temp1 = word(data1, data2);
23    word temp2 = word(data3, data4);
24
25    // Is the reading negative?
26    bool neg = false;
27    if (temp1 & 0x8000)
28    {
29      neg = true;
30    }
31
32    // Is the MAX31855 reporting an error?
33    if (temp1 & 0x1)
34    {
35      Serial.println("Thermocouple error!");
36      if (temp2 & 0x1)
37        Serial.println("Open circuit");
38      if (temp2 & 0x2)
39        Serial.println("VCC Short");
40      if (temp2 & 0x4)
41        Serial.println("GND short");
42    }
43
44    // Keep only the bits that interest us
45    temp1 &= 0x7FFC;
46
47    // Shift the data
48    temp1 >>= 2;
49
50    // Create a celcius variable, the value of the thermocouple temp
51    double celsius = temp1;
52
53    // The thermocouple returns values in 0.25 degrees celsius
```

continues

Listing 7-1: *(continued)*

```
54    celsius *= 0.25;
55    if (neg == true)
56      celsius *= -1;
57
58    // Now print out the data
59    Serial.print("Temperature: ");
60    Serial.print(celsius);
61    Serial.println();
62
63    // Sleep for two seconds
64    delay(2000);
65  }
```

On the first line, the SPI library is imported. Because this is an Arduino Due, version 1.5 or later of the Arduino software must be used. On line 3, a constant is declared, naming the pin that will be used by the Slave Select. The sketch needs this information. Because you will be using the extended library, the Arduino will activate the slave select pin; you won't have to.

On line 5, `setup()` is declared. The serial output is configured on line 7, and on line 10, the SPI subsystem is initialized for the one slave select pin declared as a constant earlier: `slaveSelectPin`.

On line 13, `loop()` is declared. This will contain all the SPI routines and print the temperature. On line 16, an SPI read function is called. By calling an SPI read with the `slaveSelectPin` variable, the Arduino Due automatically pulls the slave select pin low. For the MAX31855, this has the effect of initiating communication; the MAX31855 will wait for a valid clock to write 32 bits of data to the master. By using the `SPI_CONTINUE` variable, the slave select pin is maintained low. Because you want to read 32 bits of data, and because the `transfer()` function sends and receives 8 bits, this must be done four times. The first three are called with the `SPI_CONTINUE` parameter, but the fourth is called with the `SPI_LAST` parameter on line 19, indicating that this is the last transfer, and the Arduino should pull the slave select pin high. This is all done automatically.

The four calls have been made by sending the value zero. Because the MAX31855 is not connected to the MOSI pin, you can send any data you want; it will simply be ignored.

The data is now contained in four bytes. The first temperature reading is 14-bits, so it is now contained in 2 bytes, but how can that be used? The creators of the MAX31855 have put a lot of thought into the data output, and the data can be separated into two 16-bit values, or two "words." To create a word from 2 bytes, you can use `word()`. This function takes 2 variables in the form of 2 bytes, and concatenates them into a word, a 16-bit value. This is done on line 22 and 23.

On line 26, a boolean is declared. According to the datasheet, bit 31 corresponds to the sign of the temperature. This will be read now; the data will be transformed later. On line 27, a logical AND is made, comparing the value to `0x8000`; which is the *bitmask*, used to access a specific byte in the data (refer to the discussion of "Reading and Writing Bits" in Chapter 6 for more information on bitmasks). If the value is true, then the first bit is equal to one, meaning that the temperature reading is negative, and the `neg` variable is updated.

Bit number 16 corresponds to a fault condition; if it is true, then the MAX31855 is reporting an error and a bitwise comparison is made on the second 16-bit value where bits 0, 1, and 2 correspond to specific faults.

On line 45, a bitmask is created. The first 16 bits of data correspond to the temperature, but you will not need all that information. By creating a bitmask, you can filter out bits that do not interest you. In this case, the first bit, the sign, isn't required; it has already been placed in a variable. The last two are also of no interest and are discarded. The data is still not usable in its current state; the last 2 bits have been discarded and are equal to zero, but now the data has to be "shifted"; pushing the bits right until they are aligned as required.

On line 51, a new variable is created, a `double`. On the Due, this type of variable can contain floating point values with 64 bits of precision. Because the MAX31855 returns values in increments of 0.25 degrees, using a `double` or a `float` ensures that the decimal values are kept. First, the shifted 16-bit value is copied into this variable, and then it is multiplied by 0.25; it now contains the correct temperature in degrees Celsius.

Finally, the temperature might be negative. This is checked on line 55; if the `neg` variable is true, then the value returned was negative, and so the temperature is multiplied by –1.

On line 59, this temperature is written to the serial port, and the Arduino is told to wait for 2 seconds. The MAX31855 continues to monitor the temperature and continues to convert that temperature. When `SPI.transfer()` is next called through `loop()`, the MAX31855 communicates the temperature to the Arduino without the need for waiting.

Exercises

This sketch displays the temperature in degrees Celsius but not in Fahrenheit. Try to add a function to convert between Celsius and Fahrenheit. The conversion is a simple mathematical formula; multiply the temperature in Celsius by 1.8, and then add 32.

The MAX31855 is designed so that the first 16 bits correspond to the temperature with an additional fault bit. The last 16 bits are not normally required for normal operations; how would you modify the sketch to read the next 16 bits only if a fault is detected.

This sketch is designed to work with an Arduino Due, but you can modify it to be used on an Arduino Uno. Try to make this work on an Arduino Uno by using standard SPI commands.

Summary

In this chapter, you have seen how to communicate with sensors using the SPI bus, and you have created your first sensor board. In the next chapter, you will see another serial communications protocol commonly used on Arduino projects: the I^2C protocol.

Wire

This chapter discusses the following functions:

- `begin()`
- `beginTransmission()`
- `write()`
- `endTransmission()`
- `read()`
- `available()`
- `requestFrom()`
- `onReceive()`
- `onRequest()`

The hardware needed to use the examples in this chapter includes:

- Arduino Uno x 2
- Arduino Due
- Silicon Labs Sensor EXP board

You can find the code downloads for this chapter at `http://www.wiley.com/go/arduinosketches` on the Download Code tab. The code is in the Chapter 8 folder and individually named according to the code filenames noted throughout this chapter.

Introducing Wire

Connection wires I²C, short for Inter-IC bus, is a serial bus designed to enable access to numerous devices. The Arduino's hardware serial bus can connect only to one device at a time, and SPI (see Chapter 7) can talk to three devices. In 1982, Philips created the I²C standard, capable of addressing hundreds of devices, using only two wires. It was first used to connect peripherals together in a television set, but since then, I²C has been used in cars, computer systems, and hobbyist electronics, to name a few. It is an easy and inexpensive way to interconnect dozens (if not hundreds) of devices on a same network.

Originally, only a few I²C devices existed, but today there are hundreds of devices. Temperature sensors, pressure sensors, accelerometers, displays, and even EEPROM memory can all be accessed by I²C, using simple reads and writes. An EEPOM device controlled by I²C is illustrated in Figure 8-1.

Figure 8-1: I²C EEPROM integrated circuit

I²C is based on a master slave system; the master addresses slaves and requests information. The slave then replies and remains silent until again asked to communicate by the master. The original I⁵C specification allowed communications up to 100 kHz but numerous specifications existed. The newest in 2012 allows for 5 MHz clock speeds.

Another name for I²C is the Two Wire Interface (shortened to TWI). This is where the Wire library gets its name.

Connecting I²C

I²C requires two data wires, as well as a common ground. The two wires are called SDA (for Serial Data), and SCL (for Serial Clock). All devices in the I²C network are connected to these two wires. Both SDA and SCL lines are open drain, meaning that the devices can force their value low but cannot provide power, which will be provided directly from the main power line. For I²C to work, these two lines must be equipped with pull-up resistors, as shown in Figure 8-2. The values are not critical, and values range widely; 4.7 kilohm resistors are common. Arduinos have internal pull-up resistors that are automatically activated on both the SDA and SCL lines when the I²C connection is initialized. This is illustrated in Figure 8-2.

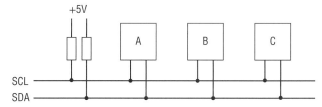

Figure 8-2: Pull-up resistors to SDA and SCL lines

Connecting multiple I²C devices is extremely easy; there is no notion of chip select, chip activate, or any other mechanism. All SDA pins are connected together, and all SCL pins are also connected together. The I²C protocol defines which circuit is to respond.

I²C Protocol

I²C is a master/slave network; the master initiates the communication, and the slave responds. Each I²C slave has a specific address, and the master must send this address to the network for a slave to answer. The I²C protocol has several specifications, so care must be taken when choosing devices, as there is a lot of confusion concerning addressing.

Address

The original I²C protocol specified 7-bit addressing and was later extended to allow 10-bit addressing. Some vendors talk about 8-bit addressing, but technically, this does not exist. Here's why.

I²C can send and receive data only in multiples of 8 bits—8 bits, 16 bits, and so on. In 7-bit addressing, addresses are (of course) 7 bits long, and the last bit is used to select a read or a write, for a total of 8 bits. In 10-bit addressing, things are a little more complicated. There is still the R/W bit, but the first 5 bits are sent as 11110, an address that is reserved in 7-bit addressing and is used only to tell the system that another byte will follow with the address complement. Figure 8-3 shows both 7-bit and 10-bit addressing.

Figure 8-3: 7-bit and 10-bit addressing methods

Some vendors give 8-bit addresses for devices, but again, technically, they do not exist. Vendors will give two values for 8-bit devices, both a read and a write address. The first 7 bits will be the same, but the last bit will be 1 for a read operation or 0 for a write operation. An example of this is shown in Figure 8-4.

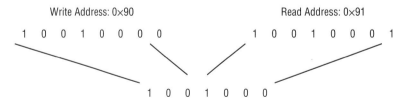

Figure 8-4: 8-bit addresses

When the master contacts a slave on the I²C network, it sends two vital pieces of information; the address of the slave, and whether it is a read or write operation. When this information is received by the slaves, each slave compares the address to its own. If a device has this address, it will send an acknowledge signal (referred to as ACK), indicating that it is present on the network and that the master can now issue instructions.

I²C devices tend to be small with few pins. (Most devices have the bare minimum.) Therefore, it is rarely possible to configure your own addresses for these devices. Most devices therefore have addresses that are specified by the manufacturer. On an ordinary computer network, it is easy to have dozens of the same type of computer with a user settable IP address unique to each machine. On an I²C network, this isn't possible; two identical sensors will use the same address. To allow developers to have several sensors in the same network, some devices allow you to change the address depending on input pins. By connecting one or several pins to either +5 V or 0 V, you can set part of the address (usually the lower bits). You might therefore have several temperature sensors, using addresses 0x90, 0x91, and 0x92, as shown in Figure 8-5.

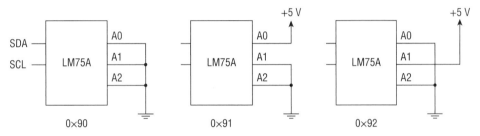

Figure 8-5: Configuring different addresses

Communication

I²C works on the master/slave scheme; a master either requests information from a slave or gives information to a slave. The master is responsible for initiating contact before releasing the bus so that a slave may communicate. Slaves cannot "talk" without permission; a slave cannot warn the system of an action; the master must poll for this information. This is the big difference between I²C and standard serial communication; it is not full duplex, meaning that devices cannot send data and receive data at the same time. Only one master is on an I²C network (except for some specific configurations).

To talk to devices, I²C uses a system of registers. A *register* is a small memory location on each device that can store data; it can be read or written to (sometimes both) depending on the type of data that is contained. For example, a temperature sensor has a register that contains the current temperature. When a master asks for information, it does not ask directly for the temperature; instead, it asks for the contents of a register. A temperature sensor will, of course, have a temperature register but might contain a configuration register (Celsius or Fahrenheit), a warning register (when this temperature is reached, an external interrupt occurs), and possibly others with different specialized functions. To read or write this data, you need to know several details:

- The slave address
- The register number
- If it is a read or write operation
- The length of the data to be received

It is important to know exactly how much data is to be sent and received. Each I²C device is different and will function in a different way. Devices that have only one writable register might accept a single byte of data directly and will place that byte into the register. Other devices with several writable registers might require you to send the register number, followed by the contents, or maybe send the contents of all the registers in multiple writes. I²C describes a way to send data and receive data, but for your own implementation, it is up to you what you need.

All Arduinos have a pair of I²C pins. The Arduino Due has two separate I²C buses, SDA and SCL, as well as SDA1 and SCL1. The pins reserved for I²C operations are listed in Table 8-1.

Table 8-1: I²C Pins on Different Arduino Boards

BOARD	SDA	SCL
Uno	A4	A5
Ethernet	A4	A5
Mega2560	20	21
Leonardo	2	3
Due	20	21

Communicating

To communicate on the I²C bus, the Wire library must first be initialized. As with all Arduino libraries, you must import the Wire library. This is done by either adding the library from the Arduino IDE (Sketch ➪ Import Library ➪ Wire) or by manually typing in the sketch.

```
#include <Wire.h>
```

To declare the Arduino as an I²C device, call `Wire.begin()`. If the Arduino is used as a slave, you must specify an address.

```
Wire.begin(address); // configures the Arduino as an I2C slave
```

Masters do not have an address because they are free to start communications whenever they want and automatically receive all responses. To declare the Arduino as a master, call the `Wire.begin()` command, without an address parameter.

```
Wire.begin(); // configure the Arduino as an I2C master
```

Master Communications

On most projects, the Arduino is configured as an I^{2}C master, sending messages to slaves and listening to the responses. To create an I^{2}C message, you must follow several steps:

1. Begin the transmission.
2. Write the data.
3. End the transmission.

This creates a custom I^{2}C message to a specific slave. When a slave answers, there is no encapsulation, and a write can be performed without beginning or ending a transmission. Data requests are also encapsulated but are made by a single function.

Sending Information

The I^{2}C protocol specifies that master communication must be done in a single transmission. To avoid breaks in the message, the message is first constructed and completed before being sent.

To start sending data, the sketch must first begin a transmission structure by using `Wire.beginTransmission()`. It takes one parameter, the destination address.

```
Wire.beginTransmission(address);
```

The sketch is then required to queue data, using `Wire.write()`. This function can be called in three different ways. It can be called with a byte as the parameter to be appended to the queue. A string can be specified, in which case each byte of the string will be appended. An array can be specified with a second parameter, the length of data to send. `Wire.write()` will return the amount of bytes appended to the message, but it's not necessary to read this.

```
Wire.write(value); // append a byte
Wire.write(string); // append a string
Wire.write(data, length); // append an array with a specified number
    of bytes
number =Wire.write(string); // store the number of bytes appended in
    a variable
```

`Wire.endTransmission()` specifies the end of the message, and sends it. This function takes an optional parameter, the bus release parameter. If TRUE, a stop message is sent, and the I²C bus is freed. If FALSE, a restart message is sent; the I²C bus is not released, and the master can continue issuing orders. By default, the bus is always freed.

```
Wire.endTransmission(); // send the message
Wire.endTransmission(stop); // send the message and close the connection
```

`Wire.endTransmission()` returns a status byte. Table 8-2 shows a list of return values.

Table 8-2: Transmit Error Codes

RETURN CODE	RESULT
0	Success
1	Data too long to fit in the transmit buffer
2	Receives a NACK on transmit of address
3	Receives a NACK on transmit of data
4	Unknown error

Requesting Information

When requesting information, the master performs a read operation, specifying the destination and the number of bytes the slave should send. The entire message is created using a single function: `Wire.requestFrom()`. This function takes two parameters and an optional third. First, the destination has to be specified—which slave is to receive this message and send data? Second, how much data is the master requesting? This is specified as the number of bytes. Finally, an optional parameter specifies if the bus should be released.

```
Wire.requestFrom(address, quantity);
Wire.requestFrom(address, quantity, stop);
```

`Wire.requestFrom()` creates a message and immediately sends it on the I²C bus. Now that the request has been sent, the master can wait for a message using `Wire.read()`.

```
data = Wire.read(); // store the information in a variable
```

`Wire.read()` returns a single byte from the input buffer. For multibyte messages, this function must be called for each byte. Requesting a certain amount of bytes does not mean that the slave will send that amount of data; it could be less. To see if any data is available in the buffer, call `Wire.available()`.

```
number = Wire.available();
```

`Wire.available()` looks at the buffer and returns the amount of bytes remaining. It can be used with `Wire.read()` to create a routine that does not block if data is not available.

```
while(Wire.available()) // Repeat as long as there is data waiting
{
  char c = Wire.read(); // Read in one byte
  Serial.print(c); // Print the byte
}
```

Slave Communications

Most people expect the Arduino to be an I²C master, controlling the network. In some cases, it can be useful to have an Arduino as an I²C slave, especially when several Arduinos are to be used. Arduinos also have a major advantage over other I²C devices; you can specify any address you see fit. You can have a total of 128 Arduino slaves on an I²C network, which should be more than enough to fully automate your house.

You do not know when an I²C master will send or request information, and a sketch cannot be told to hold indefinitely while waiting for information. To allow a sketch to continue while waiting for an I²C request, the Wire library allows you to create *callbacks*, functions that are called when an event occurs. The I²C callbacks are `Wire.onReceive()` (when the Arduino receives information) and `Wire.onRequest()` (when the Arduino is requested for information).

Receiving Information

`Wire.onReceive()` is called when a master sends information to a slave. To create this callback, you must create a function. The name can be anything you choose, but it must accept one parameter, an `int` (the number of bytes received from the master).

```
void receiveData(int byteCount)
{
  // Put your code here
}

Wire.onReceive(receiveData); // Create the callback
```

When the Arduino slave receives an I²C communication, the Wire library calls this function with the number of bytes received. To receive individual bytes, call `Wire.read()`.

```
data = Wire.read();
```

Just as when communicating as a master device, `Wire.read()` reads 1 byte from the I²C buffer and returns that data. Similarly, to know the amount of remaining bytes in the I²C buffer, call `Wire.available()`.

```
number = Wire.available();
```

It is, of course, possible to mix the two functions together.

```
while(Wire.available())
{
  data = Wire.read();
  // Do something with data
}
```

Sending Information

When a slave Arduino is asked for information, the Wire library calls the function previously registered by `Wire.onRequest()`. Again, the name of the function can be anything you want, but this one takes no parameters and returns nothing.

```
void sendData(void)
{
  // Put your code here
}
Wire.onRequest(sendData); // Create the callback
```

You must then provide the data required by the master, using `Wire.write()`, explained previously.

Example Program

For this example program, you use two Arduinos: one acts as an I²C master, and the second acts as an I²C slave. Both connect together using the I²C bus. Because Arduinos have internal pull-up resistors, the resulting schematic is extremely simple. The SDA pins of both devices are connected together, and the SCL pins are also connected together. There is one last, important stage: Both grounds are also connected—yes, three wires between the two devices. I said that I²C is a two-wire solution, and it is. It was designed to be used inside a single device, where the power supply and ground is normally identical. It can also be used for inter-device communication, like in this project, but in that case, the grounds must be connected.

The slave Arduino will turn on and off the on-board LED according to messages from the master. The master can send "0" to turn the LED off and "1" to turn the LED on. It can also request a byte of data from the slave; this data will be the current state of the LED. The master will also turn its LED on and off, so you should see a perfectly synchronized pair of LEDs.

Time to start, so start with the slave. The code is simple as shown in Listing 8-1.

Listing 8-1: The Slave (filename: Chapter8bSlave.ino).

```
1    #include <Wire.h>
2
3    #define SLAVE_ADDRESS 0x08
4    int data = 0;
5    int state = 0;
6
7    void setup()
8    {
9      pinMode(13, OUTPUT); // Internal LED
10     Serial.begin(9600);
11     Wire.begin(SLAVE_ADDRESS); // Initialize as I2C slave
12
13     // Register I2C callbacks
14     Wire.onReceive(receiveData);
15     Wire.onRequest(sendData);
16   }
17
18   void loop()
19   {
20     // Nothing to do
21     delay(100);
22   }
23
24   // Callback for data reception
25   void receiveData(int byteCount)
26   {
27     while(Wire.available())
28     {
29       data = Wire.read();
30       Serial.print("Data received: ");
31       Serial.println(data);
32
33       if (data == 1)
34       {
35         digitalWrite(13, HIGH); // Turn the LED on
36         state = 1;
37       }
38       else
```

continues

Listing 8-1: *(continued)*

```
39      {
40        digitalWrite(13, LOW); // Turn the LED off
41        state = 0;
42      }
43    }
44  }
45
46  // Callback for sending data
47  void sendData()
48  {
49      Wire.write(state); // Send the LED state
50  }
```

On line one, the Wire library is imported. On line 3, a value is declared, SLAVE_ ADDRESS. This is the slave I²C address, and it will be needed later by the master.

On line 7, setup() is defined. This function contains everything the sketch needs to function correctly. Pin 13 is set as a digital output because this is the pin that has an on-board LED. Serial communication is started, in case you want to debug anything. On line 11, the I²C subsystem is initialized, and because an address is specified (SLAVE_ADDRESS), this board will be an I²C slave. To be an effective I²C slave, the sketch requires at least one of two callbacks to be present; either when receiving or sending data. In this case, both are used.

On line 14, a callback is created to be called when data is received. This callback registers the function receiveData(), declared on line 25. The second callback is used when the slave is asked to provide data. It registers the function send- Data(), which is declared on line 25.

Nothing happens in loop(). This sketch responds only to I²C messages, and when the buffer is empty, it is not expected to do any work, so loop() is empty.

On line 25, receiveData() is declared. Thanks to the callback, this function is called every time data is received on the I²C bus destined for this Arduino. It requires one parameter, the number of bytes received as the parameter byte- Count. Due to the nature of this project, only 1 byte will be received at a time, so each byte received is immediately handled. On other projects, this can be used to detect the type of transmission.

On line 27, the sketch runs a while loop and continues to iterate so long as data is available in the buffer. The byte is read into the data variable by Wire .read() on line 29. Finally, the LED is turned on if the byte received was equal to 1 and turned off otherwise.

There is a second function, called sendData(), defined on line 47. This function is simple; when a data request is received, it sends out 1 byte, the state of the LED. Because this is an answer, there is no need to create a message; the sketch is free to send a byte directly to the master, as ordered.

Now that the slave is programmed, it is time to create the master sketch. The code is shown in Listing 8-2.

Listing 8-2: Master Sketch (filename: Chapter8bMaster.ino).

```
1    #include <Wire.h>
2
3    #define SLAVE_ADDRESS 0x08
4    int data = 0;
5    int state = 0;
6
7    void setup()
8    {
9      pinMode(13, OUTPUT); // Internal LED
10     Serial.begin(9600);
11     Wire.begin(); // Initialize as I2C master
12   }
13
14   void loop()
15   {
16     Wire.beginTransmission(SLAVE_ADDRESS); // Prepare message to slave
17     Wire.write(1); // Send one byte, LED ON
18     Wire.endTransmission(); // End message, transmit
19     digitalWrite(13, HIGH); // Turn the LED on
20
21     delay(10); // Give the slave time to react
22     printLight(); // What is the slave's status?
23
24     delay(1000);
25
26     Wire.beginTransmission(SLAVE_ADDRESS); // Prepare message to slave
27     Wire.write(0); // Send one byte, LED OFF
28     Wire.endTransmission(); // End message, transmit
29     digitalWrite(13, LOW); // Turn the LED off
30
31     delay(10); // Give the slave time to react
32     printLight(); // What is the slave's status?
33
34     delay(200);
35   }
36
37   void printLight()
38   {
39     Wire.requestFrom(SLAVE_ADDRESS, 1); // Request 1 byte from slave
40
41     data = Wire.read(); // Receive a byte af data
42     switch (data)
43     {
44       case 0:
45         Serial.println("LED is OFF");
46         break;
47       case 1:
```

continues

Listing 8-2: (*continued*)

```
48        Serial.println("LED is ON");
49        break;
50      default:
51        Serial.println("Unknown status detected");
52        break;
53    }
54  }
```

This sketch starts the same as the slave sketch; the Wire library is imported, and the address of the slave is defined. `setup()` is almost identical, except on line 11, `begin()` does not take an address parameter because this is the master.

Unlike the slave sketch, the master sketch uses `loop()`. It is designed to tell the slave to turn on its LED, wait for a few milliseconds, and then tell the slave to turn off its LED. After each transmission, it requests a byte of information to know the current state of the LED.

On line 16, the sketch begins creating a message. `Wire.beginTransmission()` requires one parameter, the destination address, which in this case is the slave Arduino. A message is created in a buffer but not sent. The Arduino automatically formats the message as required. On line 17, a byte is added to the message—a simple value: 1. According to the project specifications, sending a 1 to the slave turns on the LED. The instruction is added, but the message is not complete. Another step is required: `Wire.endTransmission()`. On line 18, that is exactly what is done. By using default settings, the message is sent and the I²C bus is freed.

To illustrate what is going on, the master also turns its LED on and off. This is what is done on line 19. On line 22, `printLight()` is called. This function is declared on line 37. It requests a byte from the slave, and prints the result in readable format.

To request data from a slave, `Wire.requestFrom()` is called. This is done on line 39. The first parameter is the address; in this case, the slave. The second parameter is the number of bytes to return—in this case: a single byte. When the order is sent, the sketch waits for a `read()` operation to complete, on line 41. That data is then fed into a `switch` statement, and the data is printed to the serial line.

When the sketch finishes turning the slave's LED on, the entire process is repeated with an order to turn the LED off.

Exercises

This sketch can control one LED by sending 1 byte, telling the slave to either turn the LED on or off. By sending 2 bytes, you could tell the slave to turn on one of several LEDs. Try to modify this sketch to turn on several LEDs. Remember that the I²C protocol can send bytes and request bytes. It is up to you to decide how to inform the slave of your intentions. What solution did you come up with?

Traps and Pitfalls

The I²C protocol is rather complex, and as such, problems can arise. They are normally easily fixed, and most electronic components use the standard I²C revision, simplifying usage.

Voltage Difference

Most Arduinos are powered by 5 volts, but some I²C circuits can be powered by 3.3 V, sometimes even lower. If you need to use 3.3-V devices (like the example in this chapter), then you have three choices. You could use a 3.3-V device like the Arduino Due. This was the solution chosen for this chapter. You could also use a level shifter, an electronic component that can convert a 3.3-V signal to a 5-V signal. The third option is to use a 5-V device anyway, but there are risks.

The I²C is an open drain bus, meaning that power is not supplied by the components, but rather by the power lines themselves using pull-up resistors. The Arduino's I²C pins have internal pull-up resistors that are automatically activated, pulling the line to 5 V. If you include external pull-up resistors to a 3.3-V power rail (like the one supplied by an Arduino), then the end result will be a voltage level slightly above 3.3 V. Most devices can handle up to 3.6 V without a problem.

The input voltage is also a problem. The Atmel AVR specifications say that an I²C input is considered high when it reaches and surpasses 0.7 times the power voltage. For a 5-volt system, this means the signal must reach 3.5 volts. With two external pull-up resistors to a 3.3-V rail, this is achieved, but there is little margin for error. It could work, and in practically all cases, it does, but be aware of the technical implications. I have never heard of either an I²C device or an Arduino being damaged by this technique, but if you are making a long-term project or a professional board, you might want to consider using other techniques.

Bus Speed

Numerous bus frequencies exist for I²C; the original bus speed was 100 kHz, but additions allowed 400 kHz, 1 MHz, 3.4 MHz, and 5 MHz speeds. Components using the Ultra Fast Mode transfer speed (5 MHz) are rare and heavily specialized.

Most standard components use the 100 kHz bus speed. Be aware that you cannot mix bus speeds; all components use the same bus speed as defined by the
master. Arduinos are programmed to use a 100 kHz clock speed. It is possible
to change this speed, but it involves editing the source code of the Arduino
programming environment, which is out of the scope of this book. For standard Arduino applications, the bus is limited to 100 kHz, which is sufficient
for most sensors.

Shields with I²C

Some shields require the presence of I²C, but this is a problem for some boards. If
you use an Arduino Uno, the I²C pins are A4 and A5. However, on the Arduino
Mega 2560, I²C is on pins 20 and 21, so shields requiring I²C that work on the
Uno will not work on the Mega 2560. Be careful if using a shield with I²C.

Summary

In this chapter, you have seen how to connect I²C devices, and how to communicate with them. You have also seen how the Arduino can become an I²C
master, and how to configure it to become an I²C slave.

In the next chapter, you will consider the Ethernet protocol and how it is used
to network computers together. I will show you how to connect your Arduino
to a local network, how to configure the board, and how to communicate both
as a client and as a server.

Ethernet

This chapter discusses the `begin()` function. The hardware required to run the examples in this chapter includes:

- Arduino Uno
- Arduino Ethernet Shield
- Light Dependent Resistor

You can find the code download for this chapter at `http://www.wiley.com/ go/arduinosketches` on the Download Code tab. The code is in the Chapter 9 folder and the filenames are:

- `Chapter9client.ino`
- `Chapter9server.ino`

Introduction

The first personal computers were not connected to each other; they were stand-alone devices, designed to calculate input from a user and to output the result of calculations to the same user. When files needed to be transferred from one machine to another, floppy disks were used.

The advances made in computer science also meant that files became bigger; because computers had more memory and could do faster calculations, the results could also be bigger. Soon, disks became too small to exchange information. Precious time was lost when data was to be retrieved; a desktop computer simply could not store all the information it required, and when modifications were made to a file on one computer, other computers would not be aware of changes. It became obvious that this had to change and that computers had to talk between themselves.

Serial communication had been used before computers existed and was an early means of connecting two computers. However, its speed made this type of link impractical. In addition, it could connect only two computers to each other. Engineers designed some interesting ways to connect three or four computers together using serial links, but the technology simply could not link computers the way they are today.

Again, it was a military need that boosted the industry. In the late 1950s, one of the first uses of networked computers was with military radar. Soon afterward, the aviation sector took over, and two airline-booking mainframes were connected. The question remained, how many computers would need to be connected? Dozens? Hundreds? Thousands, maybe? At the time, nobody could have imagined the impact of what they were working on and could certainly not have dreamed of the Internet. In 1969, three universities and a research center were linked together using 50-kilobit network lines. Research notes could be shared, and messages could be sent from researcher to researcher.

More and more companies and institutions saw the need to connect their offices and centers, and thousands upon thousands of machines were being networked into small, independent networks. With the need for more and more computers on the same network, the original networking designs could not keep up with the rise in traffic. Networking architectures became a system administrator's nightmare; in some cases, adding a computer onto a network forced all the other devices to disconnect before attempting to reconnect. Something needed to be done, both in making networks larger and allowing them to connect over greater distances. In 1973, the Ethernet standard was proposed in Xerox PARC. It was commercially introduced in 1980 and standardized in 1983. The original version proposed a high-speed throughput—10 megabits, or ten million bits of data per second. This speed was later increased to 100 megabits and then 1 gigabit—the highest speed available in home networks. Ethernet supports speeds up to 100 gigabits per second.

Ethernet

Ethernet describes the physical connection between two or more computers; the electronic signaling between devices, and the physical format of the cables.

Several other network technologies have been used in computing, such as token ring and ARCNET, but Ethernet remains the dominant system in place today.

Ethernet Cables

Ethernet describes both twisted cable and fiber optic cables, but for most home and office use, you will find only a twisted pair cable, a cable where the two elements are twisted around each other to cancel out electromagnetic interference. The cable comes in several categories, but the physical connectors are the same as shown in Figure 9-1.

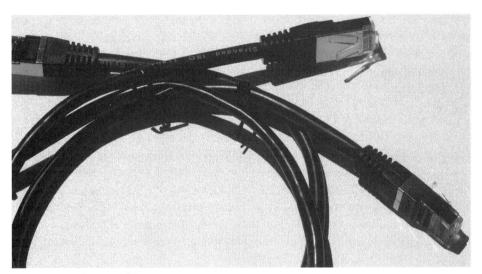

Figure 9-1: Ethernet cables

The advantage to Ethernet cables is their flexibility. Both ends have the same connector, and either end can connect to any device. Cables come in many different lengths—from the shortest (used to connect switches together) to the longest (used sometimes to connect two buildings together to form a network).

Category 6 cables are used on gigabit networks or networks that can send one thousand million bits of data per second. They have strong electromagnetic shielding, making them heavier and harder to bend than the previous Category 5 and 5e cables, and they are more expensive. Category 5e can be used on gigabit networks, but they have a lower signaling speed and are more susceptible to electromagnetic interference. Arduino Ethernet interfaces normally operate at 10- or 100-megabit speeds, so Category 5e cables are sufficient.

Switches and Hubs

A standard Ethernet cable can be used to connect two computers together, but to connect more than two computers, you must use a special device.

Hubs are relatively old technology and are used to connect multiple computers and devices together. An eight-port hub could connect eight computers, or even be used to connect to more hubs, allowing large networks of devices. Hubs were cheap but had a downside; they took *packets*, small pieces of information that are assembled together to form a larger message, and forwarded them to every device in the network, even to those that were not supposed to receive this information. All computers on a network therefore filtered all incoming traffic, and multiple communications could not happen at the same time. To avoid this, switches were developed.

A *switch* is a network device that receives packets of data and can inspect that packet to know where it is supposed to go. When it has that information, it sends that packet to the correct port—and only to that port. All other devices on the switch are free to communicate during this time. Today, it is becoming hard to find hubs, but switches are readily available. On the back of your modem, you probably have some RJ45 connectors for Ethernet cables; the chances are, that is a switch.

PoE

Power over Ethernet, or PoE, is a way of powering remote devices directly by the Ethernet cable.

Power is transmitted over a twisted pair, and as such, cables using PoE are not normally gigabit-capable. There are exceptions, but they are currently expensive.

Arduinos are not normally PoE devices and cannot be used with a PoE-powered cable, unless an optional module is supplied. The Arduino Ethernet has an option to allow PoE, allowing the Arduino to be powered directly from the cable. This means that your Arduino does not need to be powered by a battery, USB, or through the barrel jack connector, but it does require the Arduino to be powered by a PoE-capable switch or injector. Imagine a network cable running through your garden, powering an Arduino sensor in a place where you do not have mains power.

TCP/IP

Ethernet is a physical means of connecting computers together in small or large networks, but to allow programs to talk to each other, an application layer is required. The most commonly used is TCP/IP.

The TCP/IP protocol is relatively complex, but for most day-to-day usage, it is easy to understand. Each device has an address, and data is sent to that address.

MAC Address

The MAC address is the hardware address of the network connector. Each device has its own specific address, and in theory, no two devices should have the same MAC address.

IP Address

This address is defined by the user or by the network administrator. It is the address used to identify a network device, both for sending information and for receiving. It is possible to have devices that use the same address, and indeed, this happens every day. Your modem probably has a local address like 192.168.0.1, and your neighbor might have this address, too.

IP addresses are made out of 4 bytes. Normally, the first 3 bytes are the network, and the fourth is the machine on that network. The network 192.168.0.XXX is an "internal" network, one that is shielded from the Internet. You can add any devices.

DNS

Humans are good at remembering text but not so good at remembering numbers. When you want to connect to Wiley's Internet site to get more information about new books, you can enter http://www.wiley.com into your browser. This address, however, does not name a machine; machines can be contacted only by their IP address. You can almost certainly remember the text www.wiley .com, but could you remember 208.215.179.146? Probably not. To counter this, DNS was invented. DNS, short for Domain Name Service, is a large database that translates human readable domain names (like www.wiley.com) into the more difficult IP address system. All the code presented in this book is available on Wiley's website, and to download the code, you need to enter Wiley's web address into your browser. Your browser might not know Wiley's IP address, and if it doesn't, it will send a request to a DNS server. The DNS request will say, "Hey, could you please tell me the address of www.wiley.com?" The DNS server will respond with either the IP address of the request, or an error message if it does not exist. Your browser can then contact Wiley's server.

Port

To connect to a server (a machine that will provide a service), a client (something that requires this service) requires two things: the address of the server (or a domain name that will later be converted to an IP address) and a port. It is not something physical; it is represented only in software.

Imagine you want to create a web server. You install the required software, and your computer is connected to the Internet. You are now ready to go. Computers can now connect to your server and view your web pages. Now imagine you want to create an FTP server on the same computer as the web server. How can you do that? How can the server understand what the client wants? This is where ports come in.

A server program creates a port, and a client connects to that port. Some ports are standard; others are created randomly. A web server will always be opened on port 80, and your Internet browser will automatically attempt to connect to port 80 when you add an Internet address beginning with http. When using secure HTTP, the browser connects to port 443. It is also possible to tell the browser to which port you want to connect by specifying the port; just add a colon and the port number at the end.

Port numbers range from 1 to 65535. Port numbers 1024 and below are reserved, and most computers require administrative rights to open a low port. High ports, from 1025 upward, can be opened with non-administrator programs. When playing a multiplayer game, the server almost certainly uses a high port, and clients know which port to connect to. (For example, Minecraft uses port 25565 by default.)

Ethernet on Arduino

Most Arduinos do not come with Ethernet support. The Arduino Ethernet is an exception; it remains close to the Arduino Uno design and has an Ethernet port with optional PoE support. The Arduino Yún also has an Ethernet connector, but the Arduino Yún is two machines in one. An Arduino "talks" to an Atheros processor, running a Linux distribution that handles network connectivity. The Arduino Tre has a similar interface; an Arduino "talks" to a Cortex-A8 microprocessor that has an Ethernet connector. This chapter covers only Arduino boards with an Ethernet chip addressed directly by an Arduino-compatible microcontroller: the Arduino Ethernet and any Arduino with an Ethernet shield.

Importing the Ethernet Library

To import the Ethernet library, you can use the Arduino IDE. Go to Sketch ➪ Import Library ➪ Ethernet. Doing so imports a relatively large amount of libraries:

```
#include <EthernetClient.h>
#include <EthernetServer.h>
#include <Dhcp.h>
```

```
#include <Ethernet.h>
#include <Dns.h>
#include <EthernetUdp.h>
#include <util.h>
```

Depending on your application, you may not need all these libraries. Some projects might not use an Ethernet server or might not require DNS, but it is best to start off with all the libraries and remove them later if required.

Starting Ethernet

Like many libraries, the Ethernet library is initialized with `begin()`. This function can be called in different ways, depending on your needs:

```
Ethernet.begin(mac);
Ethernet.begin(mac, ip);
Ethernet.begin(mac, ip, dns);
Ethernet.begin(mac, ip, dns, gateway);
Ethernet.begin(mac, ip, dns, gateway, subnet);
```

In all cases, `begin()` requires a MAC address. The MAC address is either supplied on a sticker attached to the Arduino or Ethernet shield, or you have to invent your own.

WARNING   Do not use the same MAC address for multiple devices. These numbers are designed to be unique, and two identical MAC addresses on the same network will result in both devices having connectivity problems. Switches have an internal MAC table, and when it receives a packet, it updates the table. Packets will then be forwarded to this host until the switch receives a packet from the other device. On most switches, this will cause intermittent reachability, and on some advanced switches, one device will be deactivated and cannot connect.

The MAC address is typically represented as an array of six hexadecimal bytes:

```
// The MAC address for this shield:
byte mac[] = { 0xDE, 0xAD, 0xBE, 0xEF, 0xFE, 0xED };
```

For projects where multiple devices will be used or sold, consider placing the MAC address in EEPROM. (EEPROM is presented in Chapter 6.)

If `begin()` is not supplied an IP address, it issues a DHCP request to configure itself automatically. `begin()` returns an `int`; 1 if the DHCP server was contacted and DHCP information was received. Otherwise, it returns 0. All other uses of `begin()` require an IP address, and do not return anything. To use this functionality, you must import "Dhcp.h" and make sure your router can assign IP addresses through DHCP.

The IP address is supplied in the form of an array of bytes:

```
// The IP address for this shield:
byte ip[] = { 192, 168, 0, 10 };
```

This IP address will be used on the local network. The DNS and gateway parameters are optional; if omitted, they default to the same IP address with the last octet set to one. The subnet parameter is also optional; if omitted, it defaults to 255.255.255.0.

When the IP address has been obtained by DHCP, you can retrieve the IP address from the Ethernet controller via localIP().

```
Ethernet.localIP(); // Retrieve the IP address
```

If no parameters are specified, the IP address is returned as a string.

```
Serial.println(Ethernet.localIP());
```

It is, however, possible to obtain the IP address in byte format, by specifying a byte to read.

```
Serial.print("My IP address: ");
for (byte thisByte = 0; thisByte < 4; thisByte++) {
  // print the value of each byte of the IP address:
  Serial.print(Ethernet.localIP()[thisByte], DEC);
  Serial.print(".");
}
Serial.println();
```

DHCP leases are only available for a certain time; to maintain a DHCP lease, you must specifically request a renewal. On most servers, this will re-issue the same IP address, but on some systems this might result in a change of IP address. To renew a DHCP lease, call Ethernet.maintain().

```
result = Ethernet.maintain();
```

maintain() returns a byte, depending on the DHCP answer. Table 9-1 lists the values returned by this function.

Table 9-1: maintain() return codes

RESULT	DESCRIPTION
0	Nothing happened
1	Renew failed
2	Renew success
3	Rebind fail
4	Rebind success

In the previous connection example, the IP address was defined as an array of bytes:

```
byte ip[] = { 192, 168, 0, 10 };
```

It is possible to use the `IPAddress` class to simplify writing a list of IP Addresses. The IP Address class takes four parameters; the four parts of an IP address.

```
// The DNS server IP
IPAddress dns(192, 168, 0, 1);
// The Router's address (the gateway)
IPAddress gateway(192, 168, 0, 1);
// The IP subnet
IPAddress subnet(255, 255, 255, 0);
// The Arduino's IP address
IPAddress ip(192, 168, 0, 10);

Ethernet.begin(mac, ip, dns, gateway, subnet);
```

Arduino as a Client

The Arduino is an excellent Ethernet client; it can reliably initiate connections to servers, send data from sensors, and receive data from the server. When using the Arduino as a client, you must use the `EthernetClient` object.

```
EthernetClient client;
```

A client connects to a server. The term "server" designates any network connected device that a client connects to fetch or upload information. On a home network, this can be just about anything. Most home modems have an internal web server that allows you to configure it and to look at statistics. Your computer might have a server application installed (either a web server or an FTP server), and even if your PC is a client to the modem, it can still be a server for other devices.

A server is therefore just about anything—a computer, a network device, even another Arduino. A client is also just about anything, even a piece of hardware that requires the service provided by a server. The client must connect to the server, and in Arduino you make a connection with `connect()`. To connect to a server, you need one of these two things: either the IP address of the server or the domain name and the port.

```
result = client.connect(ip, port);
result = client.connect(dns, port);
```

The `ip` parameter is either an array of 4 bytes or an IPAddress object. The port parameter is an `int` and is the port on the server to which you want to connect.

The `dns` parameter is a string and is the domain name to connect to. It is automatically converted to an IP address via a DNS query.

`connect()` returns a boolean: `true` if the connection is made, otherwise it returns `false`.

It is possible to check the status of a connection calling `client.connected()`.

```
result = client.connected();
```

This function does not take any parameters and returns `true` if the client is still connected and `false` if it is no longer connected. Note that if data is still waiting to be read, then this function returns `true`, even if the connection has been severed.

To disconnect from a server, use `stop()`.

```
client.stop();
```

This function takes no parameters and does not return any data. It simply severs the network connection.

Sending and Receiving Data

Sending and receiving data is done through a stream; data can either be written in binary format or in text format. To send text data, use `print()` and `println()`.

```
client.print(data);
client.print(data, BASE);
client.println();
client.println(data);
client.println(data, BASE);
```

The difference between `print()` and `println()` is that `println()` adds a new line character to the end of the string. The data parameter is the string or data to print, and the optional `BASE` argument is the numerical system to use. The `data` parameter is either a `String` or an array of `char`.

To write binary data, use `write()`.

```
client.write(val);
client.write(buf, len);
```

The `val` parameter is a byte to send over the TCP/IP link. The `buf` parameter is an array of bytes, and the `len` parameter specifies the number of bytes to send.

To read from the network socket, use `read()`.

```
data = client.read();
```

This function does not take any parameters and returns the next byte in the stream, or –1 if no data is available. To check if data is waiting to be read, use `available()`.

```
result = client.available();
```

This function does not take any parameters and returns the number of bytes waiting in the buffer.

This allows an Arduino to connect to a server and to exchange stream information, but how exactly is that useful for your application? Almost all protocols rely on an exchange of stream information, including HTTP, FTP, and other common protocols.

Connecting to a Web Server

Web servers also stream data. Each connection is made to port 80 of the web server and can be done in plaintext. After all, before graphical interfaces, all the web was viewed as simple text.

To help as an example, I have uploaded a file to my web server called helloarduino.html. It is located at the following address:

```
http://packetfury.net/helloarduino.html
```

If you open this in a web browser, you will be greeted by a simple sentence: Hello, Arduino! To understand how an Arduino, and indeed any web browser works, try to connect to the web server using telnet, a protocol used to connect to a server using a text-oriented message. This utility is standard on Linux and Mac OS systems, and can be run by opening a terminal and entering `telnet <IP> <port>` as a command. `IP` is the IP address of the server you want to connect to, and `port` is the port of the service you want to connect to. For a web browser, this will be 80. For a Windows machine, a download is required. PuTTY is a very nice, free application that lets you connect to services. It is available at `http://www.putty.org`.

```
telnet packetfury.net 80
```

This program creates a connection to the specified host on the specified port. Here, you connect to packetfury.net on port 80. Normally, a web server listens to connections on port 80. You should be greeted with something that looks like this:

```
jlangbridge@desknux:~/Downloads$ telnet packetfury.net 80
Trying 195.144.11.40...
Connected to packetfury.net.
Escape character is '^]'.
```

After a short time, you will get another message:

```
HTTP/1.0 408 Request Time-out
Cache-Control: no-cache
Connection: close
Content-Type: text/html
```

```
<html><body><h1>408 Request Time-out</h1>
Your browser didn't send a complete request in time.
</body></html>
Connection closed by foreign host.
```

Web servers expect a request fairly quickly after creating a connection. It keeps the number of connections low, but also web browsers are supposed to be fast and connect only when the user has specified an address. You still have a few seconds to send a message, though.

To get a web page, you must inform the web server that you want to GET a document. Afterward, specify the document name. Then, specify the protocol; in this case use HTTP/1.1. Finally, specify the host. Remember, some web servers host multiple websites. For example, you want to GET the webpage called helloarduino.html from my website. You first tell the server that this is a GET request, then specify the web page itself, followed by the protocol. On a second line, you specify which web server you want the page from. The formatted http request looks like this:

```
GET helloarduino.html HTTP/1.1
Host: packetfury.net
```

To do this, open up a telnet application. Telnet requires two things: the server to connect to and a port. The server is packetfury.net, the name of the website. The port is 80. Enter the request text:

```
GET helloarduino.html HTTP/1.1
Host: packetfury.net
```

Remember, you have little time in which to do this. You might want to copy the text first and then paste it into your telnet client. Validate your request by pressing enter twice. The web server requires a blank line to run a request. If everything goes well, you should be greeted with the following:

```
HTTP/1.1 200 OK
Date: Mon, 28 Apr 2014 15:02:17 GMT
Server: Apache/2.2.24
Last-Modified: Mon, 28 Apr 2014 14:46:54 GMT
ETag: «6181d54-10-4f81b62f60b9b»
Accept-Ranges: bytes
Content-Length: 16
Vary: Accept-Encoding
Content-Type: text/html

Hello, Arduino!
```

Now that you know how to fetch a webpage, you can also write a sketch for your Arduino to fetch information directly from a web page. You can, of course, create your own web server on your local network. You don't even need any complicated software; although you can create a real web server, you can also get great results from Python scripts. Your Python script could then inform Arduinos of the temperature that you want for your living room or when to turn on the automatic sprinkler system.

Example Program

Now that you have fetched a web page from a web server, it is time to tell the Arduino to do the same thing. The sketch will look like Listing 9-1.

Listing 9-1: Fetching (filename: `Chapter9client.ino`)

```
1  #include <SPI.h>
2  #include <Ethernet.h>
3
4  // If your Arduino has a MAC address, use that instead
5  byte mac[] = { 0xDE, 0xAD, 0xBE, 0xEF, 0xFE, 0xED };
6  char server[] = "www.packetfury.net";    // name of server
7
8  // Set a static IP address to use if the DHCP fails to assign
9  IPAddress ip(192,168,0,42);
10
11 // Initialize the Ethernet client library
12 EthernetClient client;
13
14 void setup()
15 {
16   // Open serial communications and wait for port to open:
17   Serial.begin(9600);
18
19   // Start the Ethernet connection:
20   if (Ethernet.begin(mac) == 0)
21   {
22     Serial.println("Failed to configure Ethernet using DHCP");
23     // Can't get an IP, so use another one
24     Ethernet.begin(mac, ip);
25   }
26   // Give the Ethernet shield some time to initialize:
27   delay(2000);
28   Serial.println("Connecting...");
29
30   // Are we connected?
31   if (client.connect(server, 80))
32   {
33     Serial.println("Connected");
34     // Make a HTTP request:
35     client.println("GET helloarduino.html HTTP/1.1");
36     client.println("Host: www.packetfury.net");
37     client.println();
38   }
```

Continues

Listing 9-1 *(continued)*

```
39    else
40    {
41      // Warn if the connection wasn't made
42      Serial.println("Connection failed");
43    }
44  }
45
46  void loop()
47  {
48    // Check for incoming bytes
49    if (client.available())
50    {
51      char c = client.read();
52      Serial.print(c);
53    }
54
55    // If the server disconnected, then stop the client:
56    if (!client.connected())
57    {
58      Serial.println();
59      Serial.println("Disconnecting.");
60      client.stop();
61
62      // Now sleep until a reset
63      while(true);
64    }
65  }
```

This sketch requires two libraries, SPI and Ethernet, and they are imported on lines 1 and 2. On line 5, a MAC address is created. All Ethernet devices have a MAC address, and they should be unique. If your Arduino has a MAC address sticker, please use that value instead. On line 6, the server name is defined; this is the server that you will be connecting to. The Arduino will attempt to talk to a DHCP sever to get network information automatically. If this fails, the sketch will tell the Arduino to use a default IP address; this is specified on line 9. Please adjust as required.

The `EthernetClient` object is declared on line 12. Since this Arduino will connect to a server, it will be a client, and as such requires initializing the `EthernetClient` object; the resulting object is called `client`.

The `setup()` function is declared on line 14. Like the previous sketches, it starts by initializing a serial communications channel so that you can connect and see what is going on. This is also how the contents of the web page will be displayed. On line 20, the sketch calls Ethernet's `begin()` function. The result is used to tell if the Arduino has received a message from the DHCP server or not. If it has, a message is printed to the serial channel; if it hasn't, the Arduino will attempt to use the default address. This is done on line 24.

Once the network configuration has been made, the next step is to connect to the server. This is done on line 31 using the `connect()` function. Once again, the result is used to see if the Arduino has connected or not. If it has, then on line 35 the sketch sends three lines to the web server. First, a `GET` instruction. Second, the server name. Finally, an empty line to inform the web server that there is nothing else you want to send. It should reply. If the connection wasn't made, an error message is printed on the serial port.

The `loop()` function is declared on line 46. First it detects to see if any bytes are waiting in the buffer using the `available()` command. If there is data waiting, then each byte is read from the buffer and printed to the serial port. This is done on lines 51 and 52. On line 56, the sketch checks to see if it is still connected to the server; once the server responds with a web page, it is free to terminate the connection before serving another client. If the server has indeed terminated the connection, a message is printed to the serial port and the sketch sleeps until a reset is performed.

Arduino as a Server

You can use the Arduino as a network client, but it is also a capable network server. Instead of connecting to a server, it becomes a server, waiting for clients to connect before sending or receiving information.

To use your Arduino as an Ethernet server, you must initialize the `EthernetServer` object.

```
EthernetServer server = EthernetServer(port);
```

It takes one parameter: the port to listen for incoming connections. Web servers connect to port 80 and telnet on port 23. Remember, ports below 1024 are reserved for specific applications, and ports above are free to be used. If you create your own protocol, use one of the high ports.

To listen for a client, you must create an `EthernetClient` object.

```
EthernetClient client;
```

This function is nonblocking, that is to say, if a client is not available, the object will still be created and the rest of the sketch will continue to run. To verify if a client has actually connected, test the client object. If a client has connected, it will return `true`.

```
if (client == true)
{
  // Client has connected, send data
}
```

From here, it is possible to send and receive data using the `client()` object. The server is only responsible for opening a port and accepting connections on that port; data will be read from and written to the client object.

Servers spend most of their time waiting for connections and responding to connections before waiting for another connection. As such, they are usually in `loop()` waiting for a connection before acting. When an exchange has completed, close the connection using the `stop()` function.

```
client.stop();
```

To wait for connections, send data, and then close the connection, you can use code that looks like this:

```
void loop()
{
  EthernetClient client = server.available();
  if (client == true)
  {
    // Client has connected, send data
    client.println("Hello, client!");
    client.stop();
  }
}
```

Serving Web Pages

Web servers are the most visible ways of connecting to an Arduino over a network to get data and also great fun! They can be seen on computers, tablets, and mobile telephones and can easily be tweaked to produce some visually stunning interfaces.

When a web browser connects to a web server, it expects some specific information. It not only just receives a web page, but also some headers that you do not normally see. The server informs the web browser if the page is accessible (remember those 404-error messages you see from time to time?), the sort of data that is to be sent, and the connection status after the data has been delivered. Additional headers can be added if needed.

A typical exchange might look like this:

```
HTTP/1.1 200 OK
Content-Type: text/html
Connection: close
```

The `200` return code means that the page was found and is available. The content type of this page is HTML, sent as text data. Finally, the connection will be closed after the page has been sent. If the web browser wants another page, it must reconnect. To tell the browser that the content is about to be sent, the server sends a blank line, and then sends the HTML data.

Example Program

For this program, you use an Arduino Uno with an Ethernet shield. This is a continuation of the previous chapter and still uses the light sensor. You can now read light conditions in real time by connecting to your Arduino from a web browser.

When a connection is made, the Arduino first reads the analog value on A3 before displaying that value in HTML.

Sketch

Now it's time to write the sketch, as shown in Listing 9-2.

Listing 9-2: Server Sketch (filename: `Chapter9server.ino`)

```
1    #include <SPI.h>
2    #include <Ethernet.h>
3
4    // Enter a MAC address and IP address for your controller below.
5    // The IP address will be dependent on your local network:
6    byte mac[] = { 0xDE, 0xAD, 0xBE, 0xEF, 0xFE, 0xED };
7    IPAddress ip(192,168,0,177);
8
9    int lightPin = A3;
10
11 //Initialize the Ethernet server to listen for connections on port 80
12   EthernetServer server(80);
13
14   void setup() {
15     // Open serial communications
16     Serial.begin(9600);
17
18     // start the Ethernet connection and the server:
19     Ethernet.begin(mac, ip);
20     server.begin();
21     Serial.print("Server up on ");
22     Serial.println(Ethernet.localIP());
23   }
24
25   void loop() {
26     // Listen for incoming clients
27     EthernetClient client = server.available();
28
29     if (client)
30     {
```

Continues

Listing 9-2 *(continued)*

```
31      Serial.println("New connection");
32      // An HTTP request ends with a blank line, wait until the
         request has finished
33      boolean currentLineIsBlank = true;
34      while (client.connected())
35      {
36        if (client.available())
37        {
38          char c = client.read();
39          Serial.write(c);
40       // if you've gotten to the end of the line (received a newline
41       // character) and the line is blank, the HTTP request has ended,
42          // so you can send a reply
43          if (c == '\n' && currentLineIsBlank) {
44            // send a standard http response header
45            client.println("HTTP/1.1 200 OK");
46            client.println("Content-Type: text/html");
47            client.println("Connection: close");
48            client.println("Refresh: 5");
49            client.println();
50            client.println("<!DOCTYPE HTML>");
51            client.println("<html>");
52
53            // Get a light level reading
54            int light = analogRead(lightPin);
55
56            // Send this data as a web page
57            client.print("Current light level is ");
58            client.print(light);
59            client.println("<br />");
60
61            client.println("</html>");
62            break;
63          }
64          if (c == '\n') {
65            // you're starting a new line
66            currentLineIsBlank = true;
67          }
68          else if (c != '\r') {
69            // you've gotten a character on the current line
70            currentLineIsBlank = false;
71          }
72        }
73      }
74      // Wait a second for the client to receive data
75      delay(1);
76
77      // Close the connection
78      client.stop();
79
```

```
80    Serial.println("Client disonnected");
81    }
82  }
```

Summary

In this chapter, you have seen how Ethernet works as well as the difference between a server and a client. You have seen how to connect to a web server from an Arduino, as well as how to become a server for other devices to connect and retrieve data.

In Chapter 10 you will see how the Arduino can connect wirelessly using Wi-Fi technology. You will also see the differences between Ethernets, and how to create a wireless client and server.

This chapter discusses the following functions of the WiFi library:

- `begin()`
- `macAddress()`
- `BSSID()`
- `RSSI()`
- `scanNetworks()`
- `SSID()`
- `encryptionType()`
- `disconnect()`
- `config()`
- `setDNS()`
- `WiFiClient()`
- `WiFiServer()`

The hardware needed to use these functions includes:

- Arduino Uno
- SainSmart WiFi shield

- DHT11 humidity and temperature sensor
- Breadboard
- Wires
- 10 kilohm resistor

You can find the code download for this chapter at `http://www.wiley.com/go/arduinosketches` on the Download Code tab. The code is in the Chapter 10 folder and the filename is `chapter10.ino`.

> **NOTE** The Wireless technology name is Wi-Fi with a hyphen, but in the Arduino library, where it is unable to use hyphens, it is called WiFi. For this chapter, Wi-Fi refers to the technology, and WiFi to the Arduino library capable of using WiFi cards.

Introduction

All aspects of computers have evolved at an incredible rate. A high-end computer from 10 years ago is, by today's standard, easily surpassed by a mobile telephone. Processors, memory, and storage have all increased, and component size has drastically decreased. Mobile computers used to be rare; today, laptop computers are seen just about everywhere, as are tablets, smartphones, and even smart watches. The need for mobility has been driving the industry for years, but the need for data even more so.

Early networks were slow, complicated, cabled systems. Today, Ethernet technology can be found in almost every house. On the back of most Internet modems is a small Ethernet switch, providing four or more "ports"; connecting a computer is as simple as plugging an Ethernet cable in the ports. To add another computer, just plug in another cable in the next open port. This is perfect for households, and the same technology also powers huge companies with thousands of computers, including the Internet. Networks have become fast and reliable, but until recently, the need for physical wiring conflicted with mobility.

Mobile users had data on the go. Commercial teams could have documents on their computer with them, and engineers could have development tools and diagnostics with them. However, to get access to the Internet, or even to transfer documents, they had to plug in their laptop to the company's network. Most meeting rooms had an Ethernet switch with a few cables, just in case anyone needed quick access. Mobile devices would never be truly mobile until they got rid of the cables tethering them to the desk, and so Wi-Fi was born.

The WiFi Protocol

Wi-Fi standard devices use a wireless local area network (LAN). The technology is managed by the Wi-Fi Alliance, a group of some of the leading companies in wireless and networking products that did not actually create the technology itself.

In 1985, the U.S. Federal Communication Commission opened up part of the wireless spectrum for unlicensed use. The original wireless protocol was called WaveLAN, developed by NCR for cashier systems. The radio portion was hidden from operating systems, and to the drivers, WaveLAN cards were talking together via wired systems, making installation and use extremely easy.

Its successor, 802.11, was created in 1997. It had a data-rate of either 1 or 2 megabits per second and a communications distance of 60 feet. Interoperability problems were detected, notably because the Institute of Electrical and Electronics Engineers (IEEE for short) creates standards but does not test them for certification. The original 802.11 was not widely embraced, but a new version was: 802.11b. With the birth of 802.11b came the Wireless Ethernet Compatibility Alliance (WECA), which proposed rigorous certification programs. All devices sold with a Wi-Fi logo were compatible, and consumers loved the technology. WECA later changed its name to the Wi-Fi Alliance.

802.11b gave much faster data rates: 1, 2, 5.5, and 11 megabits per second. Although these speeds were good for browsing the web, they were not fast enough for video streaming or heavy data transfer. 802.11g proposed data rates of up to 55 Mbit/s, while retaining 802.11b compatibility. (When talking to an 802.11b device, the speed would be at a maximum of 11 Mbit/s). Newer versions provide even faster data rates; 802.11n can go as fast as 150 Mbit/s; 802.11ac can go up to 866.7 Mbit/s; and 802.11ad can transfer data at a staggering 6.75 Gbit/s.

Topology

Wi-Fi works with several network topologies, but there are two main types that are used: ad-hoc and infrastructure.

Ad-hoc mode is an unmanaged, decentralized mode. Wireless peers are free to connect to other peers, and the network is managed by all the peers. Wireless devices maintain network connectivity by forwarding packets to other devices when needed. All network peers have an equal status, and the network is only as reliable as the parameters of the hosts (transmit power, interference, and link-length). Ad-hoc networks are often closed networks; peers cannot always communicate outside the network.

Infrastructure mode is a managed mode. This topology requires one or several devices to "manage" the network, allowing peers to connect to it (or refuse connection depending on the security settings). Peers do not communicate between themselves; instead they send their packets to the network management devices: typically access points. Infrastructure access points often serve as access points to other networks: typically a wired network or a connection to the Internet. Multiple access points can be on a wired network, allowing for several zones, or "hot spots" where peers can connect wirelessly.

Network Parameters

For a network to function, several parameters are required. Imagine an apartment block—several neighbors are within close range. Each family has an Internet connection, and each family also wants access to wireless for their laptops, tablets, and mobile phones. Each family also wants their devices to be private. Instead of creating one large wireless network, each family wants its own small wireless network. It also wants it to work securely and efficiently, while allowing neighbors access to their wireless networks.

Channels

Wi-Fi works with two base frequencies: 2.4 GHz and 5 GHz. However, in practice, there are several frequencies; the 2.4-GHz band operates from 2.412 GHz all the way to 2.484 GHz. This spectrum is separated into different frequencies, or channels. If all wireless devices used exactly the same frequency, that frequency would soon become saturated as small networks started competing with other networks. Also, Wi-Fi is not the only wireless technology to use the 2.4 GHz band. For example, Bluetooth also uses these frequencies. To help, Wi-Fi uses channels.

A channel is a specific frequency used by one particular wireless network. Channels work in the same way as your television; information is received wirelessly and picked up through the TV antenna. By selecting a particular channel, you decide to listen to one particular frequency in the range, therefore excluding all other channels. When you finish watching a program, you can switch to another channel, receiving the information on one channel at a time. Wi-Fi channels work almost the same way except that channels can overlap each other. Each wireless controller (an Internet modem or access point) is configured to use a particular channel. Some analyze the network before initializing and automatically choose a free channel.

Encryption

Although most people don't think much about it, Wi-Fi presents a problem. You might be at home, shopping on your favorite Internet site. After you choose the articles you want, you go to pay, entering in your debit card details. Wireless information can, theoretically, be seen by anyone. Just like a regular conversation, if the person is close enough to hear, then he can get access to that information. To avoid this, infrastructure wireless communications are normally encrypted. Anyone can listen in to your conversation with your favorite Internet site but will not be able to understand because that conversation is encrypted with a special key that others do not know.

There are two forms of encryption: WEP and WPA2. WEP (short for Wireless Equivalent Privacy) is an early form of wireless encryption. Today, the standard is outdated, and Wi-Fi networks are encouraged to use the newer WPA2 encryption.

WPA2 (short for Wi-Fi Protected Access 2) is a solution to the weaknesses found in WEP and is a stronger version of the previous WPA encryption. It enables strong 256-bit AES encryption, using either 64 hexadecimal characters or 8 to 63 printable ASCII characters as a passkey. Again, several versions exist, but two main versions are used: WPA2 Personal and WPA2 Enterprise. WPA2 Personal requires a passkey and is perfect for home or small office environments. WPA2 Enterprise requires a specialized server and protects against more advanced attacks.

Not only does the encryption secure communications, it also secures the network. A wireless device that does not have the password cannot connect.

SSID

The network SSID, short for Service Set ID, is essentially the "network name," as it is known. This is the name that displays when you refresh your wireless network list, and is the name that devices attempt to connect to. SSIDs are sometimes hidden but are always present. A hidden SSID works in exactly the same way, only the name is not broadcast to devices; devices can still attempt to connect to a hidden SSID.

RSSI

RSSI is short for Received Signal Strength Indication and is an indication of signal strength. The units are arbitrary; some devices report signal strength as a percentage, others as a unit called dBm, or decibels per milliwatt of power. Reading this value gives an indication of signal strength and not distance because signal strength can be altered by physical obstructions (like walls) or electromagnetic interference.

Arduino WiFi

The Arduino WiFi library is designed to work with a large amount of network controllers through a simple system. The WiFi library "talks" to the Wi-Fi shield through the SPI bus, and communication is normally handled with a small microcontroller, "translating" messages on the SPI bus to the network controller.

Several vendors manufacture Wi-Fi shields, and there is also an official Arduino shield. Each board has its strong points: external antenna connectors, ultra-low power, and bridging possibilities. It all depends on your project. This chapter talks about standard connections without any external components or antennae.

The WiFi library can connect to a variety of Wi-Fi standards: typically B, G, and N networks. It can handle both WEP and WPA-2 Personal encryption but cannot connect to a WPA-2 Enterprise network. Also, it cannot connect to hidden SSIDs.

The WiFi library uses the SPI bus and requires the SPI pins to be free. It uses pins 11, 12, and 13 on the Arduino Uno, and 50, 51, and 52 for the Arduino Mega. Pin 10 is used as a Slave Select pin, and pin 7 is used as a digital handshake; these pins should not be used by the rest of the sketch.

The WiFi library methods are similar to those in the Ethernet library, and many of the functions are identical—only changed slightly to handle wireless networks and the subtle differences they face.

CROSS-REFERENCE Ethernet is presented in Chapter 9.

Importing the Library

To use the WiFi library, it must first be imported, which you can do in the Arduino IDE (menu Sketch ⇨ Add Library ⇨ WiFi) or by adding the library manually:

```
#include <WiFi.h>
```

You need to import other libraries, depending on your project:

```
#include <WiFiServer.h>
#include <WiFiClient.h>
#include <WiFiUdp.h>
```

The `WiFiServer.h` header file is used if the Arduino is to be a server. If a client connection is going to be made, the `WiFiClient.h` header file should be used. The `WiFiUdp.h` library should be imported if UDP communications are to be used.

Initialization

To initialize the WiFi subsystem, you must use `begin()`. It can take several parameters, depending on your configuration. To start the WiFi subsystem without any parameters (network SSID, password), just call `begin()`:

```
WiFi.begin();
```

To connect to an open SSID (one that does not require a password), use only the `ssid` parameter:

```
WiFi.begin(ssid);
```

To connect to a WPA-2 Personal protected network, specify the SSID and the password:

```
WiFi.begin(ssid, password);
```

To connect to a WEP protected network, another parameter is required. WEP protected networks can have up to four keys, and you must specify which one to use:

```
WiFi.begin(ssid, keyIndex, key);
```

Both keys and SSIDs can be written as an array of `chars`:

```
char ssid[] = "yourNetworkSSID";
char password[] = "MySuperSecretPassword";
```

Status

Of course, initialization presumes that a WiFi shield is present and correctly connected, which might not always be the case. To test for a WiFi shield, use the `status()` function:

```
result = WiFi.status();
```

This function takes no parameters and returns one of several constants, as shown in Table 10-1.

Table 10-1: Status Update Return Codes

CONSTANT	MEANING
`WL_IDLE_STATUS`	The WiFi shield is idle, without any instructions.
`WL_NO_SSID_AVAIL`	There are no networks to connect to.
`WL_SCAN_COMPLETED`	An initial SSID scan has been completed, and the WiFi shield knows about available SSIDs.
`WL_CONNECTED`	The WiFi shield has successfully connected to an SSID.
`WL_CONNECT_FAILED`	The WiFi shield was unable to connect; either the encryption key is wrong, or the connection was refused by the access point.
`WL_CONNECTION_LOST`	The WiFi shield was previously connected, but that connection has been lost (either out of range, or interference).

Continues

Table 10-1 (*continued*)

CONSTANT	MEANING
WL_DISCONNECTED	The WiFi shield has successfully disconnected from a network.
WL_NO_SHIELD	The Arduino cannot find a WiFi shield connected to the board.

Unlike Ethernet shields, WiFi shields have a fixed MAC address. To know the MAC address of the WiFi shield, use `macAddress()`. This function does not return any data but requires a parameter: a 6-byte array in which the MAC address will be placed.

```
byte mac[6];
WiFi.macAddress(mac); //Retrieve the MAC address, place it in mac
```

To retrieve the MAC address for the access point you are connected to, use `BSSID()`:

```
WiFi.BSSID(bssid);
```

Just like the `macAddress()` function, this function does not return any data but requires a data container as a parameter: a 6-byte array in which the MAC address will be placed.

To retrieve the RSSI, the signal quality indicator, use the `RSSI()` function:

```
long result = WiFi.RSSI();
```

RSSI, short for Received Signal Strength Indication, is a measurement of power in received radio signals. It is an indicator that generally goes from –100 to 0; the closer to 0, the stronger the reception. It cannot be used to estimate the range of a wireless device since interference can come not only from range, but also from electronic equipment or walls.

Scanning Networks

Due to the mobile nature of wireless, it can be helpful to scan the wireless networks around you to know which to connect to. An Arduino in a car might automatically connect to a home network when it's in range to send diagnostic information on your car but might also be configured to connect to another network, for example, a friend's house. In this case, the Arduino needs to periodically scan the available wireless networks until it finds one it recognizes. Wireless scanning on computers is frequent; open your wireless configuration panel to see a list of available networks.

To initiate a scan, use `scanNetworks()`:

```
result = WiFi.scanNetworks();
```

This function takes no parameters and returns an int—the number of wireless networks detected. A scan can take a few seconds to complete, but when done, the results are stored on the wireless chip, ready for interrogation. The chip stores several pieces of information: the SSID name, the signal strength, and the encryption type.

To retrieve the SSID of a network, use SSID():

```
result = WiFi.SSID(num);
```

It takes one parameter: the number of a network scanned with the scanNetworks() function. It returns a String: the name of the SSID.

To know the RSSI of a station broadcasting, use RSSI() specifying the network number:

```
result = WiFi.RSSI(num);
```

Exactly like RSSI() used to learn the RSSI of the current network, this function returns a long, the value in dBm, short for Decibel-milliwatts. Typical values range from −80 to 0; the higher the number, the better the reception.

Wireless networks also broadcast their security, specifically the encryption method required to connect (if any). To know the encryption of a network, use encryptionType(), specifying the network number:

```
result = WiFi.encryptionType(num);
```

This function returns a constant: the type of encryption detected. Table 10-2 lists the values.

Table 10-2: Possible Encryption Types

VALUE	MEANING
ENC_TYPE_WEP	WEP encryption
ENC_TYPE_TKIP	WPA encryption
ENC_TYPE_CCMP	WPA2 encryption
ENC_TYPE_NONE	No encryption, open network
ENC_TYPE_AUTO	Multiple encryption methods possible

Connecting and Configuring

To connect to a wireless network, use begin(), explained previously in the "Initialization" section. To disconnect from a network, use disconnect():

```
WiFi.disconnect();
```

This function does not take any parameters and does not return any information. It immediately disconnects from the current network.

By default, the WiFi shield uses DHCP to obtain an IP address and network settings. When begin() is called, DHCP negotiations begin after connecting to the network. While some wireless networks provide DHCP, others do not and require manual configuration. To perform manual configuration, use config(). This function can be called in four ways:

```
WiFi.config(ip);
WiFi.config(ip, dns);
WiFi.config(ip, dns, gateway);
WiFi.config(ip, dns, gateway, subnet);
```

In its most basic form, config() requires one parameter: the IP address to use, expressed as an array of 4 bytes, or optionally, using an IPAddress object. This object takes 4 bytes; the 4 bytes of an IP Address:

```
IPAddress ip(192.168.0.10);
```

To translate human-readable text into IP addresses, a Domain Name Server must be specified as the dns parameter, again, as an array of 4 bytes, or IPAddress. For packets to leave the current network to another network, a gateway IP must be specified with gateway. Finally, to change subnet, you must specify the subnet IP (by default: 255.255.255.0).

Calling config() before begin() forces the WiFi shield to use the settings specified. Calling config() after begin() again forces the WiFi shield to use the settings that were specified, but the begin() function will attempt to contact a DHCP server beforehand, resulting in a possible IP change.

The downside to this is that to use a specific DNS, you must specify the IP address. Some computers prefer to use an external DNS. (For example, Google allows users to use their DNS instead of their Internet provider's DNS.) To remedy this, the setDNS() function can be used.

```
WiFi.setDNS(dns_server1);
WiFi.setDNS(dns_server1, dns_server2);
```

This function requires either one or two DNS server addresses. It returns no data and immediately sets the DNS server values without changing the IP address.

Wireless Client

Just like with the Ethernet library, the WiFi library has its own client class. Remember, a client is a device that connects to a server on a specified port. A server is always on listening for client connections.

Before connecting to a server, the client must first create a client object; for the WiFi library, this is called WiFiClient.

```
// Initialize the client library
WiFiClient client;
```

This library is almost identical to the Ethernet library, though certain technical aspects are different to handle wireless connectivity. To create a socket to a server, you must use `connect()`, just like with the Ethernet library:

```
result = client.connect(server, port);
```

The function takes two parameters: `port` is an `int` and indicates the port to which you want to connect. The `server` parameter is either an `IPAddress` (or an array of 4 bytes), or a `String` containing the server name. It returns a `boolean`: `true` if the connection was accepted, and `false` if the connection failed.

Wireless Server

Wireless devices can also be servers, waiting for clients to connect before answering to requests. Again, the WiFi library has its own specialized object: `WiFiServer`:

```
WiFiServer server(port);
```

The `port` parameter is the port that you want to open, expressed as an `int`. When the port is opened, the server waits for incoming connections with `begin()`:

```
server.begin(); // Wait for clients to connect
```

Example Application

I'm terrible with plants. Taking care of most kinds isn't that complicated; I just need to keep the dirt moist, keep them out of direct sunlight (but still enough sunlight) and change the dirt from time to time. Just keeping the dirt moist seems to be too much for me, and this is where technology can help.

The DHT11 is a popular temperature and humidity sensor; it is inexpensive, reliable, and fairly easy to use. It comes with a plastic cover offering protection from most environments, and as long as you don't put water directly onto it, it can live happily with your houseplants. It is illustrated in Figure 10-1.

The DHT11 does have something unique. Previous chapters talked about serial communications, some of them requiring more wires than others, but some (I^2C especially) requiring only two wires to function. This component is different; it requires only one. There is one wire used to send and to receive data, in addition to a power and ground. Although it might sound complicated to use a single wire for both data reception and emission, it is actually fairly straightforward. The downside to this component is that you can make only one reading every 2 seconds, but that is more than enough for a houseplant, even mine.

Figure 10-1: The DHT11

This application uses an Arduino Uno and a SainSmart wireless shield. A DHT11 sensor will be connected to the board, allowing the user to get an accurate reading. Because I'm terrible with plants, I probably won't check the reading frequently, so this device must communicate with the outside world to send alerts. It will monitor the humidity of the dirt and send e-mails when the humidity level drops below a certain level. For this, it must be connected to the Internet. Because I don't have a wired access point nearby, I'll be using a wireless network.

This project requires a certain number of services to be put in place. First, it requires a DHCP server on the current network. Most Internet modems have their own DHCP server, so it should be compatible with most wireless access points. Secondly, it requires access to an SMTP server, a server used to send e-mail. Most Internet providers give you access to an e-mail server, but they may refuse e-mail that does not come from their network. Your Internet provider or e-mail service provider can give you information on how to access its mail servers.

The DHT11 is an interesting component in that it uses only one wire for communication. The Arduino is able to switch between input and output, so that isn't a problem.

The DHT11 communication protocol is slightly complicated. The data pin is normally at a logical high. To read from the DHT11, the Arduino must pull this data line down to zero for more than 18 milliseconds (ms) before returning it to a logical high for 40 μs. As a response, the DHT11 pulls the data line low for 54 μs and then pulls it high for 80 μs. This is an acknowledgment; it tells the Arduino that the request has been received and that data will follow. The DHT11 then sends 5 bytes for a total of 40 bits.

The timing of the data is the complicated part. The difference between a 1 and a zero is the amount of time that the data line remains high; 24 μs means a zero, and 70 μs means a 1, as shown in Figure 10-2.

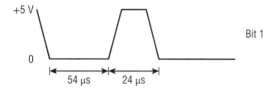

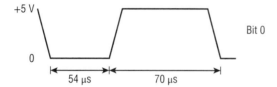

Figure 10-2: DHT11 sending a logical zero and a logical 1

At the end of the communication, the DHT11 pulls the data line back to a logical high.

Hardware

The hardware configuration is fairly straightforward. For this, you need an Arduino Uno. The WiFi shield is socketed on top of the Arduino. The DHT11 will be connected to +5 V and ground, and the data pin will be connected to digital pin 10. There is also a 10-kilohm pull-up resistor on the data line. Digital output 13 will also be used to turn on and off the internal LED for status indication. If the LED is on, then there is a problem with the board. The setup is shown in Figure 10-3.

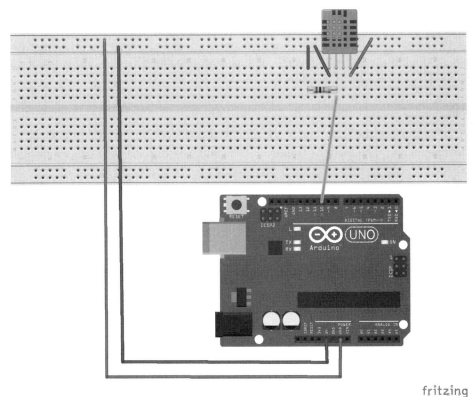

Figure 10-3: Hardware schematic (Image created with Fritzing)

Sketch

Time to get to work! Now that the hardware is complete, it is time to write the sketch. The sketch will look like that shown in Listing 10-1.

Listing 10-1: Wireless Sensor Sketch (filename: `Chapter10.ino`**)**

```
1    #include <WiFi.h>
2    #include <WiFiClient.h>
3
4    const int DHTPin=10;
5    const int LEDPin=13;
6
7    const int MINHumidity=25;
8
9    char ssid[] = "yourNetwork"; // Your network SSID (name)
10   char pass[] = "secretPassword"; // Your network WPA2 password
11   char server[] = "smtp.yourdomain.com"; // Your SMTP server
12
```

```
13  boolean firstEmail = true;
14
15  int status = WL_IDLE_STATUS;
16
17  WiFiClient client; // Set up the wireless client
18
19  void setup()
20  {
21    Serial.begin(9600);
22
23
22    Serial.println("Plant monitor");
23
24    // Configure the LED pin, set as output, high
25    pinMode(LEDPin, OUTPUT);
26    digitalWrite(LEDPin, HIGH);
27
28    // Is there a WiFi shield installed?
29    if (WiFi.status() == WL_NO_SHIELD) {
30      Serial.println("ERR: WiFi shield not found");
31      // No point continuing with the sketch
32      while(true);
33    }
34
35   // Attempt to connect to the WiFi network
36    while ( status != WL_CONNECTED) {
37      Serial.print("Attempting to connect to WPA SSID: ");
38      Serial.println(ssid);
39      // Connect to WPA/WPA2 network:
40      status = WiFi.begin(ssid, pass);
41
42      // Wait 10 seconds for connection:
43      delay(10000);
44    }
45
46    // If we got here, then the connection is good. Set LED pin low
47      and display information on  serial
48    digitalWrite(LEDPin, LOW);
49    Serial.println("Connected!");
50  }
51
52  void loop()
53  {
54    // Get a humidity reading
55    int val = getDht11Humidity();
56
57    // Print it out to the serial port
58    Serial.print("Current humidity: ");
59    Serial.print(val);
60    Serial.println("");
```

Continues

Listing 10-1 *continued*

```
61    if (val < MinHumidity)
62    {
63      // Below minimum humidity. Warn!
64      Serial.println("Plant is thirsty!");
65      sendEmail();
66      firstEmail = false;
67    }
68    else
69    {
70      // All OK
71      Serial.println("Humidity OK");
72      firstEmail = true;
73    }
74
75    // Wait for half an hour
76    delay(1800000);
77  }
78
79
80  int getDht11Humidity()
81  {
82    byte data[6] = {0};
83
84    // Set up variables
85    byte mask = 128;
86    byte idx = 0;
87
88    // Request a sample from the DHT11
89    pinMode(DHTPin, OUTPUT);
90    digitalWrite(DHTPin, LOW);
91    delay(20);
92    digitalWrite(DHTPin, HIGH);
93    delayMicroseconds(40);
94    pinMode(DHTPin, INPUT);
95
96    // Will we get an ACK?
97    unsigned int loopCnt = 255;
98    while(digitalRead(DHTPin) == LOW)
99    {
100     if (--loopCnt == 0) return NAN;
101   }
102
103   loopCnt = 255;
104   while(digitalRead(DHTPin) == HIGH)
105   {
106     if (--loopCnt == 0) return NAN;
107   }
108
109   // Acknowledged, read in 40 bits
110   for (unsigned int i = 0; i < 40; i++)
```

```
111   {
112     // Pin will go low. Wait until it goes high
113      loopCnt = 255;
114      while(digitalRead(DHTPin) == LOW)
115      {
116        if (--loopCnt == 0) return NAN;
117      }
118
119      // What is the current time?
120      unsigned long t = micros();
121
122      // Pin will go high. Calculate how long it is high.
123      loopCnt = 255;
124      while(digitalRead(DHTPin) == HIGH)
125      {
126        if (--loopCnt == 0) return NAN;
127      }
128
129      // Is this a logical one, or a logical zero?
130      if ((micros() - t) > 40) data[idx] |= mask;
131      mask >>= 1;
132      if (mask == 0)    // next byte?
133      {
134        mask = 128;
135        idx++;
136      }
137    }
138
139
140    // Get the data, and return it
141    float f = data[0];
142    return (int)f;
143 }
144
145
146 boolean sendEmail()
147 {
148    // Attempt to connect
149    if(!client.connect(server,25))
150       return false;
151
152    // Change this to your IP
153    client.write("helo 1.2.3.4\r\n");
154
155    // change to your email address (sender)
156    client.write("MAIL From: <plant@yourdomain.com>\r\n");
157
158    // change to recipient address
159    client.write("RCPT To: <you@yourdomain.com>\r\n");
160
```

Continues

Listing 10-1 *continued*

```
161    client.write("DATA\r\n");
162
163    // change to recipient address
164    client.write("To: You <you@yourdomain.com>\r\n");
165
166    // change to your address
167    client.write("From: Plant <plant@yourdomain.com>\r\n");
168
169    client.write("Subject: I need water!\r\n");
170
171    if (firstEmail == true) // First email
172    {
173      client.write("I'm thirsty!\r\n");
174    }
175    else
176    {
177      int i = random(4);
178      if (i == 0)
179        client.write("You don't love me any more, do you?\r\n");
180      if (i == 1)
181        client.write("All I know is pain...\r\n");
182      if (i == 2)
183        client.write("I would have watered you by now...\r\n");
184      if (i == 3)
185        client.write("My suffering will soon be over...\r\n");
186    }
187
188    client.write(".\r\n");
189
190    client.write("QUIT\r\n");
191  client.stop();
192
193    return true;
194 }
```

This sketch has four functions: the `setup()` and `loop()` that are present in every sketch and two others, `getDht11Humidity()` and `sendEmail()`.

At the start, the sketch includes two libraries: `WiFi.h` and `WiFiClient.h`. On lines 4 and 5, two pins are defined: the pin connected to the DHT11 data pin and the pin connected to an LED. On line 7, another pin is defined: `MINHUMIDITY`. This is the value that will be used as a warning level for the sensor; if the humidity falls below this level (expressed as relative humidity), the user will be warned.

On lines 9, 10, and 11, three variables are defined as `char arrays`. These need to be changed depending on your network setup; they are the SSID the Arduino will connect to, the password to use, and the SMTP server that will be used to send e-mails.

On line 13 is a variable: `thirsty`. This is a boolean: `true` if the plant needs water, and `false` if the dirt has enough humidity. Finally, you have an `int` named `status`. This is the status of the wireless connection and will be used later.

`setup()` is declared on line 19. `setup()` needs to do several things: configure the serial port for debug messages (line 21), set the LED pin correctly and turn the LED on (line 26), test to see if a WiFi shield is connected (line 30) and attempt to connect to a wireless network (line 37). It loops until the sketch connects to the designated network. When it does, the LED is turned off, and a message is sent to the serial port.

`loop()` is declared on line 53 and does one simple task. It gets a humidity reading from the DHT11 (on line 56), prints out the data to the serial port (line 59), and then calculates if the sensor reading is less than the minimum humidity level. If it has, then the plant is thirsty, and the user is warned. It sends out a message to the serial connection on line 58 and then calls a function: `sendEmail()`. Finally, the variable `thirsty` is set to `true`. If the minimum humidity level has not been reached, the plant is probably happy as it is, and the thirsty variable is set to `false`, telling the sketch that all is well. Finally, a `delay()` tells the Arduino to wait for one-half an hour before taking another reading.

`setup()` and `loop()`, required by all Arduino sketches, have been written, but two more are required; one of them reads in data from the DHT11 and reports the humidity level, and the second one sends an e-mail. The first function is `getDht11Humidity()`. This function is responsible for initiating communications with the DHT11, requesting data, receiving that data, and parsing part of it. It's a complicated function, but don't worry; it isn't that hard.

First off, there needs to be some variables to manipulate and hold data from the sensor, an array named `data`, and two bytes named `mask` and `idx`. To request a sample from the DHT11, the data line must be pulled low for at least 18 milliseconds and then set high. This is done on line 89 by setting the pin as an OUTPUT. It is pulled LOW; then a `delay()` function waits for 20 ms before setting the pin HIGH again. The sketch waits for 40 microseconds and then switches the DHT pin to INPUT. The DHT11 can now transmit data.

First, the DHT confirms that it has received an order by replying with an *ACK*. According to the datasheet, when the DHT11 is ordered to send data, it first responds by first driving the data pin low for 80 µS, and then high for 80 µS. It then again pulls the data pin low, ready to send data. This is its way of acknowledging the order, and informing the microcontroller that it will soon send data. The sketch waits until the line is set HIGH, and then it waits again until the line is pulled LOW. This is done on lines 98 and 104. Both portions of the sketch have a time-out; if 255 cycles have passed, the sketch reports a time out. The 255 cycles correspond to more than 80 µs, so if the time out occurs, there was indeed a problem; the ACK wasn't sent.

On line 110, a `for` loop is created. When the DHT11 has finished acknowledging reception, it will send 40 bits of data. This loop repeats 40 times once for each of the 40 bits the DHT11 should send. First, the pin is set LOW. Remember, the DHT11 sends and receives on a single wire. Previously, the Arduino had control of the wire, but when the signal was sent, it also signaled the DHT11 that it will be responsible for setting the state of the digital pin. To allow it to do this, the pin must be set LOW, and now becomes an input.

The state of the input is read on line 114; as long as the pin is low, this portion of the code repeats (unless a time-out occurs). When the line is set HIGH by the DHT11, this is where the work starts. First, the current system clock time is stored in a variable. This is the amount of microseconds the system has been powered on. A `while()` loop is created on line 125 and repeats as long as the pin is at a logical one, or HIGH. When the DHT sets the pin LOW, another time reading is made, and the difference between the two is calculated. If the data line was high for 24 μs, it was a logical zero. If the line was high for 70 μs, it was a logical one. The Arduino can't tell exactly when the pulse started and when it stopped, but it can guess closely. The easiest thing to do is to split the values: say, 40 μs. If the pulse were calculated as lasting more than 40 μs, the DHT11 sent a logical one; otherwise, it sent a logical zero. This is done on line 131. Afterward, the value is masked into the data buffer. Each bit is masked on each byte, incrementing the bit until the byte is complete and then moving on to the next byte.

So what is this NAN that is returned if something goes wrong? NAN is short for Not A Number, and is a good way of returning an error message for functions that expect numerical returns. If the function returns something that is not a number, that means there was an error reading one of the return bits.

The DHT11 sends the relative humidity value as a byte, an `int` is created from the first byte sent to be returned to the main program This `int` will contain the relative humidity, directly in percent.

Now, all that is left to do is to create a function to write e-mails. The function is declared on line 144. On line 149, the WiFi client attempts to connect to an e-mail server, on port 25. It uses an `if` statement, but checks for the result of a function, and not a variable. The exclamation mark in front of the function means NOT; it will execute the contents of the `if` statement if the result of the function is NOT TRUE. If the connection is refused, the function returns `false`.

Despite what might be thought of the complexity of e-mails, the SMTP protocol is extremely simple. The user must first authenticate, tell the server who he is, who he wants to contact, and then send the data. That's it! Almost… Some servers will require authentication, this will be explained below.

This function has all the lines necessary for communication with an SMTP server. You must specify your own "from e-mail", the "to e-mail", and a few other parameters. Remember the `firstEmail` variable? This is where it is used. If `firstEmail` is `true`, the sketch is sending its first email, so a nice e-mail should be sent. This is done on line 173. If the `firstEmail` variable is `false`, this isn't the first time an e-mail has been sent to the user, and he probably needs a gentle reminder. On line 177, a random number is generated, and then one of four messages are used. The user was warned, wasn't he? Well, in that case, the plant has the right to insist a little more by sending some different messages.

Finally, the client sends a message informing the SMTP server that it has sent all the data required and then quits. The `client.stop()` function makes sure that the Arduino disconnects from the SMTP server. The function then returns `true`, informing the sketch that everything went well.

Exercises

The `sendEmail()` function sends all the required information to an SMTP server, but SMTP servers also send information, including information that could be useful in case of a disconnection (wrong e-mail, server full, and so on). Have a look at the SMTP documentation, or a few examples of how SMTP servers work, and add some functions to verify the data sent by the server. Many examples are on the Internet, including some examples using Telnet with SMTP, which might be a good place to start. An example of SMTP exchanges is available at `http://packetfury.net/index.php/en/Arduino/tutorials/251-smtp`.

When placing a WiFi shield on the Uno, the internal LED is probably hidden. Try adding an external LED to the device to show that an error has occurred, and a second external LED to indicate the plant needs water.

While some SMTP servers will not require authentication, there are more and more servers that do. This adds one additional step. A login requires three elements: the user login, the password (of course), but also a step to tell the server what type of authentication you are requesting. The most common authentication is LOGIN. The server will request a simple login and password. To request a LOGIN authentication, you must send a new line:

```
auth login
```

The server will respond with a strange line, something like this:

```
334 VXNlcm5hbWU6
```

So what is this? This is an encoded word, written in Base64. This is a way of including special characters like accents and non-Latin letters in ASCII. You must first convert your login and password to Base64, using one of the numerous web pages available. You can find a Base64 encoder at `http://packetfury.net/index.php/en/Arduino/250-base64.php`.

The exchange with the server will look like this:

```
Client: auth login
Server: 334 VXNlcm5hbWU6
Client: <login>
```

```
Server: 334 UGFzc3dvcmQ6
Client: <password>
```

In your sketch, add some form of authentication, maybe like this:

```
client.write("auth login");
client.write("<Base64 login>");
client.write("<Base64 password>");
```

Summary

In this chapter, you have seen how to install and use Arduino's WiFi board, how to scan for wireless networks, and how to connect to a wireless network. I have shown how to read from a sensor using a single wire, and how to connect to an SMTP server to send an e-mail. In the next chapter, you will see more about SD cards: what they are, how they can be used, and how to read and write data to and from these devices using an Arduino.

LiquidCrystal

This chapter discusses the following functions of the LiquidCrystal library:

- `LiquidCrystal()`
- `begin()`
- `print()`
- `write()`
- `clear()`
- `home()`
- `setCursor()`
- `cursor()`
- `noCursor()`
- `blink()`
- `noBlink()`
- `rightToLeft()`
- `leftToRight()`
- `scrollDisplayLeft()`
- `scrollDisplayRight()`
- `autoscroll()`

- `noAutoscroll()`

- `createChar()`

The hardware needed to use the examples in this chapter includes:

- Arduino Mega 2560

- SainSmart LCD Shield

- HC-SR04 ultrasonic distance sensor

You can find the code download for this chapter at `http://www.wiley.com/go/arduinosketches` on the Download Code tab. The code is in the Chapter 11 download folder and is named `Chapter 11.ino`.

Introduction

For computers to be effective, they require two things: a way to input data and a way to output data. Data output can be in several forms; sometimes, it is invisible, communicating with other devices, such as safety systems in transportation. They are busy keeping you safe, but you will never see them. Other forms are slightly more visible: devices designed to turn on other devices, such as a timer designed to turn on a coffee machine at a particular time. They have the capacity to interact with the outside world but can be difficult to see.

Of all the human senses, sight is probably the most powerful. The best way for a computer to communicate data to the user is visually. Lights are often used for small quantities of data; a small light on your television set can tell you if it is receiving information from a remote control, and the amount of devices that tell you if they are powered with a simple red light is staggering. When more data needs to be displayed, other methods need to be used.

One of the most frequently used methods of displaying data is the liquid crystal display. Liquid crystal displays (or LCDs for short) can be found in digital watches, calculators, agendas, and vending machines, and the same technology is used for computer screens. They get their name from the thin film of liquid crystal contained inside the screen, wedged between two conductive plates. When in their natural state, the crystals inside the liquid are twisted, and light can pass through. When the crystals are subjected to an electrical current, they untwist, blocking the light. This makes the portion of the screen black.

LCD technology is fast and reliable, and uses little energy. Solar powered calculators allowed the user to make calculations with a minimal amount of light, and the solar panel was more than sufficient to power the processor and the LCD screen.

The earliest LCD screens were used to display numbers, typically for pocket calculators or wristwatches. To simplify the design, a format was created, one that allows the display of all numbers from 0 to 9. When decimal points were added, it became the perfect screen for calculators. An example is shown in Figure 11-1.

Figure 11-1: LCD screen of a calculator, displaying numbers

Although this works great for numbers, it doesn't work as well for letters. Some letters can be approximated, and some words can be guessed. Hands up; how many of you used calculators to write words? For example, entering 77345993 on a calculator and turning it upside down for EGGSHELL? I did.

To allow letters to be printed, the previous system was modified, adding more segments. This did indeed work, even if it increased the complexity of the LCD screen and the electronics needed to control it. It still wasn't perfect, and some letters were slightly difficult to read: for example, the letter V. Also, it did not allow for uppercase and lowercase letters to coexist; only uppercase letters were displayed and not every lowercase letter could be easily displayed. An example is shown in Figure 11-2.

Figure 11-2: LCD screen showing text

Electronics became smaller and smaller, while still becoming more and more powerful. New production techniques allowed LCD screens to become more and more advanced, and a new generation was born.

Modern LCD screens can display numbers and letters: both uppercase and lowercase. Much like the fonts on a computer screen, text and numbers can be written using a matrix of dots. By creating a simple matrix of 5 x 7 points, every single letter in the Latin alphabet can be displayed, and this even works on other alphabets. The downside to this is the complexity of the electronics involved to create connections for a matrix of 5 by 7 squares for every letter required, but most displays come with an integrated controller making the task much easier. Just tell the display what you want to print, and the controller does all the hard work for you.

This type of LCD screen does not talk about *resolution*. A typical desktop or laptop screen talks about a resolution in pixels, but these screens talk about the number of letters; 16 x 2 means 16 letters on two lines. It does not talk about resolution because this isn't how these screens work; they are composed of several small 5 x 7 screens, but with space between each segment. It isn't possible to display graphics on this type of screen.

LiquidCrystal Library

The Arduino LiquidCrystal library has been designed specifically for one controller: the Hitachi HD44780. Numerous boards exist with this controller, and it is so popular that other controllers also have HD44780 compatibility.

Before using the library, it must first be imported. To import the library, go into the Arduino IDE, and select the menu Sketch ➪ Import Library ➪ LiquidCrystal. Alternatively, you can manually add the header file into your sketch:

```
#include <LiquidCrystal.h>
```

To use the LiquidCrystal library, you must first create a named `LiquidCrystal` object. Numerous parameters are required, and values depend on the device that you will be using.

```
LiquidCrystal lcd(rs, enable, d4, d5, d6, d7);
LiquidCrystal lcd(rs, rw, enable, d4, d5, d6, d7);
LiquidCrystal lcd(rs, enable, d0, d1, d2, d3, d4, d5, d6, d7);
LiquidCrystal lcd(rs, rw, enable, d0, d1, d2, d3, d4, d5, d6, d7);
```

The `rs` parameter is short for Register Select and indicates the pin that is connected to the LCD's RS input. The `enable` parameter allows selection of the LCD device and indicates the pin that is connected to the LCD's ENABLE connector.

The r/w parameter is an optional parameter used to indicate if the Arduino is reading from or writing to the LCD screen. Some applications will write only to the LCD screen, in which case the R/W pin can be omitted. Otherwise, it must be connected to the LCD's R/W pin.

The remaining parameters are the data pins. Two options are available: either selecting four data pins or eight. This means that data sent to or received from the LCD controller is either in 4-bit mode or 8-bit. Originally, all data was written in 8 bits, but 4-bit mode allows programmers to send two 4-bit messages to be interpreted as an 8-bit message. This allows the designer to save four digital I/O pins when designing devices.

> **NOTE** There are several misunderstandings about the difference between 4-bit mode and 8-bit mode. One of them is about speed. It is indeed "faster" to send a single 8-bit message instead of two 4-bit messages, but with more than 90 percent of alphanumeric LCD screens, speed is not an issue. They have a relatively low refresh rate, meaning that it is possible to send an entire 2 x 16 message to the LCD screen before it has time to refresh the screen, even when using 4-bit mode.

When the LiquidCrystal object has been correctly created, it is necessary to initialize it. This is achieved with begin().

```
lcd.begin(cols, rows);
```

This function requires two parameters: the amount of columns and rows that the LCD device supports. Typical LCD screens are 2 x 16, but numerous models exist, and it isn't possible to ask every device what size they are. This information must be given.

Writing Text

The main function of an alphanumeric LCD screen is, of course, to display text. Because these screens have a built-in microcontroller, they perform almost exactly like serial terminals. When you send ASCII text to the controller, it prints those characters to the LCD screen. Just like a serial console on your computer, it continues to display those characters until you send more text than can be displayed, or until you send it an instruction.

To write text directly to the LCD screen, use print().

```
result = lcd.print(data);
result = lcd.print(data, BASE);
```

The data variable is of any data type; typically this would be a chain of characters, but it can also be numerical data. If it is numerical data, it will be printed as decimal by default, but this can be configured using the optional BASE parameter by selecting one of BIN, DEC, OCT, or HEX. This function returns a byte, the number of bytes written to the LCD device.

To print a single character, use write().

```
result = lcd.write(data);
```

The data parameter is a character that will be printed to the LCD. This function returns a byte; the number of bytes written to the LCD device (in this case, either 1 if successful, or 0 if there was an error).

To clear the screen, call clear().

```
lcd.clear();
```

This function takes no parameters and does not return any information. It sends a command to the LCD microcontroller to erase any text on the screen and to return the cursor to the top-left corner.

Cursor Commands

Cursor functions work similarly to the cursor on a spreadsheet; you may set the cursor to be at any position, and the text you enter will be printed at that position. By default, the cursor is set at the top-left side of the screen when initializing and will be updated to be placed at the end of any text that you write. When adding text to the display (by using multiple print() calls, for example), it will be added to the end of the line. So, for example:

```
lcd.print("Hello, ");
lcd.print("world!");
```

These two lines will result in printing a single line: "Hello, world!" This is useful when calling print() several times if displaying numerical values:

```
lcd.print("Temperature: ");
lcd.print("temp, DEC");
```

However, you can return the cursor to the top-left of the screen using home():

```
lcd.home(); // Returns the cursor to row 0, column 0
```

You can also place the cursor precisely where you want using the setCursor():

```
lcd.setCursor(col, row);
```

By default, the cursor itself is invisible. To make it visible (as an underscore at the position where the next character will be printed), use cursor():

```
lcd.cursor();
```

To disable the cursor again, use `noCursor()`:

```
lcd.noCursor();
```

These two functions do not take any parameters and do not return any data. To display a blinking cursor, use `blink()`:

```
lcd.blink();
```

To hide the blinking cursor, use `noBlink()`.

```
lcd.noBlink();
```

Using `cursor()` or `blink()` may produce unexpected results; the exact results depend on the screen's manufacturer. Consult your documentation.

Text Orientation

Text can be oriented both left to right and right to left. By default, LCD alpha-numerical displays are configured to be left to right. On startup, the cursor is placed at the far left, and each character makes the cursor move one step to the right. To configure the LCD screen to be in right-to-left configuration, use this function:

```
lcd.rightToLeft();
```

This function takes no parameters and returns no data. To change the orientation back to left to right, use the following function:

```
lcd.leftToRight();
```

Neither function affects previously written text, and the cursor's position is not updated.

Scrolling

LCD displays are used on numerous devices; they are cheap and reliable. You see them often on cash registers in supermarkets; an LCD device can tell you what item the cashier has just scanned and the cost of the item. At the end, it gives you the grand total to double-check with your calculations. Assuming that you want to print the total and that you need room for two decimal places, a decimal point, a dollar sign, and the remaining room for digits, then a standard 16 x 2 LCD device can be used for some expensive shopping. Sixteen characters are more than enough to display prices but become far too small if you want to place your company name or even some text. "Thanks for shopping with us; have a nice day!" is far too large for a 16 x 2 LCD screen, even on two lines.

So how can you print all that? The answer lies with scrolling, pushing existing characters out of the way for new text.

Text can be scrolled in two directions: left and right. The following functions shift both the text and the cursor by one space, either left or right:

```
lcd.scrollDisplayLeft();
lcd.scrollDisplayRight();
```

Automatic scrolling enables a simpler approach; text is automatically shifted when a character is printed to the screen. Automatic shifting can be done in both left-to-right or right-to-left configurations and depends on the current position.

To enable autoscroll, call `autoscroll()`:

```
lcd.autoscroll();
```

From here on, subsequent writes to the screen will result in previous characters to be automatically shifted. To disable autoscroll, use `noAutoscroll()`:

```
lcd.noAutoscroll();
```

Note that the cursor is also autoscrolled; this has the effect of always writing new characters to the same position.

Custom Text

Alphanumeric LCD screens are widely used, and it is not possible to imagine every use case before production. Although most simply display the time or short text, some require more advanced use. Imagine a home wireless telephone; the LCD screen is designed to print simple text, phone numbers, and why not a menu system to configure the telephone, but the constructor also wanted to add some information: the current battery level. It would be possible to display the battery level as a percentage or simply to ignore the battery if it is more than 25 percent charged, but maybe you would like to create your own character, something that resembles a battery. Maybe an elevator in a high rise building has an intelligent system. If you want to go to floor 42, the elevator will tell you to use a particular elevator. For example: Floor 42, →. The arrow will indicate that you should use the elevator on the right. It is more visual than writing text and might even be more economical to use such a solution because a smaller screen can be used. LCD screens already have a large amount of characters prerecorded, but there is still room for eight custom characters.

To create custom characters, an array of binary data must be created. This data is arranged in eight lines of 5-bit binary data, like so:

```
byte smiley[8] = {

  B00000,
  B10001,
```

```
  B00000,
  B00100,
  B00100,
  B00000,
  B10001,
  B01110,
};
```

Now, to attribute that data to a character, use `createChar()`:

```
lcd.createChar(num, data);
```

The `num` variable is the number of the character; slots 0 to 7 are available. The `data` parameter is the data structure you created previously. For example:

```
lcd.createChar(0, smiley);
```

Finally, to use the custom character, use `write()` specifying the byte to use:

```
lcd.write(byte(num));
```

Example Program

For this example, you build a distance sensor: a small device that displays the distance of the closest object to the device. Distance sensors are found in daily life; for example, they are used on building sites to know the distance between two walls or by real estate agents to calculate the size of a room. They are also used by robots to detect obstacles and used by cars in exactly the same way to help you reverse into a tight parking space.

There are several ways to achieve this, but they all rely on the same principle: bouncing waves. By emitting a certain frequency, the device calculates the time taken to receive a "copy" of that wave. Imagine yourself in a large open space: a stadium or in the mountains. When you shout, you wait for a small period of time before hearing your echo. Sound has traveled from your mouth and propagates. When it hits a solid surface, it reflects and is dispersed in different directions. Some of that sound returns to you, and your ears hear the sound. By calculating the time it took to hear your echo and factoring in the speed of sound, you can get a rough estimate of the distance. However, this doesn't work for small distances; the speed of sound is so fast that it is impossible for a human to calculate the distances inside a house, but for electronics, it isn't a problem. The HC-SR04 is one device that can do this.

The HC-SR04 is an ultrasonic distance sensor, as illustrated in Figure 11-3. Ultrasonic distance sensors are easily recognizable by their shape. When placed on a robot, it looks like two "eyes," and in a way, they are. One "eye" is an ultrasonic speaker, and the second is an ultrasonic microphone. Ultrasound waves are created, and the device calculates the time taken for those waves to return to the device. This results in surprisingly accurate results and is good for distances up to four meters away.

Figure 11-3: HC-SR04 Ultrasonic Sensor

The sensor has four pins: one for the power, one for the ground, one to issue a pulse, and the final pin to read the distance. The result is not in a binary format; this pin will not output text or data in a serial fashion. Instead, the pulse length is proportional to the time taken to receive a result. Fortunately, the Arduino can handle this with a single command.

To allow the user to read the data easily, an LCD screen will be used. This setup could easily be used with a serial device, but that doesn't make sense. The serial port displays text and so does an alphanumeric LCD screen. Only LCD screens are significantly more user-friendly.

This example uses a SainSmart LCD Keypad shield. This shield contains a 16 x 2 LCD screen with a nice blue backlight. It contains all the electronics necessary to use an LCD screen: power, the backlight control, all connected to the Arduino on digital pins. It uses four data pins, and therefore will use 4-bit commands. The example is not specific to this shield, but if you use a different screen, make sure your code and wiring reflects the necessary changes.

Hardware

The SainSmart LCD Keypad shield is a fairly large device. A normal 16 x 2 LCD screen is about as long as an Arduino Uno, and this shield covers the Uno completely, making it difficult to add additional peripherals. For this reason, the Arduino Mega2560 was chosen. It is longer than the Uno, and even with the shield present, there are still a large amount of I/O pins available. The HC-SR04 ultrasonic distance sensor is a small device, and by chance, is exactly as wide as the extended digital outputs of the Arduino Mega2560. To create a self-contained device, the sensor will be placed directly into the header pins, bypassing the need for a breadboard. Let me explain.

By reading the datasheet of the HC-SR04, available at `http://packetfury` `.net/attachments/HCSR04b.pdf`, you can find the requirements for powering the sensor: one pin for power and one ground connection. The maximum current used by the sensor is 15 mA. The maximum power delivered by the Arduino's I/O pins can't exceed 40 mA. That is more than double, a comfortable safety margin. The pin connected to the sensor's VCC sets as output and sets HIGH. The pin connected to the sensor's ground also is an output but sets LOW. Just as LED lights can be powered by an I/O pin pulled HIGH, the sensor will be powered by these pins. Similarly, the ground can be an I/O pin pulled LOW. The sensor will be sufficiently powered by the board, but remember that this is a prototype and designed for simplicity. It is possible to do what you are about to do, but if you end up creating your own shield with an LCD screen and ultrasonic distance sensor built in, it is good practice to route the shield so that the sensor is powered by the main power, not powered by the Arduino.

WARNING Don't connect the sensor just yet! The reason for this is explained later in this chapter when I talk about the sketch.

Software

The sketch is shown in Listing 11-1.

Listing 11-1: Sketch (filename: `Chapter 11.ino`)

```
1   #include <LiquidCrystal.h>
2
3   const int vccPin=40;
4   const int gndPin=34;
5   const int trigPin=38;
6   const int echoPin=36;
7
8   // Initialize the library with the numbers of the interface pins
9   LiquidCrystal lcd(8, 9, 4, 5, 6, 7);
10
11  void setup()
12  {
13    Serial.begin (9600);
14
15    // Set up the LCD's number of columns and rows
16    lcd.begin(16, 2);
17
18    // Configure the pins
19    pinMode(trigPin, OUTPUT);
```

Continues

Listing 11-1: (*continued*)

```
20    pinMode(echoPin, INPUT);
21    pinMode(vccPin, OUTPUT);
22    pinMode(gndPin, OUTPUT);
23
24    // Trigger set to low
25    digitalWrite(trigPin, LOW);
26
27    // VCC and GND
28    digitalWrite(vccPin, HIGH);
29    digitalWrite(gndPin, LOW);
30
31    // Prepare LCD screen text
32    lcd.print("Distance");
33  }
34
35  void loop()
36  {
37    long duration, distance;
38
39    digitalWrite(trigPin, HIGH);
40    delayMicroseconds(10);
41    digitalWrite(trigPin, LOW);
42
43    duration = pulseIn(echoPin, HIGH);
44    distance = duration / 58;
45
46    // Set the cursor to column 0, line 1 (beginning of second line)
47    lcd.setCursor(0, 1);
48
49    if (distance >= 400 || distance <= 0)
50    {
51      // Inform the user that we are out of range
52      lcd.print("Out of range");
53    }
54    else
55    {
56      // Tell the user what distance has been detected
57      lcd.print(distance);
58      lcd.print(" cm        "); // Extra space overwrites any text
59    }
60
61    // Wait for half a second before repeating
62    delay(500);
63  }
```

From the start, on line 1, the LCD library is imported. Afterward, four pins are defined as constants: vccPin, gndPin, trigPin, and echoPin. These pins correspond to the pins found on the HC-SR04 sensor board. The vccPin and the gndPin are the power pins, and `trigPin` and `echoPin` are the data pins. Later, `trigPin` will be an output, and `echoPin` will be an input.

On line 9, the LCD display is configured, creating an `lcd` device. This function uses six parameters, which tell the sketch that it will use four data lines and does not use the optional read/write parameter. It is called using six integers: 8, 9, 4, 5, 6, and 7. The first value corresponds to the RS pin. On the SainSmart LCD Keypad shield, RS is pin 8. The second value is the enable pin, and this is wired to pin 9. Finally, 4, 5, 6, and 7 are the data pins. As with the rs and enable pins, these are hardwired on the shield.

On line 11, `setup()` is declared. On line 13, the serial port is initialized. It isn't used in this example, but it is ready in case you need to start debugging your application. The LCD device is already activated, but the sketch knows only what pins the LCD device is connected to. It still doesn't know how many lines and columns the device has. This is done on line 16 with `begin()`; it has 16 columns and two lines. On lines 19 to 24, the four pins for the sensor are configured. One pin, echoPin, will be configured as INPUT, and the three others will be OUTPUT. On line 25, the trigger pin is set LOW. On line 28, the vccPin is set HIGH; it will now supply 5 V. On line 29, the gndPin is set LOW; it is now a ground connection. Finally, on line 32, some text is sent to the LCD device: one word—"Distance." This is printed at the default cursor position: (0,0), located at the top-left corner of the screen. This text will be present at all times, and the text on the second line will be updated in `loop()`.

On line 35, `loop()` is declared. This is where all the sensor reading and text writing takes place. It starts by declaring two variables: `duration` and `distance`. The HC-SR04 requires a pulse on the `trigPin` pin of at least 10 microseconds. To do this, the sketch first sets `trigPin` HIGH, waits for 10 microseconds using `delayMicroseconds()`, and then sets `trigPin` to a logical LOW.

After receiving a pulse, the HC-SR04 starts working. It emits a number of ultrasonic bursts and listens to the results. After the distance has been calculated, the result is returned via the `pulsePin`, a variable length pulse. So how can the Arduino know how long the pulse is? The answer is simple: `pulseIn()`. This function was presented in Chapter 4. Put simply, it waits for a pulse to appear on the designated pin. It waits for the logic level to change and then starts counting. When the logic level changes back to its original setting, it stops counting and returns the length of the pulse in microseconds. This is done on line 53, placing the result into a variable: `duration`. On line 54, a small calculation is made; the variable duration is divided by 58. This value comes from the sensor's documentation. Divide the number by 58 to get a result in centimeters and by 148 to get the result in inches. Now that you have the distance, it is time to print the results.

The results will be printed on the second line of the LCD screen, so the coordinates must be set. This is done on line 47; the position is set to column 0, line 1. Remember, most numbers start with 0, so this is actually on the first column on the second line. The HC-SR04 can give results up to 4 meters away; values greater than that will be ignored. A quick check is done on line 49 with an `if()` statement. If the result is greater than 400 centimeters or if the result is negative, the sketch writes "Out of range" if the `distance` value is out of range. If it is not out of range, the value is printed. This is done in two steps: first, the decimal value is displayed. Afterward, some text is displayed with a leading space and several spaces after the text. Why? Because if the previous text were "Out of range," the end of that text would still be visible. Writing text on a line does not automatically delete all the text at the end of the line. Just like using the insert function in a word processor, each keypress deletes one character and inserts the character you want in that text, but it does not delete text afterward. To make sure that no trailing text is displayed, several spaces are included.

The last thing that happens is waiting for one-half a second before repeating the process. This is done on line 62. Figure 11-4 shows the finished product.

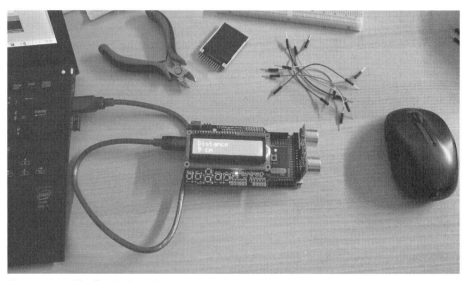

Figure 11-4: The finished product

NOTE It is vitally important to double-check the Arduino before connecting components. It is tempting to connect the sensor before uploading the sketch to the Arduino, but what would happen if the previous sketch used the I/O pins for something else? In the worst case, the VCC and GND pins could be inverted, essentially reversing the polarity of the component, damaging or destroying it. I have a dozen Arduino boards at home, and it is impossible to remember exactly which board has which sketch. Remember to upload the proper code of your Arduino before connecting external devices.

Exercises

This sketch gives surprisingly accurate results with inexpensive hardware, but a few quick tricks might make this sketch even better. It is currently written for the metric system, using centimeters. You could change the output to meters when the distance value is more than 100. For people using the imperial system, the sketch can be modified to print the data in inches, not in centimeters.

   One good way of changing between inches and centimeters would be to use something that the SainSmart LCD Keypad shield already has: a keypad. Look at the documentation; the keypad is an analog device connected to pin A0. When the keypad is pressed, the voltage on A0 changes, and that is how the sketch knows that a button has been pressed. Try to create something that would change the output when one of the buttons is pressed. `analogRead()` would be useful here for reading the results of keypresses.

Summary

In this chapter, you have seen not only how to connect liquid crystal displays, but you have learned how to create special characters for your device, and how to display data onto the screen. In the next chapter, I will show you the SD library, how it talks to SD cards, and how it can be used to read and write data to a card. You will see a data logging application that will allow you to write thousands of samples to a card, and how to read them back.

This chapter discusses the following functions of the SD library:

- `begin()`
- `open()`
- `exists()`
- `close()`
- `read()`
- `peek()`
- `position()`
- `seek()`
- `size()`
- `available()`
- `print()`
- `println()`
- `write()`
- `mkdir()`
- `rmdir()`
- `flush()`
- `isFolder()`

The hardware needed to run the examples in this chapter includes:

- Arduino Uno
- Ethernet shield (Arduino, SainSmart, or similar board)
- Micro-SD Card

You can find the code download for this chapter at `http://www.wiley.com/go/arduinosketches` on the Download Code tab. The code is in the Chapter 12 download folder and the filename is `Chapter12.ino`.

Introduction

The hunger for storage has increased exponentially. Early computers did not have hard drives; the operating system and applications were stored on a floppy disk. The first commercially available floppy disk was an 8-inch disk, which became available in 1971. It could store an enormous 175 KB of data. In 1976, the standard became 5 ¼ inch (ironically known as the minifloppy). The original model could store 87.5 KB, but newer models could store more than 1 megabyte. The large slots on your desktop computer that house a DVD drive or Blu-ray drive are that size because of floppy disks; the size of the minifloppy disk drive became standard.

As technology advanced, so did the storage capacity of disks, and 5 ¼-inch disks were considered too big; the computer industry turned to 3 ½-inch floppies, known as micro-floppies. Early models could store 360 KB, but later models could either be single density (720 KB) or double density (1.44 MB). Those are the disks that powered the computer industry, storing and exchanging data. Operating systems were sold on floppies, and the first thing that users were told to do was to copy this floppy and keep the original safe. A single floppy disk was more than enough to hold an operating system and a few programs. Figure 12-1 shows examples of three different types of early floppy disks.

Figure 12-1: Floppy disks

Technology continued to advance, and more and more files were created digitally. Businesses could find themselves submerged with floppies, and data retrieval could be extremely slow because a lot of time was taken finding the right floppy. Also, floppy disks were not the most reliable medium possible. (Older readers might remember the infamous Abort, Retry, Ignore message.) The solution came, and it was called the hard drive.

A hard drive is, essentially, a floppy disk that cannot be removed. Original models could hold just a few megabytes, but it didn't take long to increase storage space—from 20 megabytes to 40, 120, 340, 540.... The gigabyte barrier was broken in the early 1990s. However, this was not the end of floppies, far from it. Operating systems and programs were still sold on floppies, and backups used floppy disks. However, another problem was noticed.

With the advance into the digital era, everything ended up on a computer— letters, books, photos, images, and music. It was easy to add a few hard drives onto a computer until internal space ran out, but the industry's main problem was data exchange; the ability of transferring data from one computer to another. A simple Word document could be just a few kilobytes in size, but add a few images or photos, and it could become bigger than a floppy disk, the only medium used to transfer data from one location to another. The Internet wasn't available everywhere and most certainly not at the speeds required to transfer megabytes of data. We would have to wait a few years for high-speed devices like USB. I can remember receiving parcels containing dozens of floppy disks containing programs. (Windows 3.1 came on 7 floppy disks; Windows NT 3.1 came on 22.)

CD drives offered a solution, the medium is capable of storing 650 to 700 MB of data. Applications could be shipped on a single CD, and the increase in size meant that applications became more and more multimedia-oriented. Microsoft Encarta was a revolution for its time—an entire encyclopedia on a CD. However, it wasn't the most effective data transfer device possible, being a write-once read-many media. After a CD was "burned," it couldn't be erased. Different techniques were used, including the possibility to rewrite CD media, but a new technology put a stop to all that.

The Universal Serial Bus (USB) is an extension for PCs and mobile devices. Developed in the mid-1990s, the final USB 1 specification was released in January 1996. Until USB, shopping for peripherals was a nightmare. A printer would use a parallel port, but so would a scanner and a Zip drive. A mouse might use a serial port, but so would a modem and a programmer. Expansion ports were sold, adding serial ports, parallel ports, PS/2 ports, and so on. USB revolutionized all this—printers, scanners, mice, modems, even some floppy drives. All these peripherals could use USB, and it was embraced by the industry. However, the industry was about to try something else. In the year 2000, the first USB flash drive was created, as shown in Figure 12-2.

Figure 12-2: USB flash drives

The first commercial product could hold 8 MB of data, more than five times that of a floppy disk. It was solid and robust, and could survive spending days in a pocket, falling off desks, or being subjected to temperature differences. It had a high transfer speed compared to floppy disks (1 MB/second) and was better than floppies in almost all fields.

In 2000, USB 1.1 was surpassed by USB 2.0, adding higher transfer speeds. USB 2.0 could transfer up to 35 MB/s; huge files could finally be transferred quickly and efficiently. A second generation flash disk used USB 2.0, which was significantly faster than USB 1.1—approximately 20 times faster.

Speed increased and so did storage capacity. Every so often, capacities doubled. Sixteen-megabyte versions were soon available, replaced by 32 megabytes, and so on. Fourteen years later, terabyte-sized flash drives are available. Despite their huge growth and advances, flash drives have remained relatively unchanged. They rely on a small controller and flash memory.

Flash memory is different from floppies and hard drives. Floppy disks have a thin, flexible disk of magnetic storage plastic, encased in a rigid plastic case. A motor inside the disk drive turns the disk, and *heads* are placed above the surface of the disk. To fetch data, the heads are placed at a specific location and the motor turns the disk. The heads read the data stored on the disk, but the heads must wait for the disk to rotate to the right position to do so. Hard drives function in the same way, only the motor is included inside the drive.

Both floppies and hard drives are susceptible to damage; for example, a hard drive falling from your pocket might destroy the device. Flash memory works differently. Unlike floppies and hard drives, flash memory has no moving parts, and is therefore much more resilient to shocks and impacts. It requires very little energy to function, and some forms of flash memory have read and write speeds far greater than the fastest hard drive available.

USB flash drives still aren't the answer to our needs. We can now easily transfer data from one computer to another, but mobile devices are becoming more and more present. Mobile telephones, digital cameras, camcorders, and mp3 players all require storage. Early devices had a fixed amount of storage, and although it might have been more than enough for some, for others the storage wasn't close to being enough. My first digital camera had 16 megabytes of memory, more than enough for a quick photo shoot, but not enough for my holidays. Users wanted choice, so companies turned back to a format that had existed for as long as USB itself. Multiple mobile memory storage devices were created, but the most dominant format is the SD card.

SD Cards

SD, short for Secure Digital, is an evolution over the previous MultiMediaCard standard. The SD Card Association manages the format, specifications, and evolutions, and uses a trademarked logo to enforce compatibility. If your device has the same logo as the one on your SD card, you know that they will be compatible.

Physically, SD cards are available in three formats: standard size, mini, and micro (see Figure 12-3). Today, most devices use either the standard size format (for larger devices, like cameras, camcorders, and personal computers) or the micro-size format (for smaller devices, such as e-book readers, telephones, and mp3 players).

SD cards are not only used for data storage, but also for data transfer. You can transfer photos from your camera either with a USB cable or directly by taking out the card and connecting it to your PC. Some desktop computers have an SD-card reader, as do many laptops. For micro-SD cards, you have several choices. There are USB readers that can read several types of cards or USB keys that can accept a micro-SD card and be used as a regular USB flash drive. Adapters also exist to convert a micro-SD card into a standard full-size SD card.

Figure 12-3: SD cards, micro-SD cards, and SD-card readers

Capacity

SD cards have gone through numerous changes to their specification since their release in 1999. The original SD specification allowed cards with capacities up to 2 gigabytes. When the 2 gigabyte barrier became a problem, SD-HC was introduced. Short for SD High Capacity, it specified a way of storing up to 32 gigabytes of data. It does not simply integrate more space; the protocol had to be changed to allow for higher capacity. Again, the size barrier became a problem, and SD-XC (for eXtended Capacity) was born. The standard insists that newer formats accept older cards, but the opposite is not true; some SD-compatible devices will not accept SD-HC cards, even if they can fit physically.

The card capacity is only one factor. To use a card's capacity, the system normally needs to use a filesystem. A *filesystem* is a way of preparing the space on a physical storage medium (SD-card, floppy, or hard drive) to allow files and folders to be stored in a hierarchal way. SD cards can be used to transfer data between devices and operating systems with different specifications. From this variety of formats, FAT has emerged as the most common filesystem.

FAT, short for File Allocation Table, has been used since the early days of PCs. It has undergone several changes over the years. The original FAT specification, FAT8, is no longer in use. FAT16 uses 16 bits to define sector entries (a method of storing file information) and is limited to 2 gigabyte partitions. FAT32 was released after this, and storage space was theoretically increased to 2 terabytes; although in practice, few systems used it beyond 32 gigabytes. Newer systems use the exFAT filesystem, a new but incompatible filesystem that allows huge storage capacity; in theory, up to 64 zettabytes. For comparison, in 2013, the entire World Wide Web was estimated at 4 zettabytes.

FAT32 has been surpassed technically by several filesystems, including exFAT and NTFS, but still remains in use for its simplicity. NTFS adds several interesting features such as journaling, linking, and quotas; features that are not required by a digital camera. The code required to interact with a FAT32 filesystem is extremely small, making it ideal for embedded systems.

Speed

There is also another factor to consider when choosing SD cards: their speed. The SD Speed Class Rating is a simple way of understanding the minimum speed of a card. Visible by either a letter C with a number inside, it shows the number of guaranteed megabytes-per-second transfer speed. A Class 2 card (A C with the number 2 inside) guarantees that the write transfer speed will not drop below 2 megabytes per second. A Class 10 will not drop below 10 megabytes per second. The newer speed category is shown by the letter U, and to date, two categories exist. UHS-1 (a U with the number 1 inside) guarantees read/write performance of 10 megabytes a second, and UHS-3 (a U with the number 3 inside) is guaranteed for 30 megabytes read/write per second. Please note that these figures are stated only as a minimum; some Class 2 cards are more than capable of being branded as a Class-6 or higher but have not gone through certification.

Using SD Cards with Arduino

Arduinos cannot natively use SD cards; they need a shield or a breakout board to provide an SD slot. Fortunately, several shields exist with SD capacity. Most Ethernet and wireless shields provide micro-SD slots, and numerous vendors provide *datalogging shields*—a shield with a micro-SD slot and space to add your own sensor components, as shown in Figure 12-4.

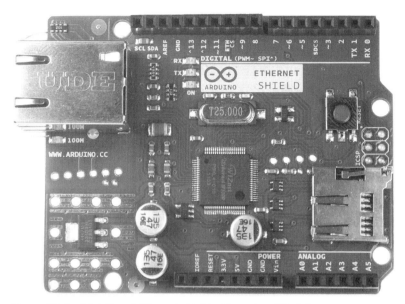

Figure 12-4: A SainSmart Ethernet shield with a micro-SD slot

Accepted SD Cards

The Arduino SD library can work with SD and SD-HC cards, all the way up to 32 gigabytes. This limitation is mainly due to the filesystem; Arduinos can use FAT16 and FAT32 filesystems but cannot use the newer, proprietary exFAT. SD-XC cards are normally formatted with exFAT, but some people have reported using SD-XC cards formatted to FAT-32.

An Arduino can work with any speed classes of SD-cards, but data throughput will be limited when writing with an Arduino. You may want to buy a faster card if you transfer data to and from a PC.

Limitations

Back in the days of Windows 3.11, filenames were harder to deal with. They were written in the 8.3 notation; filenames could consist of only 8 letters, and the extension (the text after the dot), could consist of only three letters. The filesystem did not differentiate between uppercase and lowercase letters for the system; everything was written in uppercase letters. Files were seen as WIN .COM, AUTOEXEC.BAT, and RECIPES.TXT. If you wanted to name a video of your family on holidays on a tropical island, swimming in a crystal clear sea, you had to be very creative. An extension to FAT allowed the use of LFN, short for Long File Names, but it is only an extension; it is not part of the FAT specification. There is a reason why your camera names your photos IMG_xxxx. JPG; it is probably limited to the 8.3 file-naming system. Arduinos also can use only 8.3 filenames. This isn't a problem for cameras where filenames are just numbers, and it is rarely a problem for Arduinos where files are normally configuration, or data-logging.

Communications to and from the SD card are done via SPI. The SS pin (SPI Slave Select) must be left untouched. The SD library will not work if the SS pin is not configured as an output.

Numerous shields exist and do not always use the same pin to initialize the SD card. The chip select pin can change from one design to another; consult the shield documentation to know which pin to use when initializing the SD card reader.

The SD Library

The Arduino language has an SD library built in. This library depends on three other internal libraries that handle card and filesystem-specific functions, but abstraction makes the library extremely easy to use. It is possible to use the other libraries, which is explained briefly in the "Advanced Usage" section.

Importing the Library

To be able to use the SD library, you must first import it. This can be done either automatically in the Arduino IDE by going to the Sketch ⇨ Import Library ⇨ SD menu item, or manually with this:

```
#include <SD.h>
```

Arduinos communicate with SD card controllers using the SPI protocol. Thus, you must also import that library:

```
#include <SPI.h>
```

Connecting a Card

As with many Arduino libraries, to initialize the library, you must call SD.begin().

```
result = SD.begin();
result = SD.begin(csPin);
```

SD.begin() returns true if a card is detected and the library initialized; otherwise, it returns false. The optional csPin argument is used to configure which slave select pin should be used if your application does not use the default hardware SS pin. Most shields will use the default hardware pin.

```
// See if the card is present and can be initialized:
if (!SD.begin(chipSelectPin)) {
  Serial.println("Could not initialize SD card.");
  // End the sketch gracefully
  return;
}
Serial.println("SD Card initialized.");
```

Opening and Closing Files

The SD library can create, update, and delete files on a FAT16/32 filesystem. The SD library (and indeed most programming environments) does not differentiate between creating a file and opening a file. The system is told to open a file. If the files exists, it will be opened. If it does not exist, an entry is created, and a new blank file is opened. To open a file, call SD.open().

```
file = SD.open(filepath);
file = SD.open(filepath, mode);
```

The filepath parameter, expressed as an array of char, is the name of the file to use or to create. If the file does not exist, it will be created, but this function will not create folders. To specify a folder, use the slash (/) character. The mode parameter can be one of two constants: FILE_READ or FILE_WRITE. The FILE_READ constant tells the sketch to open the file as read only. This is the default setting if the mode parameter is omitted. The FILE_WRITE constant opens the file in read/write mode. SD.open() returns a File object, something that describes and points to a file. It is used as a reference to read, update, or close files. To open a file, you must first create a File object, and then use that object on subsequent file actions:

```
File myFile;
myFile = SD.open("data.dat", FILE_WRITE);
```

It is also possible to check beforehand if a file exists. To do this, use SD.exists().

```
result = SD.exists(filename);
```

This function tests to see if a filename exists and returns true if it exists or false if it does not exist.

After you perform any read or write operations, you must close the file. This is done using close() from the File class.

```
file.close();
```

The `File` object is created when opening the file. This function takes no parameters and does not return any data.

```
File myFile;
myFile = SD.open("data.dat", FILE_WRITE);
// Perform any read or write operations here
myFile.close();
```

Reading and Writing Files

Reading files is done with a pointer to a file position. By default, when a file is opened, this pointer is set to the beginning of the file (byte 0). As each byte is read in, the pointer increments, until it reaches the end of the file. You can set the position of the pointer to any location inside the file.

Writing files is done by either appending data to the end of the file, no matter where the pointer is located, or writing data at the file pointer location.

When reading and writing to a file, you will be using the File class, which inherits from Stream, just like Serial does.

Reading Files

To read a byte from a file, use the `read()` function of the File class.

```
data = file.read();
```

This function returns 1 byte at a time (or –1 if no data is available) and automatically updates the pointer. If you do not want the pointer to be updated, you can call `peek()`.

```
data = file.peek();
```

Its use is exactly the same as `read()`, returning 1 byte, but the pointer is not updated. Several calls to `peek()` returns the same byte. To know the value of the pointer (to know which byte is the next to be read), use `position()`.

```
result = file.position();
```

This function does not take any parameters and returns an `unsigned long` indicating the current position within the file. It is also possible to set the position with `seek()`.

```
result = file.seek(position);
```

This function attempts to set the file pointer to the value of `position`, defined as an `unsigned long`. To know the size of the current open file, use `size()`. It returns the file size in bytes as an `unsigned long`.

```
data = file.size();
```

To know if there are any more bytes available for reading, use `available()`.

```
number = file.available();
```

This function returns the remaining bytes inside a file, as an `int`.

Writing Files

Three functions are used to write data to a file. `print()` and `println()` are used in the same way as the Serial functions of the same name and `write()` places bytes at the pointer position in the file.

`print()` and `println()` can be used to write formatted data: text and decimal numbers, as well as binary, hexadecimal, and octal representations using the optional `base` parameter. By specifying `BIN` as the base parameter, `print` will write binary notation. Using `OCT` and `HEX`, `print` will write octal and hexadecimal respectively. The difference between `print()` and `println()` is that `println()` automatically adds a new line character at the end. Both of these functions ignore the file pointer and append data to the end of the file.

```
file.print(data);
file.print(data, base);
file.println(data);
file.println(data, base);
```

The `write()` function is different. It can write data directly inside a file but will not insert data; it will overwrite any data present if not at the end of the file.

```
file.write(data);
file.write(buffer, len);
```

The `data` parameter can be a `byte`, a `char`, or a `string`. The `buffer` parameter is a `byte`, array of `char`, or a `String`, and the `len` parameter indicates the number of bytes to be used.

`write()`, `print()`, and `println()` also return the number of bytes written to the buffer, but reading this is optional.

Folder Operations

If no directory is specified, all operations are performed on the root folder of the SD card. It is, however, possible to create folders and work inside those folders.

Folders are used in the UNIX fashion; paths are separated by forward slashes (/), for example, folder/file.txt. All folders are named from the root folder; you cannot "cd" into a folder without first specifying the root folder(s).

Folders and files are handled differently. When creating a file, you must "open" the file, and the Arduino will create the file if it does not exist. This does not work for folders; you must first create the folder before creating the file.

To create a folder, use `mkdir()`.

```
result = SD.mkdir(folder);
```

This function returns `true` if the folder was created, or `false` if the operation did not succeed. It takes a string as a parameter and is the folder to be created (complete with forward slashes). It can also create intermediate folders if required:

```
SD.mkdir("/data/sensors/temperature"); //Will create all folders
```

To remove a folder, use `rmdir()`.

```
result = SD.rmdir(folder);
```

This deletes the folder from the filesystem but only on the condition that it is empty. The function returns `true` if the folder were deleted, or `false` if it did not complete the operation.

Folders are, in fact, special files. They can be opened with `open()`, but to know if a "file" is a regular file or a directory, you can use the `isDirectory()` function.

```
result = file.isDirectory();
```

This function takes no parameters and returns a boolean; `true` if the file is a folder, and `false` if the file is a regular file.

Card Operations

Data is buffered; that is to say that when the sketch is told to save data, that data is not necessarily written to the SD card immediately. Because SD cards have an embedded controller, write operations can be queued and the actual write can be performed a few seconds later. When the SD embedded controller receives multiple write operations, later write operations are often delayed until the card has finished current operations. To force all data to be written to a file, use `flush()`.

```
flush(file);
```

This operation is also called automatically when a file is closed with `close()`.

Advanced Usage

The SD library actually makes use of three internal libraries: Sd2Card, SdVolume, and SdFile. All the functions present in the SD library are wrapper functions that call different functions in these three libraries. The SD library follows the Arduino philosophy, making it easy to do advanced functions. However, you can still use these three libraries if you need access to even more advanced functions.

```
Sd2Card card;
SdVolume volume;
SdFile root;
```

There are numerous functions, and these functions are mainly out of the scope of this book, but there are a few that may be of interest.

To get information about the card size, you can get data about the geometry of the SD card—that is, the number of *clusters* and the number of *blocks* per cluster.

```
unsigned long volumesize = volume.blocksPerCluster();
volumesize *= volume.clusterCount();
volumesize *= 512;
```

On SD cards, blocks are always 512 bytes. You can get the amount of blocks per cluster, and the amount of clusters on the card, giving you the card size, in bytes.

More utility functions are listed in the example program: CardInfo. It is available in the Arduino IDE: Files ⇨ Examples ⇨ SD ⇨ CardInfo.

Example Program and Sketch

For this application, you build a data-logging application. The aim is to understand how sunlight evolves during a day. For this, you will require several components, but the sensor in this application is a light dependent resistor, or LDR for short. An LDR will have variable resistance depending on the amount of sunlight (or artificial light) it receives. The circuit for this example will require a pull-down resistor in order to create a circuit known as a *voltage divider*. This is illustrated in Figure 12-5. The voltage at Vin is always 5 volts, and depending on the resistance of the LDR, the voltage at Vout will be somewhere between the maximum of 5 volts and the minimum of 0 volts, depending on the light being received.

When there is no light, the resistance or the LDR will be high, and the reference voltage will be closer to zero. When there is a lot of sunlight, the resistance will be weak, and the reference voltage will be closer to 5 volts. This reference is read by an ADC on the Arduino's A3 pin. The ADC will compare the voltage on the pin to the 5 Volts the Arduino runs off. It will return a value between 0 and 1023, and depending on the component you use, it is possible to calculate the Lux value of visible light.

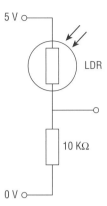

Figure 12-5: An LDR in a voltage divider setup

Knowing the present amount of light is not very useful; it would be better if the data could be logged so that you can see the evolution of light levels during the day. For that, data will have to be logged. You could use the built-in EEPROM, but EEPROM storage is limited, and getting data back onto your PC could be complicated. SD cards have much larger capacity and can easily be removed from the Arduino and read on any computer. Also, using an SD card has another benefit; the resulting file can be formatted into a specific file type. For this application, you can create a CSV file (short for Comma Separated Values). This file can be imported directly into any spreadsheet application, allowing you to use the data to create graphs.

The schematic will be simple; only a few components are required for this operation, but this application does require a shield with SD capability. The schematic is listed in Figure 12-6.

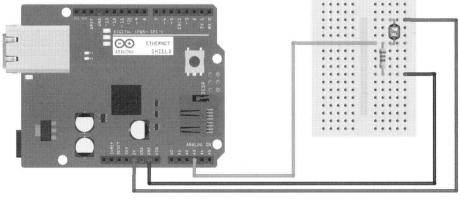

Figure 12-6: Project schematic (Image created with Fritzing)

As with most shields, the I/O lines remain accessible. You can plug in the cables straight on the Ethernet shield, and they will work in exactly the same way.

Use the code in Listing 12-1 to write the sketch.

Listing 12-1: Sketch (filename: `Chapter12.ino`**)**

```
1   #include <SD.h>
2   #include <SPI.h>
3   const int chipSelect = 4; // Change this as required
4
5   int light;
6   int lightPin = A3;
7   unsigned int iteration = 1;
8
9
10  void setup()
11  {
12    Serial.begin(9600);
13
14    Serial.print("Initializing SD card...");
15    // Chip Select pin needs to be set to output for the SD library
16    pinMode(10, OUTPUT);
17
18    // Attempt to initialize SD library
19    if (!SD.begin(chipSelect)) {
20      Serial.println("Card failed, or not present");
21      // don't do anything more:
22      return;
23    }
24    Serial.println("Card initialized.");
25  }
26
27  void loop()
28  {
29    // Get a light level reading
30    light = analogRead(lightPin);
31
32  // Open the SD data file
33  File dataFile = SD.open("light.txt", FILE_WRITE);
34
35  // Has the file been opened?
36  if (dataFile)
37  {
38    // Create a formatted string
39    String dataString = "";
40    dataString += String(iteration);
41    dataString += ",";
42    dataString += String(light);
43    dataString += ",";
44
```

```
45      // Print data to the serial port, and to the file  .
46      Serial.println(dataString);
47      dataFile.println(dataString);
48
49      // Close the file
50      dataFile.close();
51    }
52
53    // Increase the iteration number
54    iteration++;
55
56    // Sleep for one minute
57    delay(60 * 1000);
58  }
```

The sketch begins by importing the SD library and the SPI library. Three variables and one constant are defined. The chipSelect constant should refer to the pin that acts as the CS pin for the SD card on your board. On the Ethernet board specified at the beginning of this chapter, the SD card is connected to pin 4. Refer to the documentation of your shield if you're unsure. This is the pin that will be used to talk to the SD card. The light variable will hold the sensor value from the LDR. The lightPin is the pin on which these readings will take place. Finally, the iteration variable will show the number of readings; it will be used to format your data in a spreadsheet.

setup() begins with configuring the serial port for debugging, something you are probably used to by now. On line 14, a status message is sent serially from the Arduino, telling the user that the SD card is about to be initialized. The SD card initialization is done on line 19, but before that, on line 16, the Arduino's default Chip Select pin (digital pin 10) is set as an output. This is required for the SD library to work, even if the pin is not connected to your card. The SD library will fail without this.

The SD card is initialized on line 19, by using the pin previously defined in the chipSelect constant. If the SD card fails to initialize, but your card is correctly formatted in FAT32, check to see if you are using the right pin number for your board. If the initialization fails, the sketch will inform the user; otherwise a message will be printed to the serial port informing that everything went well.

loop() starts on line 27. First, the sketch reads the value on the lightPin and stores it in the light variable. When this data has been read in, it is time to open the SD file. This is done on line 33; the sketch calls the file called light.txt. If this file exists, it will be opened; otherwise, the file will be created. Because the sketch uses the FILE_WRITE parameter, it will be opened for reading and writing. The sketch then checks if the file has been opened on line 36. If it is open, a String is created, and populated with data: the iteration variable and the light variable, separated by a comma. On line 46, this string is printed to the serial port, and then, using SD.println(), appended to the data file. After this has been done, the file is closed, and all the data is flushed to the SD card.

Why is the file closed after every write? It is good practice to close a file when it is not needed, and it forces data to be flushed to the SD card. On embedded systems, you do not know when the user may unplug the system. Leaving a file open could potentially mean that data is left unwritten and therefore lost. Closing the file ensures that data is written as soon as possible, and the SD card is left in a clean state.

The result of this sketch creates a text file that can be imported into a spreadsheet, like Excel or LibreOffice Calc. The results of a sunrise in my city are shown in Figure 12-7. The ambient light level is already at 200 due to street lights, but something happened at the 16-minute mark—the visible light suddenly dropped down considerably, but only for a minute. This was probably the sensor being blocked—probably by my cat—but it shows that surprises can happen!

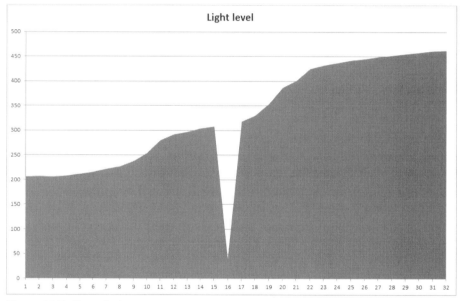

Figure 12-7: Example data output

Summary

In this chapter, you have seen how to connect an SD card to your Arduino using different methods, and how to initialize the card. I have shown how to read and write data to the card, and how that data can be used later to give visual results. In the next chapter, I will show you how to make an even more visual impact using TFT screens.

CHAPTER 13

This chapter discusses the following functions of the TFT library:

- `TFT()`
- `begin()`
- `width()`
- `height()`
- `background()`
- `text()`
- `setTextSize()`
- `point()`
- `line()`
- `rect()`
- `circle()`
- `stroke()`
- `fill()`
- `noStroke()`
- `noFill()`
- `loadImage()`

- `isValid()`
- `image()`

The hardware needed to use the example in this chapter includes:

- Arduino Uno
- LM35 Temperature sensor
- Adafruit ST7735 TFT breakout board (available at `http://www.adafruit.com/product/358`)
- Micro-SD card
- Breadboard
- Connection cables
- 10-kilohm resistor
- Light Dependent Resistor

You can find the code download for this chapter at `http://www.wiley.com/go/arduinosketches` on the Download Code tab. The code is in the Chapter 13 download folder and the filename is `chapter13.ino`.

Introduction

Computer enthusiasts love their hardware, and one of the most loved (and most feared) devices is the humble monitor. When you talk about a monitor, some people immediately think about a previous technology, known as CRT.

Cathode Ray Tubes (CRT for short) was the technology used by televisions and monitors for decades. Put simply, it is an electron canon; a device at one end blasts out electrons onto a fluorescent screen. Large magnets divert the electron beam to hit specific places on the screen, causing the screen to light up at distinct points. Of course, electrons are highly susceptible to atmospheric impurities, and even air, so the gun and the screen were encased inside a large glass shell in a vacuum. To avoid becoming too fragile, the glass was often thick, and to block most X-ray radiation, the glass used often was lead glass. Devices could be made fairly small but were often deep. (In extreme cases, CRTs were as deep as they were wide, but most were about one-half as deep as they were wide.) They have been used as televisions, of course, but also on oscilloscopes, data output, signaling, aircraft cockpits, and even as memory devices.

CRT screens could produce beautiful images but at a cost. The bigger they were, the heavier they got. A 27-inch CRT TV could weigh more than 100 lbs (40 kg). One of the largest and heaviest was a 40-inch screen that weighed in at 750 lbs (340 kg). If you wanted a big screen, you made sure you had friends available to help you install it.

The arrival of LCD screens changed home theater technology at a speed that has rarely been seen. LCD seems to have many advantages over CRT; it is relatively cheap, lightweight, robust, and easier to recycle. Screens could suddenly become bigger, but ironically, they could also become smaller. Large CRT screens were impractical for their size, but similarly, who could honestly imagine a mobile telephone with a CRT screen? Old mobile computers did have CRT screens though. They weren't the clamshell shape that you can see today; rather, they were like large bricks. The keyboard came off the top, and on one side was a CRT screen with floppy drives on the other. LCD screens not only made mobile telephones possible, but also changed the way mobile computers are used.

Technologies

Many screen technologies have been introduced since the introduction of LCD displays, each generation addressing problems and inconveniences of the previous technology.

One of the first changes was the introduction of passive matrix addressing. This technology allowed a single pixel to be changed by addressing its x-and y-coordinates, and pixels retained their state until ordered to change. This technology was reliable but offered slow refresh rates and became impractical as the screen resolution increased.

Dual Scan, known as DSTN (short for dual-scan supertwist nematic), gave faster screen refresh rates but at the cost of sharpness and brightness. DSTN screens were uncomfortable for watching films; there was visible noise and smears on these screens. I can remember taking a long-haul flight where a new multimedia system was installed on every seat but using DSTN screens. (Previously, flying was like going to a cinema, one large screen for a single cabin.) The lack of screen comfort actually made me stop watching a film and prefer reading in-flight magazines.

TFT, short for Thin Film Transistor, is another technology for displays. Originally, it was much more expensive compared to DSTN panels, but production costs were reduced as demand increased. TFT allows for crystal clear text and graphics, with superb colors. TFT panels are used in almost all mobile devices and nonportable equipment such as televisions and computer monitors.

The ST7735 is an integrated circuit that can drive small-sized TFT displays (128 x 160 pixels in size). An Arduino or other device can communicate with the ST7735 which will talk to the screen. Because the driver has on-board memory for storing a video buffer, once it sends commands to the chip, the Arduino's memory is free for sketches and variables.

ST7735-based LCD screens are available from a large number of manufacturers. SainSmart, Adafruit, and Arduino sell LCD screens based on this device.

The controller can handle a large number of colors, up to 252,000 discrete values (though the library isn't capable of accessing all of them).

TFT Library

Arduino has its own TFT library capable of controlling small-factor TFT screens. The TFT library is based on the hard work from Adafruit Industries. Adafruit originally sold a board containing a TFT screen—the ST7735—and created two libraries to accompany that device: one for the ST7735 and a graphical library common to all its LCD TFT devices. The Arduino TFT library is based on the ST7735 library and the Adafruit GFX library. The primary difference between the Arduino and Adafruit libraries has to do with the way drawing commands are called. The Arduino TFT library tries to emulate the processing programming language for its commands. It "talks" via the SPI bus and is simple to use.

CROSS-REFERENCE SPI is presented in Chapter 7.

Initialization

To use the TFT library, you must first import it and the SPI library. As it relies on SPI for communication, it is imperative. This can be done automatically by importing the library from the Arduino IDE (go to the menu Sketch ⇨ Import Library ⇨ TFT), or import the library manually:

```
#include <TFT.h>
```

Next, the TFT object needs to be initialized. For this, it requires some information: the different pins used to communicate with the controller. It requires at least three pins: CS, DC, and RESET. The DC pin is for Data/Command and tells the controller if the information being sent is data or a command. CS is for Chip Select and is used by the SPI bus. The last pin is the RESET pin and it resets the TFT screen if necessary. This can also be placed onto the Arduino's reset pin. The TFT object is initialized as follows:

```
#define TFT_CS    10
#define TFT_DC    9
#define TFT_RESET  8

TFT screen = TFT(TFT_CS, TFT_DC, TFT_RESET);
```

The ST7735 is an SPI device, and as such, it uses the SPI MOSI, MISO, and CLK pins. These are already present on fixed pins on the Arduino, so it is not necessary to define them. If necessary, you can use software SPI, in which case, you need to define the MOSI and CLK pins. While hardware SPI is significantly faster for drawing objects on the screen, sometimes you may have to use those pins for other reasons. (MISO is not required for this controller.) Using software SPI, you would be declare pins as follows:

```
#define TFT_SCLK 4
#define TFT_MOSI 5
#define TFT_CS    10
#define TFT_DC    9
#define TFT_RESET 8

TFT screen = TFT(CS, DC, MOSI, SCLK, RESET);
```

NOTE The Arduino Esplora has a socket that is designed specifically for TFT screens. As such, it uses fixed pins and is not initialized in the same way. For more information on the Esplora, and how to use a TFT screen with the Esplora, see Chapter 21.

The last thing you need to do is to begin the TFT subsystem; to do this, use the `begin()` function:

```
screen.begin();
```

This function does not take any parameters and does not return any data.

Screen Preparation

For most graphics to work, it is essential to know the screen's size, that is, its *resolution*. The resolution is the number of pixels wide and the number of pixels high. Not all screens are the same size, both in terms of physical screen size and pixels. It is not always possible to know the physical screen size, but you can ask the library the screen's resolution. There are two functions for this: one that returns the screen height and one that reports the screen width. For this, use `width()` and `height()`.

```
int scrwidth = screen.width();
int scrheight = screen.height();
```

Neither of these functions take any parameters, and both return `int` values—the size in pixels.

Before using the screen, it is often necessary to clear the screen of any text and graphics. Performing a screen wipe is good practice when initializing an LCD screen. It might be a cold boot (where the system was powered off before use) in which case the screen is probably blank, or a warm boot (where the system was reset but was already powered) in which case there may be text and graphics on the screen. To clear the screen of any graphics, use the `background()` function:

```
screen.background(red, green, blue);
```

This function requires three parameters: the red, green, and blue components of the color to be used. The `red`, `green`, and `blue` parameters are `int` variables and contain 8-bit color levels (from 0 to 255). The screen does not display colors with full 8-bit colors per channel. The red and blue values are scaled to 5 bits (32 steps each), while the green is scaled to 6 bits (64 steps). The advantage of scaling these values in the library means that the Arduino can read in graphics data with 8-bit components without the need to modify them.

Text Operations

The Arduino TFT library has support for text operations enabling you to write text directly onto the screen without having to do any complicated calculations. Writing text is as simple as specifying the text and the coordinates. The TFT library does the rest.

To write text to the screen, use `text()`.

```
screen.text(text, xPos, yPos);
```

The `text` parameter is the text to be written on the screen as a `char` array. The `xPos` and `yPos` coordinates are integers and correspond to the top-left corner of the text.

Computer screens use an x,y coordinate system, but unlike coordinates that you see in mathematics, computer screens use a slightly different way. The origin or coordinate 0,0 is the top-left corner of a screen. The x-value increases the further to the right it goes, and the y-value increases the further down it goes. This is illustrated in Figure 13-1.

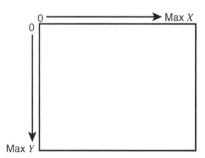

Figure 13-1: Computer screen coordinate system

Unlike in serial consoles, text written to the TFT screen does not wrap automatically. That is to say, if the length of the text written to the screen is wider than the screen's width, it is not automatically put onto the next line. You must be sure not to write too much data. Text written outside the screen is ignored.

Text can be printed in several sizes; for this, use `setTextSize()`:

```
screen.setTextSize(size);
```

The `size` parameter is an `int` between 1 and 5. It corresponds to the height of the text in pixels divided by 10: text size 1 is 10-pixels high, text size 2 is 20-pixels high, and so on. The size can go up to 5 for text that is 50-pixels high. By default, text size is set to 1. This function does not change any text already present on the screen but sets the size for all future calls to the `text()` function.

Basic Graphics

The Arduino TFT library also has functions for graphical operations: drawing lines, circles, and dots. It is with these simple tools that you can create advanced graphics, graphs, and interfaces.

The most basic of all drawing functions is the point. This simply places one pixel at the specified coordinates:

```
screen.point(xPos, yPos);
```

The `xPos` and `yPos` parameters are `int` values and represent the location of the pixel to be drawn on screen.

The next drawing function is the line, which connects a pair of coordinates to each other. It is called like this:

```
screen.line(xStart, yStart, xEnd, yEnd);
```

The `xStart` and `yStart` parameters are `int` values and specify the start coordinates. The `xEnd` and `yEnd` parameters are also `int` values and specify the end coordinates. A solid line is drawn between these two points.

You can create a rectangle with four lines, but Arduino offers a way to do this automatically using `rect()`.

```
screen.rect(xStart, yStart, width, height);
```

Just like `line()`, this function takes a pair of coordinates as `int` values that corresponds to the top-left corner of a rectangle. The `width` and `height` parameters correspond to the width and height of the rectangle, in pixels. The lines will be drawn parallel to the screen edges. All four angles will be right angles.

To draw circles, use `circle()`:

```
screen.circle(xPos, yPos, radius);
```

The xPos and yPos parameters are int values and specify the center of the circle. The radius parameter, also an int, is the radius of the circle to print, in pixels.

Coloring

All the graphical functions take coordinates and parameters to define their size and shape but do not take parameters for color. This is done through different functions. The philosophy is this: you tell the controller what color you want to use, and all subsequent drawing will use that color.

Color functions aren't used only for lines but also for any filled spaces. A rectangle can have one color for the lines defining its boundary, while the interior of the rectangle could be a different color. By specifying a fill color, anything present inside the rectangle would be erased by a solid color. The color can be any RGB value. It's also possible to declare no color, in which case the color is "transparent"; where any existing pixels are left untouched.

This is accomplished using two functions: stroke() and fill(). To define the color of points and lines, use stroke():

```
screen.stroke(red, green, blue);
```

This function takes three int values; 8-bit values for the red, green, and blue components. Again, these values are scaled down to what the TFT screen is capable of displaying. When this function is called, no previous drawings are modified; only future calls to drawing elements will be affected. This function works only on points, lines, and outline graphics for circles and rectangles. To specify how to fill a circle or rectangle, use fill():

```
screen.fill(red, green, blue);
```

Again, it takes three int values: the red, green, and blue components expressed as 8-bit values.

To set the outline color as transparent, use the noStroke() function:

```
screen.noStroke();
```

To set the fill color as transparent, use the noFill() function:

```
screen.noFill();
```

Graphic Images

If you were creating a weather station with graphic icons on an LCD screen, it would be possible to create a basic geometric image representing the Sun. Lightning would be a little more difficult to render and clouds are quite complicated. It is much easier to use a ready-made image file to load and display on the screen. The TFT library can do this off of an SD card.

Most modules and shields that use the ST7735 controller also have an SD-card slot that can read micro-SD cards. They are an excellent way to store large amounts of data like images. Because SD-card controllers use SPI and the ST7735 device is also an SPI device, it is easy to combine the two; they both share the MOSI/MISO/CLK lines. All that is needed is another slave select pin.

CROSS-REFERENCE   SPI is explained in more detail in Chapter 7. SD card usage is explained in Chapter 12.

To load an image directly from an SD card, use `loadImage()`:

```
PImage image = screen.loadImage(name);
```

The name parameter is the filename to be loaded from an SD card. This function returns a `PImage` object. A `PImage` object is the base class used to draw bitmap images onto a TFT screen. It contains the image data and can be used to write an image to a specific place on the screen. When this object has been loaded, you can retrieve information about it. You can use two functions to get the image width and height, and another function verifies the validity of the data.

```
width = image.width();
height = image.height();
```

These two functions are called on the `PImage` object, and both functions return an `int`, corresponding to the width and height of the image in pixels.

To verify that the `PImage` object is valid, use `isValid()`:

```
result = image.isValid();
```

This function, called on the `PImage` object, returns a boolean; `true` if the image is valid and `false` if there is a problem.

To display an image at specific coordinates, use `image()`:

```
screen.image(image, xPos, yPos);
```

The `image` parameter is the `PImage` object created when using the `loadImage()` function. The `xPos` and `yPos` parameters are the coordinates where the top-left corner of the image will be displayed.

Example Application

In the previous chapter, you created a system capable of data logging the level of sunlight. It is time to take that example a little further and to create a visual data logger application. Just how much light is there outside? And what is the temperature? Now you can put that together visually on a TFT screen.

The temperature will be a real-time readout, but the light levels will be over a period of time shown as a graph. To make things look nice, a background image will display. The graph displays from left to right, and when the graph reaches the far right side, the screen refreshes, and the graphs starts over again.

Hardware

The screen used in this example is the Adafruit ST7735 breakout board. Adafruit sells an LCD screen by itself, but this is not what you want. A screen without any additional hardware may be great for creating your own device after a prototype has been made, but to create this sketch, you need the ST7735 breakout board, a more complete version that is hosted on its own PCB, with pins that can be placed onto a breadboard. As an added bonus: the breakout board also has a micro-SD slot, which will come in handy for this project.

The breakout board must be hooked up to the SPI bus. It has two chip select pins: one for the embedded SD-card controller, and one for the TFT screen itself. The SD-card reader is also an SPI device, and therefore it will share the SPI bus with the ST7735, but it needs its own chip select pin. The device also has a Lite pin, allowing the Arduino to turn on the TFT backlight.

To get a temperature reading, use an LM35 temperature sensor connected to A0, and to get a light level reading, use a photo-resistor on A1.

The assembly is shown in Figure 13-2. The SPI MISO and MOSI pins are connected to the TFT breakout board's SPI pins, as well as the clock line. The backlight pin is connected to the 5-volt rail, turning the TFT's backlight on as soon as it is powered. The SD–controller chip select is connected to the Arduino's D4 pin, and the TFT chip select is connected to D10. There are two remaining pins—D/C, combined with the SPI pins, will be used to tell the TFT screen if this is a command or data, and the Reset pin is also used to reset the TFT screen if required.

Sketch

Now comes the fun part; it is time to put everything together. The sketch that you will be using to start off with is shown in Listing 13-1.

Listing 13-1: TFT Sketch (filename: `Chapter13.ino`)

```
1    // Required headers
2    #include <SD.h>
3    #include <TFT.h>
4    #include <SPI.h>
5
6    // Pin definitions
7    #define TFT_CS    10
8    #define SD_CS      4
```

```
9    #define DC      9
10   #define RST     8
11
12   int lightPos = 0;
13   int currentTemp = 1;
14
15   PImage backgroundIMG;
16
17   // Create an instance of the TFT library
18   TFT screen = TFT(TFT_CS, DC, RST);
19
20   // Char array for printing text on the screen
21   char tempPrintout[10];
22
23   void setup()
24   {
25     // Initialize the screen
26     screen.begin();
27
28     // TFT screen will first be used to output error messages
29     screen.stroke(255, 255, 255);
30     screen.background(0, 0, 0); // Erase the screen
31
32     // Initialize the SD card
33     if (!SD.begin(SD_CS))
34     {
35       screen.text("Error: Can't init SD card", 0, 0);
36       return;
37     }
38
39     // Load and print a background image
40     backgroundIMG = screen.loadImage("bg.bmp");
41     if (!backgroundIMG.isValid())
42     {
43       screen.text("Error: Can't open background image", 0, 0);
44       return;
45     }
46
47     // Now that the image is validated, display it
48     screen.image(backgroundIMG, 0, 0);
49
50     // Set the font size to 50 pixels high
51     screen.setTextSize(5);
52   }
53
54   void loop()
55   {
56
57     // Get a light reading
58     int lightLevel = map(analogRead(A1), 0, 1023, 0, 64);
59
```

Continues

Listing 13-1 *continued*

```
60   // Have we reached the edge of the screen?
61   if (lightPos == 160)
62   {
63     screen.image(backgroundIMG, 0, 0);
64     screen.stroke(0, 0, 255);
65     screen.fill(0, 0, 255);
66     screen.rect(100, 0, 60, 50);
67     lightPos = 0;
68   }
69
70   // Set up line color, and draw a line
71   screen.stroke(127, 255, 255);
72   screen.line(lightPos, screen.height() - lightLevel,
73       lightPos, screen.height());
74   lightPos++;
75   // Get the temperature
76   int tempReading = analogRead(A2);
77   int tempC = tempReading / 9.31;
78
79   // Has the temperature reading changed?
80   if (tempC != currentTemp)
81   {
82     // Need to erase previous text
83     screen.stroke(0, 0, 255);
84     screen.fill(0, 0, 255);
85     screen.rect(100, 0, 60, 50);
86
87     // Set the font color
88     screen.stroke(255, 255, 255);
89
90     // Convert the reading to a char array, and print it
91     String tempVal = String(tempC);
92     tempVal.toCharArray(tempPrintout, 4);
93     screen.text(tempPrintout, 120, 5);
94
95     // Update the temperature
96     currentTemp = tempC;
97   }
98
99   // Wait for a moment
100  delay(2000);
101 }
```

On the first few lines of the sketch, you import the libraries that will be required for this project: the TFT library for the LCD screen, the SD library for the SD card reader, and the SPI library, which is required for communication by the other libraries.

On the following lines, some pin declarations are made; these are the pins that will be used for the TFT screen. RST is the reset pin that will be used to reset the TFT screen when the TFT subsystem is ready, or as required by the sketch. DC is used as an extension to SPI to tell the TFT screen if the incoming message is either data, or an instruction. Also, the chip select pins for both the TFT screen and the SD card reader.

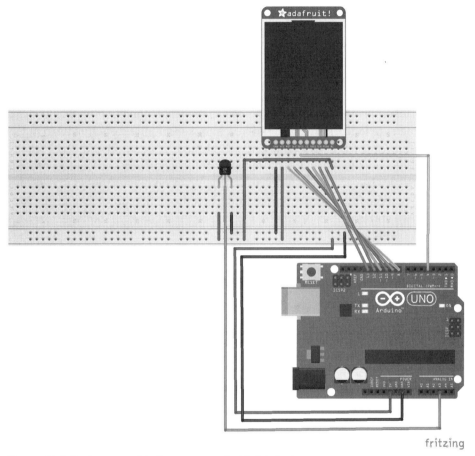

Figure 13-2: Project assembly (Image created with Fritzing)

On lines 12 and 13, two int variables are declared: lightPos and currentTemp. These two variables contain the graph position and the current temperature, respectively.

On line 15, a PImage object is created, called background. This is where the sketch loads an image into memory and allows you to display a background image on the screen.

On line 18, a TFT object, named screen, is created. It is instantiated with three arguments, the three pins used to control the screen. The SPI wires are not specified because they are on fixed pins. Because they cannot be changed, there is no need to specify them.

On line 21, another variable is created, a `char` array called `tempPrintout`. This will be used to store the temperature that will be printed out on the screen.

On line 23, `setup()` is declared. There are a lot of things to configure in this sketch, so `setup()` will have a lot of work to do. First, communication with the screen is started on line 26. In this example, the TFT screen is used for debug messages, so it must be set up to display any status messages before proceeding. On line 29, `stroke()` is called, informing the TFT screen of the color that should be used for future drawing events, including text messages. To make sure that any text is readable, `background()` is called, setting the screen to black.

On line 33, the sketch attempts to initialize the SD library. In case of failure, `text()` is called with a message at coordinates 0,0. This results in some text being displayed on the top-left corner of the screen. If the SD library did start, the next step is to load an image. The sketch looks for a file called bg.bmp in the root directory of the SD card. If it finds the image, it places it into the PImage object `backgroundIMG`. The sketch then tests the contents of `backgroundIMG` for a valid graphics file. If the contents are not valid, a text error message displays on the TFT screen. If the contents are valid, then the background image displays on the screen starting at coordinates 0,0, the top-left corner. Finally, text size is set to 5; 50 pixels high.

`loop()` is declared on line 54. This function begins by reading in the light level the voltage on pin A3. The analog-to-digital converter returns values varying from 0 to 1023, but the sketch would like a different value. Ideally, these values should not exceed 64. The screen is 128 pixels high, and the graph takes up the lower portion of the screen, so 64 is an excellent maximum. The ideal function to do this is `map()`. Next, the sketch needs to print a new line on the graphs, but before doing that, there is one question that needs answering; has the graph reached the edge of the screen? This is checked in the `if()` statement on line 61. If the graph has reached the edge of the screen, several things need to be done. First, the background image is refreshed, erasing anything present on the screen. Next, both the stroke and fill graphics are set to blue. Then, a rectangle is printed, where the temperature is supposed to go. Finally, the `lightPos` variable is set to 0, the left side of the screen.

On line 72, a line is drawn on the screen. The first set of arguments are the *x* and *y* starting coordinates of the line, and the second set of coordinates is screen and *y*-end coordinates of the line. `height()` and the value from the light sensor are used to determine the length of the line on the *y*-axis.

Now that the light level has been calculated and drawn on screen, it is time to look at the temperature. The analog value of the LM35 is read in, and a small conversion is made to transform the value into a temperature in Celsius. Now the sketch checks if the temperature has changed. Erasing a portion of the screen and printing a new number can cause a visible flicker. Because the temperature shouldn't vary that much, a simple system has been put in place to print the temperature when a change is detected. The comparison is made on line 80, using an `if()` statement. If the temperature has changed since the last reading, in lines 85 through 88 a background color is declared, the stroke color is changed, and a portion of the screen is erased. Before the text is displayed, the color is changed back to white.

Text must be supplied as a `char` array, but it is often much easier to print text into a `String`. On line 91 a `String` object called `tempVal` is created, storing the temperature as a `String`. The next line converts the `String` into a `char` array, storing it into the `tempPrintout`. This array is printed on the TFT screen at coordinates that match up with the rectangle you drew earlier.

Finally, the sketch is told to wait for 2 seconds before repeating.

Exercises

The temperature display is visible on the screen, but it could do with being a little prettier—or maybe even more colorful. Modify the sketch to change either the foreground or the background of the text according to the temperature; 15 degrees could be a cool blue and 35 a bright red.

Summary

In this chapter, you have seen what a TFT screen is, how it can be used for your projects, and how an Arduino communicates with it. You have seen how to initialize the screen, how to print text and pictures to the screen, as well as basic graphics in black and white and in color. In the next chapter, I will talk about servo motors and how to control them using an Arduino with just a few lines of code.

CHAPTER

14

Servo

This chapter discusses the following functions of servo motors:

- `attach()`
- `attached()`
- `write()`
- `writeMicroseconds()`
- `read()`
- `detach()`

The hardware needed to run the examples in this chapter includes:

- Arduino Uno
- USB Cable
- Breadboard
- LM35
- HYX-S0009 or equivalent servo motor

You can find the code download for this chapter at `http://www.wiley.com/go/arduinosketches` on the Download Code tab. The code is in the Chapter 14 download folder and the filename is `Chapter14.ino`.

Introduction to Servo Motors

Most motors are simple devices that turn on their axle when current is supplied. When a motor turns, the user generally has no idea about the angle or speed; to get this information, sensors are required. Servo motors differ by knowing exactly the angle that they are at and adjusting their position as required. Most servo motors cannot turn 360 degrees; instead, they are often limited to a range. Most servo motors have 180 degrees of rotation, as shown in Figure 14-1.

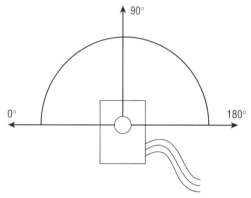

Figure 14-1: Servo motor movement

To know the exact position, servo motors can use a wide variety of techniques. Most use a potentiometer, using electrical resistance to understand how far the arm has turned, while more advanced systems use a coded optical wheel to get precise information.

Servo motors were originally designed in the dark times of war. They were used in radar and anti-aircraft artillery during World War II. Radar requires the angle of the emitter and receiver to be known because the position of the aircraft needs to be calculated and displayed on a screen. Anti-aircraft artillery needs to be placed at a precise angle depending on the results of the calculation, and servo motors could place heavy loads at the right angle much faster than humans and with more reliability.

Although it might seem strange to have a motor that does not make complete turns, servo motors have a wide range of uses. They are used in industrial systems to open and close valves; they are still used on radar or tracking equipment to point a device in the right direction with a high level of precision; and robots use servo motors to keep arms at a precise angle, while providing enough force to keep the arm in place with a high load. Hobbyists making remote controlled vehicles are familiar with servo motors because they are used to control steering. When the front wheels of a car turn left or right, this is a servo-motor acting, keeping the direction in place despite resistive force.

A servo motor is a motor assembly with additional sensors and logic. In short, an embedded microcontroller reads the angle of the output shaft, and controls a small motor.

Controlling Servo Motors

Most motors require only two wires: one for the power and one for the ground. Stepper motors are slightly different, having several wires to move a motor by a specific number of degrees, but still have no embedded intelligence. (Stepper motors are explained in Chapter 15.) Servo motors are different; most require three wires. One wire is for power, one is for the ground connection, and the third one is for sending orders to the servo motor.

Servo motors use pulse width modulation (PWM) to receive instructions. Pulse width modulation uses short and precise pulses of digital signals to transmit information. PWM was first presented in Chapter 4.

A servo expects a pulse every 20 milliseconds. The length of the pulse instructs the servo motor to move to a specific angle. The PWM signals vary between a ½ and 2 ½ milliseconds. A ½ millisecond pulse instructs the servo motor to move to its minimum position, and a 2 ½ millisecond pulse tells the Servo motor to move to its maximum position. A 1 ¼ millisecond pulse will move to the central position.

The question is, "How exactly can this be done in an Arduino?" The PWM interface on an Arduino does not have the same timings as servo motor controls, and it is easy to make a mistake and make a pulse longer than 2 milliseconds. Fortunately, the Arduino abstraction layer makes this extremely easy, requiring only a few instructions.

Most boards allow up to 12 Servo motors to be connected at any one time, with the exception of the Arduino Mega, which can control up to 48 motors. However, this comes at a small price. Using the Servo library automatically disables PWM operations on pins 9 and 10. Again, the Arduino Mega is an exception and can happily use up to 12 Servo motors without interference. Any more than 12 servo motors results in PWM being disabled on pins 11 and 12.

NOTE In Arduino 0016 and earlier, only two servos were supported, on pins 9 and 10.

Connecting a Servo Motor

Servo motors typically have three wires. The power wire, usually red, is connected to the power rail. The ground wire, usually black or brown, is connected to the ground rail. The third wire, usually yellow or orange, is the signal wire and is connected directly to a digital pin on the Arduino. The Arduino can normally directly supply power to a servo motor, but when using several servo motors, you need to separate the Arduino power supply to the servo power supply to avoid brown outs. Servo motors, even if they do not always act like typical motors, still have a small motor inside and can draw large amounts of current, far more than what the ATmega can deliver.

Before using servo motors, you must import the Servo library. You can do this either by importing the library through the Arduino IDE menu (Sketch ⇨ Import Library ⇨ servo) or by manually typing:

```
#include <Servo.h>
```

In your software, you must first create a new servo object before issuing instructions. You must create one object per servo motor (or group of servo motors) to control.

```
Servo frontWheels;
Servo rearWheels;
```

To tell the Arduino which pins the servo motors are connected to, call `attach()`, specifying the pin, and optionally, specifying the minimum and maximum pulse size.

```
servo.attach(pin)
servo.attach(pin, min, max)
```

By default, Arduino uses 544 microseconds as the minimum pulse length (equivalent to 0 degrees) and 2,400 microseconds as the maximum pulse width (equivalent to 180 degrees). If your servo motor has different settings for a maximum and minimum pulse, you can change the values in `attach()` by specifying the durations in microseconds. For example, a servo motor that uses a 1 millisecond minimum and 2 millisecond maximum can be configured like this:

```
servo.attach(pin, 1000, 2000);
```

From then on, the Arduino automatically calculates the length of the pulse according to the wanted angle but will not issue commands until a function specifically orders the servo motor to move.

Moving Servo Motors

Telling a servo motor to move to a specific angle is easily accomplished using `write()`. The Arduino will do all the necessary calculations; determining the length of the pulse to generate and sending the pulse on time:

```
servo.write(angle);
```

The `angle` parameter is an integer number, from 0 to 180, and represents the angle in degrees.

If you require precision, you can specify the length of the pulse by using the `writeMicroseconds()` function. This eliminates the need for calculation by the Arduino and specifies the exact pulse length, an integer, expressed in microseconds:

```
servo.writeMicroseconds(microseconds);
```

It does not matter what the original position was, the servo motor automatically adjusts its position. The Arduino does not need to calculate this either; all the intelligence is embedded inside the motor assembly. It does, however, keep the last angle that it was instructed to use, and this value can be fetched with `read()`:

```
int angle = servo.read()
```

Remember that servo motors can receive only instructions and not return information. The value returned by `read()` is the value inside the Arduino. When connecting a servo motor, there is no way to know what position it was in initially. It can be helpful to set a servo motor to a default position before starting your application. (For example, a remote-controlled car should probably have the wheels turn so that they are at 90 degrees; without adjusting the steering, the owner would expect the car to go straight and not at an angle.)

Servo motors and other physical objects take time to get to where you want them to be, so it's considered good practice to give your motor a bit of time to get where it wants to go. Some motors move faster than others, if you're unsure of how much time you'll need, it's best to check your motor's documentation.

Disconnecting

If required, servo motors can be disconnected inside sketches. To disconnect a servo, use `detach()`:

```
servo.detach()
```

Subsequent calls to `attached()` return `false`, and no more signals will be sent until the sketch calls `attach()` again.

Servo motors can be attached, detached, and re-attached in software. Sometimes a sketch needs to know the status of the devices connected at that time. To see if a servo motor is connected, you can use `attached()`:

```
result = servo.attached();
```

This function returns 1 (or `true`) if a servo motor has been declared as attached, and 0 (or `false`) otherwise. Note that this won't tell you if your motor is physically attached or not, just that it is connected in software.

Precision and Safety

Controlling multiple servo motors can be rather processor-intensive, and this can sometimes affect precision if you have a large amount of servos controlled by one Arduino. In extreme cases, slight angular distortion may be visible on servo motors with the lowest angular value. This is often in the range of 1 to 2 degrees.

There are situations in which using servo motors can be a safety issue. If used with robotics, one of the most basic rules of robotics is to never get in the way of a robotic arm. Imagine a robotic arm powered by servo motors that is to place an object in the user's hand. The movement must be precise and not go above or below a certain angle.

Using the Servo library does not stop interrupts. You can still respond to interrupts, and timing functions such as `millis()` still work, but remember that the end of a servo motor pulse can be lengthened by the time it takes to execute an interrupt handler. If your interrupt handler takes 200 microseconds to complete and is called close to the end of a servo's pulse, in the worst case, the pulse sent to the servo motor can be lengthened by 200 microseconds, meaning that the resulting angle is not what you expected. It will be corrected the next time a pulse is sent, and the servo motor will move to the correct angle. In most applications, this will not be a problem, but just keep this in mind if your application has an absolute limit that must not be exceeded.

Example Application

Servo motors can be used for a variety of projects, from remote controlled cars to robotics. To keep things simple, this section uses a servo motor to create a retro-style thermometer. In the digital age, you might sometimes forget what these devices used to look like. Mercury thermometers are usually long glass objects, with a straight line, but some thermometers are round, and have a hand similar to clocks. A servo motor can be used to move the hand, controlled by an Arduino that gets a temperature reading from an external component, perfect for indoor or outdoor temperature readings.

This example uses an LM35. The LM35 is an inexpensive and readily available precision temperature sensor calibrated in Celsius, and illustrated in Figure 14-2. It can be used to sense temperatures between –55° C and +150° C by adding a resistor and a reference voltage, but without any additional resistor, it can sense temperatures between 0° C and 100° C. The LM35 outputs 10 mV for each degree, from 0 V for 0° C to 1,000 mV (or 1 V) for 100° C.

Figure 14-2: An LM35

However, the Arduino's analog-to-digital converters are normally calibrated from 0 to 5 volts, but the LM35 will never output 5 volts. To compare analog values, the Arduino will compare the input to something called a *reference*—a voltage. Generated inside the microcontroller, this reference is normally set to the same voltage as the Arduino's power. The reference voltage can be changed so instead of sampling values between 0 and 5 volts, the Arduino can be told to sample between 0 and 1.1 volts. You do this by calling `analogReference (INTERNAL)`. This will give more precision for this application, but it comes at a price. If using the `INTERNAL` constant, this sketch will not run correctly on an Arduino Mega; it will require changing. When this example is complete, it will be up to you, the designer, to choose if you want to sample on 5 V and keep compatibility or to use a different sample range and only use specific boards.

By using a reference of 1.1 V, the 10-bit ADC will have a sampling precision of 1.1 divided by 1,024, or 1.07 mV. The LM35 outputs 10 mV per degree, so 10 divided by 1.07 is approximately 9.31. So, a change of 9.31 in the analog reading equals 1 degree. To get a reading in Celsius, simply get the return value and divide by 9.31.

The sketch can now retrieve temperatures between 0 and 100 degrees Celsius, but this range is too large. If your internal thermometer is showing 100 degrees, your house might be on fire, and you shouldn't be looking at your thermometer. If the outside reading is 100 degrees, something is wrong. In both cases, there is no use in displaying the temperature, so everything above 50 will be ignored.

Finally, the last part will be to convert a temperature into the servo motor movement. For this example, the servo motor will be mounted so that the 0–180 degrees line is parallel to the floor. Ninety degrees will be straight up. The temperature hand will move only between 45 degrees and 135 degrees.

This brings a question: How should the temperature be converted to an angle? This sounds like a lot of complicated calculation; 0 degrees Celsius is 45 degrees for the Servo motor, and 50 degrees Celsius will be an angle of 135 degrees. The truth is, there is no need to make any calculations; the Arduino will do that for you using `map()`, explained in Chapter 4. As a reminder, `map()` works like this:

```
result = map(value, fromLow, fromHigh, toLow, toHigh);
```

This function maps a number from one range to another, and that is exactly what is in this example: two ranges. Temperature values vary from 0 to 50, and angles vary from 45 to 135. Therefore, with a single function, the Arduino will automatically calculate the output to the stepper motor, converting a temperature range to an angle range.

Schematic

This application uses an Arduino Uno. The LM35 will be connected to analog pin 0, and the servo will be connected to digital pin 9. The wiring that should be used is shown in Figure 14-3.

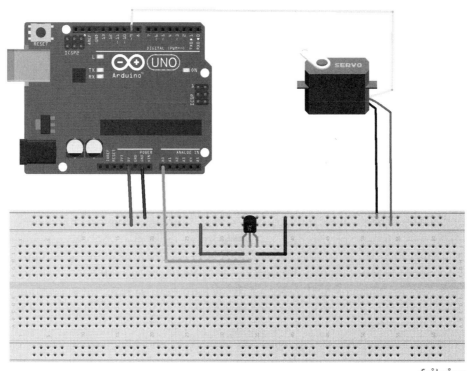

Figure 14-3: Temperature sensor application schematic (Image created with Fritzing)

Sketch

Time to write the sketch, as shown in Listing 14-1.

Listing 14-1: Sketch (filename: `Chapter14.ino`**)**

```
1    #include <Servo.h>
2
3    float tempC;
4    int angleC;
5    int reading;
6    int tempPin = A0;
7    int servoPin = 9;
8
9    Servo thServo;
10
11   void setup()
12   {
13     analogReference(INTERNAL);
14     Serial.begin(9600);
15     thServo.attach(servoPin);
16     thServo.write(90);
17     delay(1000);
18   }
19
20   void loop()
21   {
22     reading = analogRead(tempPin);
23     tempC = reading / 9.31;
24     angleC = map(tempC, 0, 50, 135, 45);
25     Serial.print(tempC);
26     Serial.print(" Celsius, ");
27     Serial.print(angleC);
28     Serial.println(" degrees");
29     thServo.write(angleC);
30     delay(500);
31   }
```

The work starts right from line 1. On the first line of the sketch, the Servo library is imported. On lines 3 to 7, variables are defined. The temperature is defined as a floating-point number, and all other variables are defined as integers.

On line 9, a `Servo` object is created, called `thServo`, short for thermometer Servo. This is the instance on which instructions will be called.

On line 11, the setup function is created. In this function, three things will be done. First, the reference voltage is set to `INTERNAL`, meaning the analog-to-digital converter will compare against a 1.1 V reference, not 5 volts as it would normally. This works for all analog inputs, and therefore, no pin is specified.

Second, a serial interface is created for debugging. Finally, the sketch is told to attach a servo motor on pin 9 (`servoPin`), and a default value is written. Ninety degrees is specified, moving the arm to a default position in the middle of the reading. The sketch is given 1 second to move, which is more than enough time.

On line 20, the `loop()` function is defined. First, the sketch reads the voltage from A0 , comparing it to 1.1 V. The result, returned as an integer, is stored in `reading`. Next, the variable `reading` is divided by 9.31 (calculated previously), and the result is stored in a floating-point number, called `tempC`. Next, the angle must be calculated. This is done through `map()`, by first indicating the values that are expected for the temperature (0 to 50) and next, the values expected as an angle (135 to 45). The numbers are inverted because this servo motor turns counterclockwise, and the lowest temperature is expected to be on the left.

On lines 25 to 28, data is printed to the serial port. This is used as debug information and can be omitted in a final version.

Finally, on line 29, the angle is written to the servo pin, and the sketch waits for one-half a second before repeating.

Congratulations, you have just created a retro thermometer!

Exercises

This sketch is fully functional but requires some tweaking to be optimal. For example, the servo motor movement may sometimes be a little erratic. Now look at the serial output to have a better idea:

```
22.34 Celsius, 86 degrees
22.77 Celsius, 86 degrees
23.20 Celsius, 88 degrees
```

So, the difference between 22.77 and 22.34 degrees Celsius does not result in a movement, but the difference between 22.77 and 23.20 degrees Celsius results in a 2-degree movement? This is the result of the `map()` function, and because it "translates" a 50-unit range to a 90-unit range, it will lose a little precision. If you need more precision, you will have to look at another way of controlling the servo motor. Try using `writeMicroseconds()` for greater accuracy.

Also, there is one requirement that was not put into place. Temperatures above 50 degrees Celsius should be ignored, but they aren't. `map()` specifies values between 0 and 50, and will "map" them to values between 45 and 135, but this does not mean that values are limited. If the input value is outside of the input range, it will also be outside of the output range. Try to limit input or output values, using `min()` and `max()`, or even better, use `constrain()`.

What solution did you come up with?

Summary

In this chapter, you have seen what a servo motor is and how it differs from typical motors. You have seen how it is controlled, and how to position it as required. In the next chapter, you will see another type of motor—the stepper motor—the functions used to control it, and an example application to put it all together.

Stepper

This chapter discusses the following functions of the Stepper library:

- `Stepper()`
- `setSpeed()`
- `step()`

The hardware needed to use these functions includes:

- Arduino Uno
- 1 x L293D
- 1 x 5-V bipolar stepper motor
- Breadboard
- Cables

You can find the code downloads for this chapter at `http://www.wiley` `.com/go/arduinosketches` on the Download Code tab. The code is in the Chapter 15 download and the filename is `Chapter15.ino`.

Introducing Motors

Electric motors generally work by creating electromagnetic fields from coils, forcing magnets on an axle to move, therefore driving the axle. By generating electromagnetic fields, a motor turns continuously until current is removed.

Servo motors (presented in Chapter 14) function a little differently, but even if their usage is different, a servo motor is still controlled by an ordinary electric motor managed by a small microcontroller to ensure the servo motor can move to a precise position.

Stepper motors are different. They have several coils inside, and the internal axle is "toothed." When applying current to one of the coils, the closest "tooth" is attracted to the coil, and the axle moves by a few degrees. Current is then removed from the coil and sent through another coil, again attracting a tooth and moving the axle by a few degrees. By repeating this operation, a stepper motor can be controlled to turn continuously in either direction, but this is not normally a stepper motor's main function. Stepper motors can have precise movement and as such can drive gears with equal precision.

Imagine a printer. Paper is fed into the printer, and the printer begins to print one line. A print head moves across the paper and deposits ink in precise locations according to the image that was sent to it. When the print head arrives at the far edge of the paper, the paper is fed into the printer, and the printer heads returns in the opposite direction, continuously printing until the end of the page. Feeding paper into the printer is extremely precise; too much paper and white lines appear on the sheet. Too little, and the resulting image will be squashed. The movement has to be precise and feed exactly the right amount of paper. Chances are, the motor feeding the paper into the printer is a stepper motor. Also, because the printer head requires precise positioning, there is a good chance that the belt used to attach the printer head assembly is also controlled by a stepper motor.

Stepper motors have several characteristics, but the most important one is the angle per "step." This can vary greatly in the different models, but ranges of between 2–5 degrees are common.

Controlling a Stepper Motor

Stepper motors are different from standard electrical motors, and as such, can be difficult to control. They require both software and hardware to be used. Fortunately, the hardware isn't difficult to use, and the Arduino software library is even easier.

Hardware

Stepper motors come in different sizes, and more important, different power ranges. It is common to find 12-V models, but this can be complicated for 5-V systems. Also, stepper motors tend to require higher current than what a microcontroller can provide. For most applications, a microcontroller cannot control a stepper motor directly; it must be interfaced with additional hardware. An H-Bridge is one type of component that can help use a stepper.

An H-bridge is an electronic component (or configuration of transistors) designed initially to control electric motors, as shown in Figure 15-1.

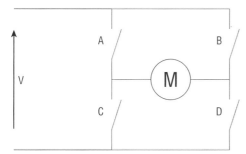

Figure 15-1: An H-bridge driver

By activating A and D, current can flow from the 12-volt rail, through a motor's electromagnet, to ground. This turns the motor in one direction. When activating B and C, the current flows in the opposite direction, and therefore the motor also turns in the opposite direction. This configuration also has the added bonus of allowing the motor to turn freely, by deactivating all inputs, or even to brake the motor by activating C and D.

Because an H-bridge controls one electromagnet and because stepper motors are composed of two or more electromagnet coils driven in sequence, a dual H-bridge can be used to drive a stepper motor. This is achieved by turning on specific coils and giving the motor enough time to align to that coil before turning it off and turning on another coil. By doing this, you can have a motor turn in a precise fashion, a few degrees at a time. The downside is that stepper motors are not as fast as classic motors, but they were not designed for speed. It is still possible to vary the motor speed by changing the frequency of the inputs, and stepper motors can still achieve relatively fast rotation speeds.

Unipolar Versus Bipolar Stepper Motors

Unipolar stepper motors have coils with a *center tap*, an electrical connection in the middle of the coil. This makes current switching easier; instead of inverting current, the center tap can be used as a grounding point for the current, and one pole or the other can be powered, therefore effectively inverting polarity without the need for complicated electronics. The center taps are often joined together, so these motors often have five leads.

Bipolar motors do not have a center tap; instead, the hardware must be used to invert current. As this inversion is easily achieved with an H-bridge, managing this is no longer a major factor. Bipolar motors do present a major advantage; because they have simplified coils, they can often achieve more torque for the same weight.

NOTE H-bridge drivers are commonly used for both unipolar and bipolar stepper motors, therefore no longer requiring the center tap, maximizing the torque of unipolar motors.

The Stepper Library

The Arduino IDE has built-in support for stepper motors through the Stepper library. To import the Stepper library, either add the library automatically via the Sketch ➪ Import Library ➪ Stepper menu item, or manually:

```
#include <Stepper.h>
```

To begin using a stepper motor, you must create a new instance of the Stepper class.

```
Stepper(steps, pin1, pin2);
Stepper(steps, pin1, pin2, pin3, pin4);
```

The `steps` parameter is an `int` which indicates the number of steps that your motor must make to complete one revolution. Some motors only document the number of degrees per step; in that case, divide that number by 360 to get the number of steps. The `pin1` and `pin2` parameters are digital output pins used for two lead stepper motors. The `pin3` and `pin4` parameters are used for motors with four leads. This is done like so:

```
Stepper myStepperMotor = Stepper(84, 5, 6, 7, 8);
```

Stepper motors turn by performing single steps, and to increase the speed of the motor, you must change the frequency at which steps are performed. To do this, use `setSpeed()`:

```
Stepper.setSpeed(rpm);
```

This function does not return any data and configures the output sequence to make the motor turn at the specified speed in revolutions per minute. The rpm parameter is a `long`. The final function is used to instruct the motor to move by a specific amount of steps:

```
Stepper.step(steps);
```

This function does not return any data and requires one parameter: `steps`. The `steps` parameter is an `int` and indicates the number of steps to perform. Depending on the wiring, positive values will cause the motor to turn in one direction, and negative values will make the motor turn the opposite direction. This function does not return until the task is complete, and depending on the amount of steps to perform, this can take a long time. During this time, the sketch cannot continue to perform other actions.

Example Project

In this project, you create another thermometer, one that varies slightly from the servo motor example in the previous example. An LM35 temperature sensor will connect to A0. The stepper motor will connect to digital pins 8, 9, 10, and 11 through a double H-bridge. This project is different from the previous because it will not show the exact temperature, but a variation. A stepper motor can maintain its position and provide force to keep the angle correctly positioned. A stepper motor cannot know its exact position; an order is given to move a certain number of steps in one direction or another, but it cannot know if the motor shaft has turned correctly. Maybe there was too much force involved, and the motor couldn't overpower the force. The advantage to this is that stepper motors can be repositioned; you can force the hand into a certain position and then let the motor reposition itself as required. This thermometer will not show the exact temperature, but a variation. The user can reposition the hand into a central position at any time, and by looking at the thermometer moments later, he will know if it is getting colder or warmer.

Hardware

This project uses an Arduino Uno for the control part of the project and an LM35 temperature sensor like in the servo example. It also uses an H-bridge controller and a 5-V stepper motor. Most H-bridges can use higher power motors, but with a less powerful motor the user can change the position of the motor by hand. An illustration of the circuit is shown in Figure 15-2.

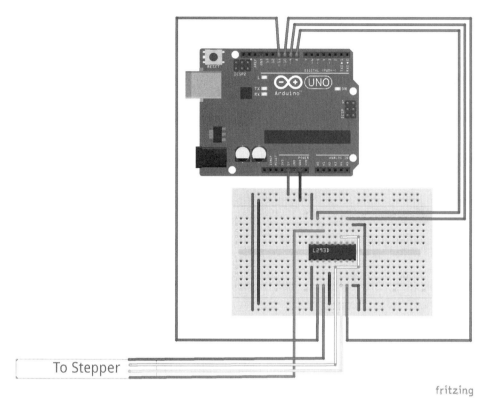

Figure 15-2: Project schematic (Image created with Fritzing)

Stepper motors often have different connections, depending on the make and model. See the documentation that came with your motor to see how to connect it.

Sketch

The sketch is the easy part of the project; this sketch simply reads the temperature and updates the position of the motor depending on temperature differences. The sketch is shown in Listing 15-1.

Listing 15-1: Stepper thermometer (filename: Chapter15.ino**)**

```
1    #include <Stepper.h>
2
3    // Set this to the number of steps your motor needs to make one turn
4    #define STEPS 100
5
6    // Stepper motor is connected to pins 8 to 11
7    Stepper stepper(STEPS, 8, 9, 10, 11);
```

```
8
9    // the previous reading from the analog input
10   int previous = 0;
11
12   void setup()
13   {
14     // Set a low stepper speed
15     stepper.setSpeed(10);
16
17     // Make a single temperature reading
18     previous = analogRead(0);
19   }
20
21   void loop()
22   {
23     // Get the sensor value
24     int val = analogRead(0);
25
26     // Move the stepper motor depending on the result
27     stepper.step(val - previous);
28
29     // Remember the previous value
30     previous = val;
31
32     delay(5000);
33   }
```

The `Stepper.h` file is required for any projects that use the stepper library, and this is included on line one of the sketch. On line 4, the amount of steps required to make a complete revolution is defined. Change this according to the stepper motor you have. On line 7, the Stepper instance is created using the amount of steps defined in `STEPS` and using digital lines 8 through 11.

`setup()` defined on line 12 does two things. First, it sets up the speed of the stepper motor to 10 rpm. This is a relatively slow speed, but the motor doesn't need to turn quickly. Secondly, it takes a reading from the temperature sensor to use as a reference value. The value is stored in `previous`, a variable defined on line 10.

On line 21, `loop()` is declared. In `loop()`, you'll first read the value of the analog pin into a variable called `val` and then change the stepper motor's position by the difference between `previous` and `val`. Finally, the contents of `previous` are replaced by the contents of `val`, and the sketch waits for 5 seconds before looping.

Summary

In this chapter, you have seen what a stepper motor is, how and where it is used, and how to control one with an Arduino. The example has given you an idea of how easy it is to use a stepper motor, and how you can use them in your own applications. In the next chapter, you will see the Firmata library, a control library that lets you read and write Arduino pins directly from a computer.

Firmata

This chapter discusses the following functions of the Firmata library:

- `begin()`
- `sendAnalog()`
- `sendDigitalPorts()`
- `sendDigital()`
- `sendString()`
- `available()`
- `processInput()`
- `attach()`
- `detach()`

The hardware needed to use the example in this chapter includes:

- Arduino Uno
- Computer
- USB cable
- Breadboard
- 4.7-kΩ resistor
- LED

Introducing Firmata

Arduinos are used in a wide variety of projects, from the most simple to some extremely complex devices. In most cases, their exact use is known; you know beforehand that digital pin 3 will be used to light an LED, and that analog input 4 will read the value of a light sensor. For some projects, you may not know what is connected, but you will still need to set pins as input or output, depending on the situation. Imagine a laboratory setup, one where you can study how new components work before deciding to use them in your projects. You could write a quick sketch each time to see how a component works, but this isn't always the best solution and certainly not the easiest. One way to easily set up your laboratory is to use Firmata.

Firmata is a protocol that communicates between computers and microcontrollers to easily access the Arduino hardware from software on a host machine. It uses standard serial commands and as such can be used on several different Arduino models. Messages are sent serially to and from the host computer, indicating pin status or requesting a pin to change state.

Firmata Library

To use the Firmata library, you must first import it. You can import the Firmata library from the Arduino IDE automatically, by going to the Sketch ➪ Import Library ➪ Firmata menu entry. Alternatively, you can write the lines manually:

```
#include <Firmata.h>
#include <Boards.h>
```

The Firmata protocol has several revisions, and if two devices use different revisions, that can lead to errors. To prevent this, you can specify which protocol revision to use with `setFirmwareVersion()`:

```
setFirmwareVersion(major, minor);
```

The `major` and `minor` parameters are `bytes`, which specify the revision to use. For most Arduino applications, this is set to major version 0 and minor version 1.

To begin using the Firmata library, you must first call `begin()`:

```
Firmata.begin();
Firmata.begin(speed);
```

This function opens a serial connection. By default, the speed is set to 57600 baud, but this can be changed by the optional speed parameter.

Sending Messages

The status of pins is sent as messages to and from the software on the host machine. Messages can be addressed to digital and analog pins. To send the status of an analog pin, use `sendAnalog()`:

```
Firmata.sendAnalog(byte pin, int value);
```

The pin parameter is the analog pin you are requesting information about. The value parameter is the value read from the pin. This function does not read the pin value directly; you must explicitly read the value first:

```
analogValue = analogRead(pin);
Firmata.sendAnalog(pin, analogValue);
```

Digital pins are sent differently. Because serial connections are slow, relative to the speed of a microprocessor, something had to be done to speed up the transfer. Digital pins are either on or off, 1 or 0. To send the maximum amount of information in the minimum packet size, multiple pins are sent in a single message.

```
Firmata.sendDigitalPorts(pin, firstPort, secondPort);
```

Up to eight pins can be sent in the pin parameter, sent as a byte. The pins must be sent in order; when starting at pin 6, it must be followed by pin 7, pin 8, and so on. To set the first pin, use the `firstPort` parameter sent as a byte. To set the number of pins sent, use the `secondPort` parameter. The pin data will be sent to the computer, specifying that the data received is the data of the pins from `firstPort` to `secondPort`.

This works well when sending a range of pin data but is not efficient if you want to send the status of a single pin or if the pins are not linear. You can also send the data of a single pin using `sendDigitalPort()`:

```
Firmata.sendDigital(pin, value);
```

This function sends the status of the pin and sends the pin input as `value`.

To send a string to the host computer, use `sendString()`:

```
Firmata.SendString(string);
```

This sends the String `string` to the host computer.

Receiving Messages

Receiving messages on an Arduino is the same as working with other types of serial information; first, you must wait until you have received data and then process that data. Data is received directly on the serial port. To see if data is waiting, use `available()`:

```
result = Firmata.available();
```

This function does not take any parameters and returns `true` if one or more bytes are waiting to be processed. To process data, use `processInput()`:

```
Firmata.processInput();
```

Typically, you would use both functions together:

```
while(Firmata.available())
{
  Firmata.processInput();
}
```

The Firmata library hides all the complicated parts of receiving data, including the data storage and processing. The library automatically decodes messages and enables you to perform actions on the data received using a system of callbacks.

Callbacks

Firmata works by using a system of *callbacks*, routines that are called when a specific action is performed, or in this case, when a specific message is received. Callbacks are highly customizable, and you can write a callback to perform almost any action you want simply by creating a function. Callbacks are put in place using an attach function; in the case of the Firmata library, it is called `attach()`:

```
Firmata.attach(messagetype, function);
```

Table 16-1 lists the `messagetype` parameter, which is one of the constants. The `function` parameter is the callback function that you have written.

Table 16-1: Callback Constants

CONSTANT	USE
ANALOG_MESSAGE	Analog value of a single pin
DIGITAL_MESSAGE	Digital value of a digital port
REPORT_ANALOG	Enables or disables the reporting of an analog pin
REPORT_DIGITAL	Enables or disables the reporting of a digital port
SET_PIN_MODE	Change the mode of the selected pin (input, output, and so on)
FIRMATA_STRING	Used for receiving text messages
SYSEX_START	Used for sending generic messages
SYSTEM_RESET	Used to reset firmware to default state

A callback requires a certain number of parameters to be defined, which is extremely specific as to the datatypes to use. The system restart callback does not require any parameters:

```
void systemResetCallback(void);
```

To receive strings, the `stringCallback` function requires one parameter:

```
void stringCallback(char *datastring);
```

`SysEx` messages require more information and have three parameters:

```
void sysexCallback(byte pin, byte count, byte *array);
```

Finally, all other callbacks use a generic format:

```
void genericCallback(byte pin, int value);
```

Callbacks must have different names. If you use both digital and analog pins, you will have two functions: one for handling digital data and the other for analog input. For example, code will allow you to receive both digital and analog instructions:

```
void analogWriteCallback(byte pin, int value)
{
  // Code goes here
}
void digitalWriteCallback(byte pin, int value)
{
  // Code goes here
}
Firmata.attach(ANALOG_MESSAGE, analogWriteCallback);
Firmata.attach(DIGITAL_MESSAGE, digitalWriteCallback);
```

A note on handling digital data: Analog data is sent one pin at a time, but this is not the case with digital pins. As seen previously, digital pin data is sent in groups of 8. This is known as a *port*. Port 1 will send the data of pins 1 to 8, and port 2 will send the data of pins 9 to 16, and so on. It is up to you to control if the pins should be written. To write all pins from a specified port, use this code:

```
void digitalWriteCallback(byte port, int value)
{
  byte i;
  byte pinValue;

  if (port < TOTAL_PORTS)
  {
    for(i=0; i<8; i++)
    {
```

```
        pinValue = (byte) value & (1 << i);
        digitalWrite(i + (port*8), currentPinValue);
    }
  }
}
```

To set a pin input or output, the `mode` parameter corresponds directly to the Arduino `pinMode()` constants. However, the trick is to know what pin corresponds to what sort of input/output. To do this, you can use some predefined data for each board. The `Boards.h` file details how many digital and analog pins a board has. For example, the Arduino Mega has the following line defined in the source code:

```
#define TOTAL_PINS 70 // 54 digital + 16 analog
```

To know if a pin is digital, use `IS_PIN_DIGITAL()` and `IS_PIN_ANALOG()`. To convert a pin to a digital or analog equivalent, use `PIN_TO_DIGITAL()` and `PIN_TO_ANALOG()`. You can use the following code to set the state of a digital pin:

```
void setPinModeCallback(byte pin, int mode)
{
  if (IS_PIN_DIGITAL(pin))
  {
    pinMode(PIN_TO_DIGITAL(pin), mode);
  }
}
```

To remove a callback, use `detach()`:

```
Firmata.detach(callback);
```

The `callback` parameter is one of the constants used to attach a callback (refer to Table 16-1).

SysEx

One of the messages that the Firmata protocol can exchange is called SysEx. Short for System Excusive, SysEx was originally used in synthesizers using the MIDI protocol to include custom commands. When writing a protocol, it is almost impossible to imagine every scenario, and to make sure that the MIDI protocol could handle just about everything, SysEx was developed. The idea was to exchange information and change settings that could not be accessed by other means. In extreme cases, memory was transferred (partitions or instruments, for example). In the Firmata protocol, it allows users to exchange information such as I²C bus data and the servo motor configuration.

To receive SysEx data, you must first create a SysEx callback, as explained in the "Callbacks" section.

An example callback might look like this:

```
void sysexCallback(byte command, byte argc, byte *argv)
{
  // Code goes here
}
```

The SysEx instruction identifier is sent as a byte, called `command`. The Arduino Firmata library defines a series of constants to describe a received message; as listed in Table 16-2.

Table 16-2: SysEx Constants

CONSTANT	FUNCTION
RESERVED_COMMAND	Reserved chip-specific instructions.
ANALOG_MAPPING_QUERY	Ask for analog to pin number mapping.
ANALOG_MAPPING_RESPONSE	Reply with mapping data.
CAPABILITY_QUERY	Ask for supported modes of all pins.
CAPABILITY_RESPONSE	Reply with capability data.
PIN_STATE_QUERY	Ask for a pin's current mode and value.
PIN_STATE_RESPONSE	Reply with pin mode and value.
EXTENDED_ANALOG	Analog write to any pin, including PWM and servo.
SERVO_CONFIG	Set servo parameters (angle, pulse, and such).
STRING_DATA	Send a string message.
SHIFT_DATA	34-bit shift out data.
I2C_REQUEST	Request I^{2}C data.
I2C_REPLY	Respond with I^{2}C data.
I2C_CONFIG	I^{2}C parameters.
REPORT_FIRMWARE	Report version number of Firmata firmware.
SAMPLING_INTERVAL	Set sampling interval.
SYSEX_NON_REALTIME	MIDI reserved.
SYSEX_REALTIME	MIDI reserved.

These constants are kept up to date at the Firmata website at http://firmata.org/wiki/V2.2ProtocolDetails.

Example Program

The beauty of Firmata is that it can adapt to so many situations. It is, of course, up to you to choose which pins will be used. If you want to expose only some pins, for example, to allow Firmata to control them, you can choose to enable just those relevant to your project. The sketch might receive Firmata instructions to update pins, but ultimately it is up to you, the developer, to decide if you should allow these instructions on all pins. Maybe you do not want a Firmata program to be able to modify certain pins. If a pressure sensor is connected to two pins, you do not want Firmata to change the pins to output and potentially damage the component.

The Arduino IDE has an excellent sketch that lets you begin working with Firmata: the StandardFirmata program. To access this program, go to Files ⇨ Examples ⇨ Firmata ⇨ StandardFirmata, and upload the sketch to your board. However, uploading the sketch to your Arduino is only one-half the project; you also need a Firmata program on your computer. Several programs exist, and one is available on the Firmata website at `http://www.firmata.org/wiki/Main_Page#Firmata_Test_Program`.

Download the version for your system (Windows, Mac OS, and Linux binaries are available), and run the program. You need to know which serial port your Arduino is connected to. After this is done, you are presented with the Firmata screen, where the status of every pin is presented. This works by sending data to the Arduino as quickly as possible; the faster the data transfer, the more responsive the output will be. The Arduino also sends data to the computer, using a clever sampling rate technique, which is described next.

Using this system, you can instruct your Arduino to perform advanced features such as turning LEDs on and off without the need to write a sketch or reading input lines without knowing in advance what will be connected (if anything). However, this has its limitations. As explained previously, if you require a device to be present on specific pins, you might want to edit the Standard Firmata sketch to not poll or update those pins. It is up to you, the programmer, to know which pins you want to expose and to create or modify a sketch to make sure that only the pins that are usable can be accessed by Firmata.

The Standard Firmata sketch is complicated and is one of the larger sketches that you will see on an Arduino, but it is well structured and can be used as the basis for your own sketches. By looking at `setup()`, you can see this:

```
Firmata.setFirmwareVersion(FIRMATA_MAJOR_VERSION,
    FIRMATA_MINOR_VERSION);

Firmata.attach(ANALOG_MESSAGE, analogWriteCallback);
Firmata.attach(DIGITAL_MESSAGE, digitalWriteCallback);
Firmata.attach(REPORT_ANALOG, reportAnalogCallback);
Firmata.attach(REPORT_DIGITAL, reportDigitalCallback);
```

```
Firmata.attach(SET_PIN_MODE, setPinModeCallback);
Firmata.attach(START_SYSEX, sysexCallback);
Firmata.attach(SYSTEM_RESET, systemResetCallback);
```

The first line sets the Firmata version, something that the Firmata application checks. It is defined using two constants: FIRMATA_MAJOR_REVISION and FIRMATA_MINOR_REVISION. These constants are set by the Arduino Firmata library. Next, a series of callbacks are defined; all seven possible callbacks are present in this sketch. This sketch can therefore react to every sort of Firmata message, or at least call a specific function when the message is received. It is then up to you to fill in the callbacks using the Standard Firmata sketch as an example.

In loop() the sketch receives and processes messages from the computer:

```
while(Firmata.available())
   Firmata.processInput();
```

One of the variables in the program is samplingInterval. This defines the rate at which Firmata polls the pins. The sketch then has a clever technique to make sure that the wanted sampling rate is maintained. Following is the code that is used:

```
currentMillis = millis();
if (currentMillis - previousMillis > samplingInterval)
{
   previousMillis += samplingInterval;
   // Code goes here
}
```

The variables currentMillis and previousMillis are each defined as an unsigned long. Each time Arduino enters loop(), the millis() function will be called, returning the number of milliseconds that the sketch has been running for. This value is then placed inside the variable currentMillis. Then, a comparison is made between currentMillis minus previousMillis and the samplingInterval. If the value of currentMillis minus previousMillis is larger than samplingInterval, previousMillis is increased by the value contained in samplingInterval, and the sketch is free to send all the pin data.

Summary

In this chapter, I have shown you the Firmata library and how it interacts with an Arduino. You have seen the different messages and the callbacks used to react to them. In the next chapter, you see how to use the Arduino GSM shield and connect to mobile data networks, transfer data to and from servers, and create your own wireless server. You also see how to place and receive telephone calls.

CHAPTER 17

This chapter discusses the following functions of the GSM library:

- `GSMAccess.begin()`
- `GSMAccess.shutdown()`
- `GSM_SMS.beginSMS()`
- `GSM_SMS.print()`
- `GSM_SMS.endSMS()`
- `GSM_SMS.available()`
- `GSM_SMS.remoteNumber()`
- `GSM_SMS.read()`
- `GSM_SMS.peek()`
- `GSM_SMS.flush()`
- `GSMVoiceCall.voiceCall()`
- `GSMVoiceCall.getVoiceCallStatus()`
- `GSMVoiceCall.answerCall()`
- `GSMVoiceCall.hangCall()`
- `GSMVoiceCall.retrieveCallingNumber()`
- `GPRS.attachGPRS()`
- `GSMClient.connect()`
- `GSMServer.ready()`
- `GSMModem.begin()`
- `GSMModem.getIMEI()`

The hardware needed to use these functions includes

- Arduino Uno
- Arduino GSM Shield
- Active SIM card
- 1 x Reed switch

You can find the code download for this chapter at `http://www.wiley.com/go/arduinosketches` on the Download Code tab. The code is in the Chapter 17 folder and the filename is `Chapter17.ino`.

Introducing GSM

One of the many things that defines the human race is our capacity to communicate. Throughout our inventions, we have developed ways to express ourselves, and to talk to more and more people, further and further away. Try to imagine life without a mobile phone, or any sort of telephone. How do you tell someone something? There are still options available to you; you could write a letter (a real letter, not an e-mail, one with pen and paper). It would take a day or two to arrive, and the recipient would read it when he arrived home (or at the office). You could also leave the house to see the person, either by going to her house, business, or a common meeting place (the town square, or even a restaurant). Neither of these options are as fast as dialing them up.

Of course, things do change. When writing this book, I am constantly in contact with my publisher and editor. I pick up my mobile phone, and call a number, and a few seconds later, another telephone rings, separated by a wide distance. I am in Europe, and they are in the United States. No matter where I am, either at home in France, or on a business trip to England, Brazil, or Singapore, people can get ahold of me. The international telephone network connects millions upon millions of people together, at distances that span the entire world, but the ability to place telephone calls is only one aspect of this network.

Mobile Data Network

Long gone are the days when a mobile telephone was used only for placing phone calls. Today, even the most basic of phones can receive network data as either text or multimedia messages. More advanced phones can receive e-mails, browse websites, or even stream high-quality videos through advanced data networks. We can be almost anywhere and still receive Facebook requests and spam messages. Times have indeed changed.

Although this may appear to be simple, it is extremely complicated to achieve. Data is sent through multiple channels, and simply walking around outside can be complicated for the mobile telephone network, as users regularly disconnect from one tower while connecting to a new tower. This is all handled transparently by the telephone and the telephone network, resulting in what appears to be a seamless network. The truth is, at any one moment, a telephone, or device in a mobile network, may not send and receive data.

GSM

The first generation of mobile communications, known as 1 G, was a simple technology that allowed full-duplex voice communication (full-duplex meaning that you could talk and listen at the same time). A simple system, it worked extremely well for people that needed to be on the move and connected continuously. Most 1 G telephones were car phones; relatively large devices that ran on a car's battery, but allowed users to do what the telephones were designed for—talking.

The 1 G network was entirely analog, but was only called 1 G when a new technology was needed; it was then known as the second generation, or 2 G and replaced 1 G.

In 1981, the European Conference of Postal and Telecommunications Administration (known as CEPT) created a new committee, the Groupe Spéciale Mobile, based in Paris. The GSM name would later be known as Global System for Mobile Communication, and its logo would become the de facto standard in almost all countries.

GSM changed quite a few technical aspects; all communications were now digital instead of analog. By using digital technology, communications could be compressed, using less bandwidth, allowing more users access to the network. Because mobile devices were becoming truly mobile and smaller, phone's radio emission strength was reduced, requiring more and more cells to allow communications. Cell towers were now cheap to produce, so this wasn't a problem, as was the cost to pay for safe devices that could be placed in a pocket and used all day.

One of the changes that the GSM specification proposed was something that is still in use: a SIM card. A SIM card contains a unique serial number, operator network information, subscriber information, temporary network information, and two passcodes for the user: the PIN and PUK. By using a SIM card, users can choose their mobile operator, and mobile operators can sometimes "lock" mobile phones to their network.

The original GSM specification did not include data transfer but was rapidly modified to allow SMS messages, just one such method that uses digital data. SMS, short for Short Message System, is a technique to send 160 characters to cell towers or to telephones. Although most people think of SMS messages as "I will be 20 minutes late," they are also an efficient way of warning people in case of an emergency, and for publicity, taxi reservations, payment systems, or even for proprietary inter-application communication. The number of SMS messages range in the billions per year, and although their use is slowly declining in favor of other messaging systems, in 2013, an estimated 145 billion SMS messages were sent.

SMS is not the only data transfer technique used by the GSM network; two other major systems exist.

GPRS

GPRS, short for General Packet Radio Service, is a packet-based data exchange technique. Although most GSM connections were circuit-switched (meaning that a connection was established and then terminated when the connection was cut), GPRS introduced a packet-switching technique, allowing operators to charge clients by the quantity of data used, and not the time spent transferring data. GPRS is an extension to the GPS 2 G technology, and as such, is often known as 2.5 G. This technology allows theoretical speeds of up to 50 Kbit/s, but true throughput is often limited at 40 Kbit/s.

EDGE

EDGE, short for Enhanced Data rates for GSM Evolution, is an enhancement over the previous GPRS data connection method. With a theoretical max speed of 250 Kbit/s, this norm was soon called 2.75 G by mobile telephone owners. It is still used today as a fallback when other high-speed networks are not available.

3 G

The third generation of mobile networks is a large change from the previous 2 G, and is not compatible with the older systems, but remains a fallback technology for current telephones. 3 G allows for higher data speeds than previous standards, ranging from 2 Mbit/s all the way to 28 Mbit/s.

The 3 G standard was created by the International Telecommunication Union, which is not the same as the GSM committee. 3 G mobile devices can use the 2 G network, but 2 G devices cannot connect to 3 G networks. They must use the older 2 G network, forcing operators to have several systems in place on the same tower.

4 G and the Future

4 G is currently the most advanced technology readily available, with extremely high speeds exceeding 50 Mbit/s. The 4 G standard allows for theoretical speeds much higher than that, but even that isn't fast enough for the future, and work has already begun on the 5 G network. Time will tell just how far the mobile network will progress.

Modems

A modem (short for modulator-demodulator) is a device that can send and receive digital data through an analog carrier. Most veteran computer experts remember modems as the trusty 56-k modem—a device that connected to a computer through a serial port and allowed the computer to connect to the Internet (or a company network) through a telephone line. Where does the 56 k come from? The speed, 56 thousand baud or 56 Kbit/s data rate. If everything went well (which it usually didn't) this meant that users could download data at a blistering 4 to 5 kilobytes per second. Don't laugh; they were fast modems, yet most were slower.

Although the trusty 56-k modems have been mostly replaced by broadband, it is interesting to know how they work. Modems are serial devices, and most were instructed to operate using the Hayes command set: simple ASCII messages instructing the modem to perform specific actions. Most commands start with "AT", short for Attention. A modem is instructed to configure itself in a specific way, to call a number and to get information using simple text messages. When the connection is made, the modem is switched from *command mode* to *data mode*, and from there on, the modem sends each byte of data it receives. It is also possible to change from data mode to command mode again to issue more instructions to the modem (for example, to hang up). Again, this is performed by sending AT commands.

The 56-k modem is indeed a dying technology, but its legacy is still with us and will be for a long time. The AT command idea was so well implemented that most radio peripherals still use them; Bluetooth devices, for example, are configured using AT commands. Bluetooth does not connect through telephone lines, but the modem principle is the same; a digital device transmits digital data over an analog medium—in this case, radio waves. Even the most modern 4 G telephone is also a modem, accepting serial data, transmitting and receiving data over radio waves. GSM devices are exactly the same.

Arduino and GSM

There are multiple ways to connect to devices wirelessly and exchange information: Wi-Fi, Bluetooth, and Zigbee to name but a few. Most of these technologies require the user to create an infrastructure, but there is no wireless infrastructure as extensive and as widely used as the mobile telephone network. Also, Arduinos are small, lightweight, and mobile, making them perfect for mobile network use. A GPS tracker on a car is only useful if it can send information through an existing network, and is useless if it leaves your Wi-Fi zone (which probably happens a lot for a car). However, there is a good chance that your car will go through at least several mobile network cells during its trip, allowing it to send data at will.

Several shields exist to achieve this. Arduino produces its GSM shield, one that comes bundled with a SIM card from Movilforum Telefonica. The GSM shield is unlocked, meaning that it can be used with any mobile operator, but Movilforum Telefonica's service is international, and it has a large partner network, allowing for GSM communication just about anywhere.

GSM shields connect to GSM networks but will not work on 3 G and 4 G networks. Although on a 2 G network, the shield enables you to make and receive telephone calls, send and receive SMS messages, and enables data connectivity.

> **NOTE** Data connectivity means that you can access the entire Internet, but most mobile operators have their own internal network, meaning that your telephone is not directly visible from the Internet. This adds a level of security to your applications but makes it difficult to "listen" for incoming connections. A GSM device should always initiate a connection and wait for a response.

GSM devices are often power-hungry and usually require an external power supply. USB ports that supply 500 mA cannot keep a GSM shield powered under heavy load; these devices often require a power supply between 700 and 1,000 mA.

To use a GSM shield, Arduino has developed a library to create connections, send and receive data, and even manage the SIM card.

Arduino GSM Library

The Arduino GSM library is available in Arduino 1.0.4 and later. The GSM library is a complex library with multiple header files. It can be imported automatically in the Arduino IDE by going to the menu Sketch ⇨ Import Library ⇨ GSM, but doing this adds a large number of files:

- `#include <GSM3MobileMockupProvider.h>`
- `#include <GSM3ShieldV1BaseProvider.h>`

- `#include <GSM3ShieldV1ModemVerification.h>`
- `#include <GSM3ShieldV1PinManagement.h>`
- `#include <GSM3ShieldV1SMSProvider.h>`
- `#include <GSM3MobileClientService.h>`
- `#include <GSM3ShieldV1CellManagement.h>`
- `#include <GSM3ShieldV1MultiServerProvider.h>`
- `#include <GSM3ShieldV1BandManagement.h>`
- `#include <GSM3ShieldV1DataNetworkProvider.h>`
- `#include <GSM3ShieldV1.h>`
- `#include <GSM3CircularBuffer.h>`
- `#include <GSM3MobileCellManagement.h>`
- `#include <GSM3MobileAccessProvider.h>`
- `#include <GSM3MobileClientProvider.h>`
- `#include <GSM3SMSService.h>`
- `#include <GSM3MobileDataNetworkProvider.h>`
- `#include <GSM3ShieldV1ServerProvider.h>`
- `#include <GSM3MobileServerService.h>`
- `#include <GSM3VoiceCallService.h>`
- `#include <GSM3MobileServerProvider.h>`
- `#include <GSM.h>`
- `#include <GSM3MobileVoiceProvider.h>`
- `#include <GSM3ShieldV1VoiceProvider.h>`
- `#include <GSM3ShieldV1ScanNetworks.h>`
- `#include <GSM3ShieldV1ClientProvider.h>`
- `#include <GSM3ShieldV1DirectModemProvider.h>`
- `#include <GSM3MobileNetworkProvider.h>`
- `#include <GSM3MobileSMSProvider.h>`
- `#include <GSM3MobileNetworkRegistry.h>`
- `#include <GSM3ShieldV1ModemCore.h>`
- `#include <GSM3ShieldV1MultiClientProvider.h>`
- `#include <GSM3ShieldV1AccessProvider.h>`
- `#include <GSM3SoftSerial.h>`

Don't be frightened by the large number of files. For most applications, you can simply include the GSM library `#include <GSM.h>`.

Because the GSM library is complex, its different usage is separated into classes. There are classes to manage GPRS connections: SMS messages, and voice calls, to name but a few.

GSM Class

The GSM class is responsible for initializing the shield and the on-board GSM device. It is initialized like this:

```
GSM GSMAccess
GSM GSMAccess(debug)
```

The `debug` parameter is optional. It is a `boolean` and is `false` by default. If set to `true`, the GSM device outputs AT commands to the console.

To connect to the GSM network, use the `begin()` function:

```
GSMAccess.begin();
GSMAccess.begin(pin);
GSMAccess.begin(pin, restart);
GSMAccess.begin(pin, restart, sync);
```

The `pin` parameter is a character array that contains the PIN code for the SIM card connected to the GSM shield. If your SIM card does not have a PIN code, you can omit this parameter. The `restart` parameter is a `boolean` and specifies if the modem is to be restarted. By default, this parameter is `true`, resulting in a modem restart. The `sync` parameter is a `boolean` and sets the synchronization to the base station. In a synchronous configuration, the sketch can tell if an operation has completed. In an asynchronous configuration, operations are scheduled, and their result isn't always immediately available. By default, it is set to `true`. All the return codes listed in this chapter correspond to a synchronous configuration.

This function returns a `char` indicating the status of the modem: `ERROR`, `IDLE`, `CONNECTING`, `GSM_READY`, `GPRS_READY`, or `TRANSPARENT_CONNECTED`.

This can be used as follows:

```
#include <GSM.h>

#define PINNUMBER "0000" // SIM card PIN

GSM gsm(true); // Debug AT messages

void setup()
{
  // initialize serial communications
```

```
    Serial.begin(9600);

    // connection state
    boolean notConnected = true;

    // Start GSM shield
    while(notConnected)
    {
      if(gsm.begin(PINNUMBER)==GSM_READY)
        notConnected = false;
      else
      {
        Serial.println("Not connected");
        delay(1000);
      }
    }

    Serial.println("GSM initialized");
}
```

To shut down the modem, use `shutdown()`:

```
GSMAccess.shutdown();
```

This function does not take any parameters and returns a `boolean`: `true` if the modem was shut down and `false` if the function is currently executing. If this function returns `false`, it does not mean that the function failed, only that the shutdown operation has not yet completed.

SMS Class

GSM modems can, of course, be used to send and receive SMS messages. To enable SMS message services, use the GSM_SMS class:

```
GSM_SMS sms;
```

An SMS message is sent in three steps; first, the destination number is required. Second, the text is entered. Finally, the message is confirmed.

To set a destination telephone number, use `beginSMS()`:

```
sms.beginSMS(number);
```

The `number` parameter is a `char` array, the telephone number that will receive the SMS message.

To fill in the SMS body, use `print()`:

```
sms.print(message);
```

The `message` parameter is again a `char` array and contains the message to be sent. Note that SMS messages are limited to 160 characters. This function returns the amount of bytes sent, expressed as an `int`.

To complete an SMS message and to instruct the modem to send the message, use `endSMS()`:

```
sms.endSMS();
```

This function does not take any parameters.

When the SMS message has been assembled, the SIM card is told to send the message as soon as possible. The SIM card coupled with the modem make an autonomous unit which acts independently from the Arduino. Assembling and sending a message through the Arduino API does not guarantee that the message is sent; it is queued to be sent.

Because the device is autonomous, it also receives SMS messages without warning; there is no callback and no interruption. The sketch must periodically poll the GSM shield to see if a message is present. This is done with `available()`:

```
result = sms.available();
```

This function returns an `int`, the number of messages waiting on the SIM card. To begin reading a text message, you must first retrieve the number of the sender, which is done with `remoteNumber()`:

```
sms.remoteNumber(number, size);
```

The `number` parameter is a `char` array, a memory location where the sender ID will be stored. The `size` parameter is the size of the `char` array.

When the sender ID has been retrieved, the next thing you must do is to retrieve the message body. You can do this with `read()`, which works the same way as with file functions and serial buffers. It reads one character at a time.

```
result = sms.read();
```

You can read the entire content of a message with the following code:

```
// Read message bytes and print them
while(c=sms.read())
Serial.print(c);
```

SMS messages that have been previously read are marked with a hashtag. To see if a message has been read without actually fetching the first character, you can use `peek()`. Just like with serial buffers, this function returns the first character but does not increment the index. Subsequent calls to `peek()` or even `read()` will return the same character.

```
if(sms.peek()=='#')
   Serial.println("This message has been discarded");
```

To discard a message, you can use `flush()`:

```
sms.flush();
```

This function deletes the SMS at the current buffer index from the modem's memory.

VoiceCall Class

You can use the `VoiceCall` class to place and to answer voice calls. An Arduino can place voice calls but cannot send voice data without additional hardware. Most shields have an audio input and output port, allowing users to add additional components as required. This can be in the form of a microphone and speaker, or for distress calls, it can also be an electronic component capable of outputting wave audio. The GSM component accepts text instructions and encodes/decodes the audio as required. Instructions include dialing numbers, picking up and hanging up, as well as caller identity functions.

The first thing you must do is create an instance of the `GSMVoiceCall` class:

```
GSMVoiceCall vcs;
```

To place a phone call, use `VoiceCall()`:

```
result = vcs.voiceCall(number);
```

The `number` parameter is a `char` array and is the telephone number to call. The function returns an `int`: 1 if the call were placed or 0 if it were unable to call. This can be used as follows:

```
// Check if the receiving end has picked up the call
if(vcs.voiceCall(phoneNumber))
{
   Serial.println("Call Established");
}
Serial.println("Call Finished");
```

This function places only the call and returns if the call were established. To check on the call status, use `getVoiceCallStatus()`:

```
result = vcs.getVoiceCallStatus();
```

This function takes no parameters and returns `IDLE_CALL`, `CALLING`, `RECEIVINGCALL`, or `TALKING`, which is described in Table 17-1.

Table 17-1: getVoiceCallStatus() Return Codes

CONSTANT	DESCRIPTION
IDLE_CALL	The modem is idling: no incoming calls, no outgoing calls, and no call in progress.
CALLING	The modem is currently calling a number.
RECEIVINGCALL	The modem is receiving an incoming call.
TALKING	A call has been placed (incoming or outgoing) and communication is established.

The other end of a telephone call can hang up whenever it chooses (or even when network conditions no longer allow a call to continue), and the Arduino can also instruct the GSM device to hang up with hangCall():

```
result = vcs.hangCall();
```

This function takes no parameters and returns an int: 1 if the operation succeeded and 0 otherwise. This function not only hangs up a connected call, but can also hang up on an incoming call.

Arduinos can also receive calls, but the GSM modem does not warn the sketch of incoming calls; the sketch must poll the GSM device with getVoiceCall-Status() when there's an incoming call expected. When an incoming call is detected (when getVoiceCallStatus() returns RECEIVINGCALL), you can retrieve the calling number and decide to accept/refuse the call. To get the incoming telephone number, use retrieveCallingNumber():

```
result = vcs.retrieveCallingNumber(number, size);
```

The number parameter is a char array and can store the incoming number. The size parameter is the size of the array. This function returns 1 if the phone number is retrieved, and 0 if it is unable to retrieve the phone number.

To pick up an incoming call, use answerCall():

```
result = vcs.answerCall();
```

This function does not take any parameters and returns 1 if the call is answered, or 0 if it is unable to answer. Incoming calls can also be refused with hangCall().

GPRS

GPRS is the method used to send and receive data using a GSM mobile device. It does not require an active voice call but does require authentication. When the SIM card has been told to create a connection, it maintains the connection and automatically reconnects if needed. Before using a GPRS connection, you must use the GPRS class:

```
GPRS gprs;
```

Then, to initiate a connection, you must use `attachGPRS()`:

```
grps.attachGPRS(APN, user, password);
```

This function takes three parameters, all three are `char` arrays. The `APN` parameter is the Access Point Name, the name of the connection point between the GPRS network and the Internet. Each GPRS network should have one; check with your SIM card provider for more information. The `user` and `password` parameters are optional username and password details that are sometimes required to connect to an APN. Again, the documentation that comes with your SIM card should give more details. Not all providers use the username and password fields; in which case they may be left blank. This function returns the same constants as `begin()`; it returns `GPRS_READY` when the connection is established.

```
if (gprs.attachGPRS(GPRS_APN, GPRS_LOGIN, GPRS_PASSWORD)==GPRS_READY)
   Serial.println("Connected to GPRS network");
```

When the connection to the GPRS network is established, you need to create either a server or a client. A server waits for incoming connections, and a client connects to external servers. A server uses the `GSMServer` class, and a client uses the `GSMClient` class. Both work almost the same as an Ethernet connection, with a few differences; the GSM library attempts to be as compatible as possible with the Ethernet library.

CROSS-REFERENCE   The Ethernet library was presented in Chapter 9.

To create a client, that is to say a device that will connect to another Internet device, use the `GSMClient` class:

```
GSMClient client;
```

When that is done, you must connect to a server. To connect to a server, use `connect()`:

```
result = client.connect(ip, port);
```

The `ip` parameter is a 4-byte IP address, and `port` is an `int` specifying the port that the sketch wants to connect to. This function returns a `boolean`: `true` if the connection is established, and `false` if the connection fails.

When a connection has been made, you can send and receive data. Sending data is done with `print()`, `println()`, and `write()`:

```
result = client.print(data);
result = client.println(data);
result = client.write(databyte);
```

These functions are presented in Chapter 9.

To become a server, that is to say a device that will listen to incoming connections, use the `GSMServer` class:

```
GSMServer server(port);
```

The port parameter is an `int`; it tells the server which port to listen on for connections.

One difference between the GSM library and the Ethernet library is the nature of the connection. GSM connections are sometimes unstable; network coverage may not be available in some locations (for example, inside a building or under a bridge). To know if a command were successfully executed, use the `ready()` function:

```
result = client.ready();
```

This function does not take any parameters and returns an `int`; 1 if the previous operation has completed, and 0 if it has not (yet) completed.

Many network providers do not allow incoming connections on their network, making it impossible to run servers with the GSM shield. Check with your provider to see if there are any such limitations with your network.

Modem

The modem class is used primarily to perform diagnostic operations on the modem component. To use it, you must use the `GSMModem` class:

```
GSMModem modem;
```

To initialize the modem subsystem, you must first use `begin()`:

```
result = modem.begin();
```

This function returns `true` if the modem subsystem was initialized or `false` if there was a problem with the initialization. (For example, the shield has not been correctly installed.)

To retrieve the IMEI number, the International Mobile Equipment Identifier, a unique number identifying the shield's modem, use `getIMEI()`:

```
result = modem.getIMEI();
```

This function does not take any parameters and returns a `String`, the IMEI number of the GSM modem.

Example Application

One of the domains where Internet-connected devices are in constant demand is home security. Most security devices use a home's Wi-Fi connection, but these devices are vulnerable to attack. For this reason, many security systems also have a backup GSM system, allowing devices to communicate even if the physical line to the Internet is severed.

For this application, you will create a system that monitors a door or window. In the event of this entrance opening, a warning message is sent via text message. To make sure that the system works, every few minutes a "heartbeat" is sent to an Internet server. This message is just a small bit of information that shows that the system works. If the server does not hear from the Arduino within a certain timeframe, then it knows that something is wrong.

This example uses an Arduino Uno and a GSM shield. One entrance is monitored by means of a reed switch, button, or other contact-based switch. This switch must be configured as NC, normally closed, and connected to the Arduino's ground. Normally this would require a resistor to pull either the 5-V power rail or the ground, but Arduinos have internal pull-up resistors that can be activated in code, and that is what will be done here. If the door is open, the connection is severed, and the Arduino's internal pull-up registers an intrusion. Also, if the wires are cut, the Arduino also registers that as an alert. The schematic is shown in Figure 17-1.

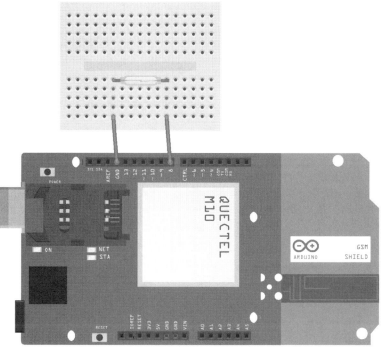

Figure 17-1: Project schematic

Your sketch should look like Listing 17-1

Listing 17-1: Sketch (filename: `chapter17.ino`)

```
1   #include <GSM.h>
2
3   #define PINNUMBER "0000" // Replace with your SIM card PIN
4   #define CONTACT "01234567" // Replace with your mobile telephone
        number
5   #define GPRS_APN       "GPRS_APN" // Replace your GPRS APN
6   #define GPRS_LOGIN     "login"    // Replace with your APN login
7   #define GPRS_PASSWORD  "password" // Replace with your APN password
8   #define SERVER "yourhomesecurity"
9   #define PORT 8080
10
11  // initialize the library instance
12  GSM gsmAccess;
13  GSM_SMS sms;
14  GSMClient client;
15  GPRS gprs;
16
17  // Variables
18  bool intrusion = false;
19
20  void setup()
21  {
22    // initialize serial communications and wait for port to open:
23    Serial.begin(9600);
24
25    // connection state
26    boolean notConnected = true;
27
28    // Start GSM shield
29    // If your SIM has PIN, pass it as a parameter of begin() in
          quotes
30    while(notConnected)
31    {
32      if((gsmAccess.begin(PINNUMBER)==GSM_READY) &
33        (gprs.attachGPRS(GPRS_APN, GPRS_LOGIN, GPRS_PASSWORD)
34              ==GPRS_READY))
35          notConnected = false;
36      else
37      {
38        Serial.println("Not connected");
39        delay(1000);
40      }
41    }
42
43    pinMode(8, INPUT_PULLUP);
44  45    Serial.println("GSM initialized");
46  }
```

```
47
48  void loop()
49  {
50    for (int i = 0; i < 600; i++)
51    {
52      delay(500); // sleep for half a second
53      if (digitalRead(8) == HIGH)
54      {
55        if (intrusion == false)
56        {
57          // An intrusion has been detected. Warn the user!
58          intrusion = true;
59          sendWarningSMS();
60        }
61        else
62        {
63          // The user was already warned about an intrusion, do
                nothing
64        }
65      }
66      else
67      {
68        // Everything looks OK
69        intrusion = false;
70      }
71    }
72
73    // It has been 10 minutes, send a heartbeat
74    if (client.connect(SERVER, PORT))
75    {
76      Serial.println("connected");
77      client.print("HEARTBEAT");
78      client.stop();
79    }
80    else
81    {
82      // if you didn't get a connection to the server:
83      Serial.println("Connection failed");
84    }
85  }
86
87  void sendWarningSMS()
88  {
89    sms.beginSMS(CONTACT);
90    sms.print("Intrusion alert!");
91    sms.endSMS();
92  }
```

This sketch begins by importing the GSM library, and then defining the necessary parameters for this sketch: the PIN number, the contact number, and different connection parameters.

On line 12, the different objects are created: `gsmAccess` is used to talk to the Arduino GSM board, `sms` is the object used to send SMS messages, client is used to create a GPRS client connection, and `gprs` is used to attach the GPRS connection.

The `setup()` function is declared on line 20. The serial connection is configured on line 23, and on line 26 the variable `notConnected` is set to `true`. As long as this variable is `true`, a `while` loop attempts to attach to the GPRS network, with the `attachGPRS()` function on line 33. Finally, on line 43, pin 8 is set as an input with an internal pull-up resistor.

On line 88 a function is declared: `sendWarningSMS()`. This function will send an SMS message to the specified contact. The SMS message is created on line 90 using the `beginSMS()` function. On line 91, text is sent to the SMS engine—this will be the content of the message. Finally, on line 92 the `endSMS()` function will send the message.

The `loop()` function is declared on line 49. It starts with a `for()` loop and iterates 600 times. Each loop will start by waiting for a second, and then looking at the state of the digital input on pin 8. If the result is false, that means that the reed switch has been activated, and the variable intrusion is set to true before calling the `sendWarningSMS()` function.

Once this loop iterates 600 times, or close to 10 minutes, the sketch will attempt to connect to a server. If the connection is successful, the sketch will send a message to the server telling it that the security system is still up and running. If the sketch cannot connect, then a warning message is sent to the serial console.

The sketch is simple and needs protection. A warning light could be added, or at least an output to a relay for a siren of some sort. Also, the device can send SMS messages to warn people, but it can also receive messages—you can write a routine that can receive messages to turn the security on if the user leaves the house without activating his alarm.

Summary

In this chapter, I have shown you just how flexible a GSM shield can be and the different ways it can be used. You have seen an example using just some of the many functions, and explored an idea about how to increase connectivity. In the next chapter, I will show you the Audio library, a powerful library that adds function to an Arduino Due to output audio files. You will see how audio files are composed and how to create a device that will output audio to a loudspeaker.

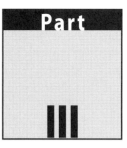

Part

III

Device-Specific Libraries

In This Part

Audio

This chapter discusses the following functions of the Audio library:

- `begin()`
- `prepare()`
- `write()`

The hardware needed to use the examples in this chapter includes:

- Arduino Due
- Ethernet Shield (Arduino, SainSmart, etc.)
- Micro-SD card
- Breadboard
- LM35 Temperature Sensor
- Wires
- 3.5-mm audio jack
- An audio amplifier

NOTE The Audio library is only found in Arduino IDE version 1.5 and later. It is still considered experimental and under development.

You can find the code download for this chapter at `http://www.wiley.com/go/arduinosketches` on the Download Code tab. The code is in the Chapter 18 folder and the filename is `Chapter18.ino`.

Introducing Audio

Science fiction films from the 1980s were full of strange machines with lots of flashing lights and annoying beeps. The first PCs sold had only a buzzer, and the first versions could only do that, buzz. A while later, people played with the buzzer, making tones and even music for games. There are various videos on YouTube that show what games used to be like. Don't laugh; we really did play like that, and we liked it!

The gaming industry was driving sound development at the time, and gamers wanted more advanced music. It wasn't long before MIDI sound cards were released. MIDI is a protocol for connecting musical devices together. (A computer can also be a musical instrument.) Some sound cards could be programmed with "instruments" to be played back at different notes. Although the sound fidelity was much better than the original internal buzzers, it could still be better. Music was certainly much better, but recorded sounds still were not possible—or at least, not easily. You could listen to high-quality music, but the explosions created by your rocket launcher wouldn't sound quite right. The industry turned to another solution.

A new generation of sound cards was born: Creative Lab's Sound Blaster series. It had the features of MIDI sound cards but also had digital signal processors (DSP for short) that could create complex digital audio signals. Computer processors were more and more powerful, and finally powerful enough to create complex sounds by digitally interpreting an analog signal through the sound card. We could hear music, and explosions sounded great. We stayed up all night hurling rockets at each other.

Again, new technology had its benefits but also had a problem: space. Digital sound files took up a lot of space, and space wasn't readily available at the time. High-end hard drives were just more than 1 gigabyte in size, and a 3-minute song recorded from the radio could be hundreds of megabytes in size. If music were to become digital, we needed larger hard drives or to find a way to compress music, preferably both. Today, a song can be compressed into 4 or 5 megabytes and placed onto a music player with gigabytes of space. However, it also requires something else: faster processors.

Digital Sound Files

One of the first digital audio formats is known as *wave*: an uncompressed digital file that represents an analog signal. Where analog signals can have almost every value possible between their maximum and minimum values, digital cannot. It requires a resolution: the amount of values it can handle. On a scale of 0 to 10, an analog signal would create a 7.42, but a digital signal from 0 to 10 in steps of 1 would not; the closest it can do is 7, as shown in Figure 18-1.

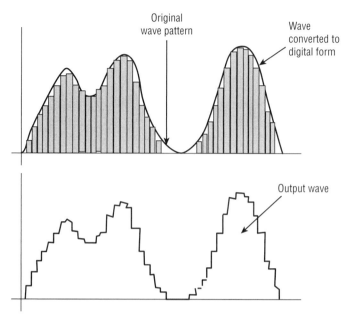

Figure 18-1: Digital resolution

As you can see, the analog signal flows through different values, but the digital representation creates a "step" effect; the representation of the data is not precise, and quality is lost. Thankfully, sound cards do not have values that go from zero to 10; most are 16 bits for a total of 65,536 values. Previous generations had 8-bit sampling for a total of 256 values, and 256 values are too low for an accurate representation. However, the 16-bit value of 65,536 is considered to be more than enough for most audiophiles. This is the quality found on CDs and even some Blu-ray audio files. However, the resolution is not the only factor to take into consideration.

Sound waves are a mixture of different frequencies; the higher the frequency, the higher the pitch. Humans can normally hear sounds from as low as 20 Hz all the way to 20 kHz and above. To digitally sample frequencies as high as 20 kHz, the *effective sampling rate* (the speed at which the sound is sampled) must be at least doubled or 40 kHz. For typical applications, a sampling rate of 44.1 kHz is used. A microchip was already on the market that used this frequency for sampling, designed by Sony Corporation. For professional applications, sampling was done at rates as high as 48 kHz. 44.1 kHz and 48 kHz are common sample frequencies found on computers, as are multiples of 44.1 kHz; 22.05 kHz, and 11.025 kHz. 8 kHz was used for a long time for telephone systems, where audio quality was adequate to understand human voice conversations. Professional sampling devices can sample at a high rate for even more accurate results; DVD audio is sampled at 192 kHz, and other devices can go as high as 2 MHz.

The higher the sampling rate, the more accurate the result will be. The effects of sampling speed are shown in Figure 18-2.

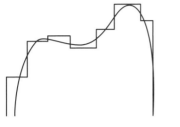

Slower, less accurate sampling   Faster, more accurate sampling

Figure 18-2: Sampling rates

Higher sampling rates also create more data, meaning more space is required.

Music on the Arduino

Arduinos can create musical tones because music is, put simply, repeated frequencies. A musical A has a frequency of 220 Hz, a musical A' is double that, or 440 Hz. By knowing the frequencies of notes, it's possible to program an Arduino to create simple musical tones. For example, the famous song "Happy Birthday" can be written in musical tones as: "CCDCFE CCDCGF CCC1AFED BBAFGF." By using `tone()`, you can generate a musical tune to impress your friends, but it remains a simple musical tone. The sound is clearly artificial and does not resemble piano tones or any other musical instrument.

CROSS-REFERENCE   `tone()` **is presented in Chapter 4.**

Arduino Due

The Arduino Due is a different kind of Arduino. It is based on Atmel's implementation of an ARM Cortex-M3, a powerful microcontroller and has more processing power than most Arduinos. It is a 32-bit microcontroller, runs at 84 MHz, and has more input and output pins than most Arduinos, including some advanced functions. Audio output on Arduinos is normally done by varying the frequency of a square wave, but the Arduino Due has two Digital to Analog Converters (DAC) that can output a true analog signal, like the pulses produced by `tone()`.

Pulse width modulation is an "all or nothing signal;" the output alternates between a logical high and a logical low. High fidelity sound is different; it requires a signal that has multiple values between the minimum and maximum voltage to control the volume, and to provide a clearer audio signal. The `tone()` function generates a square wave, but unlike pulse width modulation, it has a 50% duty cycle, that is to say, it oscillates between a logical high and a logical low, both phases being equal in length. It results in an audible tone, but cannot represent a complex audio signal like voice.

CROSS-REFERENCE   PWM is presented in Chapter 4.

Digital to Analog Converters

Digital to Analog Converters (DAC) can be used to generate waveforms and are often used to create sine, triangle, and sawtooth waves. Because these devices can create custom waveforms and because sound is also a waveform, they can be used to create sound—and with relatively good precision.

WARNING   Microcontrollers and DACs can generate signals but are not powerful enough to power devices; they require an amplifier to create a signal powerful enough for a speaker to use. Connecting a speaker directly to the microcontroller can, and probably will, damage the pin, maybe even the microcontroller.

A DAC is the opposite of an Analog to Digital Converter (ADC) but it uses the same properties. A digital signal has a resolution; the amount of bits that are used to create a signal. On the Arduino Due, the two DACs have 12-bit resolutions; they can write values from 0 to 4,095. The analog output varies from one analog value to another; on the Arduino Due, it varies from 0 V to +3.3 V, the voltage of the Cortex-M microcontroller. Because the voltage range is 3.3 V and because there are 4,096 possible values, the DAC has a precision of 3.3 divided by 4,096, or approximately 0.000806. Each increment on the digital side will result in a change of 0.8 mV on the analog side.

Digital Audio to Analog

Digital audio files are essentially a representation of analog signals. It is therefore easy to take each value and to write that value into a DAC, creating a waveform that is close to the original audio. There are several factors to consider:

- **Resolution**—The resolution of the digital audio file is important; on most computers, they are either 8 bits or 16 bits, but the Arduino Due's DAC has a 12-bit resolution.

- **Speed**—The original file was sampled at a precise speed, and playing back the audio data at a different speed would change the pitch.

- **Stereo or mono**—Audio can be recorded as mono (single channel) or stereo (dual channel). The Arduino Due can play only mono files, so stereo files play back as mono; both channels convert to a single channel.

Creating Digital Audio

You can create digital audio files using numerous tools, from programs on your computer to your smartphone. Most operating systems have at least one application you can use to record your voice. Digital audio can also be "converted"; converting one format to another is also possible with a large range of applications, but because some audio formats are licensed, some of these applications are either shareware or commercial.

A third option is the capability of some more advanced programs to "speak" directly, using voice synthesis. This can later be used to create new files containing the voice. This is an interesting solution if you are looking for a robotic voice system.

For most audio recording, limited resources are required. For nonprofessional applications, a simple multimedia headset is often more than enough; some USB models have good sampling rates and offer noise reduction. Try to record your voice inside with no other ambient noises. Choose a time when you know you will not receive a phone call or have a visit from someone. Having a break of even one-half an hour can result in a slightly different voice, so try to record all the files you need in a single session.

Storing Digital Audio

Digital audio files can be extremely large, and wave files are not compressed. For a typical desktop computer, this will not be a problem. Audio CDs containing wave files could hold 80 minutes of stereo music in 700 megabytes, which is normally more than sufficient for most projects. Most audio files can exceed the Arduino Due's internal memory and flash, so another storage medium is required. To store (and play) digital audio on the Arduino Due, you must use an SD card with a shield that has SD-card capability.

> **WARNING**   The Arduino Due is not a 5-V device; it is a 3.3-V device. Some shields that are designed for 5-V Arduinos will not work on the Arduino Due, so check compatibility.

The shield can be any type that supports an SD card; some sensor shields and most Ethernet shields have an SD-slot present on the board. For more information on SD cards, see Chapter 12.

Playing Digital Audio

To play back audio files, you must first import the library: `Audio.h`.

```
#include <Audio.h>
```

To play back Audio files from the SD card, you will also require the SD and SPI libraries; import `SD.h` and `SPI.h`.

```
#include <SD.h>
#include <SPI.h>
```

NOTE   The Arduino Due is supported only in the versions of the Arduino IDE. Version 1.0 does not support the Due, and you cannot import the Audio library from the menu. Version 1.5 and above support both the Arduino Due and the Audio library.

To initiate the Audio library, you run `begin()`.

```
Audio.begin(rate, size);
```

This function takes two arguments: the `rate` and a `size`. The audio rate is the number of samples per second; for example, 22050 or 44100 are typical values. For stereo audio files, you must double the audio rate (44100 for 22.05 kHz and 88200 for 44.1 kHz). The `size` parameter indicates the size of an audio buffer that will be created by this function, in milliseconds. For example, to prepare the Arduino Due to play a 44.1-kHz stereo file with a 100-millisecond buffer, use the following:

```
// 44100Khz stereo => 88200 sample rate
// 100 mSec of prebuffering.
Audio.begin(88200, 100);
```

When the Audio library is ready, you must prepare your samples to be played. This is done with the `prepare()` function:

```
Audio.prepare(buffer, samples, volume);
```

The `buffer` parameter is the name of a buffer created by your sketch; it is not the audio buffer created by the `begin()` function. The `samples` parameter is the number of samples to write, and the `volume` parameter is the volume of the audio output, expressed as a 10-bit number; 0 is a silent output, and 1023 is the maximum volume possible.

The final step is to write the data into the audio buffer using the `write()` function.

```
Audio.write(buffer, length);
```

The `buffer` parameter and the length parameter are identical to the parameters used in the `prepare()` function. This function writes the samples to the internal audio buffer. If the audio file is not played, playback commences. If the file is currently played, this adds the samples to the end of the internal buffer.

Example Program

For this application, you create a digital thermometer, using an LM35, a small thermometer that is first presented in Chapter 14. The schematic is almost identical, but for this application, there is a change. When the user presses a button, the Arduino does not display the time; it says it out loud.

To do this, you have quite a bit of work to do. The Arduino cannot "speak" directly; to say "The temperature is 22-degrees Celsius," it requires several sound files. The first part, "The temperature is" will be one file, and the last part, "degrees Celsius" will also be one file. In between, you have to record your voice or get a friend to record theirs. Don't worry; you don't have to record every number between zero and 100; like the previous example in Chapter 14, this application does not go above 40. You can choose later on if you want to go higher. Also, the English language does come to your rescue in this example; every number between zero and 20 will have to be recorded, but after that, it is easier. For example, in the 30s, each number starts with "thirty," followed by 1 digit. The number 37 could therefore be a file with the word "thirty," and a file with the word "seven." This is exactly what your GPS system does in your car; "In four-hundred meters, turn right" is actually composed of several files. It is up to you to create those files or to find some free audio files on the Internet—the choice is yours.

You must decide how to proceed and with the exact wording required. For this example, you create numerous audio files. The first one, called `temp.wav`, will contain a quick phrase; "The current temperature is" or words to that effect. Afterward, you need to create numerous files; each number from 0 to 20 and named as the number they contain, plus the extension .wav. For example, the file containing the word "18" would be "18.wav." There is no need to record 21; this will be done by mixing 20 and 1. Instead, record the tens: 20, 30, and 40. For most applications, 40 should be sufficient.

The application itself will be simple, but it is something that you can use to create a nice project. When the user presses a button, the temperature is sampled. One by one, files are opened on the SD card and sent to an audio buffer. When all the files are read, the last file is closed, and the system waits for the user to press the button again.

Hardware

For this example, you will be using an Arduino Due with a shield compatible with the board that has an SD slot. The Ethernet shield used in Chapter 9 would suffice, even if the Ethernet adapter is not used; this application needs only the SD-card slot. The LM35's output will be connected to analog input 5, and the ground pin will be connected to the ground pin on the Arduino Due, but the +Vs pin is different. On previous examples, it was connected to the +5V pin because that is all that was available. However, the component's documentation states that the +Vs pin must have at least 4 V, but the Arduino Due is powered only by 3.3 V. On the Arduino Due, there are two voltage pins: 3.3 V and 5 V. For this example, the LM35 will be powered by the +5-V pin. For other components, this might have been a problem; the Arduino Due is powered at 3.3 V, and the inputs expect to have 3.3 V or lower; applying 5 V to an input could damage the microcontroller. The LM35, however, can safely be powered by +5 V in this application because the output is equivalent to 10 mV per degree Celsius, or 1.5 V for 150 degrees. Therefore, the LM35 can safely be powered by +5 V because it will not output more than 3.3 V.

The button will be connected to digital pin 2. It will be powered by 3.3 V and connected to ground through a 10-Kilohm pull-down resistor. When the button is open, the input will be connected to the ground, resulting in a logical zero. When the button is pressed, the input will be connected to 3.3 V, resulting in a logical 1.

Finally, the audio output will be connected to DAC0. Remember, this is only a signal; it is not strong enough to power a speaker. Using too much power will result in damage to the Arduino. To output audio, the schematic uses a jack connector. Most home Hi-Fi systems or mobile speakers use a jack input, usually by using a male-to-male jack cable. It uses the same connecter you would use to connect your MP3 player to the speaker.

Figure 18-3 shows the layout for this design.

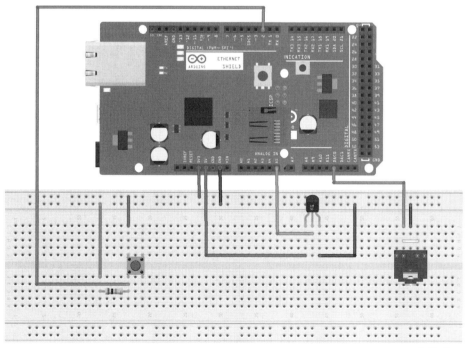

Figure 18-3: Hardware layout (Image created with Fritzing)

Sketch

The code that will be used for this sketch is presented in Listing 18-1.

Listing 18-1: Sketch (filename: Chapter18.ino)

```
1    #include <SD.h>
2    #include <SPI.h>
3    #include <Audio.h>
4
5    const int buttonPin = 2; // The pushbutton pin
6    const int sensorPin = A5; // The analog input pin
7
8    void setup()
9    {
10     // Debug output at 9600 baud
11     Serial.begin(9600);
12
13     // Set up SD-card. Check your board for the pin to use
14     if (!SD.begin(4))
15     {
16       Serial.println("SD initialization failed!");
17       return;
18     }
19
20     // Configure high-speed SPI transfers
21     SPI.setClockDivider(4);
22
23     // 44100Khz mono files, 100 mSec of prebuffering.
24     Audio.begin(44100, 100);
25
26     // Configure pins
27     pinMode(buttonPin, INPUT);
28     pinMode(sensorPin, INPUT);
29   }
30
31   void loop()
32   {
33     // Wait for a button to be pressed
34
35     if (digitalRead(buttonPin))
36     {
37       // read the value from the sensor:
38       int sensorValue = analogRead(sensorPin);
39
40       Serial.print("Sensor reading: ");
41       Serial.print(sensorValue, DEC);
42
43       // Convert the temperature (3.3V on the Due)
44       int tempC = ( 3.3 * analogRead(sensorPin) * 100.0) / 1024.0;
45       Serial.print(" Temperature: ");
```

```
46      Serial.println(tempC, DEC);
47
48      // Play the first file
49      playfile(String("temp.wav"));
50
51      // File name to read?
52      if (tempC > 20)
53      {
54        Serial.print("Open filename ");
55        String filename1 =  String(String(tempC - (tempC % 10))
56              + ".wav");
57        Serial.println(filename1);
55        playfile(filename1);
59
60        Serial.print("Open filename ");
61        String filename2 =  String(String(tempC % 10) + ".wav");
62        Serial.println(filename2);
63        playfile(filename2);
64      }
65      else
66      {
67        Serial.print("Open filename ");
68        String filename =  String(String(tempC) + ".wav");
69        Serial.println(filename);
70       playfile(filename);
71      }
72    }
73    else
74    {
75      // Button was not pressed, sleep for a bit
76      delay(50);
77    }
78  }
79
80  void playfile(String filename)
81  {
82    const int S=1024; // Number of samples to read in block
83    short buffer[S];
84    char chfilename[20];
85
86    filename.toCharArray(chfilename, 20);
87
88    // Open first wave file from sdcard
89    File myFile = SD.open(chfilename, FILE_READ);
90    if (!myFile)
91    {
92      // If the file could not be opened, halt
93      Serial.print("Error opening file: ");
94      Serial.println(filename);
95      while (true);
```

continues

Listing 18-1: *(continued)*

```
96    }
97
98    // Loop the contents of the file
99    while (myFile.available())
100   {
101     // Read from the file into buffer
102     myFile.read(buffer, sizeof(buffer));
103
104     // Prepare samples
105     int volume = 1023;
106     Audio.prepare(buffer, S, volume);
107     // Feed samples to audio
108     Audio.write(buffer, S);
109   }
110   myFile.close();
111 }
```

This sketch has three main functions: the usual `setup()` and `loop()` but also `playfile()`, the function that will be called to play audio files.

`setup()` is declared on line 8. The serial port is configured on line 11, and the SD card reader is initialized on line 14. Communication between the Arduino and the SD card controller is done via the SPI protocol, and reading wave files requires high-speed transfers. To do this, on line 21, the SPI clock divider is defined to speed up communications. On line 24, the Audio library is initialized. It will expect mono files with a bit rate of 44.1 kHz, and allocates a buffer for 100 milliseconds, more than enough for most data reads from the SD card. Two pins are then defined on lines 27 and 28; the pin used to read the state of the button is set as an input, and then the sensor pin is also defined as an input.

`loop()` is declared on line 31. This is where most of the work will be done. On line 35, the state of the button is read. If the button is not pressed, almost all of `loop()` is skipped, and the sketch pauses for 50 milliseconds on line 75 before repeating.

If the button is pressed, then the analog value on the sensor pin is read and stored as a variable. To help debugging, the value is displayed over the serial port. On line 44, a calculation is made, converting the reading from the sensor to degrees Celsius. Remember that the Arduino Due is a 3.3-V device, and therefore, the analog value is compared to 3.3 V, not to 5 V. The temperature is then output to the serial port.

To save space on the SD card, the recording of the different numbers have been separated into different files. If the temperature is below 21 degrees, then a single filename will be used; put simply, the filename is the temperature. If the temperature is eighteen degrees, it refers to a file called "18.wav". Temperatures of 21 degrees and more will cause two files to be called; one containing the 10s, and one containing the single 1s. Twenty-four degrees will cause the sketch to call two files: "20.wav" and "4.wav". After the filename is created, `playfile()` is called with the filename passed as a `String`.

`playfile()` is declared on line 80. It takes a single parameter, a `String`, the name of the file to be opened. On line 82, a `const int` is declared, which is the amount of data to be copied from the wave file per pass. On the next line, a buffer is created; this is the container where data will be placed from the file on the SD card. On line 84, another variable is created; this is again the filename, but as a `char` array; the `SD.open()` function does not accept strings, only `chars`.

On line 89, the sketch attempts to open the file on the SD card. If it fails, it prints out a message on the serial port and then halts execution. If the sketch does open the file, it carries on.

On line 99, a `while` loop is created, and loops until there is no more data left to read in the file. This is done with the `File.available()` function, which returns the number of bytes that can be read from the file. On line 102, the file is read in blocks of `sizeof(buffer)` into `buffer`. On line 105, a variable is declared and contains the value 1023. This is used on the next line, where the Audio library prepares the samples with the `Audio.prepare()` function. It takes the local buffer called `buffer`, the size of that buffer, and the volume to be applied; in this case, 1023, or the highest volume possible. The final step is to write the local buffer into the Audio buffer with the function `Audio.write()`. This function takes the same parameters as the `Audio.prepare()` function, with the exception of the volume. When the `while` loop is finished, the file is closed, and the function returns.

Exercise

This application measures the temperature from a single source. You could modify the sketch to retrieve the temperature from an inside sensor, as well as the temperature from outside. You could also add a humidity sensor or an ultraviolet sensor. By pressing a button, you could know that the outside temperature is 38-degrees Celsius, the humidity is 20 percent, and the UV index is 8, but inside you have a comfortable 24 degrees.

Not everyone uses Celsius; you could modify the sketch to use Fahrenheit, and even use the EEPROM to store your setting, making this a sketch that you can use worldwide. You could even create your own shield with sensor connectors, an SD slot, and an audio jack integrated directly onto the shield.

Summary

In this chapter, you have seen how the Due has some advanced functions that can be used to play back audio files, and the library used to perform these actions. You have seen how to wire an Arduino Due to a loudspeaker to create your own alarm clock, temperature sensor, or any sort of device that requires an audio output. In the next chapter, I will show you the Scheduler library, an advanced library for the Arduino Due that allows you to run different tasks at different times.

Scheduler

This chapter discusses the following functions of the Scheduler library for the Arduino Due:

- `startLoop()`
- `yield()`

The hardware needed to use these functions includes:

- Arduino Due
- LM35 temperature sensor
- PowerSwitch Tail II (110 V or 220 V)
- Adafruit's RGB LED Weatherproof flexi-strip (`http://www.adafruit.com/products/346`)
- 3 x TIP120 transistors
- 3 x 100-Ω ¼-W resistors

NOTE The Scheduler library is only found in Arduino IDE version 1.5 and later. It is still considered experimental and under development.

You can find the code downloads for this chapter at `http://www.wiley.com/go/arduinosketches` on the Download Code tab. The code is in the Chapter 19 folder and the filename is `Chapter19.ino`.

Introducing Scheduling

Back in the early days of computing, computers could do only one thing at a time. When you turned on your trusty PC and put in a disk, the operating system started. Then you changed the disk and ran a spreadsheet. Your spreadsheet appeared on the screen after a few seconds and you heard some dubious sounds from the disk drive, and then, finally, you could get to work. If you wanted to take a break and play a game in glorious four colors, you had to save your work and quit the spreadsheet (or in some cases, actually restart the computer) before playing a game. With disks, this didn't matter so much; you couldn't have two programs open at the same time.

When graphical systems arrived on the PC, users wanted to have windows containing their applications, but they also wanted to switch from one application to another, or even have two running at the same time. Hard drives could store several programs, and there was enough system memory to have multiple executables in memory at the same time. The question was, how do you run two programs at the same time?

Computer manufacturers started selling computers with graphical systems with a lot of memory and internal hard drives, and this became standard. The more they added on, the more users wanted. To attract users, they would say that you could run several programs at the same time and that they could run simultaneously. This is one of the biggest lies in computers, but it is close enough.

A processor cannot execute multiple programs at the same time; technically it isn't possible. A processor can execute the instructions it is given, one at a time, but the trick is in giving it the instructions it needs to run.

The operating system is the software heart of any system. An application cannot run without the help of an operating system. Even if you use only one program, you can't just install that program onto a computer without an operating system. The operating system does much more than just run programs; it sets up the hardware, including keyboard and mouse inputs, and video output, and it configures the memory as required—something a normal program doesn't need. A program can tell the operating system to print something on the screen, and it is the operating system that does all the hard work, including multitasking.

Multitasking is the art of running several programs in a way that makes users think that they are running at exactly the same time, but they aren't. The operating system gives control to an application (or thread) before either taking back control or waiting until the application gives control back to the operating system, as shown in Figure 19-1.

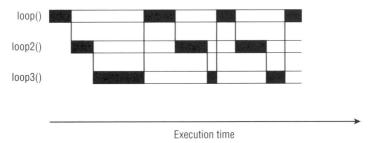

Figure 19-1: Execution of threads

This has led to some complicated situations; Microsoft Windows 3.1 used something called cooperative multitasking, where applications had to cooperate. If an application didn't cooperate (either it wasn't designed to run in Windows or crashed) then control was never given to other applications. In Figure 19-2, the thread `badloop()` takes control but never gives it back, leaving two threads unable to function.

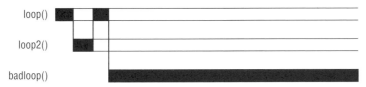

Figure 19-2: Noncooperative thread

Today, operating systems use multiple techniques to ensure that applications will run together, even if one is greedy with system resources, and the entire system keeps on going even if an application crashes.

While writing this book, I am using a text editor. In the background is a music player to help me concentrate. I am using a two-monitor setup, and on the opposite screen I have a web browser for reference, and the Arduino IDE to write the sketches that I will be using. If I need a break, I'll play a game, but I won't close any applications, I'll let the operating system keep them alive while I have a break. When I've had a break, I'll come back to my text editor and continue where I was.

Arduino Multitasking

Arduinos, by default, do not multitask. Take this simple sketch as an example:

```
// the setup function runs once when you press reset or power the board
void setup() {
  // initialize digital pin 13 as an output.
  pinMode(13, OUTPUT);
}
```

```
// the loop function runs over and over again forever
void loop() {
  digitalWrite(13, HIGH);  // turn the LED on (HIGH is the voltage level)
  delay(1000);             // wait for a second
  digitalWrite(13, LOW);   // turn the LED off by making the voltage LOW
  delay(1000);             // wait for a second
}
```

This is the Blink example found in the Arduino IDE's Examples menu. In this simple example, an LED is set to blink: one second on, one second off. The code used to switch between the different states runs quickly; it requires mere microseconds. `digitalWrite()` requires a little bit more time, but it is still fast. Next, the sketch runs a `delay()`. This function is called a *blocking* function; it prevents all other functions from running until it has completed. Because Arduinos are designed to be single-task devices, no multitasking library was originally created. An Arduino will continue to run a single task, waiting for data, or acting on data. Some libraries allow something called a callback; a function that will be run when an external event occurs. For example, an Arduino can't be told to wait forever for an I2C instruction. In this case, a callback is programmed. The Arduino can continue to do what it needs to do (for example, read sensors) and when an I2C instruction arrives, the Arduino stops what it is doing and runs the callback before returning to whatever it was doing before being interrupted. However, this is not the case of most applications; almost all functions are blocking, and other functions cannot run until it has completed.

The Arduino Due uses a different microcontroller; instead of using an Atmel AVR, it uses an Atmel ATSAM3X8, Atmel's implementation of an ARM Cortex-M3 microcontroller. It is a 32-bit device running at 84 MHz. It has some advanced features and is a powerful device. Because of its capabilities, one developer in particular decided to change the way it worked and to implement a scheduling system. The library, called Scheduler, was introduced in Arduino IDE 1.5.

Scheduler

The scheduler implementation is a cooperative scheduler. It remains powerful yet lightweight but does require some careful thinking when implementing. It can run several functions at the same time, so long as they cooperate. It also rewrites one function in particular; the `delay()` function, which is discussed later in the Cooperative Multitasking section.

The first thing you need to do is to import the Scheduler library. This can be done either from the IDE menu (Sketch ➪ Import Library ➪ Schedule) or by adding the `include` manually.

```
#include <Scheduler.h>
```

From here, use `startLoop()`:

```
Scheduler.startLoop(loopName);
```

This function takes a single parameter: the name of a function declared inside the sketch. The named function cannot take any arguments, but it can be any function that you wish. Multiple functions can run consecutively by calling `startLoop()` for each named function:

```
Scheduler.startLoop(loop1);
Scheduler.startLoop(loop2);
Scheduler.startLoop(loop3);
```

There is one other function to know about—`yield()`:

```
yield();
```

This function takes no parameters, returns no data, and from a visual stand-point, does not do anything, but this is the function that is called to yield control to another function. Remember, the Scheduler library uses cooperative multi-tasking, so control must be given back to other functions; otherwise, they will not have any CPU time.

Cooperative Multitasking

Consider the following example:

```
#include <Scheduler.h>

void setup()
{
  Serial.begin(9600);

  // Add "loop1" and "loop2" to scheduling.
  Scheduler.startLoop(loop1);
  Scheduler.startLoop(loop2);
}

void loop()
{
  delay(1000);
}

void loop1()
{
  Serial.println("loop1()");
  delay(1000);
}

void loop2()
```

```
{
  Serial.println("loop2()");
  delay(1000);
}
```

This sketch is simple; it will import the Scheduler library and run two functions: `loop1()` and `loop2()`. Remember, `loop()` is always called. The two additional loop functions will simply print a line of text to the serial port and then wait for a second.

Remember when I said that `delay()` was blocking? With the Scheduler library, it isn't; it allows functions to sleep for a set time but gives control back to other functions. In this case, one loop is called, and when it reaches `delay()`, it gives control to the other loop function. When that one reaches `delay()`, it will once again return control to the first function, and this will happen until `delay()` ends, after 1 second.

The output of the function on the serial port is a list, alternating between `"loop1()"` and `"loop2()"`.

Scheduled functions can also use global variables. Change the sketch to add the following:

```
#include <Scheduler.h>

int i;

void setup()
{
  Serial.begin(9600);

  // Add "loop1" and "loop2" to scheduling.
  Scheduler.startLoop(loop1);
  Scheduler.startLoop(loop2);

  i = 0;
}

void loop()
{
  delay(1000);
}

void loop1()
{
  i++;
  Serial.print("loop1(): ");
  Serial.println(i, DEC);
  delay(1000);
}
```

```
void loop2()
{
  i++;
  Serial.print("loop2()");
  Serial.println(i, DEC);
  delay(1000);
}
```

A global variable has been added: i. Each time a loop function is called, i is incremented, and the value is displayed. The output of this function is again a list, alternating between "loop1()" and "loop2()" with the variable i incrementing each time.

Noncooperative Functions

Now, add something else. The variable i is incremented each time a loop is called, and we would like to have a message displayed when i reaches the value 20. This can be achieved by adding a third function, one that looks at the value of i and prints a message if the value is reached.

```
#include <Scheduler.h>

int i;

void setup()
{
  Serial.begin(9600);

  // Add "loop1" "loop2" and "loop3" to scheduling.
  Scheduler.startLoop(loop1);
  Scheduler.startLoop(loop2);
  Scheduler.startLoop(loop3);

  i = 0;
}

void loop()
{
  delay(1000);
}

void loop1()
{
  i++;
  Serial.print("loop1(): ");
  Serial.println(i, DEC);
  delay(1000);
}
```

```
void loop2()
{
  i++;
  Serial.print("loop2()");
  Serial.println(i, DEC);
  delay(1000);
}

void loop3()
{
  if (i == 20)
  {
    Serial.println("Yay! We have reached 20! Time to celebrate!");
  }
}
```

The new function, loop3(), is called in the setup() function and has a single task; to monitor the value of i and print a message when i reaches the value 20. Except it doesn't. If you run the program and open a serial monitor, you'll see there is no output from this sketch, and nothing is displayed on the serial port. loop1() and loop2() do not print any values, and loop3() does not celebrate the arrival of the value 20. What happened?

The code is valid; there is no syntax error. Because the code ceased to work when loop3() was added, it is safe to say that the problem lies within this function. Time to take a closer look.

It starts with an if statement: if i equals 20, then a message is printed. And if i doesn't equal 20? Nothing, it just loops. It should work, and on most multitasking systems, it would. Most multitasking systems have a kernel that gives control to functions and then takes control away after a set period of time, or number of instructions, or whatever algorithm the system uses. On cooperative multitasking, it is up to the programs (or functions) to play nice with the other functions and to give control back. The problem with loop3() is that it continues to run but never gives control back to the other functions. It keeps on looping waiting for i to reach 20, when i can never be incremented. The other two functions are still waiting for their turn. To tell loop3() to give control back to other functions, use yield().

```
void loop3()
{
  if (i == 20)
  {
    Serial.println("Yay! We have reached 20! Time to celebrate!");
  }
  yield();
}
```

A single modification has been made; `yield()` has been added after the `if` loop. When the sketch reaches this point, it releases control of `loop3()` and looks to see if any other function needs CPU time. Now all the functions are cooperative, and the sketch functions as needed.

Cooperative multitasking is an excellent way of making reliable multitasking code, without the need for a heavy operating system. However, care must be taken to make sure that the threads are cooperative, by adding `yield()` functions or `delay()` statements.

Example Program

This example will be an aquarium temperature sensor, one that will monitor the temperature and control a lighting system and control the temperature depending on the result. Every few seconds, the sensor will send the temperature by serial.

Aquariums can be expensive, and enthusiasts often welcome devices that can help them monitor certain aspects of the water; temperature, acidity, water hardness, and oxygen levels are all critical to the well-being of the fish they contain. A mistake can often be disastrous.

The temperature sensor is simple; as with the previous chapter, you will be using an LM35 temperature sensor. Tropical fish require precise temperatures, and this application can help you achieve that. Most heating elements auto-regulate themselves, but for exotic fish, or for breeding conditions, you may want to regulate the temperature; it should be warmer in the day and slightly cooler at night. Bala sharks, also known as silver sharks, are a beautiful addition to large aquariums—and my personal favorite. They are peaceful creatures but are difficult to please, requiring a temperature between 22 and 28°C. For this application, the heater will be turned off at 26 and turned on at 24.

Also, lighting conditions are important, especially when breeding. Most lighting turns on rather violently in the morning and turns off entirely at night, instead of a more natural cycle of slowly brightening the light and slowly dimming. This sketch enables you to change that. Figure 19-3 shows the lighting strategy.

Figure 19-3: Lighting control

The light regulator will use the Arduino Due's digital to analog converter. It will be a single task; one that will wait for hours before changing the light settings.

There are two ways to make a sketch wait for a long time, either using the `delay()` function, which normally means that no other calculation can take place, or by reading the number of milliseconds since the sketch started. To make things simple, this application will use two loops; one for the temperature sensor and one for the lighting application. Both will be running independently.

Hardware

The Arduino Due will have an LM35 temperature sensor connected to A0. The LM35 will be powered by 5 volts. Even though the LM35 runs at 5 V, it will never reach 3.3 V, so it's safe to connect to the Arduino Due.

> **WARNING**   The LM35 is not waterproof! Do not place it directly in water; it could damage the component and cause oxidation of power wires, resulting in toxic water for the fish. Make sure to totally isolate the LM35 and any wires before placing them inside an aquarium. The outside glass of an aquarium is often a good indication of the temperature of the water; you can place the LM35 outside the tank, directly on the glass.

The PowerSwitch Tail II is a power cable with on-board electronics. When it receives a signal on the input pins, it lets the AC electricity through. It requires little energy to activate; at 5 V, it will draw about 10 mA, which the Arduino is more than capable of delivering. The PowerSwitch Tail II is also "opto-isolated," meaning that the low voltage is never in any contact whatsoever with the AC lines, making this device extremely safe to use. The output will be connected to digital pin 7.

To light the aquarium, you can use either an LED array or LED strip. Both of these can be found on sites like Adafruit. For this application, I recommend Adafruit's RGB LED Weatherproof flexi-strip (available at `http://www.adafruit .com/products/346`). These strips contain 60 RGB LEDs per meter, and their length can be adjusted according to your aquarium. However, they draw far more current than an Arduino can deliver, so they require an external power supply and will require three transistors to power them, one for each color channel. A transistor is like a switch: by providing a small current to the base, a much larger current can flow from the collector to the emitter, allowing the Arduino to power devices that either require far more current than what it can provide, or even power devices that require more voltage.

> **CROSS-REFERENCE**   Transistors were presented in Chapter 3 in the "Transistors" section.

To control the light intensity, you will be using PWM. The LED will essentially be turned on and off very quickly, far too fast for the human eye to see, and by varying the duty cycle—that is to say, the amount of time spent on compared to the amount of time spent off—you can adjust the light intensity. The three transistors will be controlled by pins 2, 3, and 4. The TIP120 transistor is a powerful component that can let through a large amount of current compared to what the Arduino can provide, or sink. Adafruit's flexi-strip has four connectors: one for a 12-V power supply, and one for each of the red, green, and blue components. By connecting these to the *ground*, or 0 V, they turn on each of the color components. This is what the transistor will be used for; it will allow as much current through as is required, but since the base will be connected to PWM, it will turn on and off very quickly, giving the appearance of dimming.

This device does not have a screen and does not provide any way to let the user configure the timing sequence or when it should start. By default, the sketch will begin its timing sequence as if the user had connected it at midday. Figure 19-4 shows the schematic.

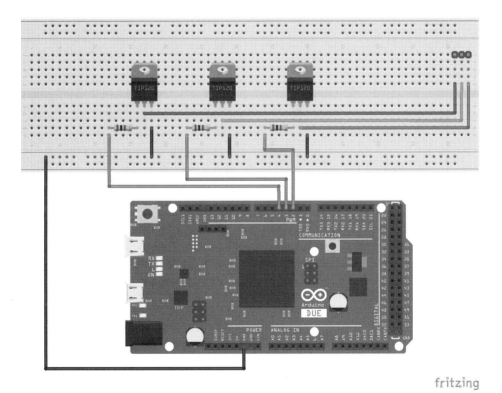

Figure 19-4: Schematic (Image created with Fritzing)

Sketch

Use the code in Listing 19-1 for this sketch.

Listing 19-1: Sketch (filename: `Chapter19.ino`)

```
1    #include <Scheduler.h>
2
3    const int sensorPin = A0; // The analog input pin
4    const int powerPin = 7; // The power socket output pin
5
6    const int rPin = 4; // Red color component
7    const int gPin = 3; // Green color component
8    const int bPin = 2; // Blue color component
9
10   const int maxTemp = 26; // Turn off heater when above this temp
11   const int minTemp = 24; // Turn on heater when below this temp
12
13   int powerPinStatus = LOW; // By default, no power on the AC circuit
14
15   int i; // Temporary variable for if statements
16
17   void setup()
18   {
19     // Serial output at 9600 baud
20     Serial.begin(9600);
21
22     // Configure sensor pin
23     pinMode(sensorPin, INPUT);
24
25     // Start heater and lighting treads
26     Scheduler.startLoop(heatloop);
27     Scheduler.startLoop(lightloop);
28   }
29
30   void loop()
31   {
32     yield(); // Releases the Arduino from the main loop
33   }
34
35   // The loop responsible for checking water temperature
36   void heatloop()
37   {
38     // Get a temperature reading from the temperature sensor
39     // 3.3V on the due
40     int tempC = ( 3.3 * analogRead(sensorPin) * 100.0) / 1024.0;
41
42     // Send the temperature reading out the serial port
43     Serial.print("Temperature: ");
44     Serial.println(tempC);
45
46     // Check to see if we need to change the output
47     if (powerPinStatus == LOW)
48     {
```

```
49      //Mains plug currently turned off
50      if (tempC < minTemp)
51      {
52        powerPinStatus = HIGH;
53        digitalWrite(powerPin, powerPinStatus);
54      }
55    }
56    else
57    {
58      // Mains plug currently turned on
59      if (tempC > maxTemp)
60      {
61        powerPinStatus = LOW;
62        digitalWrite(powerPin, powerPinStatus);
63      }
64    }
65
66    // Warn if possible heating element failure
67    if (tempC < (minTemp - 2))
68    {
69      Serial.print("CRITICAL: Water temperature too low. ");
70      Serial.println("Heating element failure?");
71    }
72
73    // Sleep for ten seconds
74    delay(10000);
75  }
76
77  // The loop responsible for lighting
78  void lightloop()
79  {
80    // Wait for 7 hours before turning the lights off
81    delay(7 * 60* 60 * 1000);
82
83    // Lower the light level over the span of one hour
84    for (i = 255; i >= 0; i--)
85    {
86      analogWrite(rPin, i);  // Write the red light level
87      analogWrite(gPin, i);  // Write the green light level
88      analogWrite(bPin, i);  // Write the blue light level
89      delay(60 * 60 * 1000 / 255); //Sleep for a few seconds
90    }
91
92    // Wait for 11 hours
93    delay(11 * 60* 60 * 1000);
94
95    // Increase the light level over the span of one hour
96    for (i = 0; i <= 255; i++)
97    {
98      analogWrite(rPin, i);  // Write the red light level
99      analogWrite(gPin, i);  // Write the green light level
100     analogWrite(bPin, i);  // Write the blue light level
```

continues

Listing 19-1 (*continued*)

```
101    delay(60 * 60 * 1000 / 255); //Sleep for a few seconds
102  }
103
104  //Wait for 4 hours
105  delay(4 * 60* 60 * 1000);
106 }
```

This sketch begins by importing the Scheduler library. On lines 3 and 4, the input and output pins are defined. On lines 6, 7, and 8, the pins used to control the color components are declared. On lines 10 and 11, two temperatures are defined; the minimum and maximum temperature. When the minimum temperature is reached, the heating element is turned on. When the maximum temperature is reached, the heating element is turned off. Change the values to suit your aquarium.

On line 13 a variable is declared, containing the status of the output pin. By default, the status is set to LOW. On line 15 a temporary value is declared. It will be used later by one of the functions.

setup() is declared on line 17. It configures the serial port at 9600 baud; it sets the sensor pin to input; and it registers two functions as threads: heatloop() and lightloop().

loop() is declared on line 30 and contains a single instruction: yield(). Every time the CPU gives control to this function, it immediately gives control back to the sketch, allowing the CPU to control the two other scheduled loops.

On line 36, heatloop() is declared. This is the function that supervises the heating element; taking measurements from the LM35 and acting upon that information. First, on line 40, it reads the temperature on the analog input in degrees Celsius. On lines 43 and 44, this temperature is printed to the serial port. On line 47, program execution enters an if statement depending on the state of the output pin. If the pin is set to LOW, it compares the current temperature to the minimum temperature. If the current temperature is too low, the pin status is inverted, and the pin is set to HIGH. If the pin is already HIGH, the current temperature is checked against the maximum temperature. If the temperature is too high, the pin status is again inverted, the pin is set LOW, and program execution continues. On line 7, another comparison is made. If the current temperature is lower than the minimum allowed temperature minus 2 degrees, the serial port issues a warning; maybe the heating element is defective and can no longer heat the water, in which case immediate action should be taken. Finally, the function sleeps for 10 seconds before continuing. Because the Scheduler library has been imported, this is no longer a blocking function; instead, control is given to other threads.

On line 76, lightloop() is declared. This function relies heavily on delay(), something that can be tricky when using threads. It has five phases. First, it runs delay() for 7 hours. Remember, this application will be plugged in at midday, and the lights will begin to dim at 7 P.M. At 7 P.M, the second phase begins; the Arduino's PWM has 256 possible values. A loop, decreases the value of each of the color outputs by 1, creating a `delay()` over 1 hour divided into 256 steps. Once this hour has passed, the sketch will wait for 11 hours. At 7 A.M, the sketch will begin to increase the light levels using the looping technique, simulating a morning sunrise over the course of an hour. The sketch then waits for another 4 hours, until midday. It then repeats the cycle.

Exercises

This application is extremely useful for fish-keepers, but connecting to the PC to get temperature information may be an unnecessary process. Also, the temperature warning function is critical, but again, if the computer is not turned on, the user never receives his warning. This application could benefit from an LCD screen to be effective—to show the temperature, output status, and any warning messages.

Turning this application on at exactly midday may not be practical for many people. A real-time clock module would be a good tool for keeping accurate timing.

The strip light contains RGB LEDs, and this sketch changes all the colors at the same rate, resulting in white light. However, in some cases you might not want white light, but maybe something more green to simulate a more realistic environment, or maybe leave some blue light on during the night. You can easily change the sketch to add the color you want.

Summary

In this chapter, you have seen how powerful the Scheduler can be with only a few instructions. You have seen how an Arduino Due can perform multiple tasks at the same time, and how to avoid possible problems. In the next chapter, you will see the USBHost library and how to connect USB input devices to your Arduino, allowing text and mouse inputs for your sketches.

USBHost

This chapter discusses the following functions:

- `keyPressed()`
- `keyReleased()`
- `getModifiers()`
- `getKey()`
- `getOemKey()`
- `mouseMoved()`
- `mouseDragged()`
- `mousePressed()`
- `mouseReleased()`
- `getXChange()`
- `getYChange()`
- `getButton()`

The hardware needed to use these functions includes:

- Arduino Due
- USB keyboard
- USB OTG micro adapter

You can find the code download for this chapter at `http://www.wiley.com/ go/arduinosketches` on the Download Code tab. The code is in the Chapter 20 folder and the filename is `Chapter 20.ino`.

Introducing USBHost

Most people do not understand the nightmares that some computer users previously had when adding peripherals. When the PC originally shipped, it did not have a mouse as standard; you needed to buy that separately. It came with a keyboard, but that is about it. The keyboard was a standard element to computers, and it still is. Since there is no need to have two keyboards connected to a computer, each PC came with a single keyboard connector, the DIN keyboard connector. It was large and bulky, and kept the connector firmly in place. Then manufacturers decided to add a mouse. Mice were normally sold with a serial connector, the highly reliable RS-232 connector. Because most computers were sold with two serial ports and one parallel port, that was easy. It left ports free.

Suppose the user wanted to add a printer. Printers were almost always connected to parallel ports, but the computer had only one. Then a 56-k modem connected to the remaining serial port. That's it. No more connectors left. This would be a problem if the user wanted to go further and connect a scanner or other device. Expansion cards existed to add a second parallel port, but what if the user wanted a scanner and two printers? Color printers existed, but they were expensive, and the cartridges were even more so. For printing in black and white, some users still preferred to have a second printer for black and white only.

Peripherals were becoming more and more common, and if the user scanned lots of text and images, sooner or later, they would require storage. Iomega's Zip drive was originally an external diskette drive, but one that had a large capacity compared to floppy disks; the original Zip drive could store 100 megabytes. Don't laugh; that was a lot of storage in 1994! The problem was that it was a parallel device requiring a parallel port.

Peripheral shopping became a nightmare. When deciding on buying a peripheral or not, people had to ask themselves, "Do I have a spare serial/parallel/SCSI port?" Mice were serial devices, and because every computer being shipped suddenly had graphical interfaces, a mouse was a requirement. Enter the PS/2 interface.

The PS/2 interface was designed for simplicity. Each computer had one keyboard and one mouse. The old DIN keyboard connector was replaced with a PS/2 keyboard connector, and mice were created with a PS/2 connector. There were two connectors on computer mainboards: one purple port for keyboards and one green port for mice. Both were physically identical: They were mini-DIN connectors. They had the same power connectors and the same data connectors, but if the user mistakenly inverted the keyboard and mouse, they would not function. Simply unplugging and replugging into the correct port resolved this. This left a serial connector free for other peripherals: modems, PC-to-PC connectors, software dongles, joysticks, circuit programmers, parallel port switchers, to name but a few—still far too many. Also, another interesting event was occurring; some users wanted something that the designers hadn't anticipated: two interface options, like one standard mouse for day-to-day operations and either a track-pad or a mouse specialized for graphical work.

To simplify everything, Universal Serial Bus (USB) was created, which is a way of connecting devices to a computer using a standard interface. Keyboards, mice, scanners, modems … just about anything could be connected to the computer using USB. Even better, if the amount of USB ports on the computer weren't enough to add another peripheral, a USB hub could be used. A single USB controller can have as many as 127 different ports by using hubs.

USB Protocol

For USB to work, it requires at least one USB host. This is the device that controls USB devices, and USB devices communicate with the host. For a standard PC setup, the PC is the USB host.

Devices connect to the host, and when they do, an enumeration occurs. Each device connected is given a number from 1 to 127. When enumerated, the device description is read, so the USB host knows what this device can do. Sometimes drivers are needed to fully use a USB device; some devices do not require drivers because the computer already knows what the device's function is. Several USB classes exist, and one of them is called HID, short for Human Interface Device. HID devices include keyboards and mice.

USB devices are *"hot pluggable"*; they can be connected while the system is running. They can also be disconnected without the need for rebooting; when unplugging your keyboard and plugging it into another USB port takes only a few seconds for the computer to recognize the new port.

For desktop and laptop computers, the USB mechanism is simple; the computer acts as the USB host, and a connected peripheral is a USB device. The computer enumerates the USB device, and a connection is established. For some devices, like mobile phones, this is a more complicated process.

Mobile phones lack the connectivity possibilities of a computer. They have a single USB port, no disk drive, no CD drive, and limited capabilities for physical input. Some phones can be used as USB drives; plug in the right kind of smart-phone to a computer, and the telephone can use an internal SD card as a disk, allowing the computer access to the files. This is great when you want to copy multimedia files onto a telephone, but it isn't always practical. What happens when you are far from your computer, when you have taken the perfect photo with your digital camera, and you want to send it via e-mail? This is where USB On-The-Go (USB OTG) comes in.

USB On-The-Go is an extension to the USB specification, allowing devices to act as either a master (host) or slave (peripheral). Technically, all USB OTG devices are masters, but when connected to another master, they can act as a slave. Some modern smartphones are USB OTG devices and act just like a normal USB device; plug them into a computer and they become USB slaves, allowing you to browse files. However, plug in a USB peripheral, and they become a master. A mobile phone can therefore be connected to a computer or to a USB drive. Your phone can then browse files on the USB key, just like a computer can.

USB Devices

There are far too many USB devices to list in a single book, and more and more devices are made each day. Practically any type of computer add-on can be found with a USB connection, from user input to screen output, from sampling graphics to playing sound. Some devices are intelligent and can communicate with a master, specifying their USB class and their capabilities. Some have no built-in intelligence and simply use the +5-V power supply that the USB bus supplies; this is often the case for some "gadget" USB devices; LED lights, fans, and so on.

Keyboards

A keyboard is one of the most useful components for any personal computer; it is the primary means of entering textual information to a computer; it is a human interface device.

Keyboards are, essentially, lots of electronic switches connected to a microcontroller. It isn't possible to have one wire per key, so keyboards use a mesh system. Essentially a giant game of battleships, a keypress causes two wires to become active, and the microcontroller senses this information and translates that into a *scancode*. It then sends this information to the computer.

A scancode corresponds to a key. The information is not sent in ASCII but in binary information. It is not sent in ASCII for two main reasons: one, not every letter can be sent as ASCII—function keys, for example. And two, a scancode does not represent a letter. Let me explain.

While writing this book, I am using a keyboard connected to my computer. I press the letter A, and the letter A appears in my text editor. I have a French keyboard which means the letters "Q" and "A" are swapped from an English keyboard. My operating system translates what I type. So while my keyboard has the letter "Q" written on it, as far as my computer is concerned (or even the embedded microcontroller), it is an "A". Anyone who has a non-English keyboard and installs operating systems knows; if the operating system has not been instructed to load a keymap, then the system defaults to QWERTY: the standard U.S. keyboard. This is something to remember.

The traditional PC keyboard is long dead; manufacturers are making friendlier keyboards with added buttons to control volume, applications, or even some laptop functions. More advanced keyboards have programmable buttons that can either be simple scancodes or preprogrammed to write several scancodes at once to the computer. Even more advanced gaming keyboards also have LCD screens and sometimes LCD keys. These are not "standard" keyboards; they require specific drivers to function but still embed part of a standard keyboard. When entering the BIOS, these special keyboards still work, but the LCD screen doesn't. To achieve this, there is often a small USB hub inside, with different components behind the hub: the keyboard, the LCD screen, and sometimes external USB ports to connect USB keys, headphones, and so on.

Mice

Mice are, today, a basic component of every computer, but it wasn't always the case. Early computers did not have a mouse, and they were added only when graphical interfaces became standard.

A mouse is a device, either mechanical or optical, that senses movement relative to the surface on which it is placed and sends movement information to the computer in x-/y-coordinates. In addition, there are also buttons (typically left, middle, and right), with a middle button often capable of scrolling. More advanced mice may have several more buttons, and gaming mice often have 10 or more buttons.

Hubs

USB hubs work like network hubs; they enable you to connect several devices onto a single port. To do this, the hub connects to the computer's USB host, and further devices are placed behind the hub. The hub dispatches messages from the host to the device, and messages from devices are sent to the host.

Arduino Due

The Arduino Due is different from other Arduinos for several reasons. It is based on Atmel's SAM3X8E microcontroller, which is in turn based on an ARM Cortex-M3, a powerful device. It has two micro-USB connectors, and runs at 3.3 V (see Figure 20-1).

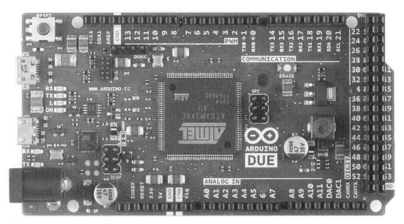

Figure 20-1: The Arduino Due

The USB connector adjacent to the power barrel, the Programming port, is a USB serial connector that is connected to an ATmega16U2 microcontroller which handles serial communication between the Arduino Due's main processor and the host computer. The other USB connector, the Native port, is connected directly to the SAM3X8E (see Figure 20-2). This means the Due has full control of this USB port, and can be connected as a slave for native serial communication. It is also USB OTG-compatible and can be connected to peripherals such as keyboards and mice using a special adapter.

Figure 20-2: USB OTG connector

These adapters have a micro-USB connector on one side and a full-size USB connector on the other, allowing keyboards and mice to be connected.

The Arduino Due can use the USBHost library, a powerful library containing routines to use keyboards and mice as input devices, but it does come at a cost. USB drivers tend to be big. To reduce the size and complexity of the driver for use with a microcontroller, it's limited to talk only to a single device: a keyboard or a mouse.

It cannot use USB hubs, and as such cannot talk to multiple devices or communicate with keyboards that have a built-in USB hub. This includes some specialized keyboards or keyboards with USB connectors for plugging in external devices.

USBHost Library

The Arduino 1.5 IDE comes with the USBHost library. To use it, you must first import it. This can be done in the menu: Sketch ⇨ Import Library ⇨ USBHost. This imports quite a few libraries, as shown here:

```
#include <hidboot.h>
#include <hidusagestr.h>
#include <KeyboardController.h>
#include <hid.h>
#include <confdescparser.h>
#include <parsetools.h>
#include <usb_ch9.h>
#include <Usb.h>
#include <adk.h>
#include <address.h>
#include <MouseController.h>
```

To initialize the USB subsystem, you must create a USBHost object:

```
// Initialize USB Controller
USBHost usb;
```

The usb object can then be given to the different software structures. To process USB events, you must use the task() function.

```
usb.task();
```

The task() function waits for a USB event and calls the necessary function as those events happen. The function is blocking; while it is running, no other functions can run. If no event is received, it will time out after 5 seconds. If no device is connected, this function returns immediately, instead of waiting for a time-out.

Keyboards

Keyboards have their own controller, the KeyboardController class. First, you must attach the KeyboardController to the USB subsystem:

```
// Initialize USB Controller
USBHost usb;

// Attach Keyboard controller to USB
KeyboardController keyboard(usb);
```

When initialized, this class calls two functions when a specified event occurs. There are two events that can be identified by the class outside `loop()`: when a key is pressed and when a key is released. These do not include modifier keys; Shift, Control, Alt, and other such keys do not call these functions, but Caps Lock does.

The two functions are `keyPressed()` and `keyReleased()`. No parameters are passed to these functions; they must retrieve pending information from other sources.

```
// This function is called when a key is pressed
void keyPressed()
{
  Serial.print("Key pressed");
}
```

This tells the sketch that a key has been pressed or released, but that is all. To know which key or combination of keys has been pressed, use `getKey()`.

```
result = keyboard.getKey();
```

This function takes no parameters and returns the ASCII code of the key pressed. Not all keys can be printed as ASCII, and for this reason, another function is available, `getOemKey()`.

```
result = getOemKey();
```

This function, unlike `getKey()`, does not return an ASCII code, but the OEM code associated with this key. This key can be one of the function keys or a multimedia key. It does not work on modifier keys: Shift, Alt, AltGr, Control, and so on. To get the status of modifier keys, use `getModifiers()`:

```
result = keyboard.getModifiers();
```

This function returns an `int`, representing a bit field with modifiers, listed in Table 20-1.

Table 20-1: Modifier values

MODIFIER KEY	VALUE
LeftCtrl	1
LeftShift	2
Alt	4
LeftCmd	8
RightCtrl	16
RightShift	32
AltGr	64
RightCmd	128

The modifiers listed in this table have been created as constants, and as such, can be used directly in your code.

```
mod = keyboard.getModifiers();
if (mod & LeftCtrl)
    Serial.println("L-Ctrl");
```

Mice

Mice are just as easy to use as a keyboard, using similar techniques. To use a USB mouse, you must attach the `MouseController` to the USB subsystem, just like with a keyboard.

```
// Attach mouse controller to USB
MouseController mouse(usb);
```

Just like the keyboard controller, the mouse controller can also call functions. There are four of them: when the mouse is moved, when the mouse is dragged, when a button is pushed, and when a button is released.

```
void mouseMoved()
{
  // Mouse has moved
}
void mouseDragged()
{
  // Mouse was moved with a button pressed
}
void mousePressed()
{
  // A mouse button has been pressed
}
void mouse Released()
{
 // A pressed button has been released
}
```

To retrieve movement information, you use `getXChange()` and `getYChange()`. Both return `int` values, indicating the relative change in direction since the last time the mouse was polled.

Computer screens use a top-left coordinate system; the (0, 0) coordinate is in the top-left side (see Figure 20-3). The *x*- coordinate increases when going right and decreases when going left. The *y*- coordinate increases when going downward and decreases when going upward.

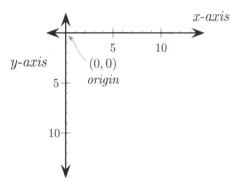

Figure 20-3: Computer graphics coordinates

The getXChange() function therefore returns a positive value if the movement is towards the right and a negative value if moving left. Likewise, the getYChange() function returns a positive value if moving upward and a negative value if moving downward.

To know which button was pressed or released, use getButton(). This function returns one of three predefined values: LEFT_BUTTON, RIGHT_BUTTON or MIDDLE_BUTTON.

```
Serial.print("Pressed: ");
if (mouse.getButton(LEFT_BUTTON))
  Serial.println("L");
if (mouse.getButton(MIDDLE_BUTTON))
  Serial.println("M");
if (mouse.getButton(RIGHT_BUTTON))
  Serial.print("R");
Serial.println();
```

Example Program

In the early days of computers, there were no graphics. "Colossal Cave Adventure" was the game that started a whole new genre: computer adventure games. More like an interactive book, these games presented the user with a text representation and asked the user what to do, again, in text. Colossal Cave Adventure was so detailed that some people visiting the cave that it was based on actually recognized their surroundings.

The game recognized simple text commands and, through these actions, completed the story through several possible paths. You might get something like this:

> You are in a small clearing. Butterflies dance in the sunlight, and there is bird song above. To the south there is a small stream, to the east you can see a small house, and to the north there is an apple tree.

```
> GO NORTH
```

You are under an apple tree. It provides comfortable shade from the sun, and the ground looks comfortable, more than enough for a quick snooze.

There is an apple in the tree.

As easy as it was to move around, the text system did have its limits. It wasn't possible to create sentences that were too complicated...

```
> IS THERE A WORM IN THE APPLE?
I'm sorry, I don't understand you. Please be more specific.
> I WANT TO KNOW IF THE APPLE IS EDIBLE
I'm sorry, I don't understand you. Try rephrasing that.
> IS THE APPLE RIPE?
I'm sorry, I don't understand you. Please be more specific.
> TAKE APPLE
You take the apple.
```

Early versions of the game actually saved time and size by analyzing the first five letters of any instruction; by using this method, the game could run on almost any computer. Later, as systems became faster, fans of the game developed versions in which each individual word was analyzed, and more complex orders could be given.

```
> HIT THE TROLL WITH THE SILVER SWORD
```

Well, he didn't see that one coming! The troll curls up into a ball, and turns back into rock.

More devious programmers had fun making games, turning some situations into textual nightmares:

```
> PUT THE RED GEM INTO THE BLUE SOCK AND PUT IT UNDER THE ALTAR
```

A voice echoes; Naribi accepts your gift! You hear a click from the other side of the door, and it slowly swings open.

Because the Arduino Due can accept a USB keyboard, it makes a perfect setup for some old-school games. You won't be designing an entire game; instead, these routines will concentrate on text input.

Remember, waiting for USB events can block the system for up to 5 seconds, so these routines will not be called all the time. They will be called only when the Arduino expects input and will continue to run until the last character is entered: the Enter key. After the text is entered, the Arduino can scan the individual words and then act according to some rules.

Hardware

This application runs on an Arduino Due because of the USB Host possibilities provided by this platform.

There are no external components for this project, with the exception of a USB keyboard, and a cable to convert the micro-USB port to a USB port. The other USB port will be connected to a computer to see the serial output. Serial communications will be at 9,600 baud.

Source Code

Time to write the sketch, as shown in Listing 20-1.

Listing 20-1: Sketch (filename: `Chapter20.ino`)

```
1   #include <KeyboardController.h>
2
3   // Key pressed
4   int curkeycode = 0;
5
6   // Initialize USB Controller
7   USBHost usb;
8
9   // Attach keyboard controller to USB
10  KeyboardController keyboard(usb);
11
12  void setup()
13  {
14    Serial.begin(9600);
15    Serial.println("Program started");
16    delay(200);
17  }
18
19  void loop()
20  {
21    keyloop();
22  }
23
24  // This function intercepts key press
25  void keyPressed()
26  {
27    curkeycode = keyboard.getKey();
28  }
29
30  // Sort the final sentence
31  void sortSentence(String sentence)
32  {
33    // Sentence logic goes here
34    Serial.println(sentence);
35  }
36
37  void keyloop()
38  {
```

```
39    String sentence = "";
40    bool waitforkey = true;
41
42    while (waitforkey == true)
43     {
44     // Process USB tasks
45     usb.Task();
46
47   // Look for valid ASCII characters
48     if (curkeycode >= 97 && curkeycode <= 122)
49     {
50       sentence += char(curkeycode);
51       Serial.write(curkeycode);
52     }
53
54     // Check for Return key
55     else if (curkeycode == 19)
56     {
57       Serial.println();
58       sortSentence(sentence);
59       waitforkey = false;
60     }
61
62     curkeycode = 0;
63     }
64  }
```

On the first line, the sketch loads the Keyboard controller library. This is the only library that will be required for this example.

The sketch defines an int, curkeycode. This variable holds the keycode from the keyboard; in most cases, it maps to ASCII, but it cannot be called ASCII because some keyboards can return non-ASCII characters. The return code will be checked later to see if it is ASCII. Until then, it is known as a *keycode*.

On line 7, the USB host is initialized, and on line 10, a KeyboardController object is created, and the previous USB object is passed to it. The USB host can now connect a keyboard to the USB subsystem.

On line 12, setup() is created, but all this does is configure the serial line. On line 19, loop() is created and is even simpler. It calls one function, keyloop(), over and over again.

There is only one keyboard event that will be of interest for this sketch: when a key is pressed. The sketch has no interest in when a key is released, so only one callback function is created: keyPressed(). This function simply updates the global variable curkeycode with the contents of the USB event.

On line 37, keyloop() is defined. This function is run whenever the sketch expects a keyboard input. First, an empty String is created, and then a boolean variable called waitforkey is set to true. While this variable is set to true, the USB subsystem waits for events. A while loop is created on line 42, and on line

45, the USB task function is run. This function either returns with an event or times out after 5 seconds. There is no way of telling exactly how this function ends, so the sketch looks at the contents of the variable `curkeycode`. If a valid ASCII character is detected (a keycode between 97 and 122), then the sketch adds that character to the end of the string. If the value 19 is received, then the sketch has received a return key press, so a new line is printed, and `sortSentence()` is called with the variable `sentence`, and the boolean variable is set to `false`, telling the loop that it is no longer expecting text input from a keyboard. If any other value is received, it is simply ignored. These include special characters, function keys, and control characters.

At the end of the `while` loop, the value of `curkeycode` is set to zero, an indication that the value has been read, and that the `while` loop expects a new value. Without this, the `while` loop might interpret this information as a key press, even if no key was pressed. Remember, the USB task function times out after 5 seconds, and then the rest of the sketch looks at the value of this variable. It has to be reset at the end of the loop.

While there's no logic for parsing the text you've entered in this example, `sortSentence()` is where you would write the code for figuring out the sequence of events in your text adventure story. To run this example, once you've uploaded the code to the Arduino, connect the keyboard to the Native USB port and your computer to the Programming port. Open the serial monitor and start typing away on the keyboard attached directly to the Due. You should see your words come up in the serial monitor once you press the return key.

Summary

In this chapter you have seen how the Arduino Due can be controlled by a USB keyboard and mouse. You have seen the functions used to get the status of inputs and to receive movement information. You have created the beginning of an interactive system allowing you to enter text to your Arduino. In the next chapter, you will see the Arduino Esplora and the library that is used to program this incredible device and use all the electronics present on this device.

This chapter discusses the following functions of the Esplora library:

- writeRGB()
- writeRed()
- writeGreen()
- writeBlue()
- readRed()
- readGreen()
- readBlue()
- writeRGB()
- readSlider()
- readLightSensor()
- readTemperature()
- readMicrophone()
- readAccelerometer()
- readJoystickX()
- readJoystickY()
- readJoystickSwitch()

- `readJoystickButton()`
- `readButton()`
- `noTone()`
- `readTinkerkitInputA()`
- `readTinkerkitInputB()`
- `readTinkerkitInput()`

The hardware needed to use these functions includes:

- Arduino Esplora
- 2 x TinkerKit 3-wire cables

You can find the code download for this chapter at `http://www.wiley.com/go/arduinosketches` on the Download Code tab. The code is in the Chapter 21 folder and the filename is `Chapter21.ino`.

Introducing Esplora

Almost all Arduino devices are physical boards that are placed on a desk or inside an enclosure. To add electronics, you must either use a shield or a breadboard. The Arduino Esplora is a different beast.

Arduino is all about getting hands-on, and the Esplora goes a step further. It is a device that ends up in your hands, not on the desk. Get ready to pick it up and play with it.

The Esplora is an excellent device for users who do not want to get too involved in electronics because it integrates an amazing amount of peripherals. Although most Arduinos only have an on-board LED on pin 13, the Esplora has an LED on pin 13, an RGB LED, a light sensor, a temperature sensor and much, much more. Here is the entire list:

- Temperature sensor
- Light sensor
- Microphone
- Two-axis analog joystick (with center-push button)
- Four push buttons
- Three-axis accelerometer
- RGB LED
- Piezo buzzer

- Two TinkerKit inputs
- Two TinkerKit outputs
- LCD screen header

So what is a TinkerKit input or output? TinkerKit is a fantastic way of connecting components without needing to know anything about electronics. There are different modules: joysticks, accelerometers, potentiometers, Hall effect sensors, LEDs, servos, and relays to name a few. These modules can be connected to a port using standard cables; the Arduino Esplora has four ports.

As you can see, the Arduino Esplora has an amazing amount of components on the device, but this comes at a cost. The Arduino Esplora is designed to be held in your hand and has the look and feel of a console game pad. As such, it does not have any shield connectors (but does have a header for an optional LCD screen). It also does not have any prototyping space, meaning that adding components is difficult. There are no electronic input and output pins, and no headers to add components to. All Arduino Esploras are therefore alike, and therefore a library was written specifically for this device.

The Arduino Esplora Library

The Esplora library is available in Arduino IDE 1.0.4 and later. To import the library, use the Arduino IDE: Sketch ➪ Import Library ➪ Esplora, or add the library manually:

```
#include <Esplora.h>
```

After this file is imported, all the devices on the Arduino Esplora become available through the `Esplora` constructor. There is no need to create this object; it is defined automatically.

RGB LED

The Arduino Esplora has a high-power RGB LED on-board. A sketch can control this LED and create different colors by varying the output to each component. This is done automatically via PWM, and writing a value to the LED once keeps the LED on at the specified color until instructed otherwise.

To set the LED to a specific color, use `writeRGB()`.

```
Esplora.writeRGB(red, green, blue);
```

The red, green, and blue parameters are ints and represent the brightness of the corresponding color. (Acceptable values ranging from 0 to 255 included.) It is possible to write a single color value using the writeRed(), writeGreen(), and writeBlue() functions.

```
Esplora.writeRed(value);
Esplora.writeGreen(value);
Esplora.writeBlue(value);
```

Again, each parameter is an int and accepts values between 0 and 255. Writing to one color does not affect the other components.

By writing an individual color, the sketch may no longer know what color value was written. For example, if the red value changes based on an external input, the main program might not know what the value of the red LED is. It is possible to read these values after writing them by using readRed(), readGreen(), and readBlue().

```
redResult = Esplora.readRed();
greenResult = Esplora.readGreen();
blueResult = Esplora.readBlue();
```

Each of these functions returns an int representing the brightness of the LED.

To turn the LED off, use writeRGB() with all parameters set at zero (the value of the red, green, and blue is off).

```
Esplora.writeRGB(0, 0, 0); // Turn the LED off
```

Sensors

The Arduino Esplora has an integrated linear potentiometer in the form of a slider. This component, connected to an analog-to-digital converter, can give values between 0 (0 Volts) to 1,023 (5 Volts). To read the value, use readSlider().

```
result = Esplora.readSlider();
```

This function does not take any parameters and returns an int, the value of the position of the potentiometer.

The Arduino Esplora also has a light sensor that is connected in the same way. It also returns values between 0 and 1,023; the more light, the higher the value.

```
result = Esplora.readLightSensor();
```

Also available on the list of sensors, the Esplora has a temperature sensor. The temperature can be read using readTemperature().

```
result = Esplora.readTemperature(scale);
```

The scale parameter is a constant, one of either `DEGREES_C` for Celsius or `DEGREES_F` for Fahrenheit. This function returns an `int`; returned values vary between –40° C and 150° C (or –40° F and 302° F).

The Esplora has something else uncommon for an Arduino; it has a microphone. The microphone is not designed to record sounds; instead, it gives an accurate reading of the amplitude of the ambient noise level. The value can be read with `readMicrophone()`.

```
result = Esplora.readMicrophone();
```

This function takes no parameters and returns an `int`—the ambient sound level—on a scale of 0 to 1,023.

Finally, the Esplora also has an accelerometer: a small device that can detect the tilt of the device. Contrary to what some people believe from the name, an accelerometer does not calculate coordinate acceleration (a change in velocity); it measures proper acceleration: acceleration relative to gravity. It can therefore detect a tilt (a change in direction relative to gravity) but also movement. (For example, a falling device has limited acceleration attempting to counter gravitational pull.)

Values can be read from the accelerometer by using `readAccelerometer()`.

```
value = Esplora.readAccelerometer(axis);
```

This function needs to be called for each axis individually. The axis is specified using the `axis` parameter and is one of `X_AXIS`, `Y_AXIS`, or `Z_AXIS`. It returns an `int` between –512 and 512. A result of zero means the axis is perpendicular to gravity: negative and positive values mean acceleration on the axis.

```
int x_axis = Esplora.readAccelerometer(X_AXIS);
int y_axis = Esplora.readAccelerometer(Y_AXIS);
int z_axis = Esplora.readAccelerometer(Z_AXIS);

Serial.print("x: ");
Serial.print(x_axis);
Serial.print("\ty: ");
Serial.print(y_axis);
Serial.print("\tz: ");
Serial.println(z_axis);
```

Buttons

The Esplora comes with an impressive array of buttons. On the left side of the Esplora is an analog joystick and on the right side are digital buttons.

The joystick can register the exact *x*-axis and *y*-axis position, and also has a center-push button.

To read the joystick inputs, use `readJoystickX()` and `readJoystickY()`.

```
xValue = Esplora.readJoystickX();
yValue = Esplora.readJoystickY();
```

These functions both return an `int`: Values range from –512 to 512. A return value of zero means that the joystick is in the center and has not been moved. Negative values mean that the joystick is pushed to the left (*x*) or down (*y*). Positive values mean that the joystick is pushed to the right (*x*) or up (*y*).

To read the center-push button, you can use `readJoystickSwitch()`.

```
value = Esplora.readJoystickSwitch();
```

The return value is an `int` and is either 0 or 1,023. Remember that `readJoystickX()` and `readJoystickY()` return 10-bit values and are shifted to make things easier. The center button also returns a 10-bit value but because it is either pushed or not, values returned are extremes. If you need something simpler to use, you can use the `readJoystickButton()` function.

```
state = Esplora.readJoystickButton();
```

This function returns a `Boolean`: `LOW` if the button is pressed and `HIGH` if the button is not pressed.

To read the status of the buttons, there is only one function: `readButton()`.

```
state = Esplora.readButton(button);
```

This function takes one parameter, the button that is to be read. The `button` parameter can be one of four constants: `SWITCH_DOWN`, `SWITCH_LEFT`, `SWITCH_UP`, or `SWITCH_RIGHT`. This function returns one of two values: `HIGH` or `LOW`. A return value of `HIGH` means the button is in the high position; that is to say, it has not been pressed. A return value of `LOW` means that the button is in the low position and is currently pressed.

Buzzer

The Arduino Esplora has a buzzer located on the top left of the device that can create simple audio outputs. To create an audio output, use `tone()`.

```
Esplora.tone(frequency);
Esplora.tone(frequency, duration);
```

The `frequency` parameter specifies the audio frequency in hertz, expressed as an `unsigned int`. The optional `duration` parameter is the duration of the tone in milliseconds, also expressed as an `unsigned int`. If omitted, the tone continues until interrupted, either by calling the `tone()` function with new parameters or by calling the `noTone()` function.

```
Esplora.noTone();
```

This function immediately stops the output of a `tone()` function.

The `tone()` and `noTone()` functions are part of the Arduino language, but these two variants are modified to be used on the Esplora. As such, it is not necessary to specify the pin; the actions are immediately applied to the correct pin.

NOTE The buzzer is controlled by high-speed PWM, as is the red component of the RGB LED. Using the buzzer may interfere with the red light.

TinkerKit

The Arduino Esplora comes with four TinkerKit connectors; two are inputs and two are outputs.

To read the TinkerKit inputs, use `readTinkerkitInputA()` and `readTinkerkitInputB()`.

```
resultA = Esplora.readTinkerkitInputA();
resultB = Esplora.readTinkerkitInputB();
```

These two functions do not take any parameters and return an `int`, the value detected on the TinkerKit input. Values range from 0 (0 V) to 1,023 (5 V). There is another way to read TinkerKit inputs, using a single function: `readTinkerkitInput()`.

```
result = Esplora.readTinkerkitInput(whichInput);
```

This function takes a parameter, `whichInput`. This parameter is a `Boolean`: if it is `false` (or `0`), then the value of TinkerKit input A is returned. If it is `true` (or `1`), then the value of TinkerKit input B is returned.

The Esplora also has two TinkerKit outputs, but currently, there are no Esplora specific functions allowing easy output. However, they are digital outputs just like on any Arduino, so it is still easy to write to their outputs—the trick is to know which output goes where.

There are two outputs: OUT-A and OUT-B. Just below the connector, next to the output identifier, is another piece of information: D3 for Output A and D11 for Output B. These are the reference to the digital outputs, and using `digitalWrite()`, you can output digital data. These two pins are also capable of PWM, so you can also use `analogWrite()`.

CROSS-REFERENCE `digitalWrite()` and `analogWrite()` are standard functions, which are explained in Chapter 4.

LCD Module

The Arduino Esplora can also host an optional TFT screen placed on the connectors on the middle of the board. This module uses the standard TFT library (as well as SPI), and there are no Esplora-specific functions for this module. However, as everything on the board is hardwired, you don't need as much code to use a screen as other Arduinos. After including the TFT, SPI, and Esplora libraries, all you need to do is reference the Esplora TFT object with `EsploraTFT`. For more information on the TFT library, see Chapter 13.

There is also another use for the LCD Module connectors. Contrary to most Arduinos, the Esplora does not support shields; apart from the TFT connector, there are no connectors capable of placing a board or shield, and there are no prototyping areas. By using this connector, it is possible to have more inputs and outputs. The connectors on the left side of the Esplora are not electronically connected; they are there solely to fix the TFT screen in place. On the right side, however, several pins are exposed. Of course, this is to allow the TFT screen to talk using the SPI protocol, but there are a few others, for example, to control the backlight. Creating a PCB for use with the Esplora is beyond the scope of this book, but you can find more information on the connector on Arduino's website.

Example Program and Exercises

The Arduino Esplora is an excellent device to get "hands-on," and the next chapter presents another unique device. The Esplora, in the shape of a handheld game controller, can also be used as a remote control. Without spoiling the next chapter too much, this project converts the Esplora into a remote control for the Arduino Robot, an interesting device that is essentially a moving Arduino. It is controlled by two motors, and can move forward, backwards, and turn around. This sketch will serve as a remote control for the Arduino Robot, by using the two TinkerKit outputs. The left TinkerKit connector controls movement to the left, and the right TinkerKit controls movement to the right. If both are activated, the device goes forward, and if neither is active, then the device stops.

NOTE If you do not have access to an Arduino Robot, this project can be adapted to other robotic kits. Several interesting devices are available at `http://www.robot-shop.com/`. This can be adapted to both vehicles and robotic arms.

To do this, the sketch sets the TinkerKit outputs to digital mode and constantly monitors the status of the buttons. This sketch will use two TinkerKit outputs: Out A and Out B. Out A will handle the left-hand side motor, and Out B will control the right-hand side motor. To go forward, both motors will be activated at the same time. To turn, only one motor will be activated. The sketch will look like Listing 21-1.

Listing 21-1: Sketch (filename: `Chapter21.ino`)

```
1    #include <Esplora.h>
2
3    #define OUTA 3    // Pin TinkerKit Out A is connected to
4    #define OUTB 11   // Pin TinkerKit Out B is connected to
5
6    void setup()
7    {
8      pinMode(OUTA, OUTPUT); // TinkerKit A to output
9      pinMode(OUTB, OUTPUT); // TinkerKit B to output
10   }
11
12   void loop()
13   {
14     boolean outputA = LOW;
15     boolean outputB = LOW;
16
17     if (Esplora.readButton(SWITCH_UP) == LOW)
18       outputA = outputB = HIGH;
19
20     if (Esplora.readButton(SWITCH_LEFT) == LOW)
21       outputB = HIGH;
22
23     if (Esplora.readButton(SWITCH_RIGHT) == LOW)
24       outputA = HIGH;
25
26     digitalWrite(OUTA, outputA);
27     digitalWrite(OUTB, outputB);
28   }
```

On line 1, the Esplora library is imported, the first thing needed for this project. On lines 3 and 4, there are some `define` directives, which define the digital pins used on the TinkerKit outputs because there are no functions available to write to the TinkerKit pins directly. Because you have to do this the old way, it requires `pinMode()` calls in `setup()`. This is done on line 8 and 9; both pins are set to `OUTPUT`.

`loop()` is declared on line 12, and this is where the buttons will be read and, if necessary, the outputs will be written to. It starts on line 14 with the creation of two variables: `outputA` and `outputB`. As you can imagine, they will be used to hold the output status. They are defined as `LOW` by default, meaning that without any modification, they will set the outputs `LOW`. On line 17, the first button read is made. If the up button is pressed, both `outputA` and `outputB` are set high.

The second read, on line 20, checks to see if the left button has been pressed. If it has, then outputB is set `HIGH`. If the user is also pressing on the up button, the sketch changes the output to `HIGH` anyway. This is why the variables were initially set to `LOW`: Reads are made to see if there is a reason to set the variable to `HIGH`. If two or more conditions update the variable, that isn't a problem; the end result is the same. A third read is made on line 23 to see if the right button has been pressed.

Finally, the two digital outputs are updated with the contents of the variables. `loop()` then repeats.

A simple sketch can turn an advanced device into a remote control, even if there are no specific TinkerKit output routines. By making the sketch use the digital outputs instead of using specific functions, you can perform more software actions than the library alone allows. The TinkerKit outputs can be used as digital output or PWM, but by knowing the exact pin number, you could use these pins as serial outputs, or for other purposes.

The output of this sketch is binary only; either the outputs are on or off. With a little bit of adjustment, this could quickly become an analog output, using the joystick. That will require a little bit of modification to the example in the next chapter as well, but you will get to that later.

You will have a remote control allowing a new device freedom of movement, but there is one button that is not used, the down button. There is no point using it to slow down, so why not use it to make beep noises? Just like a car horn, warning the cat or dog to get out of the way.

Alternatively, for advanced programmers, use the Esplora's accelerometer to control output.

Summary

In this chapter you have seen the Arduino Esplora, an interesting device with lots of embedded electronics and a rich library to read and write the components. You have seen the library and the different functions used to read from and write to the different components. You have seen how easy it is to create a project. In the next chapter, you will see the Arduino Robot and the library used to control it, and you will be able to use the sketch presented in the chapter to control its movement.

This chapter discusses the following functions of the Robot library:

- begin();
- motorsWrite()
- motorsStop()
- turn()
- pointTo()
- compassRead()
- updateIR()
- knobRead()
- keyboardRead()
- digitalRead()
- analogRead()
- digitalWrite()
- analogWrite()
- beginSpeaker()
- beep()

- playMelody()
- playFile()
- tempoWrite()
- tuneWrite()
- robotNameWrite()
- robotNameRead()
- userNameWrite()
- userNameRead()
- cityNameWrite()
- cityNameRead()
- countryNameWrite()
- countryNameRead()
- beginTFT()
- beginSD()
- drawBMP()
- displayLogos()
- clearScreen()
- text()
- debugPrint()
- drawCompass()
- parseCommand()
- process()

The hardware needed to use these functions includes:

- Arduino Robot
- 2 x TinkerKit connection cables and digital inputs
- Arduino Esplora (presented and programmed in Chapter 21)

You can find the code download for this chapter at `http://www.wiley.com/go/arduinosketches` on the Download Code tab. The code is in the Chapter 22 folder and the filename is `Chapter22.ino`.

Introducing Robot Library

Over the years, there have been several attempts to teach programming languages to children. Teachers and governments wanted to show children that programming isn't magic, and that simple logic is all that was required. The

British Broadcasting Corporation, BBC for short, even went as far as to create its own computer for schools to accompany a television series on computer programming. It was a huge success and was just one of many projects. One of these projects was the Logo programming language.

Most programming languages are mathematical: the acquisition, modification, and use of numbers. Logo was different; it was based on logic. (Hence the name Logo is derived from the Greek word *logos*, thought.) Although designed for several reasons, an entire generation remembers it for the famous turtle.

The turtle was represented as a computer rendered triangle on our large cathode-ray tubes connected to primitive computers. The turtle was free to roam across the screen but needed instructions. For some unknown reason, it had a paintbrush strapped onto its tail. It could be told to put the brush down (to start drawing) or to pick it up (to stop drawing). It then required the user to give it instructions. Anyone who has used BASIC probably knows about the first program anyone writes:

```
10 PRINT "Hello, world!"
20 GOTO 10
```

This would print out endless lines of text and was a good visual start to programming but did not go any further. The turtle, however, was different. For example, take this program:

```
FD 100
RT 90
FD 100
RT 90
FD 100
ERT 90
FD 100
```

FD is short for forward. The turtle is instructed to advance for 100 "units" and then make a right turn (RT) by 90 degrees. Then it is instructed to advance another 100 units and so on. The result? A square as shown in Figure 22-1.

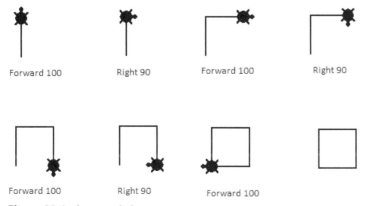

Forward 100   Right 90   Forward 100   Right 90

Forward 100   Right 90   Forward 100

Figure 22-1: A square in Logo

Squares are basic, but Logo could create hugely complex structures and teach students about programming. Imagine a flower made up of eight petals. Each petal could be one "function" and called eight times by placing the turtle in the correct position. The results were visual, perfect for young children. A lot of us started off with Logo, and I can remember having great fun in the classroom with this.

One serious attempt was made to make the turtle "physical." Created in the form of a large half-sphere, the turtle made it into the real world, but only for a short time. A turtle robot was made to show children just what could be done, but it was too early for the poor turtle. It was expensive, difficult to set up correctly, and required an exceptionally flat surface. The poor little turtle eventually disappeared, only a few programs exist today that still use it, either for teaching, or for simple nostalgia. Programmers returned to the digital world to see their little turtle. Some of us dreamed of seeing the little turtle return, and it has. Sort of.

Arduino Robot

Your Arduino Uno will be placed on your desk and will probably live there until your project is finished and you install it in its final resting place. I have one hidden behind my television, and it will stay there for quite some time. The Arduino Robot is different. It is the only Arduino that most certainly will not stay in the same place.

The Arduino Robot is an Arduino on wheels—literally. There are two large wheels on each side and two ball casters to keep it steady. It contains an impressive amount of electronics, but more important, it has enough space for you to add electronics and all the buses and connectors needed to connect components.

The Arduino Robot is, technically, two Arduinos in one. The motor board is controlled by an ATmega32u4 (the same microcontroller as on the Arduino Esplora) and contains flash memory, RAM, EEPROM, and two prototyping areas. It does not have a large amount of I/O, but what it does have is motor control circuits and power electronics to take standard batteries and power the two on-board motors. The control board on top uses the same microcontroller but has more I/O and adds a large array of electronics not seen on most other Arduinos. It has a keypad like the Arduino Esplora, an LCD screen connector that is compatible with the LCD module used on the Esplora, an 8-ohm speaker, a compass, and a large amount of external EEPROM via the I^{2}C protocol (in addition to internal EEPROM). It also has four prototyping areas.

The Arduino Robot is a complex device, and care must be taken when preparing it. Unlike most Arduinos, there is some preparation required before using it for the first time: a protective cover must be placed under the device to protect it, drivers must be installed, and the optional TFT screen must be placed in the correct position, to name but a few. Arduino keeps an up-to-date webpage on the Arduino website at `http://arduino.cc/en/Guide/Robot`.

The Arduino Robot has two boards, and both are independent. They can be programmed separately, and both have a USB connector used for programming. Note that when programming the Arduino Robot, the electric motors are automatically disabled to prevent accidents. In order to fully use your sketch, you will need to power your device with batteries.

Generally, the control board is the only one that is programmed. The Arduino Robot has a number of functions that facilitate communication between the two. It is recommended to first use the control board and to program the motor board only when you are comfortable with the control board. If you make a mistake, don't worry; the stock motor program is available in the Arduino IDE as an example. The control board can tell the motor board to perform actions but also to read sensors on the motor board (like the infrared line following sensors on the bottom of the motor board).

Robot Library

The Arduino Robot library is a complicated library and depends on a number of external libraries, mainly for the infrared sensors and audio synthesis. These libraries have been merged into the Arduino Robot library to save space and do not need to be added manually. It also depends on some Arduino standard libraries for use. (Wire and SPI need to be included separately if using the functionality of those libraries.) To import the library, you must first decide which board you will be using because they do not require the same components. To create a sketch for the control board, add the `Robot_Control` library in Sketch ➪ Import Library ➪ Robot_Control. This adds the following `include` declarations:

```
#include <Fat16mainpage.h>

#include <SdCard.h>
#include <ArduinoRobot.h>
#include <SdInfo.h>
#include <EEPROM_I2C.h>
#include <FatStructs.h>
#include <Fat16util.h>
#include <Fat16Config.h>
#include <Multiplexer.h>
#include <Fat16.h>
#include <Arduino_LCD.h>
#include <Squawk.h>
```

```
#include <Compass.h>
#include <Wire.h>
#include <Adafruit_GFX.h>
#include <SPI.h>
#include <SquawkSD.h>
#include <EasyTransfer2.h>
```

Not all these are required. Typically, you need only to include `ArduinoRobot.h`. To create a sketch for the motor board, add the `Robot_Motor` library in Sketch ➪ Import Library ➪ Robot_Motor. This adds the following `include` declarations:

```
#include <ArduinoRobotMotorBoard.h>
#include <Multiplexer.h>
#include <EasyTransfer2.h>
#include <LineFollow.h>
```

Not all these are required. Typically, you need to include only `ArduinoRobotMotorBoard.h`.

Control Board

To use Arduino Robot control board, you must use functions from the `RobotControl` class. The functions are accessed through the object directly, so there is no need to call the constructor. However, to begin using the Arduino Robot-specific functions, you must first call `begin()`:

```
Robot.begin();
```

`begin()` initializes interboard communication, sets variables to their correct values and other initializations for the Arduino Robot, but does not initialize the LCD screen or the speaker; other functions exist for those and are explained later in this chapter in the "LCD Screen" section.

Robotic Controls

The basis of any robot is, of course, movement. The Arduino Robot has an impressive amount of sensors, but its primary function is to move. The motor board has two independent motors, and although it is the motor board that drives these motors, the control board can instruct the motor board to perform actions.

To control the motors directly, use `motorsWrite()`:

```
Robot.motorsWrite(speedLeft, speedRight);
```

This function takes two parameters: two `int` values. The `speedLeft` variable instructs the left motor at what speed it should rotate; accepted values range from –255 and 255. If the value is greater than 0, the motor turns forward. If the value is negative, the motor turns backward. If the value is zero, the motor stops. The `speedRight` parameter works in exactly the same way. This function does not return any data.

To instruct both motors to stop, use `motorsStop()`:

```
Robot.motorsStop();
```

This function takes no parameters and does not return any data. It instructs both motors to stop immediately.

Turning can be achieved by varying the speed of rotation of the left and right motors. By varying the speed of each motor, you can achieve rotation, but the Arduino Robot goes a step further and has an embedded compass that can be used for greater accuracy. To tell the Arduino Robot to turn by a specific amount of degrees, use `turn()`:

```
Robot.turn(degrees);
```

This function takes one parameter, an `int`, and accepted values are between −180 to 180. Negative values make the robot turn left; positive values make the robot turn right. Entering a value of zero has no effect. This function uses the on-board compass to get a bearing to magnetic north and then turns the robot by a specific number of degrees, verified by the compass. To make the robot turn to a specific heading, use `pointTo()`:

```
Robot.pointTo(degrees);
```

Like `turn()`, `pointTo()` uses the compass to get its bearings, but instead of turning a specific amount of degrees, it tells the Arduino Robot to face a particular heading. It takes one parameter, `degrees`, which is the heading to face, where 0 is north, east is 90, south is 180, and west is 270.

The robot automatically decides if it should turn left or right, whichever is the shortest turn.

Sensor Reading

For robots to function correctly, they require multiple sensors. They need to know where they are and how they can interact with the world. You can add additional sensors to the Arduino Robot, but it already comes with a few sensors to get you started.

As seen previously, the Arduino Robot can be told to face in a specific direction, using the compass. You can also read the value of the compass using `compassRead()`:

```
result = Robot.compassRead();
```

This function returns an `int`; the degrees of rotation from magnetic north.

> **NOTE** The Arduino Robot's compass takes readings relative to magnetic north, and the compass can be affected by magnetic fields. Make sure to keep your robot away from speakers, motors, or other strong magnets that could temporarily make the compass give false readings.

The motor board also contains five infrared sensors used for line following. The motor board can access the reading for the individual sensors, but with the control board, sketches must use `updateIR()`:

```
Robot.updateIR();
```

This function takes no parameters and does not return any data. What it does is update an array, readable through `Robot.Irarray[]`:

```
Robot.updateIR();
for(int i=0; i<=4; i++)
{
  Serial.print(Robot.IRarray[i]); // Print the value of each IR sensor
  Serial.print(" ");
}
```

The control board also has a knob, a potentiometer. Powered by 5 V, it is connected to an analog-to-digital converter with 10-bit precision. It maps input voltages to an integer value between 0 and 1023, and is accessible through `knobRead()`:

```
result = Robot.knobRead();
```

This function returns an `int`, the value read from the ADC.

The control board also has a five-button keyboard. These keys can be read through `keyboardRead()`:

```
result = Robot.keyboardRead();
```

This function returns a constant reporting the button that is being pressed. See the possible values in Table 22-1.

Table 22-1: Keyboard Return Codes

VALUE	BUTTON
BUTTON_LEFT	Left button pressed
BUTTON_RIGHT	Right button pressed
BUTTON_UP	Up button pressed
BUTTON_DOWN	Down button pressed
BUTTON_MIDDLE	Middle button pressed
BUTTON_NONE	No button pressed

The Arduino Robot contains TinkerKit connectors, both on the control board and on the motor board. Most of these ports can be read as both digital and analog, depending on the function call. Two functions can be called: `digitalRead()` and `analogRead()`.

```
DigitalResult = Robot.digitalRead(port);
AnalogResult = Robot.analogRead(port);
```

The `port` parameter is a constant: the ID of the TinkerKit port to use. Accepted values are TK0-TK3, TKD0–TKD5, and B_TK1 to B_TK4. TK4 and TK5 are digital inputs only. `digitalRead()` returns either TRUE or FALSE. `analogRead()` returns integer values between 0 and 1023.

NOTE Before reading the value of a TinkerKit port, make sure that a device is connected. Reading the value of a port where no device is present can result in unexpected results.

Of course, some TinkerKit ports are not used only for input, and the control board can also set TinkerKit outputs. To write digital output, use `digitalWrite()`:

```
digitalWrite(port, value);
```

The `value` parameter is the value to write, either HIGH or LOW. The `port` parameter is the TinkerKit port, one of TKD0–TKD5, B_TK1–B_TK4, or LED1 (an LED located on the control board).

To write an analog value, use `analogWrite()`:

```
Robot.analogWrite(port, value);
```

The `value` parameter is the analog value to write, ranging from 0 to 255. The output is not true analog; it is created using PWM, as with most Arduino analog outputs. The port value is the TinkerKit port to use; it can be used only on TKD4 and cannot be used at the same time as TK0 through TK7.

Personalizing Your Robot

I love all my Arduinos, but there is something even more lovable about computers that can follow you around. Just like a pet, it deserves a name and some personal information. This information can be stored in EEPROM and retrieved through special functions.

To give the robot a name, use `robotNameWrite()`:

```
Robot.robotNameWrite(name);
```

The `name` parameter is a string and can be up to eight characters. The data will be stored into EEPROM and can be retrieved with `robotNameRead()`:

```
Robot.robotNameRead(container);
```

In the following snippet, `container` is a `char` array and stores the result of the query.

```
char container[8];
Robot.robotNameRead(container);
Serial.println(container);
```

To tell the Arduino Robot your name, use `userNameWrite()`:

```
Robot.userNameWrite(name);
```

The `name` parameter is a string and can be up to eight characters. As with the robot's name, the user's name can be retrieved using `userNameRead()`:

```
Robot.userNameRead(container);
```

The `container` parameter is a `char` array.

There are two more things the Arduino Robot can read and write—the city name and the country name:

```
Robot.cityNameWrite(city);
Robot.cityNameRead(container);
Robot.countryNameWrite(country);
Robot.countryNameRead(container);
```

As with the previous functions, the write functions take strings, and the read functions require an 8-byte `char` array.

LCD Screen

The Arduino Robot control board has a connector for a TFT screen (the same screen as used on the Arduino Esplora). The Arduino Robot also has advanced functions to make the most of the screen.

To use the TFT screen, you must first call `beginTFT()`:

```
Robot.beginTFT();
Robot.beginTFT(foreground, background);
```

By default, if called without any parameters, the TFT screen is configured with black as a background color and white as a foreground color. This can be changed by specifying the colors when calling `beginTFT()`. Valid colors are BLACK, BLUE, RED, GREEN, CYAN, MAGENTA, YELLOW, and WHITE.

The TFT screen module also contains a micro-SD card slot, and to activate it, use `beginSD()`:

```
Robot.beginSD();
```

This function is required before using functions such as `drawBMP()` (explained next) and `playFile()` (explained in the "Music" section). Be aware that this library is fairly large and should be used only if you require the SD slot; complex sketches may have unexpected results if the SD card slot is initialized.

To draw a graphics file to the screen, use `drawBMP()`:

```
Robot.drawBMP(filename, x, y);
```

The `filename` parameter is the name of the file located on the SD card. It must be in BMP format. The `x` and `y` parameters are the coordinates of the top-left corner of the image.

Displaying logos is often useful when starting a sketch, but the Arduino Robot library has a better solution. `displayLogos()` displays two logos on the screen:

```
Robot.displayLogos();
```

This function takes no parameters and automatically looks for two files on the SD card: `lg0.bmp` and `lg1.bmp`. This function first loads `lg0.bmp` and displays it on the TFT screen before waiting for 2 seconds. Afterward, it loads `lg1.bmp` and again waits for 2 seconds. These files are present on the SD card by default but can be replaced.

To clear the screen, use `clearScreen()`:

```
Robot.clearScreen();
```

This automatically clears the screen using the default background color (black, unless specified otherwise).

It is possible to write text to the screen, using `text()`:

```
Robot.text(text, x, y, write);
```

The `text` parameter can be a `String` but also an `int` or a `long`. The `x` and `y` parameters are the coordinates of the start position. The `write` parameter is a `Boolean`: `true` if the color to use is the foreground color (write) or `false` if the TFT screen uses the background color (erase).

To display debug information on the TFT screen, use `debugPrint()`:

```
Robot.debugPrint(value);
Robot.debugPrint(value, x, y);
```

The `value` parameter can be either an `int` or a `long`. The `x` and `y` variables are optional and tell the function where to print the text. By default, the text will be printed on the top-left corner. This function not only prints a value, but also refreshes it, adding a unique debugging feature.

Another debug function, and a rather pretty one, is achieved with `drawCompass()`:

```
Robot.drawCompass(degrees);
```

This function draws a compass on the TFT screen and shows the specified bearing, defined by the `degrees` parameter. Typically, this value is fetched with `compassRead()`.

Music

The Arduino Robot has a built-in speaker on the control board, and numerous functions exist to take advantage of this component. You need to include the Wire and SPI libraries to use the speaker. To use the speaker, it must first be initialized with `beginSpeaker()`.

```
Robot.beginSpeaker();
```

This function must be declared in `setup()`.

The most basic form of sound is the beep and is made using `beep()`.

```
Robot.beep(type);
```

The type parameter is one of three constants: `BEEP_SIMPLE` (a short beep), `BEEP_DOUBLE` (a double beep), or `BEEP_LONG` (a long beep).

To play simple music, use `playMelody()`.

```
Robot.playMelody(melody);
```

The `melody` parameter is a string and describes the notes to be played, as well as their length. The notes are listed in Table 22-2.

Table 22-2: Melody Notes

TEXT	NOTE
c	Play "C"
C	Play "C#"
d	Play "D"
D	Play "D#"
e	Play "E"
f	Play "F"
F	Play "F#"
g	Play "G"
G	Play "G#"
a	Play "A"
A	Play "A#"
b	Play "B"
-	Silence

To set note length, use digits as described in Table 22-3.

Table 22-3: Note Length

DIGIT	DURATION
1	Make the next notes full notes
2	Make the next notes half-notes
4	Make the next notes quarter-notes
8	Make the next notes eighth-notes
.	Make the previous note ¾-length

The Arduino Robot can make simple music, but it is also capable of more advanced playback, using `playFile()`.

```
Robot.playFile(filename);
```

The `filename` parameter is the name of a file on an SD card. The SD card reader is located on the back of the LCD screen. As such, it requires the sketch to call `beginSD()` beforehand. The file must be in *Squawk* format, a special format resembling what was used on Amiga 500 computers. This file format can generally be created using Music Trackers. For more information, see the library README located on the project GitHub page at `https://github.com/stg/Squawk`.

These files contain music information and are played back at a precise speed and pitch. You can change both these parameters using functions. To change the tempo of a music file (to make it play faster or slower), use `tempoWrite()`.

```
Robot.tempoWrite(speed);
```

The `speed` parameter is an `int`, the speed at which to play back the file. The default value is 50; lower values set the file to be played back slower, and higher values set the file to be played back quicker. This has no effect on the pitch; to change the pitch, use `tuneWrite()`.

```
Robot.tuneWrite(pitch);
```

The pitch parameter is a `float` and indicates the pitch at which the file should be played back. The default value is 1.0; higher values set a higher pitch.

Motor Board

The motor board, placed underneath the control board, is responsible for controlling the two DC motors and reading the infrared sensors. It responds to instructions sent from the control board, but the default sketch can be modified to fit your use.

Just like the control board, to use the Arduino Robot motor board, you must use functions from the `RobotMotor` class. The functions are accessed through the object directly, so there is no need to call the constructor. However, to begin using the Arduino Robot-specific functions, you must again first call `begin()`.

```
RobotMotor.begin();
```

To retrieve instructions from the control board, use `parseCommand()`.

```
RobotMotor.parseCommand();
```

This function takes no parameters and does not return any data. It is used simply to read and update internal registers. After commands have been parsed, it is necessary to act on those instructions; this is achieved with `process()`.

```
RobotMotor.process();
```

Again, this instruction does not take any parameters and does not return information. It operates the motors depending on the internal results of `parseCommand()`.

These two instructions are, in fact, the basis of the default motor board sketch.

```
#include <ArduinoRobotMotorBoard.h>

void setup(){
  RobotMotor.begin();
}
void loop(){
  RobotMotor.parseCommand();
  RobotMotor.process();
}
```

This sketch simply reads instructions from the control board and acts on those instructions. Why is there a separate board in this case? Although the microcontrollers on these boards are powerful, it is often a good idea to keep the functions separate; one microcontroller powers the control board, the other powers the motor board. The motor board performs instructions and continues to do so until instructed otherwise. The control board can perform advanced calculations or perform blocking functions while the motor board continues to monitor the DC motors.

Example Program and Exercises

The Arduino Robot is a superb platform and ready for tinkering. With a large number of inputs, it is easy and fun to create sketches giving your robot freedom of movement. For this application, you create a remote controlled Arduino

Robot. For this, two TinkerKit digital inputs are used. TK5, placed on the left of the robot controls the left motor, and TK7 placed on the right controls the right motor. A logical 1 means that the motor turns, and a logical 0 stops the motor. These inputs will be read periodically. The speed of the wheels will be controlled by the potentiometer.

The sketch looks like Listing 22-1.

Listing 22-1: Sketch (filename: Chapter22.ino**)**

```
1    #include <ArduinoRobot.h>
2
3    void setup()
4    {
5      Robot.begin(); // Start the control board
6    }
7
8    void loop()
9    {
10     // Read in potentiometer values
11     int speed = Robot.knobRead();
12
13     // Potentiometer data is 0-1023, motors expect 0-255
14     // (we won't use negative values)
15
16     int motorSpeed = map(speed, 0, 1023, 0, 255);
17
18     // Motor variables
19     int leftMotor = 0;
20     int rightMotor = 0;
21
22     if (Robot.digitalRead(TK5) == true)
23       leftMotor = motorSpeed;
24
25     if (Robot.digitalRead(TK7) == true)
26       rightMotor = motorSpeed;
27
28     // Now control the motors
29     Robot.motorsWrite(leftMotor, rightMotor);
30
31     // Sleep for a tenth of a second
32     delay(100);
33   }
```

On line 1, the Arduino Robot library is imported. On line 5 in setup(), Robot .begin() is called. From here on, the user can call Robot functions.

loop() is declared on line 8. Because the motor speed will be controlled by the value of the potentiometer, the analog value is read in on line 11. This value is stored in an int called speed. The potentiometer gives values between 0 and

1023, but the motor control requires a value between 0 and 255. (Negative values are not used.) To adapt these values, `map()` is called on line 16; the result is stored in an `int` called `motorSpeed`.

Two new variables are declared on lines 19 and 20, and default values are assigned: 0. On line 22, the input of TinkerKit connector TK5 is read, and if this value is `true`, the user instructs the left motor to operate. If so, the value of `leftMotor` is set to `motorSpeed`, ordering the motor to turn forward. The same thing is done with the right-side motor on line 25. Finally, the motors are programmed on line 29 with `motorsWrite()`.

Now that the motors have been activated or deactivated, the sketch waits for 1/10th of a second through a `delay()` on line 32 before continuing.

Multiple TinkerKit connectors are available, and you can use TK6 in the same manner to control the speaker. How about making the Arduino Robot beep on command to tell pesky cats and humans to get out of the way?

The TinkerKit inputs are set as digital but can also be set as analog, allowing the user to control the speed of the Arduino Robot. Change the inputs to make them analog.

Summary

In this chapter you have seen one of the most fascinating Arduinos, the Arduino Robot. You have seen the two boards that together make the Robot—the Control Board and the Motor Board. You have seen the library used to control both and how simple sketches can result in a fully functional mobile device. You have also seen how the Arduino Robot can use external sensors to be controlled. In the next chapter you will learn about the Arduino Yún and the Bridge library used to exchange messages between the Arduino microcontroller and a more powerful microprocessor running Linux.

CHAPTER 23

This chapter discusses the following functions of the Bridge library:

- `Bridge.begin()`
- `Bridge.put()`
- `Bridge.get()`
- `Process.begin()`
- `Process.addParameter()`
- `Process.run()`
- `Process.runAsynchronously()`
- `Process.running()`
- `Process.exitValue()`
- `Process.read()`
- `Process.write()`
- `Process.flush()`
- `Process.close()`
- `FileSystem.begin()`
- `FileSystem.open()`
- `FileSystem.exists()`

- ■ `FileSystem.rmdir()`

- ■ `FileSystem.remove()`

- ■ `YunServer.begin()`

- ■ `YunClient.connected()`

- ■ `YunClient.stop()`

The hardware needed to use these functions includes:

- ■ Arduino Yún

- ■ 1 x Breadboard

- ■ 1 x LDR

- ■ 1 x 10 kΩ resistor

- ■ Wires

You can find the code download for this chapter at `http://www.wiley.com/go/arduinosketches` on the Download Code tab. The code is in the Chapter 23 folder and the filename is `Chapter23.ino`.

Introducing Bridge Library

There is often confusion as to the name of a microcontroller. A microcontroller (as the name implies) controls, whereas a microprocessor processes data. This becomes apparent for the Arduino Yún, where both are present.

In December 2002, Linksys released its WRT54G residential wireless router. It was a small device with two antennae behind a blue-and-black cover. Behind were four Ethernet LAN ports and an uplink port. It was an easy way to add high-speed Wi-Fi to a home network and was used by a large number of people, including myself. My WRT54G increased my wireless range at home and allowed me higher speeds than what my Internet modem provided. (The WRT54G provided Wi-Fi-G instead of the aging Wi-Fi-B.) It was also a device destined to be tinkered with.

These devices were based on a 125-MHz MIPS microprocessor with surprisingly good characteristics. With 16 MB of RAM and 4 MB of flash memory, it was more than capable of running a complete Linux distribution which shipped with the device. The Linux distribution was delivered under the GPL license, and as such, Linksys had to make the source code available on its site. This sparked a group of people to look at that code, and to modify it, allowing more and more features to be added. Within the space of a few months, a consumer-level router had functions reserved for top-of-the-line industry-level routers. Although most routers simply allowed home devices to connect, this new software allowed for advanced frequency scanning programs, traffic shaping, firewall, scheduling, and mesh networking, to name but a few. All that the user had to do was to overwrite the original firmware—something that could be undone later if needed. An entire generation of routers were designed around this initial product, and the new firmware was released under the name OpenWRT.

The power of OpenWRT was not only that it added advanced features, but it also contained a package manager, meaning users could install their own programs. The filesystem is also read/write-capable, meaning that users could create and update files. A simple WRT54G device could be placed anywhere, act as a sensor, and log the results to a data file. The router was no longer a router but a small computer.

Since its early days, OpenWRT has been under heavy development, becoming an extremely complex distribution, no longer limited to Linksys devices. One device to which the OpenWRT has been ported is the Arduino Yún. This board is actually two devices in one; on one side, it has an ATMega32u4, which is the "Arduino" side. The other side is based on an Atheros AR9331. This chip, with its corresponding RAM, Ethernet, and Wi-Fi chip, hosts an OpenWRT distribution called Linino. To allow the AVR to communicate with the Atheros, a library was created: Bridge.

> **NOTE** You can modify files on the root filesystem of the Yún; however, it is strongly advised to use external storage. The Arduino Yún has an on-board micro-SD slot to expand filesystem space.

Bridge

The Arduino side of the Yún can send commands and data requests to the Linux-side of the device; these instructions are interpreted by a Python 2.7 interpreter on OpenWRT. In order to begin communications, you must import the Bridge library. This can be done inside the Arduino IDE, by going to the menu Sketch ⇨ Import Library ⇨ Bridge, or by adding the include lines manually:

```
#include <Bridge.h>
#include <YunClient.h>
#include <Process.h>
#include <Mailbox.h>
#include <HttpClient.h>
#include <Console.h>
#include <YunServer.h>
#include <FileIO.h>
```

The first include, `Bridge.h`, is required for intersystem communication. The other includes are required only when using specific portions of the library. The `YunClient.h` include is required for HTTP client operations, similar to Ethernet client includes. Similarly, `YunServer.h` is required when the Arduino becomes an Ethernet server. The `Process.h` include is required when running processes (or commands) on the Linux side. The `Mailbox.h` include is required when using the mailbox interface system. The `Console.h` include is required when simulating a console on the Linux side, and `FileIO.h` is required when reading and writing files to the micro-SD card and when reading files from Linux.

To begin the Bridge library, use `begin()`:

```
Bridge.begin();
```

This function does not take any parameters and does not return any values. It must be called in `setup()` and is a blocking function; it does not return until the operation has finished and stops the sketch until it has completed. It takes roughly 3 seconds to initialize the Bridge system.

To exchange information between the two devices, a put/get system exists. `put()` places data into a Python *dictionary* on Linino. It requires two elements: the key and a value. The key is a name; the value can be numerical or text but is stored in text format. Stored data may look like this:

```
username: john
age: 42
profession: programmer
highscore: 880
```

To place data on the Linux side, use `put()`:

```
Bridge.put(key, value);
```

This function requires two parameters: the `key` and the `value` and does not return any data. This information is sent to the Atheros processor and placed inside the Python dictionary. If the key does not exist, it is created, and the contents of `value` are stored. If the key already exists, the contents of `value` are stored and replace whatever was previously there. To fetch values stored in the dictionary, use `get()`:

```
int result = Bridge.get(key, buffer, buffer_length);
```

This function takes three parameters: `key` is the text key to search for in the dictionary; `buffer` is a `char` array that will be used to store the result; and `buffer_length` is the size of `buffer`. This function returns an `int`, the amount of bytes that have been placed into the buffer. If no data is available, this function returns 0.

The Bridge class is a simple way to transfer data to and from the Linux side, and includes features like error correction to ensure that data is always correctly transferred.

Process

The `Process` class runs and manages applications running on Linux. To begin using the `Process` class, you must first create a `Process` object:

```
Process p;
```

Next, you must specify the command to run. This is done with `begin()`:

```
Process.begin(command);
```

The `command` parameter is a text representation of the command or program to execute; for example, `cat`, `ls`, `curl`, and such. To add one or more parameters, use `addParameter()`:

```
Process.addParameter(param);
```

This function takes one parameter, a string with the parameter to add:

```
Process p; // Create a Process class
p.begin("cat"); // Prepare a program
p.addParameter("/proc/cpuinfo"); // Add a parameter
```

The final step is to run the application with the required parameters, which is done with `run()`:

```
Process.run();
```

This function does not take any parameters and executes the program. This is a blocking function; the function does not return until the Linux program finishes. If you run a program that will not exit by itself, your sketch will freeze and will not continue. To run a program that does not exit, use `runAsynchronously()`:

```
Process.runAsynchronously();
```

This function does not take any parameters, executes the Linux application, and returns immediately. The application may or may not be running. To check the status of a program, use `running()`:

```
result = Process.running();
```

This function does not take any parameters and returns a `boolean`: `true` if the application is still running and `false` if it has terminated.

When an application terminates, it often returns a *return code,* which is a numerical value that can give information about the return conditions. (For example, curl will return 2 if the application failed to initialize, 3 if the URL was malformed, and 7 if it failed to connect to the host.) To get the return code, use `exitValue()`:

```
result = Process.exitValue();
```

This function returns an `unsigned int`: the return code of the Linux application. It is not necessary to read the return code for every application. You can call this only when it's needed.

Some applications require text input to operate correctly, asking the user for certain parameters before executing actions. Before asking information from the user, applications normally display text information. To help exchange data, read-and-write functions are available.

To read data from a process, use `read()`:

```
data = Process.read();
```

read() returns an unsigned int, the first byte of data available from the serial output of the process, or –1 if no data is available. To write serial data to a process, use write():

```
Process.write(val);
Process.write(str);
Process.write(buf, len);
```

The val parameter sends a single byte to the process. To send data as a String, use the str parameter. Finally, you can send data by specifying a char array as buf and the length of the buffer as len. This function returns a byte, the number of bytes written to the process.

To flush the buffer, that is, to delete any data waiting to be read, use flush():

```
Process.flush();
```

This function does not take any parameters and does not return any information. It flushes the incoming buffer after all pending output has been written.

To terminate a process, use close():

```
Process.close();
```

FileIO

The Arduino Yún has an integrated micro-SD slot, allowing users to expand the filesystem. This card is handled by Linux, but the FileIO library provides a convenient way to interact with files—creating, reading, writing, and deleting. These functions send instructions through the Arduino Yún bridge.

WARNING   The following functions work only with files on the SD card.

Before using filesystem instructions, you must first use begin():

```
// Setup File IO
FileSystem.begin();
```

This function must be called inside setup(). Next, you must create a File object. To do this, you must open() a file. If the file exists, it will be opened. If the file does not exist, it will be created, but the folder it is in must exist.

```
File datafile = FileSystem.open(filename);
File datafile = FileSystem.open(filename, mode);
```

The filename parameter is a String and indicates the file to open. It can include directories so long as they are separated by a forward slash (for example, "data/log.txt"). The optional mode parameter indicates how the file should be opened, in the default read-only mode (specified by FILE_READ), or in read/write mode (specified by FILE_WRITE). This function returns a File object and is used to perform read-and-write functions. If the file cannot be opened, the `File` object evaluates to `false`; it is therefore possible to test if the file was opened:

```
File datafile = FileSystem.open("/data/log.txt", FILE_WRITE);
if (!datafile)
  Serial.println("ERROR: File could not be opened!");
```

File operations are exactly like the SD-card library; functions such as `read()`, `write()`, `seek()`, and `flush()` exist. This library is similar in structure to the SD library; only the underlying routines change. For more information, see Chapter 12.

However, not every function works on files. `open()` requires a folder to exist, but it does not work if the folder does not exist and does not create a folder if it is missing. To remedy this, various filesystem instructions exist that do not require a file to perform actions.

To check if a file exists without opening it (or creating a new one), use `exists()`:

```
result = FileSystem.exists(filename);
```

The `filename` parameter is a `String` and is in the same format as `open()`. It returns a `boolean`: `true` if the file (or folder) exists and `false` if it does not exist.

To create a folder, use `mkdir()`:

```
result = FileSystem.exists(filename);
```

This function returns a `boolean`: `true` if the folder were created, `false` otherwise. To delete a folder, use `rmdir()`:

```
result = FileSystem.rmdir(folder);
```

This function returns a `boolean`: `true` if the folder were deleted, `false` if the function were unable to delete the folder. It requires the target folder to be empty; any files present must be removed. To remove files, use `remove()`:

```
result = FileSystem.remove(filename);
```

This function, like the previous functions, returns a `boolean`: `true` if deleted, `false` otherwise. This function is a wrapper for the system command `rm` and as such can delete both files and folders.

YunServer

The YunServer class is used when creating a server on the Arduino Yún's Linux distro. This allows the Arduino side of the Yún to receive requests and to answer those requests.

To create a server, you must first create a YunServer object:

```
YunServer server;
```

When the object has been created, you must tell the Arduino who can connect. Contrary to most Arduino Ethernet shields, you will not want external connections, only local connections. The Arduino will wait for connections from the local host, but the local host is also the Linux side of the Arduino. This means that when incoming connections arrive, they will be routed through the Linux processor, leaving the AVR microcontroller side of the Arduino free to do what it does best—control your sketches. To do this, use `listenOnLocalhost()`:

```
server.listenOnLocalHost();
```

The last step, after the object has been created, is to use `begin()`:

```
server.begin();
```

The server has now been created, and you can wait for clients to connect. The difference between the Arduino Yún and other models using Ethernet or Wi-Fi shields is the multitasking capacity. Although other Arduinos have to wait for a client to connect, the Yún doesn't need to wait, The Linux server can handle connections, and the Arduino can see how many clients are waiting and handle connections as required. Your sketch is free to continue between connections. All you have to do is wait for a client.

YunClient

The YunClient interface is used for all client-based calls on the Yún. Just like the server, you must first create a YunClient object:

```
YunClient client;
```

To accept an incoming connection, you can talk with the YunServer:

```
YunServer server;
YunClient client = server.accept();
if (client)
{
  // Client has connected
}
```

You can verify if a client is still connected using `connected()`:

```
result = client.connected();
```

This function returns a `boolean`: `true` if the client is still connected and `false` if it has disconnected.

When a client has connected, you can read and write using standard `stream` functions:

```
String data = client.readString();
client.println("Thanks for connecting to my Yún");
```

When you finish talking to a client, you can terminate the connection using `stop()`:

```
client.stop();
```

Example Application

In Chapter 12, you created a light sensor that was capable of logging data to an SD card. In this chapter, you again use a light sensor, but one that can log the temperature to a data file with a timestamp and that can be read over a wireless connection.

To do this, you need an Arduino Yún and a micro-SD card to use for data logging. A standard LDR will be connected to your Yún through the analog pin A3. The sketch will wait 20 seconds between each measurement. During this loop, the sketch will listen to connections from a web navigator.

Hardware

This sketch uses an Arduino Yún connected to a light-dependent resistor. One pin of the LDR is connected to +5 V, and the other one is connected to a 10-kΩ resistor that is connected to ground. The analog reading is made where the LDR and the fixed value resistor are connected. The breadboard example will look like Figure 23-1:

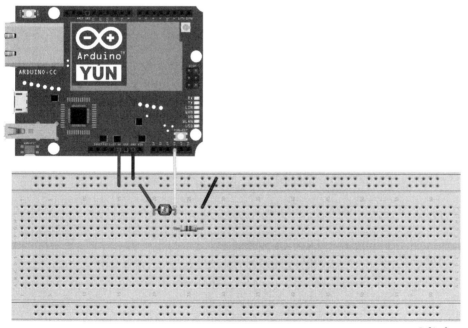

Figure 23-1: Project schematic (Image created with fritzing).

Sketch

The sketch will look like Listing 23-1.

Listing 23-1: Sensor sketch (filename: Chapter23.ino**)**

```
1    #include <Bridge.h>
2    #include <FileIO.h>
3    #include <YunServer.h>
4    #include <YunClient.h>
5
6    YunServer server;
7    String startString;
8
9    int iteration = 0;
10
11   void setup()
12   {
13     Serial.begin(9600);
14     Bridge.begin();
15     FileSystem.begin();
16
17     server.listenOnLocalhost();
18     server.begin();
19   }
20
21   void loop ()
22   {
23     String dataString;
24     YunClient client;
25
26     dataString += getTimeStamp();
27     dataString += ", ";
28
29     int sensor = analogRead(A3);
30     dataString += String(sensor);
31
32     Serial.println(dataString);
33
34     iteration++;
35     if (iteration == 20)
36     {
37       boolean result = logResults(dataString);
38       if (result == false)
39       {
40         // Uhoh, couldn't write!
41         Serial.println("ERR: Couldn't write data to file");
42       }
43       iteration = 0;
44     }
45
```

```
46    for (int i = 0; i < 20; i++)
47    {
48      client = server.accept();
49      if (client)
50      {
51        client.print(dataString);
52        client.stop();
53      }
54      delay(1000);
55    }
56  }
57
58  boolean logResults(String dataString)
59  {
60    File dataFile = FileSystem.open("/mnt/sd/log.txt", FILE_APPEND);
61
62    if (dataFile)
63    {
64      dataFile.println(dataString);
65      dataFile.close();
66      return true;
67    }
68    return false;
69  }
70
71  // This function return a string with the time stamp
72  String getTimeStamp() {
73    Process time; // The process instance
74    String result; // The String the result will be stored to
75
76    time.begin("date"); // The command to run is "date"
77    time.addParameter("+%D-%T"); // The parameters to add
78    time.run(); // Run the command
79
80    delay(50); // Give the instruction some time to run
81
82    // Get the output from the command line
83    while (time.available() > 0) {
84      char c = time.read();
85      if (c != '\n')
86        result += c;
87    }
88
89    return result;
90  }
```

On lines 1 to 4, you import the necessary header files. `Bridge.h` is used for almost everything on the Arduino Yún. `FileIO.h` is used for saving data to the SD card, and `YunClient.h` and `YunServer.h` are used to handle client/

server operations. On line 6, an instance of the YunServer is created. This will be used later.

setup() is declared on line 11. First, the serial port is initialized, and then the Bridge and filesystem subsystems are initialized. Finally, the server starts.

loop() is declared on line 23, but before describing its functionality, let's look at the two other functions it calls. One is used to write data to the SD card, and the other retrieves the timestamp from Linux.

getTimeStamp() is declared on line 74. When it runs, it creates an instance of the Process class. It also creates a variable called result; this is the variable that holds the result of a Linux command. This command runs inside a process called time. The function that it calls is named date; when executing the date command, it returns something like this:

```
jlangbridge@desknux:~$ date
Fri 29 Aug 15:01:00 UTC 2014
```

This contains a little bit too much information, you need only a short date and time. This is achieved by adding some parameters to the instruction:

```
jlangbridge@desknux:~$ date +%D-%T
08/29/14-15:01:00
```

To call date, the sketch calls time.begin() on line 78 using date as an argument. To add parameters, addParameter() is used on line 79. The command is run on line 80. The next few lines wait for a fraction of a second and then read the output of the command. This data is placed in a String, which is then returned to the loop().

The second function is called logResults(), and it is declared on line 60. This function takes a String and places that data onto an SD card. It begins by attempting to open a file on the SD card in the FILE_APPEND mode. On line 64 a verification is made to see if the file were opened. If it were opened, the data is written, and the file is closed before returning true. If the file weren't opened, the function returns false.

Back to loop(). A variable called dataString is declared and then a YunClient object is created. The dataString variable holds the date, time, and light sensor reading. On line 28, the date and time is added from the return value of get-TimeStamp(). Next, the analog value on pin A3 is read, converted to a String, and added to dataString. On line 36, the variable iteration is incremented. If the value equals 20, then the value is written to the data card. Finally, on line 50, the sketch checks to see if a client is connected. If it is, the dataString displays, and the connection is closed before returning the iteration value to zero.

Exercises

This sketch is the basis for a compact sensor, and together with a temperature sensor and barometer, it can be used to create a wireless weather station. Add some components to the device, and display their value on the web server.

Summary

In this chapter you have seen the Arduino Yún and the Bridge library used to exchange messages between the Arduino microcontroller and the Linux microprocessor. You have seen the different ways in which information can be exchanged, and how to issue commands and fetch data to and from the Linux operating system. In the next chapter, you will see how users and companies have added functionality to Arduinos in the form of user libraries, and how to import those libraries to add functionality to your own projects.

Part

IV

User Libraries and Shields

In This Part

Importing Third-Party Libraries

This chapter requires the following:

- Arduino Uno
- Adafruit Si1145 breakout board

As you have seen throughout this book, the Arduino libraries add an impressive amount of functionality to the platform. They facilitate the use of a large number of electronic components and breakout boards. In some cases, using a shield is as simple as selecting the correct library, but this isn't always the case. The Arduino ecosystem has grown immensely over the years; it has been used for an unbelievably large amount of projects. Not all use "standard" components; some need more specific hardware.

When you import a library, the Arduino has access to more functionality. For example, the SD library enables you to easily write to large storage formats with an Arduino, something that would otherwise be difficult to do. This is done by adding functions, pieces of code that help you talk to hardware, or performing software calculations and actions. Libraries facilitate this by *importing* these functions and making them available to the sketch. Sketches can, of course, add existing standard Arduino libraries, but they can also add libraries written by third parties.

Libraries

So what exactly is a library? Sketches are written in a form of C, and a library is simply an extension, written in either C or C++. When you create a function in your sketch, you can call it inside the same sketch. A library has a collection of functions that can be reused in multiple sketches. When you import a library: functions are made available, and you can call one, several, or all the functions in the library as needed. You could also call none of the functions, but that would be a bit of a waste.

There are several advantages to libraries; by hiding away all the long functions, your sketch is made simpler. For example, if talking to a new external component, the library can tell your sketch how to read the data from the component. First, pull this output high, then send some binary data, wait for a few milliseconds, retrieve binary data, sort that data, perform some calculations, and then return the data. All this, just to return the temperature or the ultraviolet index? Well, you always need to follow the same process, but it can be taken care of by a function. By putting all this code in a function, your sketch is clearer, and you even use less memory because the sketch can call one piece of code several times, instead of having different copies of the same function in memory. It also makes maintenance easier; if you have several sketches that use the same functions, updating the library makes those changes immediately available to the sketches that use them.

Finding Libraries

Often, the most difficult part of using an external library is finding it in the first place, and even that isn't hard. Some hardware manufacturers develop libraries designed specifically for their shields or breakout boards, and these are available on the company's site. For example, Adafruit often has a tutorial for the breakout boards that it sells, showing how to connect it and typically with some example code. On these pages, you often find a link to download the library they created to interface with the component.

Some electronic components do not require breakout boards but are still complex enough to merit their own library. In Chapter 10 you saw how to create a wireless device that helps keep houseplants happy. The DHT-11 humidity sensor is a rather complex device, and the code was a little difficult. I don't expect every Arduino user to write code like that. To help beginners use these devices, a DHT-11 library exists. The same goes for other electronic components. To use these libraries, you need to search online to see if there is something available.

Libraries are, put simply, source code files. There are sites that are dedicated to hosting open source projects and handling source code. These sites allow other users to retrieve the source code and to suggest modifications and corrections if required. A single open source project can have hundreds of developers, each proposing a change or adding their code to an existing project. One such site is GitHub (`http://github.com`).

NOTE GitHub gets its name from the open-source code management program, Git. It allows users to use this application to download the source code, upload changes, and to create parallel versions. Although the site is optimized for Git, you do not need to use this program; projects can be downloaded as a Zip file.

On the top of the screen, GitHub allows you to make a search of the available projects. Give it a try. This chapter will use Silicon Lab's SI1145 UV sensor. Enter **Arduino si1145** in the search field, and then press Search. There are dozens of responses, but you can change the order of the results, either by stars (the amount of popularity a project has), forks (the amount of times this library has been used to create another project), or recently updated (the last time the project was updated). Best Match, the default setting, uses all three to create the best solution and displays those results first.

NOTE Adafruit also uses Github for its libraries.

One of the best sources of information, not only for libraries but for everything to do with Arduino, is the Arduino Forum.

Importing a Library

To import a third-party library, you can use the Arduino IDE. When you go into the Sketch ⇨ Import Library menu, you have the choice of importing a standard Arduino library, but there is also an Add Library menu item, as shown in Figure 24-1.

Clicking this menu item opens a new window, prompting you to select a Zip file or folder containing the library you want to import. A Linux computer shows a window like the one in Figure 24-2.

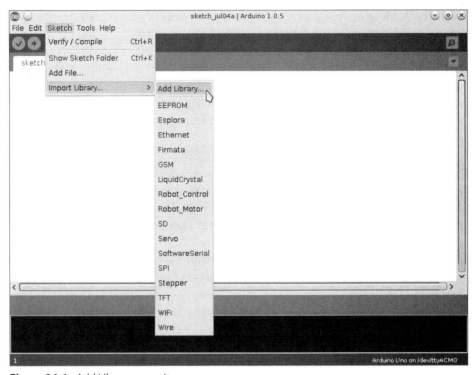

Figure 24-1: Add Library menu item

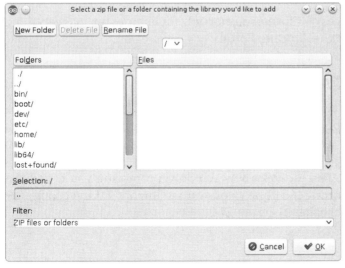

Figure 24-2: Select archive window

The Arduino IDE can recognize two different formats: either a compressed Zip file or a folder. You must either select a zipped archive or the folder you want to import.

If the Arduino IDE can import the library, a message displays informing that the import has completed and that the library is now accessible from the Add Library menu. If the Arduino IDE cannot import the library, a message displays in the information bar at the bottom of the application with a brief explanation of the issue.

NOTE The Arduino IDE can import libraries with properly formatted names—it can handle only ASCII characters such as letters and numbers, and a library cannot start with a number. Also, dashes ("-") are not supported, but underscores ("_") are. Check the library's name before you try to import it.

It is also possible to manually import a library. To do this, first start by downloading the library you want to import. It will normally be available in a compressed format, so after downloading the compressed file you must decompress it. The result should be a folder with the name of the library you want to import. Inside this folder, there should be one or more files: the .cpp file is the source code, and the .h file is the header file. (It may also contain other files.) You will need to copy (or move) the folder that contains these two files.

To manually import a library, you must first quit the Arduino IDE if it is running. Next, locate the Arduino library folder. On Windows machines, it is most likely placed in your Documents or My Documents folder, inside a subfolder called Arduino. On Macintosh, it will be in your Documents folder, again in a subfolder called Arduino. Inside the Arduino folder will be another folder called "libraries." This folder may or may not contain subfolders, depending on if you have already imported other libraries or not. Copy and paste your decompressed archive into this folder, and the next time you start the Arduino IDE your library will be visible under the Sketch ⇨ Import Library menu item.

Using an External Library

Now that you have imported your library, it is time to use it. But where do you start? You can import your library just like you would import any standard Arduino library. New libraries appear at the bottom of the Import Library menu, as shown in Figure 24-3.

This imports the library, but that is all it does. So how exactly do you get your hardware to work? Most libraries come with at least one example application, sometimes several. This is the case with the SI1145 written by Ladyada, Adafruit's founder. Here is an extract of her example sketch:

```
Float UVindex = uv.readUV();
// the index is multiplied by 100 so to get the
// integer index, divide by 100!
UV index /= 100.0;
Serial.print("US: "); Serial.println(UVindex);
```

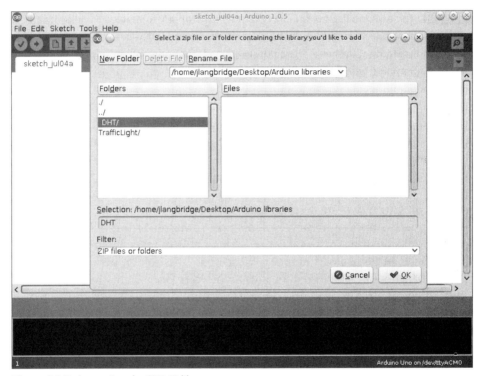

Figure 24-3: Importing the Si1145 library

This example code is extremely simple. A single function is called: `readUV`. Ladyada also explains why the returned data is divided by 100. This function is called on a `uv` object. This object is created at the beginning of the sketch, as follows:

```
Adafruit_SI1145 uv = Adafruit_SI1145();
```

After that, another function is called inside the `setup()` function:

```
uv.begin();
```

And that's it. Everything you need to use the SI1145.

If there are no examples available, then all is not lost. With the open source nature of Arduino, most libraries are also open source, so you can read the contents of the library. These files are written in C++ but are easily readable and can be opened with any text editor. Opening the SI1145 library header (the .h file) shows the following lines in the source code:

```
class Adafruit_SI1145 {
public:
  Adafruit_SI1145(void);
  boolean begin();
  void reset();
  uint16_t readUV();
  uint16_t readIR();
  uint16_t readVisible();
  uint16_t readProx();
private:
  uint16_t read16(uint8_t addr);
  uint8_t read8(uint8_t addr);
  void write8(uint8_t reg, uint8_t val);
  uint8_t readParam(uint8_t p);
  uint8_t writeParam(uint8_t p, uint8_t v);
  uint8_t _addr;
};
```

The `class` name is a reference to a C++ *class*. This becomes an object in your sketch. This object contains both variables and functions. It consists of several parts. The `private` section includes functions and variables that will be visible only inside the class. The sketch cannot see them and cannot modify the variables, or call these functions. What the sketch can see are the members of the `public` part. As you can see, the previous function is found here, `readUV()`, but there are others: `readIR()`, `readVisible()`, and `readProx()`. Although the function of `readVisible()` seems obvious, `readProx()` isn't clear and wasn't used in the example sketch. Header files rarely have comments, so you may not know immediately what this function does. This is a declaration; it tells the compiler that somewhere in the .cpp file there is a function called `readProx()`, so that is where you need to look for the answer.

This is the first few lines of the function found in the C++ file:

```
// returns "Proximity" - assumes an IR LED is attached to LED
uint16_t Adafruit_SI1145::readProx(void)
{
  return read16(0x26);
}
```

Just a few lines of comments, and you can tell what the function does. So this function calculates the Heat index, the human-felt equivalence temperature—an interesting addition that could be useful for weather stations.

Example Application

For this example, you will import a third-party library to use a piece of hardware.

The Si1145 from Silicon Labs is a digital UV sensor. Targeted for the wearable market, it is compact, light, and ultra-low-powered. It is a highly professional solution, but like most professional solutions, it does come at a price. That price is configuration. This device is not like the LM35 temperature sensor that requires a simple analog read; it requires a little bit of configuration before you can use it. When set up, it provides a highly reliable readout. It doesn't just read UV; it can read visible light, infrared light, and when used with an infrared LED, it is also a proximity sensor. All in all, a highly advanced sensor that is great fun to use.

The Si1145 is difficult to use on a typical Arduino project. The component is *surface-mounted*, meaning it cannot be placed directly on a breadboard. It is designed to be as small as possible to keep electronic projects small, and as such, it is difficult to solder the component to a board by using household equipment. It takes some skill and a good setup to solder this component by hand. Also, it is powered by 3.3 V, not the 5 V that an Arduino typically uses. To make this device easier to use, Adafruit has developed a breakout board for the Si1145 sensor, adding standard-sized pins, allowing it to be used on a breadboard, and voltage shifters, making it compatible with 5-volt Arduinos. To make it even easier to use, Adafruit has also created a nicely designed and easy-to-use library.

The first thing you require is the Adafruit Si1145 library. You can find the Si1145 breakout board information page here:

```
https://learn.adafruit.com/adafruit-si1145-breakout-board-uv-ir-visible-
sensor/overview
```

From that page, you can visit the "Wiring and Test" link where you will find a link to Adafruit's GitHub repository:

```
https://github.com/adafruit/Adafruit_SI1145_Library
```

On that page, there are a few things to note. Figure 24-4 displays the webpage.

Repositories can be in a constant state of change; developers can add, change, or delete portions of code, and although some projects are updated daily, others may be updated hourly. You can see the contents of the repository, the filenames, folders, and the last time they were updated. At the bottom, the contents of README.txt are displayed, giving some important information on the project. To the right, there is some statistical information, the number of bug reports, and different ways to connect to the server to retrieve the source code. Some of these involve using the Git software package, but the easiest way is to click the Download Zip button on the bottom right. This takes a snapshot of the current project, compresses it into a Zip file, and downloads the compressed file to your computer.

Figure 24-4: Adafruit's Si1145 GitHub page

Now that the Zip file has been downloaded, it has to be imported. For now, try to import the library as it is currently; the filename is `Adafruit_SI1145_Library-master.zip`. Open the Arduino IDE, go to the Sketch ➪ Import Library ➪ Add Library menu item, as shown in Figure 24-5.

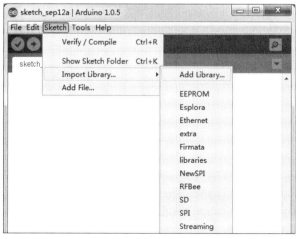

Figure 24-5: Import a library

A new window opens. Select the Zip file that you downloaded. Didn't work, did it? You should have an error message at the bottom of the screen.

This is one of the problems when importing libraries: the naming convention. The Arduino IDE cannot read the dash in the filename, so why was it there? Adafruit did not name its library like that; if you look at the Adafruit and Github pages, the repository name is `Adafruit_SI1145_Library`, no dash. The dash is added by a Git convention, adding `-master` to the end of the compressed file-name. Git repositories can have several "branches," different areas of code that can be modified independently from the rest of the code. This is used from time to time to test new functionality, and if everything goes to plan, that branch is then merged back into the main repository, called master.

The Zip file cannot be used as it is. You cannot simply rename the Zip file because it contains a folder with a dash in the name. To import this library, you have to try something else: extract the contents. Most operating systems have native support for Zip files. Extract the contents of the Zip file to a location on your hard drive. The result should be a folder name called `Adafruit_SI1145_Library-master`. Rename this folder **`Adafruit_SI1145_Library`**. Now, import this folder. As before, go to the Sketch ➪ Import Library ➪ Add Library menu item. Select the folder (without going inside the folder) and press OK. If everything goes well, you will have a new message on your Arduino IDE, like the one shown in Figure 24-6.

Figure 24-6: Successful library import

Now that your library has been imported, you can use it. It becomes available immediately and is listed in the Import Library menu. This library also adds an example, available for use immediately in the File ⇨ Examples menu. Note that for both the Import Library and the Example menu items, external libraries are separated from standard libraries.

Now, load the Si1145 example sketch shown here:

```
1    /*****************************************************
2      This is a library for the Si1145 UV/IR/Visible Light Sensor
3
4      Designed specifically to work with the Si1145 sensor in the
5      adafruit shop
6      ----> https://www.adafruit.com/products/1777
7
8      These sensors use I2C to communicate, 2 pins are required to
9      interface
10     Adafruit invests time and resources providing this open source
        code,
11     please support Adafruit and open-source hardware by purchasing
12     products from Adafruit!
13
14     Written by Limor Fried/Ladyada for Adafruit Industries.
15     BSD license, all text above must be included in any redistribution
16     *****************************************************/
17
18   #include <Wire.h>
19   #include "Adafruit_SI1145.h"
20
21   Adafruit_SI1145 uv = Adafruit_SI1145();
22
23   void setup() {
24     Serial.begin(9600);
25
26     Serial.println("Adafruit SI1145 test");
27
28     if (! uv.begin()) {
29       Serial.println("Didn't find Si1145");
30       while (1);
31     }
32
33     Serial.println("OK!");
34   }
35
36   void loop() {
37     Serial.println("====================");
38     Serial.print("Vis: "); Serial.println(uv.readVisible());
39     Serial.print("IR: "); Serial.println(uv.readIR());
40
41     // Uncomment if you have an IR LED attached to LED pin!
42     //Serial.print("Prox: "); Serial.println(uv.readProx());
```

```
43
44    float UVindex = uv.readUV();
45    // the index is multiplied by 100 so to get the
46    // integer index, divide by 100!
47    UVindex /= 100.0;
48    Serial.print("UV: ");  Serial.println(UVindex);
49
50    delay(1000);
51  }
```

Now, it's time to have a closer look at that sketch. On lines 1 to 16, the author begins with a comment. This is a general explanation of the example, what component it is used for, and some licensing information for the software. The BSD license allows you to use the source code for your projects. You can use this library as long as you credit the original author and agree not to take legal action against them if it does not work as expected.

On line 18, the Wire library is imported. This is used to communicate through the I²C protocol, and this is how the Si1145 communicates. On line 19, the Adafruit SI1145 library is imported.

On line 21, an `Adafruit_SI1145` object is created called `uv`. This is the object that will be used to access the sensor's information.

On line 23, `setup()` is declared. Like most test sketches, it opens up the serial port to allow for simple debugging. On line 28, `begin()` is called to the `uv` object. Typically, `begin()` functions are called to initialize hardware pins, to set voltages to a required state, or to send configuration data to microchips. The Si1145 is an I²C device, so there is no need to configure the I²C bus; it is done via the Wire library. It has a fixed address, so there is no configuration required. It does not require any external pins so that isn't done either. What it does require is a lot of parameters to be sent to the device for it to function correctly. This is what `begin()` does. For this library, it also detects if the device is present, a nice addition. It is all too easy to incorrectly connect a device. The function returns `true` if the sensor is present, making sure that you have set everything up correctly before proceeding with the rest of the sketch.

On line 36, `loop()` is declared, and this is where the fun begins. Several functions are called: `readVisible()` on line 38, `readIR()` on line 39, and `readUV()` on line 44. The `readVisible()` function returns the current ambient light level, and `readIR()` returns the current infrared light level. Adafruit's Si1145 breakout board does not come with an IR LED, but it has a connector if you want to use one. For those who do, another function is available (but commented out in the example): `readProx()` on line 42.

This is an example of a well-designed library; one that is easy to import includes board detection in the `begin()` function, and works well with a fantastic piece of hardware. The Si1145 is an excellent sensor, and Adafruit has worked hard to create a good breakout board and a great library to go with it.

Exercises

You have seen that with this library, you can use new hardware with only a few lines of code. The Si1145 is a powerful device, capable of replacing a light-dependent resistor (LDR) in most applications, with the advantage of including a proximity sensor. Of course, having a device that can give the exact UV level is a huge advantage for wearable devices that can be used for skin protection, both for adults and children. You can monitor when you have had enough sun, or when it is unsafe for children to play outside. Try to add this device onto one of the projects that you have created while reading this book. A UV sensor is always a great addition to weather stations and nice to have for outdoor sensors.

Summary

In this chapter, you have seen what a third-party library is, where you can find one, and how to run example programs, all of which is designed to get you up and running. You have seen how to get information about the different functions the library has—what they do and the values they return. You have seen how to import them into the Arduino IDE and how to use them in your own applications. Libraries are typically used to add functionality from shields, and in the next chapter you will see how to design and create your own shield for use in your projects.

Creating Your Own Shield

As you have seen throughout this book, Arduinos are powerful devices. With a large amount of input and output pins, they can perform advanced functions, but the real power comes with shields. *Shields* expand the functionality of an Arduino by adding electronic components or connectors. Hundreds of designs exist, adding Wi-Fi connectivity, Ethernet, LCD and TFT screens, more input and output, robotics, or simply prototyping.

   Even if hundreds of shields exist, sometimes it is worth creating your own. Don't worry; this isn't magic. Some hobbyists are frightened of creating printed circuit boards, but new tools exist that make this simple. There are no expensive machines to buy and no messy chemicals to use. Even the software used to create these boards is free. If you can create a circuit on a breadboard, you can create a shield.

Creating a Shield

There are hundreds of boards available, either through Arduino, through Arduino-compatible vendors, or through hobbyists and makers. If so many shields are available, why would you want to create your own? Put simply, to have your own hardware the way you want it. A data-logging shield might miss a component that you want, or maybe that fancy input and output shield has a few components that you don't need. Also, the satisfaction of creating your own shield is indescribable. You'll see.

The Idea

It all starts with an idea. The idea is normally the project you have on your desk— a breadboard with dozens of wires linked to a few components. Large projects can have 100 or more wires connected to dozens of components. Although this works great for evaluation and development, it won't last long. Imagine that you have just finished a project for your house. You want to place a data-logging Arduino in the ceiling, hidden away from sight behind some plaster, or in a small hole in the wall. You have already thought of everything; a network cable has been run through the wall to this location, providing a network connection and power to the Arduino. All you have to do is to place the Arduino and the breadboard that contains your project: temperature sensors, humidity sensors, EEPROM data-logging, barometric sensors, and a few other components. You place the Arduino, you place the breadboard, and you connect everything. A job well done! You are about to take a break when you notice a wire on the floor. Where did it come from? It must be from a component when you installed the breadboard; but where? From which component? There are more than a dozen components, possibly 100 small wires, and even if the project works great, the breadboard is a mess. Finding out where the wire came from could be a huge task. Even worse, this device gives information about a single room; you still have to install the ones for the kitchen, bedroom, garage, and attic. Imagine snagging a wire on each. This could take hours, if not days.

Because each breadboard is identical, it is easy to create a shield. Because you created a breadboard design, it is easy to create an electronic schematic, which is explained in the section, "Your First Shield." Having all the components on a shield instead of a breadboard makes the design much more resilient; no more wires to catch on clothes or nails. No more components ready to fall off. A nice, clear design, smaller than a breadboard, which can probably last years (if not decades). Even better, if you ever get that extension to your home finished, you already have the design for the shield, and you can add a sensor to the new room as soon as the work is done.

The Required Hardware

If you have the Arduino IDE set up on a computer, you already have all the hardware that you need. Back in the old days, you had to have transparent film, a UV lamp, ferric chloride, and a steady hand. When not created on a computer, connections and lanes were drawn by hand or by using stickers. This was printed or drawn onto a transparent film and then placed onto a photoresist copper-clad board. Exposing this to UV light removes the photoresist that was not protected by markings, revealing the copper. The board is then dipped into ferric chloride, a nasty chemical that can stain just about anything bright orange. When this was complete, the board needed to be cleaned, and the last thing to do was to drill holes where you were to place components.

This is still done frequently today, but companies have been created that do the work for you, resulting in a board that is professionally created with a much higher standard than anything you can make with home equipment. One of these companies is Fritzing.

The Required Software

Fritzing has been used throughout this book to create images of breadboards with the circuit connections. You can use this free, open-source application for a variety of things, from creating a breadboard connection diagram, to an electronic schematic, all the way to hardware design. Fritzing is available for Windows, Mac OS, and Linux and is available on the Fritzing website at `http://fritzing.org/`.

Fritzing comes with a large collection of components, including the standard resistor, LED, breadboard, most of the Arduino boards, and more advanced components such as the PCF8574, which is explained in the section, "Your First Shield." Of course, there are hundreds of thousands of components available, and it isn't possible to list them all, so some companies and makers create user libraries of components. For example, Adafruit supplies a component library that Fritzing can use to help you use its components and breakout boards.

A Fritzing project contains several elements: the breadboard design, the electronics schematic, and the printed circuit board. This file can then be sent to the Fritzing website for production; you can order your shield directly through the application.

Fritzing has an easy-to-use interface. When you open the application, you are presented with the main screen. On the top, you see four buttons that correspond to four activities. By default, you will be on the Welcome screen. Next, the Breadboard view allows you to create projects with a virtual breadboard, using visual components that resemble what you have used until now. Next, the Schematic view can create an electronic schematic from the Breadboard view. Finally, the PCB view allows you to create a printed circuit board from the Breadboard and Schematic views.

To the right are two views: Parts and Inspector. Parts is where you can find electronic components like resistors and wires, but also breadboards, Arduino, and breakout boards. Anything that you want to place is present there. The Inspector panel is used to change component characteristics; you can change the value of components, for example, change the resistance of a resistor.

Your First Shield

Throughout this book, you have used libraries and shields created by other people. Now you are ready to take that a step further and create your own shield! This chapter describes the steps necessary to design and create your own shield. To use that shield, you need to create a software library, which is discussed in the next chapter.

So, what kind of shield can be made? It would be easier to ask what kind of shield cannot be made; there are so many different shield designs that it is impossible to list them all. For this chapter, you create an I/O shield, increasing the capacity of the Arduino by another 16 pins. Why would you want to create more I/O? Doesn't the Arduino have enough I/O? I've seen projects where the makers would clearly say that no, even the Arduino Mega 2560 does not have enough input and output, and more is always welcome. It would be even better if the shield could use the I²C protocol, therefore using up few pins.

There are many I²C-compatible components on the market. The component that you use for this project is the PCF8574AP. This component is an 8-bit I/O expander, capable of adding eight input and output pins to an I²C bus. The Arduino already has a built-in I²C bus, so no other components are required.

The first thing to do when using a new component is to download the datasheet. This device is created by NXP, and their website contains a link to datasheets. This specific datasheet is available at `http://www.nxp.com/documents/data_sheet/PCF8574_PCF8574A.pdf`. Here is an extract from that datasheet.

The devices consist of eight quasi-bidirectional ports, 100 kHz I²C-bus interface, three hardware address inputs, and interrupt output operating between 2.5 V and 6 V. The quasi-bidirectional port can be independently assigned as an input to monitor interrupt status or keypads, or as an output to activate indicator devices such as LEDs. System master can read from the input port or write to the output port through a single register.

A single paragraph tells you a lot about the component. First is the I²C speed, 100 kHz, something that the Arduino can use. The I²C has three address inputs, meaning that 3 bits of the address can be set, allowing several components to be used at the same time, or simply to configure the address on a heavily populated I²C bus.

Another important detail; inputs and outputs can function between 2.5 V and 6 V. Arduinos use two voltages: 3.3 V and 5 V. This shield will be compatible with both types of Arduino, without the need to add voltage-shifting hardware.

Next, it talks about quasi-bidirectional ports. What exactly is a quasi-bidirectional port? An input port is one that can read the voltage on a pin. An output port is one that can set a voltage on a pin. In theory, a bidirectional port is one that can do both at the same time: set output voltage and read input voltage. The problem arises when, for example, the output is set to a logical one, 5 volts, and the input is a logical zero, ground. In this configuration, that would result in a pin set too high to be in direct contact with the ground, resulting in a short circuit, cutting power to the board and potentially damaging the component and the board. Quasi-bidirectional solves this and allows the component to work in this fashion. Quasi-bidirectional pins can sink a rather large amount of current (tens of milli-amps, more than enough for an LED) but can source only a small amount of current (sometimes tens of micro-amps). In the case of a short circuit, the device simply limits the current, as if a large resistor was placed in the circuit. The advantage is, of course, ease of use. There is no need to set a pin to be specifically input or output, but the disadvantage is that this pin cannot be used to power all components; it will not deliver enough power to turn on an LED. So why does the datasheet talk about output devices such as LEDs? Well, they can still be used, but they should ground to the device, turning the LED on when the output is a logical zero or be used with a transistor that requires much less current to activate than an LED. That part will be left to the end user; your job is to create the shield that will contain the components and connectors.

Step 1: The Breadboard

Breadboards are an excellent way to test circuits and ideas. It is extremely easy to add wires, to change connections, and to duplicate part of the circuit if required. Most projects start as an experiment on a breadboard, even the most professional Arduino applications.

To create a simple circuit, you can use a breadboard to create a design almost immediately. There is, however, a slight difference between this breadboard design and the designs that you have been using. In previous designs, the output of a component was simply left as it is; to use that output, you need to place a wire in one of the breadboard connectors. When designing a shield, you should always use the type of connector that will be on the final design. There is a good reason for this; one that you will see in the section "The PCB."

This design requires two PCF8574AP integrated circuits, one 16-pin or two 8-pin headers, and optionally, additional headers to specify the I²C addresses.

Remember, the PCF8574AP needs to be configured by either pulling pins high or low to define the address. This can either be done "hard" by physically wiring the pins on the shield, or "soft" by placing jumpers on the board. For this example, they will be hard-wired. You can add headers and jumpers as an exercise. The pin layout is shown in Figure 25-1.

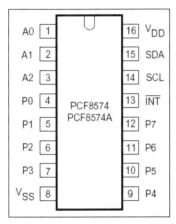

Figure 25-1: PCF8574AP pin layout

Open up Fritzing and enter the Breadboard view. By default, a new project already has a breadboard placed in the center of the view. Go to the Parts panel and search for the PCF8574AP chip by entering the text "PCF8574" next to the magnifying glass. The result will be displayed below. To place a component, you can drag the component from the Component view directly onto the breadboard. Place the two PCF8574AP chips and headers on the breadboard. Connect +5 V and GND pins of the Arduino to the power rails of the breadboard, and then wire power to the integrated circuits.

Pin 16 is V_{DD}, supply voltage, and pin 8 is V_{SS}, supply ground. This is a common layout for integrated circuits.

Next, connect the I²C bus wires. Remember, pin A4 is for SDA, and A5 is for SCL. Connect these two pins to the breadboard. Figure 25-2 shows my layout.

Next, set the addresses of the two integrated circuits. Pins 1, 2, and 3 are used for the address. For this example, device 0 (on the left) will use 000b (all low), and device 1 (on the right) will use b001; that is, A0 and A1 will be low, and A2 will be high. This can still be achieved without the breadboard view becoming too complicated by using both the top and lower power rails, as shown in Figure 25-3.

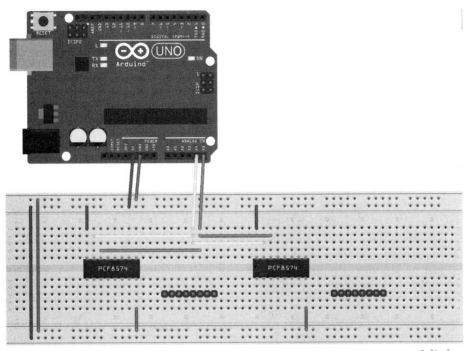

Figure 25-2: Power and I²C connected (Image created with Fritzing)

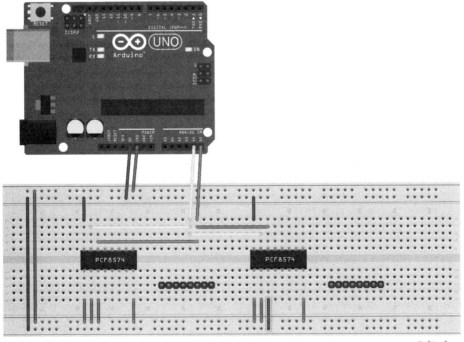

Figure 25-3: I²C address set (Image created with Fritzing)

The breadboard view is still visible and not too complicated. That is about to change. The last thing to do is to connect the two headers, each one requiring eight wires. The view will be extremely complicated, but don't worry; you will see that there is a better way of looking at your circuit when this is done.

Connect all eight input/output pins of the two devices: P0 to P7 to each header. My breadboard looks like the one illustrated in Figure 25-4. Note that I made the wires a little clearer on the right but not on the left. With the I²C wires in the way, it isn't easy to make something that is elegant. It might be possible by spending a lot of time, but remember that breadboard schematics are all about getting things done and not about understanding the electronics behind a design.

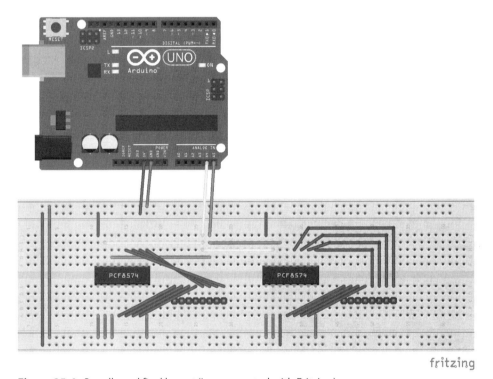

Figure 25-4: Breadboard final layout (Image created with Fritzing)

You now have a working breadboard design, but how do you turn this into a shield? You can do this directly, but just before, it is time to look at the schematic.

Step 2: The Schematic

Reading breadboard designs isn't easy. The bottom left pin on both integrated circuits are pulled low, but is this pin the ground? Is it an address? It is difficult to know without extensive knowledge of the integrated circuit itself, and there are tens of thousands of designs. To understand what a circuit does, you have to look at the schematic.

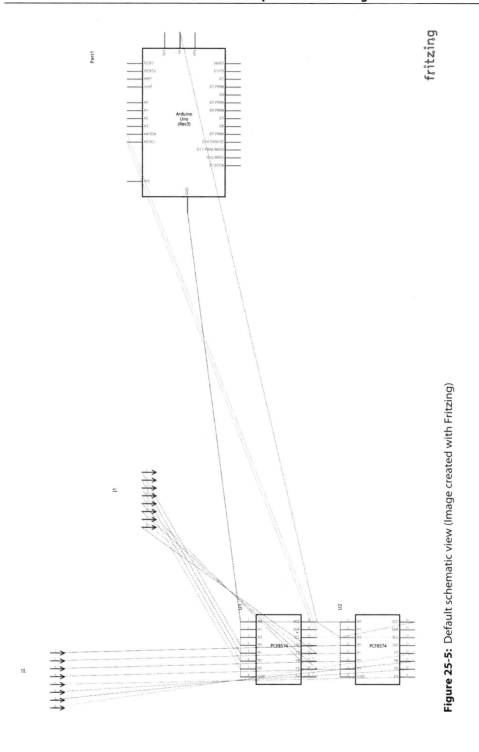

Figure 25-5: Default schematic view (Image created with Fritzing)

Fritzing also has a schematic view that updates automatically. To view the schematic view, click the Schematic tab. (You are currently on the Breadboard tab.) Figure 25-5 shows my schematic.

Whoa. What is this? This is an engineering nightmare, completely unreadable. There are dotted lines going from pin to pin, crossing over each other. This is actually a valid layout; each connection has been made, but it still needs to be sorted out. This takes some time but is a useful part of any project.

In the schematic view, your job is to re-create the connections in a way that is easily readable by others (and by yourself). When you mouse over a component, it is "selected" by a gray background. Right-clicking this component opens a menu allowing you to perform certain actions. The most useful are the rotate and mirror actions. By left-clicking and dragging, you can move the components around. Attempt to move the components in a way that creates the least amount of crossing lines. You won't make it perfect, so don't worry if a few do cross over; this will be sorted when creating the PCB. In my view, I have moved the components in a way that looks better, and I have also started to make some connections between the Arduino and the two integrated circuits, as shown in Figure 25-6.

A connection is already made between the different pins according to what was done on the breadboard, and now your job is to make a solid, visible line between the different pins. To do this, Fritzing helps you out. Place your cursor above one of the pins, and it changes to blue. Click and hold down the mouse, and you can start to create a wire. Fritzing also highlights pins that need to be connected in red, making it easier to know what pins need to be connected.

This draws a straight line between the two pins, possibly crossing over other wires or even components. Don't worry. You can add bendpoints by clicking the wire that was created. Try to keep wires horizontal and vertical to make the schematic easier to read. If you need to move a bendpoint, select the bendpoint by hovering over it with your mouse, and then drag and drop the bendpoint to the new location. To delete a bendpoint, hover over and then right click it, and select the Remove Bendpoint option from the menu. Moving a component automatically moves the first part of the wire up until the first bendpoint.

After 10 minutes, this is what I created, illustrated in Figure 25-7. It is much clearer than the first version and can be shown to other makers to share ideas or to ask for advice if needed.

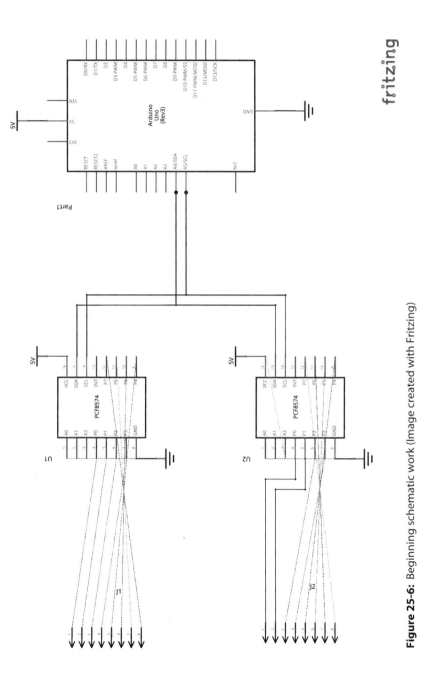

Figure 25-6: Beginning schematic work (Image created with Fritzing)

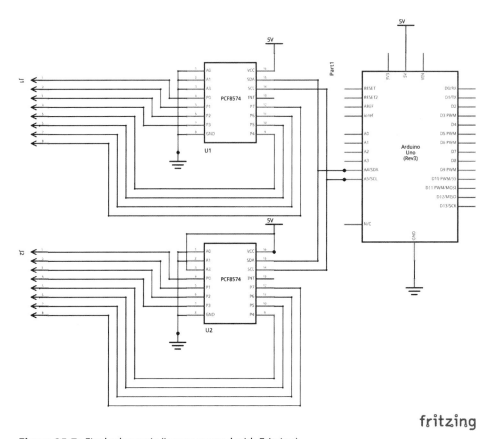

Figure 25-7: Final schematic (Image created with Fritzing)

Although you can create a shield only from a breadboard example, creating a schematic does help. Did you notice those INT pins on the integrated circuits? The PCF8574AP can "warn" a device through an interrupt that one of the inputs has a changed state. On a breadboard, this was impossible to notice, but on a schematic, it is clearly visible. It might be a good idea to connect these to the Arduino in a next version. For now, it is time to create the shield.

Step 3: The PCB

The most rewarding part of creating a shield is designing the PCB, the Printed Circuit Board. It is also the most complicated part, but it isn't overly difficult, and Fritzing helps you a lot.

Designing a PCB is all about the physical world; in the schematic view, it doesn't matter if the connectors go on the left side or on the right side. It is more a question of preference, and if I put the connectors on the left, it was mainly because that is what Fritzing started with. For the PCB, it is different. The Arduino headers, for example, are placed in a specific position and cannot be moved. Fortunately, this is just one of the many ways in which Fritzing helps you.

When opening the PCB view, you are presented with a black screen with individual components placed on the screen. Again, there are dotted lines connecting the different pins and components. In the middle of the screen, Fritzing has placed a shield layout. By default, it will be for the Arduino Uno, but this can be changed. Fritzing can help you create shields for almost all Arduino types. To select a board, click the board on the screen, and select the board type in the Inspector on the bottom right side, and select the type. For this example, you create a shield for the Arduino Uno without the need for the ISCP headers.

This particular shield design already has the correct header placement, so you do not have to place those. However, you have to place the integrated circuits and the two headers. This is why you had to use headers for the breadboard view so that the component is visible. If you had used wires only to connect other devices, the header would not have been added.

Place the headers on the left in a line close together but not too close. Next, place the integrated circuits on the board, somewhere where the dotted lines don't cross over too often. Remember to use the rotate function to place the components in the best possible location.

Printed circuit boards have one or several copper plates on their sides or inside. Basic printed circuit boards have one copper side, known as the single layer. More advanced circuit boards have copper on both sides and are known as dual-layered. The mainboard inside your personal computer can sometimes have up to a dozen "layers" of copper and are extremely advanced. Instead of the wires on your breadboard, there will be copper "lanes" going from one component to the other. Fritzing can provide double-layer printed circuit boards, meaning that there can be connections on both sides.

Contrary to the schematic view, wires cannot cross each other on the same side. If you cannot go around a wire, you can go underneath or above. This makes routing slightly difficult, but luckily, Fritzing has yet another tool to help you, known as autoroute. Autoroute attempts to create wires between the components and normally does a good job but does need a little bit of tweaking.

My solution is available at `http://www.wiley.com/go/arduinosketches`. Have a look, and compare with your own.

The final step to making your shield is to send it for fabrication. This is done automatically by clicking the Fabricate button on the bottom-right side. After selecting the amount of printed circuit boards, the design is sent to the Fritzing Fab.

Fritzing checks your design, but only for major problems: short circuits, design problems, or missing connections. After a few days, you will receive a professionally made printed circuit board, ready to go! Place it on your Arduino, and prepare yourself for another adventure; after you have created a shield, you have to create the software for the shield. You do this in the next chapter.

Creating Arduino shields is an excellent way of learning electronics but can also be a source of income. Several companies sell Arduino shields but also individuals shields on dedicated electronics sites. Arduino shields work, of course, on Arduinos, but not only. Several boards exist with Arduino-compatible connectors, even if they are not Arduinos and are not programmed by the Arduino IDE. One example is Atmel's SAMA5D3 evaluation board. Atmel supplies most of the microcontrollers on Arduino boards but also creates advanced processors for professional designs. The SAMA5D3 is one example of a processor that can run a full Linux or Android system, but with Arduino shields.

Summary

In this chapter you have seen just how easy it is to create your own shield using Fritzing, an open-source application to create schematics and help you create professional quality shields. You have created your own project and developed a solution to increase the input/output of your Arduino beyond its initial design point. However, to use your shield, you will require software to control the components, something that will be presented in the next chapter. You will see how to create your own library using the Arduino IDE, and how to package it to distribute to other people and projects.

Creating Your Own Library

This chapter discusses how to create your own library. You can find the code downloads for this chapter at `http://www.wiley.com/go/arduinosketches` on the Download Code tab. The code is in the Chapter 26 download and individually named according to the filenames noted throughout this chapter.

The Arduino project has had an immense success since its creation, and there are several reasons. The cost is, of course, an important criterion to any project. Continuous R & D has also helped, but one of the primary reasons today is simple: the openness of the project. The Arduino community is extremely active. Just look at the Arduino forums: Google+ groups or Arduino events organized in cities throughout the world. This is the community that drives the ongoing evolution of the platform, either by getting the tools to work with new electronic components and breakout boards, or finding and creating their own when nothing exists. In Chapter 25 you created your own shield, now you will create your own library.

Libraries

You can use libraries for several applications, but two main uses exist. One is to have specific routines such as temperature conversion, data processing, or hardware I/O. The second use is to allow the use of specific hardware, hiding away any long routines, and making hardware easy to use. This chapter looks at both of these kinds of libraries.

Library Basics

When you import a library, you import an .h file, the header file. This is a text file that describes what is in a C++ file (that ends with the .cpp extension). Header files are used in most C and C++ projects. They are not required for sketches but are required for libraries. They are a simple way of telling the compiler what to expect in the C++ file and how to use it. It is also an excellent way for developers to know what is contained in a library; everything is listed in just a few lines.

Simple Libraries

Function libraries are an easy entry into writing a library; they contain simple functions similar to ones you might write in your main sketch. Don't worry, you'll look at making some with advanced capabilities in the "Advanced Libraries" section. For now, these contain only simple functions, and their header file is straightforward.

You can demonstrate the use of a potential library with a function call. You can use an Arduino to calculate the answer to the Ultimate Question of Life, the Universe, and Everything. Luckily, Douglas Adams has already answered this question in *The Hitchhiker's Guide to the Galaxy*; a super-computer calculated this question for 7.5 million years before coming up with the answer: 42. Luckily, the Arduino is a lot faster to come up with the answer, and the function looks simple:

```
int theAnswer()
{
  return 42;
}
```

Looks simple, doesn't it? The only difficulty is making this function usable as a library. It requires a few things to set up before it is useable. First, you must think of a name for the library, as well as the folder that will contain your files. The choice of the name is important because it will also be used for the name displayed on the Import Library menu item. Try to think of a name that clearly identifies the library you will create—either the component name, function, or application. Users of your library will depend on this. For this example, use **theAnswerToEverything**.

Create a folder with this name on your desktop or anywhere you have easy access to. Next, you need to create two files: the source file and the header file. The Arduino IDE cannot directly open or save C++ and .h files. These can be created with a standard text editor or with an IDE. Code::Blocks is a freeware

IDE that works on several platforms, including Windows, Linux, and Mac OS. It is available from `www.codeblocks.org/downloads/`.

The header file is a file that contains a description of the functions that you will be writing. Its name is just as important as the name of the library and folder it lives within. For example, when you import the EEPROM library, you add this line:

```
#include <EEPROM.h>
```

This is the header file. Typically, it has the same name as the folder it is held in, but not always. For example, when importing the Wi-Fi library, you may see this:

```
#include <WiFi.h>
#include <WiFiServer.h>
#include <WiFiClient.h>
#include <WiFiUdp.h>
```

Several header files are located inside this folder, and if you use the Import Library functionality in the IDE, all header files are automatically imported. If named well, they clearly state what they do, so anyone using the library can know what the headers do and if they are needed. Imagine another sort of name:

```
#include <stuff.h>
```

This isn't clear, and users will have no idea what this library does. Remember to keep your library name precise and clear.

First, create a source file named **theAnswerToEverything.cpp**. The source file is written in C++ and has the extension `.cpp`. Add the following contents to the file and save it:

```
int theAnswer()
{
  return 42;
}
```

There is just this one function; it takes no parameters and returns an `int`. The Arduino IDE still does not know about this function; it has to be *declared*. This is the role of the header file. Create a new file named `theAnswerToEverything.h` and add the following:

```
int theAnswer();
```

Did you see the difference? It is the same structure, only instead of having source code within brackets, the line is immediately ended with a semicolon. This is the *declaration*. It tells the compiler that this function exists, that it returns an `int`, and that it takes no parameters. If called, the compiler will know that it can find the source code within the `.cpp` file.

There is also one other line that is required and that should be placed at the very beginning of the file:

```
#include "Arduino.h"
```

This imports the Arduino header file, giving you access to Arduino constants and types. It is automatically included for your sketches, but for libraries, you must manually add this include statement.

All that is left to do is to import your new library. From the Arduino IDE, go to Sketch ➪ Import Library ➪ Add Library, as shown in Figure 26-1.

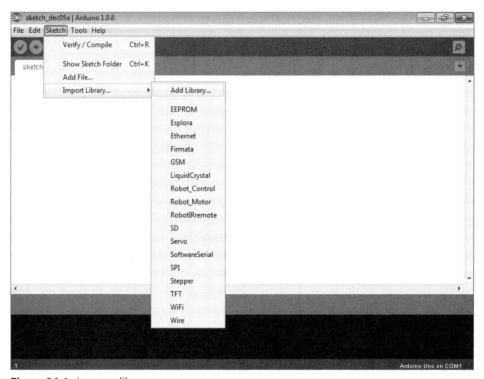

Figure 26-1: Import a library.

Select the folder that contains your library, and import it. If everything goes well, the Arduino IDE should tell you that the import has finished. You can see your library by navigating back to Sketch ➪ Import Library where you see a new library listed, as shown in Figure 26-2.

Now that the library has been imported, it is time to test it. Create a new sketch, and add your library by going to the menu Sketches ➪ Add Library ➪ **theAnswerToEverything**. This should add the following line:

```
#include <theAnswerToEverything.h>
```

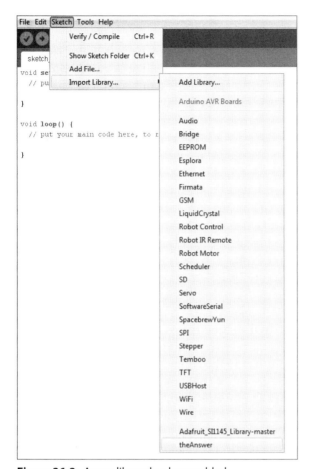

Figure 26-2: A new library has been added.

With that in place, it is now time to use the function you created previously. Add the following lines to setup(), calling the library's function:

```
void setup() {
  // put your setup code here, to run once:
  Serial.begin(9600);
  Serial.print("The answer is ");
  Serial.println(theAnswer());
}
```

Compile it to make sure that everything works well. Then upload it to your Arduino, and have a look at the serial output. Congratulations! You have just created your first library.

Advanced Libraries

The previous example used only simple functions, but Arduino libraries are capable of much, much more. You have seen how to initialize external hardware with the Arduino, usually by specifying some hardware pins. For example, when using the Servo library, the user must specify which pin is connected to the servo. Afterward, functions are available to control the servo, but the user does not have to tell the driver which pin to use. The reason is simple: the driver has stored that data in memory, so the user does not need to specify it every time. How? C++ classes.

C++ development is oriented around objects. What is an object? It can be many things, but mainly, it is a collection of variables and functions, all rolled into a C++ class. A class provides blueprints; it does not define any data, but defines data types. An object is then created by using the class blueprint.

Imagine a traffic light. It has three lights: red, yellow, and green. Physically, three lights are connected to a microcontroller, and the microcontroller issues instructions to each output pin; turn on the red light, and turn off the yellow light. The traffic light is physically an object. If you make a second traffic light, it is a copy of the first; it does exactly the same thing, has the same hardware, and will be used for the same applications as the first traffic light, but it operates independently of the first. This is similar to the concept of a software object. In software, an object is a structure in memory that contains the data and functionality all wrapped up in one package. In this case, imagine an object called `trafficLight`. It will have several functions to allow it to work and several variables to help it keep track of its state. If you create a traffic light and connect it to an Arduino, you could create a `trafficLight` object. Connect a second one, and you could create a second `trafficLight` object, and so on.

An object is defined by a C++ class. A *class* is a structure of code that contains functions, variables, and a constructor. Here's an example.

A traffic light requires three pins to work: one to activate the red light, one for the yellow, and one for the green. Under normal conditions, only one light should ever be on at the same time. This is easy to accomplish, but it requires you to do two things; turn off the previous light, and turn on the new light. This is easy enough with one traffic light, but with multiple lights, it would become increasingly difficult to manage all the pins and variables to keep track of their states. To make things easier, you could make an object.

To create an object, you need several things. First, you need a way to configure the object; telling it which pins to use. Then, it requires at least three functions for manipulating the lights. Naming them after the color they control can make it more intuitive: `red()`, `amber()`, and `green()`. When creating this library, start with the header file, and "describe" the object before building the different parts. This is what the object in the header file `TrafficLight.h` might look like:

```
1   class TrafficLight
2   {
3     private:
4       int _redpin, _yellowpin, _greenpin;
5
6     public:
7       TrafficLight(int redpin, int  yellowpin, int  greenpin);
8       void begin();
9       void red();
10      void yellow();
11    void green();
12  };
```

First, the class TrafficLight is defined. This is the object that will be created in your sketch. Next, it has two parts: one called public and one called private. The public section is where you will place functions and variables that will be visible to the sketch. This includes functions for controlling the state of the lights that you (or someone else using your library) will call in the main sketch. The private section contains functions and variables that are not visible to the sketch, only to the object. You can see how this works in a few paragraphs.

On line 7, there is an interesting function. It is called TrafficLight, the same name as the class. It takes three parameters, does not return any data, and isn't even declared as void. This is known as the *constructor*, which is a function that is automatically called when the object is created and is even called before setup(). The constructor is vitally important because it initializes any variables that need to be set up before the sketch has a chance to execute any functions. Typically, constructors take parameters, in this case the pins that will be used.

There is another important requirement for header files. When a header file is imported, the file is parsed, and the compiler knows what functions are available. If the same file is imported again, it can lead to confusing results, and compilers will complain. To make sure this does not happen, it is common to wrap up the header file in a construct:

```
#ifndef TrafficLight_h
#define TrafficLight_h

// Include statements and code go here

#endif
```

This construct prevents problems if somebody includes the library twice. In the sketch, the TrafficLight object would be created like this:

```
const int redNorthPin = 2;
const int yellowNorthPin = 3;
```

```
const int greenNorthPin = 4;
TrafficLight northLight = TrafficLight(redNorthPin, yellowNorthPin,
    greenNorthPin);
```

When this object is created, the constructor is called with the three variables. Now it is time to write the constructor. This function would be included in `TrafficLight.cpp`:

```
TrafficLight::TrafficLight(int redpin, int yellowpin, int greenpin)
{
  _redpin = redpin;
  _yellowpin = yellowpin;
  _greenpin = greenpin;
}
```

The function is extremely simple, but it does differ from functions that have been previously written in this book. First, the function name: `TrafficLight::TrafficLight`. The first part, `TrafficLight::`, is the name of the class that the function will belong to. The second part is the function name. Because this is a constructor, it must have the exact same name as the class. It takes three `int` variables. Inside the function, the parameters it was given are stored in three variables: `_red`, `_yellow`, and `_green`. Where do they come from? They were defined in the header file on line 4. Because they are in the `private` section, they cannot be called from the sketch but are used inside this particular class object. Let the user have access to the required functions, and keep the rest hidden away. Imagine that you have two traffic lights, a northbound light and a southbound light. They are created like this:

```
TrafficLight northLight = TrafficLight(1, 2, 3);
TrafficLight southLight = TrafficLight(9, 8, 7);
```

Both have been created with different variables. When these objects were created, each called the constructor independently. Their private variables are also different: `northLight`'s `_red` variable contains the value 1, but `southLight`'s `_red` contains the value 9. You can create many objects with the same functionality but with different variables. This makes it possible to turn the northbound light red, stopping all traffic, while turning the southbound light green, allowing traffic to go straight, or to turn at a rather difficult junction, without any other traffic.

On line 8 of the header file, there is another function, `begin()`. You have seen functions with the same name throughout this book, which are used when a device is ready to be used. The constructor set up only the variables; it did not set any outputs, or even declare any pins as output. Typically, this is done in a `begin()` function. The sketch might need those pins for something else before using a traffic light, so it is often good practice to wait until the `begin()` function is called. A `begin()` function might look like this:

```
Boolean TrafficLight::begin(void)
{
  // Set pins as outputs
  pinMode(_redpin, OUTPUT);
  pinMode(_yellowpin, OUTPUT);
  pinMode(_greenpin, OUTPUT);

  // Set Yellow and Green off
  digitalWrite(_yellowpin, LOW);
  digitalWrite(_greenpin, LOW);

  // Set Red on
  digitalWrite(_redpin, HIGH);

  return true;
}
```

The `begin()` function sets the traffic light pins as outputs, and sets the yellow and green lights to off. As a security, these traffic lights will start with the red light on, halting traffic, adding a level of security before deciding which direction should be green. Next, you need to create functions to turn on individual lights. When activating the green light, both the red and yellow light are to be turned off. The `greenLight()` function might look like this:

```
void TrafficLight::greenLight(void)
{
  // Set Red and Yellow off
  digitalWrite(_redpin, LOW);
  digitalWrite(_yellowpin, LOW);

  // Set Green on
  digitalWrite(_greenpin, HIGH);
}
```

Adding Comments

Comments are a critical part of any code and are unfortunately often omitted. They serve several purposes and are particularly useful in libraries.

Most comments are used inside code to explain the function of a portion of code. Of course you know what the code does; you have spent an hour writing it, and even more debugging it, and it has become perfect: elegant and functional. Would co-workers understand what you have done? They might have come up with another way and may be confused by your code if it isn't explained a little, no matter how elegant it is. Also, would you read your code 1 year from now? You might have done dozens of different projects, and your coding style might have changed since this project. Be nice to people; don't hesitate to write a comment if you think it could be helpful.

Ironically, one of the problems with comments is when there are too many comments, or even useless comments. If a variable called `inputPin` is declared as an `int`, there is no point writing a comment to say that it is an input pin and that it is declared as an `int`.

Comments are not just about functionality but also about the project. Someone reading the traffic light header file may understand what the library does, but there are several types of traffic lights. Most of the time, two traffic lights are identical; if the northbound light is green, then the southbound light is too, allowing traffic to flow in both directions. This isn't the case for this library; the advantage is that you can control both lights independently, but the disadvantage is that it generates more work. Tell the user that!

```
/*****************************************************
This library is used to control a single traffic light,
it does not allow you to create pairs, instead, you have
full control over the way you want the traffic light to
behave.
It requires three pins per traffic light

Written by an Arduino Sketches reader
BSD license, all text above must be included in any redistribution
*****************************************************/
class TrafficLight
{
  private:
    uint8_t _redpin, _amberpin, _greenpin;

  public:
    TrafficLight(uint8_t redpin, uint8_t amberpin, uint8_t greenpin);
    void begin();
    void red();
    void amber();
   void green();
};
```

It is now clear what the library is used for. Also, you get to add your name to a project to let people know who did this amazing library, which allows you to set a license. All the code available in this book has the BSD license—either code written by myself or by other parties. The BSD license makes the code free to use, but without any guarantee. It is free to redistribute, but the original license must remain. It allows code to be used in part or in whole in any software project, free or commercial. Remember that the Arduino project is open source; be nice and give back to the community when possible.

Adding Examples

Now that you have read through this example and added functions to turn on the different lights, it is time to move on. Before distributing your library, your users need to know how the library works. You can spend time writing documentation, but the easiest way to show people how a library works is to create an example program. From there, they can upload the example to an Arduino, modify the code to see how it works, and then copy/paste parts of the example into their own projects.

An example program is simply a sketch that uses your library. Again, make sure to comment your code to make it readable, and explain what is being done. Don't use a variable that hasn't been explained.

To add an example, first, write a sketch that uses the library. Next, go to the folder that you are creating for your library. Inside this folder, create a folder, **"examples"**. This is where the examples will be placed. Inside that folder, create another folder, the name of the example you want to create. Some libraries might require several examples. (Remember, the Ethernet library in Chapter 9 has multiple examples for servers and clients.) Now, paste your sketch inside this folder, keeping the same name as the folder but with the extension .ino (for Arduino sketch). Alternately, you can use the Arduino IDE to create the files and save them to disk directly. When the folder is imported, the Arduino IDE automatically adds any examples it finds into the Examples menu. For example, Figure 26-3 shows my TrafficLight library folder with two example sketches.

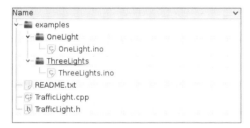

Figure 26-3: Traffic lights folder layout

Read Me

Most projects contain a README file—a text file that contains information about files in a folder. Historically, they were used to describe the contents of a folder, and were sometimes called README.1ST to inform the user that the contents should be read first. The README file should contain information about the project, the functionality that the library adds, what the user needs to make it work, and the examples included. This gives the user a good idea about what your library does without having to look at the source code.

Coding Style

To make it easier to both use and to distribute libraries, certain coding styles should be followed. These general rules make everything simpler and to make sure that everyone has a great time when programming Arduino. You can find the official API style guide here at `http://arduino.cc/en/Reference/APIStyleGuide`.

Use CamelCase

Sooner or later, you will need to write a function that is two or three words long. To put several words into a single compound phrase, there are several techniques possible. Programming languages are full of examples; using underscores results in functions like `this_function()`, and some languages even went as far as to put the first word in uppercase and the second in lowercase, but `THESEfunctions()` isn't easy to read.

The Arduino style uses CamelCase: each word starts with a capital with the exception of the first letter. Functions are easier to read that way; functions such as `readFile()` or `openImage()` are immediately clear and remain perfectly readable. CamelCase is even used for multiple everyday objects; the first known use of CamelCase is in a 1950s technology called CinemaScope. Some readers might be reading this book on an eReader, another example of CamelCase.

CamelCase does have one disadvantage; it can be difficult to read functions that contain several uppercase letters: `ReadID()` for example. Of course, the function can read an ID, but functions such as `GetTCPIPSocketID()` become complicated. Should you write `GetTCPIPSocketID()` or `GetTcpIpSocketId()`? Generally, you should avoid abbreviations, but when they are inevitable, it is often better to write them as capitals.

Use English Words

Don't shorten words for your functions. If you can't explain it in three words, look for another way. Always use complete words: `deleteFile()` is always clearer than `delFile()`, and `oFile()` doesn't mean anything, where `openFile()` does. Again, it is better to avoid abbreviations because only some abbreviations are clear to most people. You have probably heard of HTML, and writing "Hyper Text Markup Language" is going to make some ridiculously long function names. You can find a perfect example in the Arduino libraries; they don't talk about PWM, they called the function `analogWrite()`.

Don't Use External Libraries

If you are writing a library, make sure that it uses only the Arduino standard libraries, or if absolutely necessary, board-specific libraries. If you have a great idea for a function, but one that can run only on an Arduino Esplora, then you can use the Esplora libraries. However, if it can be used on any Arduino, it would be a shame to limit it to one device. Similarly, don't rely on third-party external libraries; you are creating an external library, and users might not want to use your library if it depends on another one. Importing several libraries makes the code bigger.

Use Standard Names

Most hardware-related drivers use a `begin()` function in their code. Don't try to find synonyms; keep the same names as other functions. For example, if obtaining data, always use read: `readInput()` or `readStatus()`. When outputting, use write: `writeData()`.

Distributing Your Library

When the coding is complete and the testing has been done, it is time to distribute your library. You can create a Zip file of your library and post it on your homepage (or the page you use to sell your hardware). This makes the library available to buyers (or visitors to your site) but does not increase visibility.

To make your library as visible as possible, consider putting it on one of the many sites designed specifically for source code, such as Sourceforge, GitHub, or Google Code. There are dozens of sites available for free, so long as your project is open source. This also automatically adds your library to search engines and allows users to help add new features, be alerted to updates, and make comments and requests.

Closed Source Libraries

A closed source library is one where you distribute binary code, and users are not allowed to see the source code. They cannot see the work you have done and therefore cannot modify the library. This also adds the possibility of requesting payment for use of your library, but it goes against everything the Arduino project is trying to do and is also technically extremely difficult to achieve.

Compilers and linkers take source code and transform it into machine code, code that can be executed on a microcontroller or processor. This is generally the format in which closed source libraries are distributed. The problem is that binary files are created for one specific processor and cannot be used on another. A program compiled for an AVR cannot be run on an ARM-based device such as the Arduino Due or an Intel-based device such as the Galileo. It has to be recompiled. Even worse, not all AVRs are the same; there are differences in models that make binary code imports impossible. In short, releasing a binary-only library makes that library usable on a single Arduino model.

Example Library

In Chapter 25, you created a shield for Arduino based on the PCF8574AP. Now it is time to write a library to use this device. If you haven't created your shield yet, or if you haven't received it, don't worry; you can still use the breadboard version presented in that chapter, which works in exactly the same way.

The Library

The I^{2}C expander shield contains two PCF8574AP chips, both of which have configurable addresses. Therefore, you must select two addresses to use for your devices. You can choose which device will be the first selected—either chip 0 or chip 1 depending on the application. This will be handled in the constructor. The two addresses must be stored inside the class for the rest of the application to work. To do this, they will be saved as two 8-bit variables called _chip0Address and _chip1Address. Part of the job of the expander shield is to provide extra outputs: two banks of 8 pins. To make this easier to the user, the library should be designed to allow three different write operations: bit by bit, 8-bit writes, or 16-bit writes. The Arduino naming convention states that these operations should be called write, and the functions will be called writeBit(), writeByte(), and writeWord(). To write a bit, two values are required: the bit to write and its position. The bit will be a boolean, and the position will be an 8-bit value. To write a byte, again, two values are required: the byte to write and which device to use. The byte will be coded as a byte (naturally), and the device will be a Bool: 0 for device 0 and 1 for device 1. To write a 16-bit word, only one parameter is required, the word itself. All three functions should return a boolean: true if the operation succeeded and false otherwise.

The other part of the expander's job is to read data. Three functions need to be created to read data. The Arduino naming convention states that they should be called read: readBit(), readByte(), and readWord(). The readBit() function should require one parameter, the bit to read, and output a boolean. The readByte() function requires one parameter, the chip ID, as a boolean, and returns a byte. The readWord() function does not require any parameters and returns a word.

Since these devices are I^{2}C devices, they will also require the Wire library.

There is one thing that should be taken into account. The user might want to write a bit of data to one of the chips, but how do you do that without affecting the other bits? Well, as far as the chip is concerned, you can't. You can write only

8 bits of data at a time, the entire output of the chip. To achieve this, two more variables will be needed; `_chip0Output` and `_chip1Output` will both contain 8-bits of data, the data that will be sent to the chip. The user does not need to worry about how a bit of data is sent, or even be aware that the library cannot send a single bit, which is one of the reasons why libraries are so powerful. The library takes care of the details, letting the user concentrate on the sketch.

Finally, a `begin()` function will be written. This function will initialize the chip to a power-on state and will be called when the user is ready.

By simply thinking about what the user would need the shield to do, you'll have a good idea of what the header file should contain. It will look something like this (filename: `PCF8574AP.h`):

```
#include "Arduino.h"

class PCF8574AP
{
  private:
    int _chip0Address;
    int _chip1Address;

    int _chip0Output;
    int _chip1Output;

  public:
    PCF8574AP(int chip1, int chip2);
    void begin();

    bool writeBit(bool bit, int pos);
    bool writeByte(int data, bool chipSelect);
    bool writeWord(int data);

    bool readBit(int pos);
    int readByte(bool chipSelect);
    int readWord();

};
```

Now that the structure is created, it is time to work on the C++ file, called `PCF8754AP.cpp`. First, add references to the libraries it depends on—`Arduino.h` and `Wire.h`—as well as the library header, followed by the constructor:

```
#include "Arduino.h"
#include "Wire.h"
#include "PCF8574AP.h"

PCF8574AP::PCF8574AP(uint8_t chip0, uint8_t chip1)
{
    _chip0Address = chip0;
    _chip1Address = chip1;
}
```

And that's it. All that needs to be done is to copy the values sent as parameters into private variables. Configuration of the chip is done in `begin()` and will look like this:

```
void PCF8574AP::begin()
{
    Wire.begin();

    // Set all pins of chip 0 to HIGH
    _chip0Output = 0xFF;
    Wire.beginTransmission(_chip0Address);
    Wire.write(_chip0Output);
    Wire.endTransmission();

    // Do the same for chip 1
    _chip1Output = 0xFF;
    Wire.beginTransmission(_chip1Address);
    Wire.write(_chip1Output);
    Wire.endTransmission();
}
```

The function begins by calling `Wire.begin()`. Why does it do that? Although the device requires the Wire library for communication, the user doesn't need to know exactly how the shield is connected. It's up to this function to initialize the I²C library and start communication with the chips. Next, the function then sets both output variables to `0xFF` (or, in binary, `1111 1111`). It then proceeds to write that value to each of the two chips. When the chips first power on, this is their default state. So why does this function do that, if this is what is expected? There is no guarantee that the device was powered on; it might just have been reset, or the device is in an unstable state. This makes sure that the device is in a known configuration before continuing.

Now to read data. The easiest function to accomplish is `readByte()`. It simply reads the 8 bits of the chip and returns that data.

```
uint8_t PCF8574AP::readByte(bool chipSelect)
{
    byte _data = 0;

    if(chipSelect == 1)
        Wire.requestFrom(_chip1Address, 1);
    else
        Wire.requestFrom(_chip0Address, 1);

    if(Wire.available())
    {
        _data = Wire.read();
    }
```

```
        return(_data);
}
```

This function requests 1 byte of data from either chip, depending on the value of `chipSelect`. If data is present in the I²C buffer, that data is copied into the local variable `_data` and then returned. If no data is available, the function returns zero.

Reading words is just like reading bytes, only 2 bytes are read. This function obtains a byte of data from both chips, merges them into a word, and then returns that data. This is accomplished with the following:

```
uint16_t PCF8574AP::readWord(void)
{
    byte _data0 = 0;
    byte _data1 = 0;

    Wire.requestFrom(_chip0Address, 1);
    if(Wire.available())
    {
        _data0 = Wire.read();
    }

    Wire.requestFrom(_chip1Address, 1);
    if(Wire.available())
    {
        _data1 = Wire.read();
    }

    return(word(_data1, _data0));
}
```

Things become slightly more complex when reading a specific bit, requiring bitwise operations:

```
bool PCF8574AP::readBit(uint8_t pos)
{
    byte _data = 0;

    // Is the bit requested out of range?
    if (pos > 15)
        return 0;

    if (pos < 8)
        Wire.requestFrom(_chip0Address, 1);
    else
    {
        Wire.requestFrom(_chip1Address, 1);
        pos -= 8;
```

```
    }
    if(Wire.available())
    {
        _data = Wire.read();
    }

    return(bitRead(_data, pos));
}
```

The function reads in data from one of the chips with `Wire.requestFrom()`, depending on the bit position. If the requested bit is between 0 and 7, the request is sent to chip 0; otherwise it is sent to chip 1. Then, the Arduino function `bitRead()` is called, extracting the bit that was requested and returning it as a boolean value.

All the read functions have been completed, but it isn't over yet. The write functions need to be written. Writing a byte is straightforward:

```
bool PCF8574AP::writeByte(uint8_t data, bool chipSelect)
{
    if (chipSelect == 0)
    {
        Wire.beginTransmission(_chip0Address);
        _chip0Output = data;
        Wire.write(_chip0Output);
    }
    else if (chipSelect == 1)
    {
        Wire.beginTransmission(_chip1Address);
        _chip1Output = data;
        Wire.write(_chip1Output);
    }
    else
    {
        return false;
    }
    Wire.endTransmission();

    return true;
}
```

As with `readByte()`, `writeByte()` selects only one chip. If `chipSelect` is 0, an I²C transmission begins at chip 0. `data` is copied to `_chip0Output`, and its contents are sent to the device. If chip 1 is selected, the same operation occurs, but for chip 1. Finally, the data is sent, and the function returns `true`.

Writing a word is similar:

```
bool PCF8574AP::writeWord(uint16_t data)
{
    Wire.beginTransmission(_chip0Address);
    _chip0Output = ((uint8_t) ((data) & 0xff));
```

```
Wire.write(_chip0Output);
Wire.endTransmission();

delay(5);

Wire.beginTransmission(_chip1Address);
_chip1Output = ((uint8_t) ((data) >> 8));
Wire.write(_chip1Output);
Wire.endTransmission();

return true;
}
```

By now you should be accustomed to using both chips. The logic behind this is that both variables are updated, and both chips are updated with those variables. The trick comes in separating a word into 2 bytes; this is done with masks and shifts. The first conversion transforms a word into a byte, by omitting the first 8 bits using a mask. The second conversion does the same; only it shifts the first 8 bits to the right, essentially pushing the first 8 bits to the place of the second 8 bits, and then masking.

The last function that you need is writing individual bits:

```
bool PCF8574AP::writeBit(bool bit, uint8_t pos)
{
    // Is the bit requested out of range?
    if (pos > 15)
        return false;

    if (pos < 8)
    {
        //Chip 0
        if (bit == true)
        {
            bitSet(_chip0Output, pos);
        }
        else
        {
            bitClear(_chip0Output, pos);
        }
        Wire.beginTransmission(_chip0Address);
        Wire.write(_chip0Output);
        Wire.endTransmission();
    }
    else
    {
        //Chip 1
        if (bit == true)
        {
            bitSet(_chip1Output, pos - 8);
        }
```

```
            else
            {
                bitClear(_chip1Output, pos - 8);
            }
            Wire.beginTransmission(_chip1Address);
            Wire.write(_chip1Output);
            Wire.endTransmission();
        }

    return true;
}
```

Because the PCF8574AP can't actually read what it is outputting, when the user wants to modify a single bit, the function needs to know what the data is on the bus and then modify it. This is why it was necessary to save the output as a variable. This is the benefit of using a library, hiding a detail that end users don't need to know. Users can just see that they can modify a bit with a single instruction.

Examples

It doesn't matter how clear function names are; libraries are always better with examples. Example sketches also serve another purpose—to test the hardware. One of the best ways to test if the hardware is correctly set up is to open up an example and see it run. Even if the shield it drives is basic, users will still use example sketches as a basis for their own. Put simply: Example sketches need to clearly demonstrate the functionality of the library.

This library has two examples: one for writing outputs and the other for reading. Of course, the shield can do both at the same time, so comments need to be put in place to tell the user that. Also, critically important, the PCF8574AP can read inputs correctly only if the output is set to high; this needs to be clearly explained in a comment.

First, for the example to write outputs, you must think about what the user needs. Of course, he needs to understand the library. He will also need to set up an example. LCD screen examples are easy to set up; if you are using an LCD library, you probably already have the LCD screen. This case is different. Nothing on this particular shield is visible to the user; there are no LEDs, no LCD screens, nothing that can tell the user what is going on. To see what the shield can do, a user will have to add his own components. What should you use? Nothing too fancy. An awesome example would be to use an 8x8 LED matrix, but not everyone will have that. Don't use specific hardware in examples; use tools that are readily available. The cheapest, most readily available, and most robust component available to makers is the trusty LED; almost everyone has a few LEDs on their desk with the corresponding resistors. They might not have 16, so this example uses only one output, with 8 LEDs.

```
#include <Wire.h>
#include <PCF8574AP.h>

// Define the addresses of both chips on the expander board
#define EXPANDER_CHIP0 B0111000
#define EXPANDER_CHIP1 B0111001

// You must provide two I2C addresses, one for each chip on the shield
PCF8574AP expanderShield = PCF8574AP(EXPANDER_CHIP0, EXPANDER_CHIP1);

byte output;

void setup()
{
  Serial.begin(9600);
  expanderShield.begin(); // Start the expander shield, set all outputs
      to 1
}

void loop()
{
  // Write a 16-bit word to the expander shield, all ones
  expanderShield.writeWord(0xFFFF);
  delay(1000);

  // Time to begin the light show
  // Make the lights go towards the center by writing bytes
  expanderShield.writeByte(B01111110, 0);
  delay(1000);
  expanderShield.writeByte(B00111100, 0);
  delay(1000);
  expanderShield.writeByte(B00011000, 0);
  delay(1000);
  expanderShield.writeByte(B00000000, 0);
  delay(1000);

  // Now make the lights go towards the edges by writing individual bits
  // Bits can be set by writing a 1 or a 0 to a specific location: bits
      0 to 15
  expanderShield.writeBit(1, 0); // Write a logical 1 to bit 0 of the
      expander shield
  expanderShield.writeBit(1, 7); // Write a logical 1 to bit 7 of the
      expander shield
  delay(1000);
  expanderShield.writeBit(1, 1);
```

```
expanderShield.writeBit(1, 6);
delay(1000);
expanderShield.writeBit(1, 2);
expanderShield.writeBit(1, 5);
delay(1000);
expanderShield.writeBit(1, 3);
expanderShield.writeBit(1, 4);
delay(1000);

// turn off all the lights
expanderShield.writeByte(0, 0);
delay(1000);

// Create a light display by shifting a bit from one side to the
   other, increasing speed
for(int i = 0; i < 20; i++)
{
  output = 1;
  for(int j = 0; j < 8; j++)
  {
    // Write a byte to device 0 (the first I2C extender)
    expanderShield.writeByte(output, 0);
    delay(600 - (i * 30));
    output = output << 1;
  }
}
}
```

This example shows the user how to use the PCF8574AP I/O expander shield, and the very first thing it does is to include that library. To be able to use that library, the user must provide two pieces of information: the address for each component. To make this clear, the addresses are included as define statements on lines 5 and 6.

On line 9, the PCF8574AP object is created, called `expanderShield`. By using the defined addresses, the code becomes more readable, and the user understands what is required to get started. On line 13, the `setup()` function is declared, as with any sketch. Inside, the serial connection is configured and `expanderShield` is initialized with a `begin()` function.

The `loop()` function is declared on line 20, and this is where the example code will be placed. To show how the library can write words (or 16-bit numbers), the example uses the `writeWord()` function. This sets all the outputs to HIGH, turning the LEDs off.

Next, the user is presented with an example on how to use `writeByte()`. A series of four commands are run, each time setting more and more outputs to 0. The effect of this is to turn on the LEDs from the edge towards the center.

The next series of instructions demonstrates how to write individual bits using the `writeBit()` function. Once again, a visual effect is created, this time turning the LEDs off from the edge towards the center.

Finally, to make the example even more visually appealing, a final phase is used. By using two `for` loops and using one value for the output and another value for the delay between operations, the result is a racing light going from one side of the LEDs to the other, going ever faster and faster.

Multiple comments have been placed in the file to explain to the user what the sketch is doing. So long as LEDs are connected to the board (cathodes connected to the pins) the user will be presented with a nice light show.

README

Every project should have a README file, a simple text file that describes the project. When you look at a project on GitHub, the text you see on the project page comes directly from the README file in the project. Here is mine:

```
/************************************************
ArduinoSketches Expander Shield Driver

This library is used to control the two PCF8754APs
present on the expander shield. They can perform both
reads and writes, but to perform a read, the output
on that pin must be high.

This library accesses those devices through bit-wise,
byte-wise or word-wise reads and writes.

Written by James A. Langbridge, enhanced by a reader of
Arduino Sketches.

Released under BSD license

To run the examples in this library, you will require
at least 8 LED lights, and corresponding resistors
(for red LEDs, use 150 ohm resistors). The anode should
be connected to the resistor and power supply, and the
cathode should be connected to the input/output of the
shield.
************************************************/
```

The first line tells the user what this library is for: the Arduino Sketches expander shield. It contains a little more detail on the project, what it does, how it achieves that, who originally wrote it, and the license the project is distributed under. I wrote the original library, but you will continue the project. This library is distributed under the BSD library; use it in any way you see fit.

Secondly, the file also includes the list of components required to run the examples, if required. For this example, the user requires 8 LEDs, and the corresponding resistors.

Finishing Touches

As usual, the source code here is functional but could do with a little bit of tweaking. Remember those write functions that tell if the information was written correctly? They all return true for the time being, but you can enhance that by looking at the amount of bytes written to the I²C bus. Use that data to give a more accurate response.

One thing is missing from this library: to perform a read, the user must first make the output high. What would happen if that weren't done? The reading would not be accurate. You could add this to the read functions; because the outputs are known through a global variable, make sure that the output is high before reading.

You have your shield, and you have your library, hopefully with your name on both. Make this your project, and be creative with the applications you come up with. Don't forget to tell me all about your projects!

Summary

In this chapter you have seen how to create your own library, and how to make it easy to use by other users, by creating examples and other files. You have seen the importance of writing clear comments, how users will read your library, as well as the importance of naming your functions. Now you have a working library, ready to use with your own shield. All that is left to do is to imagine new applications!

Index